THE NOMADS OF THE BALKANS

PLATE I

IN CAP AND BELLS. A VLACH MASQUERADER AT VERRIA

THE NOMADS OF
THE BALKANS

AN ACCOUNT OF LIFE AND CUSTOMS AMONG
THE VLACHS OF NORTHERN PINDUS

BY

ALAN J. B. WACE

AND

M. S. THOMPSON

WITH FORTY-TWO ILLUSTRATIONS AND TWO MAPS

BOOKS FOR LIBRARIES PRESS
FREEPORT, NEW YORK

First Published 1914
Reprinted 1971

INTERNATIONAL STANDARD BOOK NUMBER:
0-8369-6705-4

LIBRARY OF CONGRESS CATALOG CARD NUMBER:
70-37358

PRINTED IN THE UNITED STATES OF AMERICA
BY
NEW WORLD BOOK MANUFACTURING CO., INC.
HALLANDALE, FLORIDA 33009

PREFACE

IN writing Vlach phonetically we have used as simple an alphabet as possible and endeavoured to avoid the use of diacritical marks. The symbols used are to be pronounced as follows :—

a, e, i and *u* as in German,

o as a closed *o* as in the French *côte*,

oa as an open sound as in the French *bois*,

ea to resemble the Italian *ia* in words such as *pianta*,

ai as in the English *i* as in *mice*,

ei as the English *ay* in *play*,

ao and *au* as the German *au*,

ĭ and *ŭ* as whispered sounds, the latter like a half uttered English *w*,

ă like the English *er* in *better*, while *ā* is a vowel sound peculiar to Roumanian and its dialects which cannot be described,

p and *b* as in English,

t and *d* as in English,

g as the hard English *g* as in *gape*, *k* as the hard English *c* in *care*, *y* as in *yacht*, *gh* (the Greek *γ*) like the *g* in North German words such as *Tage*, *h* like the Scottish *ch* in *loch*,

m and *n* as in English and *ñ* as the English *n* in *finger*,

l as in English and *r* as in Scottish,

f and *v* as in English, *th* (the Greek *θ*) as the *th* in *thorough*, *dh* (the Greek *δ*) as *th* in *then*,

s and *z* as in English, *sh* as in English and *zh* as the *z* in *azure*, *tsh* like the English *ch* in *church*, and *dzh* like the English *j*,

g' as in *ague* or in *argument*, *k'* as in *Kew* or the *c* in *cue*,
h' as in *hew* or *huge*, *n'* like the Italian *gn* and *l'* like the
Italian *gl*.

Although the name *Sāmārína* is in Vlach pronounced as the
spelling indicates we have written throughout *Samarina*, and
this, if spoken so as to rhyme with *semolina*, is sufficiently
accurate for practical purposes.

As regards Modern Greek we have attempted to trans-
literate the language phonetically, but in the case of well-
known names and places we have retained the conventional
spelling.

We have to thank Professor E. G. Browne, Dr. Braunholtz,
Mr. E. H. Minns and Mr. E. C. Quiggin for help and advice on
many linguistic questions.

Of the literature on the Vlachs we have consulted all that
was accessible to us. The notes at the end are intended to
indicate only the chief sources where further information can
be obtained.

Si furim shi eu ka tine vream si mi duk Sāmārina.

A. J. B. W.
M. S. T.

August 15th, 1913

CONTENTS

LIST OF ILLUSTRATIONS

THE NOMADS OF THE BALKANS

THE NOMADS OF THE BALKANS

CHAPTER I

MAINLY INTRODUCTORY

Viniră di t alte lokuri
Tră z veadă anoastre tropuri.

They came from other places to see our customs.

VLACH SONG

O F the various races that inhabit the Balkan peninsula the Vlachs are in many ways one of the least known. Though at one time of sufficient importance to give their name to the greater part of Northern Greece, during the last few centuries their existence as a separate people has almost been forgotten. At the present day they are to be found widely scattered over the more mountainous and remote parts of the peninsula from Acarnania in the south to as far north as the mountains of Bulgaria and Servia. Their settlements are all small, there is no such thing as an exclusively Vlach town and nowhere do they occupy any large continuous tract of country. One of their chief districts in the south is along the wooded slopes of Northern Pindus between Epirus and Southwestern Macedonia. The higher of the villages on Pindus are under snow each winter and each year as soon as summer ends most of the inhabitants move down to the plains with their flocks and herds, taking with them whatever is needed to carry on their trade. Thus for the six winter months there is a large Vlach population living in the plains of Thessaly and Macedonia ; Velestinos for the time being becomes almost a Vlach town, and numerous Vlach families take up their abode in Trikkala, Larissa, Elassona

I

and the other towns and villages near by. The villages in the hills however are always regarded by the Vlachs as being their real home; they are essentially a mountain people and as soon as they begin to settle permanently in the plains, as many have done in the past, far away from their native hills and woods and streams they lose their national characteristics and rapidly become merged into the surrounding races. Their language both in its vocabulary and structure is clearly descended from Latin—so much so that a Latin grammar solves many of the difficulties—and is closely allied to Roumanian, of which it is in fact a dialect. But like all the Balkan languages in their common spoken forms Vlach contains a large number of foreign words and phrases, borrowed from Greek, Slavonic, Turkish and Albanian, the proportion from each varying in the different districts. The earliest record of spoken Vlach goes back to the sixth century A.D., but it seems not to have been written till the eighteenth century when a Greek script was employed. Since the beginning of the national movement about the middle of last century the Roumanian alphabet has been adopted.

Excepting some of the women in certain of the more remote villages all the Vlachs of both sexes know in addition to their native language at least one other tongue, either Greek, Bulgarian, Albanian or Serb. In the case of the women however this is largely a modern development for only fifty years ago in an accessible village like Metsovo few knew any other language but Vlach ; the men on the other hand owing to the necessities of trade have almost certainly been bilingual for many generations. The Vlachs call themselves ' Romans,' or in their own dialect Arumāni, which is really the same word, just as the Greeks still commonly call themselves ' Romei ' and their language ' Romeika.' By the Bulgarians, Serbs and Albanians the Vlachs are known as Tsintsars which is a nickname derived from the numerous hissing sounds in Vlach suggestive of mosquitoes. Thus the Roumanian cinci (five) is in Vlach tsintsi.

By the Greeks the Vlachs are known as Vlakhi or more accurately as Kutsovlakhi. The name Vlach which is a shortened form of Wallach occurs in many languages and is perhaps in origin connected with the name Welsh. In Greek it is now and has been for some time past often applied to all wandering shepherds without denoting any particular race, so that its meaning is not always clear. We have nevertheless used it throughout, but always with a racial meaning as it is the most familiar name in Western Europe. The origin of the name Kutsovlach, which invariably has a racial significance, has been disputed. According to one theory the first part of the word comes from the Turkish *kuchuk* little, and in this case the Kutsovlachs would be the little Vlachs of the Balkans as opposed to their more numerous kinsmen north of the Danube. A second theory which finds more favour with philologists derives it from the Greek κουτσός a word originally meaning ' lame ' or ' halting ' which occurs in many compounds often with a depreciatory sense. Thus κουτσοπατάτα ' a poor sort of potato ' we have heard applied to the bulb of the Cyclamen ; and κουτσοδάσκαλος similarly means ' an ignorant schoolmaster,' In other cases the original meaning of ' lame ' is more clearly preserved ; February for example is called κουτσός or ' halting February.' On this theory the Kutsovlachs would be the halting or lame Vlachs again in contrast with those further north ; the allusion being to the same peculiarity of speech that has won them the name of Tsintsar among the Slavs.

The position of the Vlach villages high up in the hills of Macedonia, in districts rarely visited, the departure of the Vlachs from the plains in early spring before the time when travelling is most common, their use of a second language in all intercourse with the outer world and lastly the double meaning of the name Vlach in Modern Greek have all helped to restrict and confuse outside knowledge of their life and conditions.

Our own acquaintance with the Vlachs began quite by chance. In the winter of 1909-10 we were travelling in Southern Thessaly in the district between Almiros and Mt. Othrys in search of inscriptions and other antiquities. In Almiros itself and in one or two of the villages to the west are a

number of Farsherots or Albanian Vlachs who formerly came
from Pleasa. We happened to employ one of these as muleteer
and from him began to learn a few words of Vlach. Though
a resident in Thessaly our informant possessed a detailed
knowledge of the Macedonian hills, as he had more than once
been employed in Greek bands and failing these had made
expeditions of his own. A few weeks later while looking for
inscriptions in the plain of Elassona we spent the night at
Vlakhoyianni a winter village of the Pindus Vlachs and there
heard more details of Samarina and the other villages on
Pindus. The tales told proved of interest, so that a few days
later we employed another Vlach muleteer, this time a native
of Samarina, and plied him with various questions as to Vlach
life in general. He told us of mountains covered with grass
and pasture for large flocks of sheep, of forests of oak and
beech and pine and of innumerable mountain streams that
never failed in summer and were almost too cold to drink.
How every one at Samarina ate meat every day and wine was
brought up from Shatishta three days' journey with mules.
We had spent the previous July excavating in the Thessalian
plains amid heat, mosquitoes and dust, so these tales of woods
and streams proved all the more enticing. There were other
attractions also of a less material kind, a church with a miraculous pine tree growing on the roof (Plate XIV 1) ; a festival
(Plate IV 2) at which all the marriages for the year were celebrated, and all wore their best clothes (Plate XIX) and danced
for five consecutive days. Further God Almighty, when he
made the world, dropped one of his four sacks of lies at
Samarina. These either—the excuses vary—ran down hill
to other parts of the globe or else being merely masculine
became extinct. The attractions proved too strong and we
determined to visit the Pindus villages the following summer.
The obvious course was to travel up with the Vlach families
who leave for the hills each year about the same day. We
found the muleteer and his family willing to have an addition
to their party ; and so agreed to meet at Tirnavos in time to
start with them. Our first visit to Samarina and the villages
on Pindus in 1910 has led to others since and we have also seen

many of the Vlach communities elsewhere. Thus in 1911 on our way from Salonica to Samarina we went to the villages around Verria and also to Neveska and Klisura ; in the following year we visited Monastir and the Vlach communities between it and Resna, Okhridha, Muskopol'e and Kortsha. Apart from these and similar journeys made mainly to study the distribution and customs of the Vlachs while travelling in the Balkan peninsula for archæological reasons we have endeavoured to see as much as possible of Vlach life and there are few towns in Southern Macedonia where we have not some Vlach acquaintances. Outside Macedonia and Thessaly there are still several gaps in our knowledge ; of the Vlach villages in Acarnania we have visited only one ; Albania north of Konitsa and west of Muskopol'e is unknown to us, and the Farsherots or Albanian Vlachs we have met have been mostly those settled in Macedonia and Greece. When in Bulgaria we were fortunate in having introductions to the Vlach colony at Sofia, which is of Macedonian origin, but of the other Vlach communities in Bulgaria we have no personal knowledge. Lastly in Macedonia itself we have never been to the Meglen though we have met several natives of that district in other parts of the country. This book therefore can have no claim to be a complete account of all the Vlach settlements ; its aim is rather to give a detailed description of Samarina and the adjacent villages on Pindus together with some account of the Balkan Vlachs as a whole.

The recent history of the Vlachs has been complicated by political troubles, which cannot quite be ignored though it seems needless to discuss them in detail. We have therefore noted only the main effects on certain of the villages, and give here a brief account of the circumstances under which the dispute arose.

At the time when the whole peninsula was under Turkish rule in accordance with Turkish custom religion alone was recognized as the basis of nationality, so that the Greek Patriarch at Constantinople was the head and representative of all the orthodox Christians before the Sublime Porte. In 1821 came the revolt in the south which ended in the establishment of an independent Hellenic kingdom. The revolt however was far from being coextensive with the Greek race, and also was not exclusively Greek for the other Christians in the south Albanians and Vlachs too helped and became part of the newly liberated population. Thus there is in Greece to-day a considerable number of Albanians who have been from the first loyal Hellenic subjects. The Christians left outside Greece and still under Turkish rule naturally looked towards the new kingdom, and many moved southwards to come under Greek rule. Among these were numbers of Vlachs who previously partly hellenized soon became in every way Hellenic. This tendency towards Hellenism was all the greater because Greek was then not only the sole language of the church, but almost the only native language in the peninsula that was commonly written. The value of Greek at that time or slightly earlier can perhaps best be seen from a Greek reading book written by a Vlach priest of Muskopol'e in 1802. It begins with a preface in verse, the first lines of which without maligning the original may be rendered thus :—

> Albanians, Bulgars, Vlachs and all who now do speak
> An alien tongue rejoice, prepare to make you Greek,
> Change your barbaric tongue, your customs rude forgo,
> So that as byegone myths your children may them know.

Then follow a tetragloss exercise in Greek, Vlach, Albanian and Bulgarian, all in Greek script ; a dissertation on the value of learning in general and on the special advantages of the book in question ; instruction in the elements of Christian knowledge and natural physics ; a complete letter writer with model examples of letters to dignitaries of the church, parents, relations, friends, schoolmasters, rich Beys and great Pashas ; lessons in the four rules of arithmetic; and at the end is a calendar showing the chief feasts of the Orthodox Church. By about the middle of the nineteenth century or somewhat later the other subject Christian races followed the example of Greece. Servia, Bulgaria and Roumania became independent states and their nationals left under

Turkish rule demanded or had demanded for them by others churches and schools of their own. It hardly perhaps need be said that one and all of these movements were most disconcerting for the Greeks and in particular for the Greek Patriarchate which ever since 1767, when it suppressed the Bulgarian Patriarchate at Okhridha in Macedonia, has fought tooth and nail against all attempts at religious or educational freedom. Among the Vlachs the national movement began in the Pindus villages about 1867 ; it was originated by natives of Macedonia, but help was soon procured from Bucharest which became the centre of the movement. Roumanian elementary schools were founded in several of the Vlach villages and afterwards higher grade schools were started in Yannina, Salonica, and Monastir. Eventually in 1905 the Vlachs were recognized by the Turks as forming a separate ' millet ' or nationality. This however brought no real unity as the Vlach villages are widely scattered and many from their position alone are too closely connected with Greece to wish to take a course of their own. The movement however in the first instance was of an educational kind, and the purely political aspect it has at times assumed has been produced almost entirely by the opposition with which it was met.

Greek opposition at first was confined to exerting pressure by means of the church, but in 1881 when Thessaly and a considerable Vlach population came under Greek rule Roumanian education had to retire northwards and the situation became more acute. The theory had by that time been devised in Greece that the Vlachs were Vlachophone Hellenes, that is to say racially Greeks who had learnt Vlach. The arguments then and since brought against the Roumanian schools were curiously inept ; it was urged that they taught a foreign language, and were financed and staffed by Roumanians and not Vlachs. As far as language is concerned Roumanian has a close connection with Vlach while Greek has none, and in the lower forms of the Roumanian schools the Vlach dialect is used to some extent. Both schools equally in most of the Vlach villages were financed from outside and in recent years at least most if not all the school-masters employed in the Roumanian schools have been Vlachs and not Roumanians. It is interesting to note that the perfectly valid argument that the Vlachs had rapidly been becoming hellenized was not used at all.

In 1903 the Bulgarians in Macedonia revolted against the Turks; the fighting was fiercest between Klisura and Krushevo, districts now allotted to Greece and Servia, and the revolt was only suppressed with fire and sword and wholesale brutality. One result of this rising was to show the Greeks how much Hellenism had declined and Bulgarian propaganda increased since the beginning of the Bulgarian church and schools some thirty years before. Consequently with the approval of the church a committee was formed in Athens to hire bands to send into Macedonia to enforce the claims of Hellenism and destroy Bulgarian schools and churches. These bands were largely composed of Cretans and often led by regular officers, but any ex-brigand was sure of a ready welcome. Similar bands meanwhile had been dispatched from Sofia to gather all Bulgarian villages into the fold of the Bulgarian church and nationalism. In the bitter and bloody struggle that followed the Vlachs were soon involved, for the Greek bands were ordered to turn their attention to the Roumanian schools as well. Threats soon reduced the numbers of the Roumanian party, several of their schools were burnt, many of their more staunch advocates were murdered and their homes and property destroyed. One result of this was that Vlach bands soon appeared on the opposite side, but from their numbers and position were compelled to act mainly on the defensive. In July 1908 with the proclamation of the Ottoman constitution this campaign ended and comparative peace followed. One result of the recent wars has been that Roumania has secured from all the Balkan states educational and religious freedom for the Vlachs and the continuance of Roumanian schools where they are desired. This should put an end for ever to the peculiarly mean squabble in which the Vlachs have been concerned.

Owing to this deplorable dispute it has been extremely hard for any one to acquire accurate information about the Vlach villages. As Weigand found many years ago when the quarrel was in its infancy and no blood had been spilt any one enquiring into Vlach dialects was viewed with the utmost suspicion and liable to be told the most fantastic tales. Thus on one occasion we overheard the school children being ordered to talk only Greek as long as we were present ; in another village which we were assured spoke only Greek, Vlach proved to be the common tongue. Nearly all modern Greek books and pamphlets on the Vlachs which might otherwise be of extreme interest and value, are owing to their political theories almost entirely worthless. Political philology has shown that Kutsovlach means ' little Vlach ' and that ' a little Vlach ' means one who is mostly a Hellene. This result is apparently reached by deriving the word first from *kuchuk* and confounding it with the meaning of κουτσός. Another work purporting to be a sober historical enquiry ends with the wish that our foes may hate us or better still fear us. Such literature can hardly be taken seriously, but at the same time its authors, often hellenized Vlachs, possess a knowledge of the country that no stranger can hope to acquire. Roumanian books on the Vlachs like the Greek are not impartial witnesses. From the nature of the case however they are less liable to fantastic theories ; as regards the language they often minimize the number of Greek loan words in common use, in history and in folklore Rome plays a larger part at times than is either likely or possible and the numbers in the Vlach communities are calculated on a liberal basis. Estimates of population are all exceedingly doubtful ; the Turkish figures take no account of race and are only concerned with religion, so that a Greek may mean a Bulgarian, Vlach or Albanian member of the Patriarchist Church. Nationality too in the Balkans is still in a state of flux ; and classifications according to descent, language or political feeling would lead to different results. To take a simple case from Greece itself ; by descent nearly all the Attic villagers are Albanians, a linguistic test would still give a large number of Albanians, for comparatively few have entirely adopted Greek. Yet if they were asked to what nation they belonged the large majority would probably answer Greek, and all would be Greek in politics and ideals.

A Greek estimate made before political troubles began put the total number of Vlachs at 600,000 ; later Greek estimates give usually a much lower figure. An enthusiastic Roumanian has proposed 2,800,000, but other Roumanian estimates are from about 850,000 upwards. Weigand who has paid more attention to the subject than any other traveller puts the total of Vlachs in the whole peninsula at 373,520. This seems to us to err on the side of moderation, for it is based largely on the calculation of five persons to a house, which from our own experience of Vlach villages is well below the average. Including as Vlachs all those who learnt Vlach as their mother tongue we should estimate the total at not less than half a million. Of these however some will now be using Greek and others Bulgarian in everyday life and their children will not know Vlach at all. Quite apart from questions which involve politics, information of any kind is difficult to acquire. At times courtesy towards the stranger which especially in the villages as we have good reason to know is very real indeed, demands that all answers given should be adapted to the questioner's assumed desires ; on the other hand there is a deep-rooted belief, by no means confined to the villages, that all strangers being credulous the most fantastic answers will suffice. Once in the early days when our knowledge of Vlach was small we arrived at a Vlach village which had just reunited after a winter in the plains. All around were talking Vlach ; we were welcomed kindly by the schoolmaster who spoke to us in Greek. " We only talk Vlach when we first meet again after the winter " were almost his first words. It was not till a month later that we heard another word of Greek.

It is perhaps necessary to add that no dragoman or interpreter has ever been with us on our journeys; most of our wanderings have been made alone and of those many on foot.

CHAPTER II

FROM TIRNAVOS TO SAMARINA

Kānd are z yină prumuveara
S̨ easă Aɪumăul'i prî la mundza,
Lilitshe n'i di pri Maiu!

When it is the season for the spring to come, for the Vlachs to go
out on the mountains, my flower of May!

VLACH SONG

LARGE numbers of the Vlachs from Northern Pindus who pass the winter in the plains of Thessaly or Southern Macedonia arrange their departure for the hills each spring so as to pass through Ghrevena on their way home at the time of the great fair of St Akhillios which begins each year on the Monday that falls between the 16th and the 23rd of May O.S. (May 29th to June 5th N.S.), and lasts four or five days.

Several days before the date of the fair we came to Tirnavos so as to travel up with the Vlach families to Samarina, as we had arranged. We found our muleteer and his family eagerly awaiting our arrival, but some days elapsed before the journey to Samarina began. First there was some uncertainty about the date of the fair, which was proclaimed by the Turkish authorities at Ghrevena, and secondly there was a change of plan as to the route to be followed. The direct route from Tirnavos or any place in Northeastern Thessaly to Ghrevena and the Vlach villages in Northern Pindus leads through the pass of Tirnavos to Kephalovriso leaving Elassona on the right, and then turns westwards to Dhiskata and so by Dhiminitsa and Phili to Ghrevena. This road is that normally used by the Vlachs who are joined as they go by friends and relations from the villages in the valley of the Xerias, the ancient

Europos, the district being known as Potamia. In 1910 however the annual disturbance in Albania had begun somewhat earlier than usual, and all passing into Turkey were liable to be searched rigorously for arms and ammunition. It was considered advisable to avoid the pass of Tirnavos where the Turkish customs officials were reported to be very severe and instead to take a longer route by Trikkala and Kalabaka crossing the frontier at Velemishti. In fairness perhaps to our fellow-travellers it should be said that this change of plan was made in hopes of avoiding the trouble of unpacking all the baggage no light task where whole families are concerned —and not because on this particular occasion they were engaged in smuggling arms.

The few days in Tirnavos were not on the whole unwelcome. We made the acquaintance of several of the Vlach families who like ourselves were bound for the hills, began to learn a few words of their language, and to get a first glimpse of their life, manners and customs. The Vlach population of Tirnavos consists of over a hundred families, nearly all of which come from Samarina. By profession these Vlachs are muleteers, small tradesmen, cobblers, ironworkers, shepherds and butchers, but most either by leaving their business or else taking it with them manage to spend a part, if not all, of the summer in their homes in Pindus.

Thursday, May 26th, was the day finally fixed for departure. The morning and early afternoon were spent in endless preparations. In view of a long and hot journey leeches were put on the mules' hocks, and they were all re-shod. A large amount of wool, for the women to work during the summer, besides household goods and chattels, and clothes had to be stowed away in large striped sacks, and made up into bundles of equal weight, and lastly a lamb had to be roasted whole, an essential preparation for a Vlach journey. All at length being ready, the baggage was loaded on the mules and at five o'clock in the afternoon we left Tirnavos. Our own particular party consisted of our two selves, the muleteer, his grandmother, his mother, his aunt with her two little girls, Phota and Aspasia aged about seven and five, a girl relation, several

PLATE II

1. VLACH FAMILIES ON THE ROAD

2. VLACH MULETEERS

chickens, an ill-tempered kitten and a dog, all of which excepting the last were enthroned on the mules' pack saddles between the bundles of baggage (Plate II 1). One muleteer can work a team of about six mules and a horse. The average load for a mule is slightly over two hundred pounds, to which must be added the weight of the rider, but in hilly or rough ground all dismount except the old women or small children. The horse which leads the caravan usually has a lighter load, but is always ridden, for no Vlach muleteer will walk when he can possibly ride (Plate II 2). *Imnăndălui* which literally means on foot, is Vlach slang for being in the gutter. Attached to our party was a muleteer from Smiksi with his five mules, three of which were devoted to carrying an old woman, her daughter and their belongings, and the other two to transporting part of the property of our muleteer's family. Thus on leaving Tirnavos we had in all a train of ten animals. Owing to the late start the first stage of the journey was soon finished, and at 7.30 p.m. we stopped for the night at a place not far from the ferry over the Peneus at Ghunitsa, where we found several other families already encamped, who had left Tirnavos shortly before us. The mules were soon unladen, the bundles piled up in an orderly row, rugs spread on the ground, and after discussing the roast lamb we turned in for the night, while the muleteers picked up their goat's-hair capes and went to sleep and watch by their mules. Curiously enough no Vlach muleteer ever tethers or hobbles his mules at night when they are turned loose to graze. Consequently he must watch them as much to prevent straying as theft. Here as on most occasions when the night was clear conversation turned on Halley's comet which was then blazing in the western sky. It was pointing towards Macedonia, and was thought to be a sign of war.

The practice of starting late in the day and camping for the night after a journey of two hours or even less is common among Vlach muleteers, although not peculiar to them alone. At first sight there is little to recommend this plan, but in practice it is found to be the only effective means of securing an early and a punctual start on the following day.

In summer also and for the greater part of the year a night
in the open is preferable to one in a village khan, which is
sure to be stuffy and probably also very dirty.

Friday, May 27th.—All were astir long before dawn and at
4 a.m. the mules being laden we moved down to the river
bank to await our turn for the ferry boat, which took five
mules and seven or eight people each journey. Meanwhile
the sun had risen and we could see up the gorge made by the
river as it breaks through the bare limestone hills that border
the Thessalian plain. The Turkish frontier here crossed the
river and recrossing it below Kutsókhiro included a group of
hills on the southern bank. These hills to the south of the
Peneus were one of the strategic advantages obtained by the
Turks after the war of 1897, and were joined to the rest of
Turkey by a military bridge, just visible from Ghunitsa ferry.
While we waited on the bank the iniquities of a certain khan-
keeper, who had best be nameless, came under discussion.
A muleteer made a miniature grave mound, put a cross at
its head, and formally cursed the khan-keeper with the words,
" So-and-so is dead." Within a year he was robbed, abandoned
his khan, and fled. A belief in this particular form of magic
is probably common amongst both Vlachs and Greeks, but no
other example has yet come under our notice. After an
hour's delay all were safely across, and we continued our way
over the plain keeping the frontier close on the right. Soon
we overtook another family that had made an earlier start
on the previous day, and passed the river before nightfall.
Their unusual display of energy had met with its own reward,
for we found them vainly searching for two mules that had
strayed during the night. An hour and a half from Ghunitsa
we reached the Trikkala road about seventeen kilometres
west of Larissa, and following it crossed the Peneus for the
second time by the ferry at Kutsokhiro. The old wooden
bridge, that spanned the river here was carried away many
years ago by a flood. Preparations were promptly made
for a new one : an embankment was made for the road,
and piers were built in the river. The work was then
abandoned, and has not now been touched for several

years. Local opinion is undecided as to who is precisely to blame, and suggests the ferryman or the railway which is supposed to dislike road traffic. We crossed this time with little delay, but two mules jammed their bundles in the ferry boat and broke a bottle containing five okes of the best Tirnavos *uzo*. *Uzo* is the North Greek variety of rakí ; that made at Tirnavos is justly famous. We followed the road for some distance, and at 10 a.m. halted in a grove of mulberry trees by the roadside just beyond the khan of Zarkos. The village of Zarkos, which lies in a recess in the hills to the north of the road, has a considerable Vlach population mainly from Avdhela.

The midday halt lasted several hours. Fires were lit and enough food cooked to last till the next day, for the camping ground where the night was to be spent was known to be bare of fuel. On the most frequented routes the muleteers have regular camping grounds where wood, water and grass can be found together. The whole journey is often calculated by so many *kunăk'ĭ* or camps, and the length of each day's journey depends on the position of these rather than on the distance actually covered. The sun was so hot that those who could not find shade under the mulberries unpacked and set up their tents. As a race the Vlachs seem to feel the heat to an excessive degree, and even in the hills will complain of the sun on a day which most would consider only reasonably warm. A Vlach tent, which is only used for sun or heavy rain, is of a simple and effective type (Plate III 2). It consists of a long, oblong blanket, very thick and made of coarse wool, and in colour white with broad black or dark brown stripes. The narrow ends are pegged to the ground, while the centre is supported by two light poles connected at the top by a thin cross-bar. The baggage heaped up and covered by another blanket forms a back, and so a simple gable tent without a door is made. These tents have two points in their favour, first the sides can be touched without any fear of letting in the rain, and secondly they are very light and portable. The two poles and the cross-bar, hardly thicker than laths, make no appreciable difference to any mule load, and the

blanket helps to temper the hardness of a wooden pack
saddle.   In a more severe climate a Vlach tent might prove
insufficient ; a door would be an advantage, and might easily
be contrived ; but for Macedonia however they will be found
in all ways satisfactory.   As to how many each tent holds
opinions will differ, for it depends on the state of the weather
outside, but on a bad night six or seven can sleep inside with
comfort.

Breaking camp at 4 p.m. we start off again towards Trikkala
in a long procession increased by several families that had
joined us in the course of the morning from Tatár and other
villages near Larissa and Tirnavos.   The main road to Trikkala here runs along the foot of the hills, in places on a small
embankment, and in places cut out of the hill-side to avoid
some large pools and marshes fed by springs at the hill foot.
This road does not appear on the Austrian staff map, which
marks instead a presumably older road, now never used, some
distance to the south.   At 7.30 p.m. we turned off the road to
the north and camped on a small level space between the foot
of the hills and the marshes.   On a low isolated hill just behind
our camp are the ruins of a Hellenic and medieval city, known
now as Paleogardhíki.   Directly separating this from the
main range is a deep hollow in the ground called Zurpapá
where local tradition says that a priest who by a trick had
obtained his bishop's permission to commit incest with his
daughter, was swallowed up.

Saturday, May 28th.—An early start was made at 3.30 a.m.
in order to get beyond Kalabaka by evening.   We turned back
into the main road, and went straight along it to Trikkala,
the first place that merits notice on this day's journey.   Two-
thirds at least of the population of this town are Vlachs or of
Vlach extraction.   Some of the Samarina Vlachs since the
cession of Thessaly to Greece in 1881, became permanent
residents on Greek soil, and founded a New Samarina in the
southern part of Pindus due west of Trikkala above Karvuno-
Lepenitsa, to which they go in the summer.   But the majority
are still faithful to their old homes, and as we passed through
the town several families joined us increasing the caravan to

PLATE III

1. VLACH FAMILIES ENCAMPING

2. A VLACH CAMP AT MIDDAY

over a mile in length. Many more came out to say good-bye, and send messages to friends and relations at Ghrevena and elsewhere.

Beyond Trikkala we set our faces northwards. Here the character of the country changes rapidly ; trees become more common ; the wide, open plain contracts, and beyond Kalabaka gives place to a wooded valley through which the Peneus comes down from Malakási. Up this valley is the famous route that leads over the Zighós to Metsovo and Yannina and throughout history has been the main road into Thessaly from the west. In the last thirty years since the cession of Thessaly it has fallen into disuse. The creation of a frontier across this route and the high Greek customs tariff have strangled the once flourishing trade, and the villages on it, which are nearly all Vlach, have dwindled in size.

At 10.30 a.m. a halt was made on the banks of the river of Trikkala at the foot of the hill on which stands the monastery of St Theodore. Two views of this encampment showing the rocks of the Metéora in the distance are given on Plate III.

At 4 p.m. we started again, and reaching Kalabaka just before sunset followed the valley northwards. We skirt the foot of the Meteora rocks, pass the village of Kastráki, and going slowly over a rough track that had once been a paved road pass a khan, and then camp for the night at 8.30 p.m. in a field about an hour from Kastraki.

Sunday, May 29th.—There was a long delay in starting. Two mules during the night had strayed into a field of maize, and had been impounded by the watchmen. By the time they had been ransomed and all was ready it was 6 a.m.

This late start had its advantages as we had a glimpse up the Peneus valley towards Malakasi and saw the isolated monastery-crowned crags of the Meteora by daylight. From time to time on our way up from Kalabaka we passed under rocks of the same weird formation and saw others standing by the edges of the valleys like grim sentinels. Then we turned off up the bed of the Murghani river where the plane trees on either side prevented any distant view.

At about nine o'clock we leave the river bed, and at 10 a.m.

2

camp on the hill-side about an hour from Velemishti. Here
we were in the midst of a fine champaign country which was
very pleasant to the eyes after the scorched and treeless
Thessalian plains. Here were rolling hills, green and grassy,
and well covered with trees among which oaks and wild pears
were prominent. Water seemed plentiful, and the soil rich.
This, if looks go for anything, should be an ideal agricultural
and pastoral district. At 4 p.m. we were off again, and passing
through the village without stopping reached the frontier
station on the top of the ridge about half a mile further on.
The Turkish customs officer, an Albanian, did not prove quite
so amenable as had been hoped. He ordered all the mules to
be unladen, and then satisfied his conscience by making a
superficial search or rather by kicking each bundle in turn.
This and the examination of passports occupied the time till
sunset, so we stopped for the night on a grassy slope on the
Turkish side.

Velemishti is a squalid Hashiot village, which owns several
vineyards and some fields of corn and maize, and is wealthy
compared with other Hashiot villages. The district called
Hashia comprises the hill country between the Peneus and the
Haliakmon on both sides of the former Graeco-Turkish frontier.
Its western limit may be marked roughly by a line drawn
from Ghrevena to Kalabaka, and its eastern limit by a similar
line from Serfije through Elassona to Tirnavos. The name
seems to imply that the villages in this district are all chiftliks.
That is to say that each village instead of being composed of
small holdings, is the absolute property of one or more absentee
landlords. The inhabitants are thus little better than serfs,
for within their own villages they can own nothing. The
landlords are represented by resident bailiffs who collect the
share of the produce due to the landlord. The landlord's
share is usually a half, if he finds the seed and the cost of plough-
ing, and a third if the peasant finds them. Often petty acts
of tyranny take place. Some will take their third or half
before setting aside the seed corn. Others will let the whole of
the common pasturage of the village to nomad shepherds,
and refuse the peasants any right of pasture without payment,

for the usual custom is that a peasant has the right to pasture so many head of sheep, cattle or horses. The houses even when they boast two stories, are built of wattle and daub or of mud-brick, but are as a rule in a most dilapidated and filthy condition. The peasant has no interest in repairing what is not his own, and the landlord is anxious only for his income. The inhabitants, though as might be expected in hill villages, they are often sturdy and healthy in appearance, are probably the lowest type of Greek to be found. They are slow and stupid and excessively dirty. Amongst their neighbours they have a bad reputation, for they are thought to be dishonest and treacherous. In fact the name Hashiot with some is almost a synonym for a dirty and thievish beggar.

The woods in the neighbourhood of Velemishti made it a favourable place for all who wished to cross the frontier unobserved. In the autumn of 1911, when owing to the cholera in Macedonia, the Greek authorities took strict measures to see that all who entered Greece secretly should at least do quarantine, the extent of this traffic was revealed. At Velemishti alone in the space of five days over fifty such persons were found, including a band of five brigands who had spent the summer in Macedonia, and an average of ten a day was considered normal. Absentee landlordism, and the facilities once offered for brigandage by the frontier in the absence of any extradition treaty, seem to be the main reasons for the deplorable state of the Hashiot villages.

Monday, May 30th.—We start at 6 a.m. having first said good-bye to the Albanian customs officer, who is left in a state of blank amazement at two Europeans who travel with Vlachs and prefer a night in the open to one in an aged guard house. Our road leads through country similar to that below Velemishti. To the north-east we see a fine stretch of open undulating country extending as far as Dhiminitsa and the Haliakmon ; to the north-west whither our way lies, we go across rolling hills well covered with oak woods and scrub. An hour after starting we pass Mánesi unseen on the left, and shortly after a Turkish gendarmerie station just visible on a wooded ridge to the right. Four gendarmes watching by the roadside were the only sign of life till we reached Pléshia, a miserable Hashiot village. This consists of some half-dozen buildings of wattle and daub looking far less like human habitations than dissipated pigstyes. When we passed through Pleshia in August 1912 it was totally deserted.

The long procession of mules slowly climbs the ridge beyond this village, and here our fellow-travellers obtain their first glimpse of their native land. There to the north-west towering over the craggy ridge of Spíleo are the great peaks of Pindus, Zmolku and Vasilitsa, still covered with snow, and half hidden in clouds. The first sight of their home naturally caused great excitement amongst young and old.

" Have you mountains in your country ? "

" Yes, but our mountains are not so high."

" Our mountains are covered with pines and beeches."

" In England pines and beeches grow in the plains."

Chorus of children and others somewhat incredulous, " They say that they have pines and beeches in the plains, but their mountains are not so high as ours."

At 10.30 we halt in a clearing by a spring for the usual midday rest, and at 3 p.m. start again so as to reach the scene of the fair before nightfall. The country continues to be thickly wooded until just beyond Eleftherokhóri, a Hashiot village, somewhat larger than Pleshia, but equally filthy, where after a sharp descent we reach the banks of the Venetikó river, the most considerable tributary of the Haliakmon in this district. At this point there is a stone bridge over the river, but so broken that the mules had to be led across, which is usually known as the bridge of Ghrevena, though the town lies on another small river an hour to the north. The Vlachs however call the bridge Puñyea di Pushanlu, the Bridge of Pushan. As all had to dismount when crossing the bridge, and since there was some excitement over the prospect of reaching the town soon, our caravan unconsciously assumed the order usual when approaching a resting-place. First came a troop of boys of all ages from eight to fourteen hurrying on on foot, and eager to be in first. They were followed by a band of women and girls also on foot, most of whom were carrying their shoes in their hands in order to get over the rough ground more easily. The rear was brought up by the long and slowly moving procession of laden mules (Plate II 1), by side of which walked the muleteers and men urging them on with sticks, stones and curses, and ever on the look out lest a mule should get into rough ground. If a mule gets into uneven ground, the clumsy bundles balanced on its pack saddle, which is never tightly girthed, begin to sway ominously from side to side, and may turn right over to one side saddle and all, and so involve five minutes' delay while all is unfastened, and reloaded. Also should a mule stumble and fall it cannot get up again unaided ; the load is too heavy and clumsy. Then when men rush in on either side and lift the bundles to help the mule to rise, the perverse animal as often as not politely declines to do so, and rolls over on its side kicking out in a tangle of ropes, bales, chickens, cooking pots, puppies and any other small items that may have been thrown on top. Between each of the three divisions of the caravan there was a gap, and with the last mounted on the mules was all that could not walk, grandmothers, cats, babies and chickens.

Up the steep ascent on the other side of the Venetiko we pushed on ahead with the division of boys, till we came out on to a wide grassy plateau. This was covered with droves of grazing mules and horses, each in charge of a small Vlach boy, and showed that at last the fair was near at hand. In less than an hour the plateau was crossed, and suddenly on reaching its northern edge Ghrevena and the fair of St Akhillios came into view. The shelving slope beneath us was covered with groups of Vlach tents arranged according to villages. Here were the Smiksi families from Potamia, there the Perivoli folk from Velestinos, beyond the Samarina people from Elassona, below the Avdhela families, and so on. At the foot of the slope was the river of Ghrevena, a wide but shallow stream, which flows into the Haliakmon a few miles further east. Directly in front on the further bank was the town with its trees, minarets and clock tower nestling in the valley. Immediately to the east a flat, open common by the river was the actual scene of the fair, thronged with people and dotted with booths. Being late arrivals—the fair had begun that morning—it took us some time to find a vacant space to pitch our tents. This accomplished we spent the last remains of daylight in wandering through the encampment, looking at the busy crowd on the far side of the river and enquiring after the prospects, sights and shows of the morrow.

Ghrevena (Plate IV 1), which the Vlachs call Grebene and the Turks Gcrebina, is a long straggling town and of considerable strategic importance as it commands both the roads leading from Northwestern Thessaly into the upper basin of the Haliakmon, and those leading from Yannina and Konitsa towards Salonica through Southwestern Macedonia. For this reason at the beginning of the war of 1897 Greek irregular bands under Davelis with some Garibaldians under Cipriani made a fruitless raid over the frontier with the object of seizing Ghrevena and so cutting the Turkish communications between Epirus and Macedonia. The town is the seat of a Greek orthodox bishop and what we know of its history is principally due to its bishops. Pouqueville says that it is included by Constantine Porphyrogenitus in his list of the towns of Macedonia as Γρίβανα, but the Bonn text reads Πρίβανα. The bishopric was one of those subject to the independent Patriarchate of Achrida (the modern Okhridha). It was not one of the original dioceses mentioned in the golden bull of Basil II when he confirmed the privileges of this Bulgarian Patriarchate, but it occurs in two lists of the bishoprics in the eleventh and twelfth centuries. Dositheos relates that Leo Archbishop of Achrida, one Saturday ordained a certain Ἰωάννης Κοψόχειρος priest, and the next day, Sunday, consecrated him bishop of Ghrevena. Le Quien thought this referred to Leo II, who lived early in the twelfth century, but it is just possible that it might refer to Leo I who flourished in the eleventh century. Demetrios Chomatianos, Archbishop of Achrida in the first half of the thirteenth century, mentions in one of his letters the death of Theodore, bishop of Ghrevena. We next hear of the bishopric in 1382 and an ecclesiastical document of the Patriarch of Constantinople dated 1395 mentions κάστρον Γρεβενὸν λεγόμενον. From other sources we learn that on December 6th 1422 Neophytos Bishop of Ghrevena died, and that in 1538 the bishop was called Symeon. In lists giving the dioceses under the Patriarch of Achrida and in the synodical acts and other documents of the same Patriarchate of the seventeenth and eighteenth centuries the diocese and its bishops are frequently mentioned. The earliest bishop given is Gregory who was alive in 1668. He was followed by Theophanes who flourished about 1676. This energetic prelate although the synod had already chosen another Patriarch of Achrida, journeyed to Adrianople and obtained the see through the Sublime Porte. He was formally dethroned by the Patriarch of Constantinople. His accusers alleged that though only a monk he had seized the bishopric of Ghrevena and had acted as such without being consecrated. Further he was said to have induced the Patriarch of Achrida, Ignatios a man of no intelligence and ignorant of ecclesiastical law to consecrate him. He was also accused of perjury, adultery, theft and of trying to take from the Patriarchate of Constantinople and bring under his own authority the diocese of Beroea. Other bishops mentioned are Pankratios, Theophanes (this name occurs from 1683 to 1740, so probably there were two of the same name), Seraphim, Makarios and Gabriel.

After the Turkish conquest Ghrevena obtained the position which it held throughout Turkish times, as the capital of a district, first as the seat of a mudir till 1860, and then of a kaimmakam till 1912. In the sixteenth century according to Aravandinos, it was made the centre for one of the capitanliks of armatoli, a kind of christian militia maintained by the Turkish government to guard the roads and keep order. These armatoli were often brigands, who were taken into service on the principle of setting a thief to catch a thief. Robbers frequently betrayed one another to the authorities, and if any armatoli and brigands fell in a skirmish, the Turks philosophically considered that it was merely a case of dog eating dog. Ghrevena is often mentioned in the modern Greek klephtic ballads, large numbers of which refer to Vlach or Kupatshar worthies. When the armatoli system fell into disorder this region, like most of Western Macedonia, was put into the strong hand of Ali Pasha. Afterwards it formed part of the independent sanjak of Serfije, which was later attached to the vilayet of Monastir. Some interesting details about the armatoli and brigands of Ghrevena can be gleaned from Aravandinos, Lambridhis and other sources, which we have supplemented by personal enquiries on the spot. One of the most renowned was Dhimitrios Totskas, a native of Olympus, who flourished in the latter half of the eighteenth century. He built a church of Ayia Paraskevi at Alpokhori, and in 1776 at the suggestion of Ayios Kosmas gave forty fonts to forty villages, and in 1779 built a mill at Dhervizhana which produced a yearly income of twenty pounds for the church. This was only one side of his life. When urged by Ayios Kosmas to give up his robber life, he is said to have replied that in the spring his inclinations naturally turned towards brigandage and murder. In 1770 or soon after he in company with Belos the capitan of Metsovo, waylaid and cut to pieces a band of Albanians returning with plunder from the unsuccessful Greek rising in the Peloponnese, which had been instigated by the Russians under Orloff. This exploit is said to have taken place between Smiksi and Philippei, and so probably on the col of Morminde. In 1780 he was bribed by Abdi Pasha to ambush one Tsomanga of Metsovo, but only succeeded in killing his fellow-traveller K. Kaphetsis. He was murdered by the orders of Kurt Pasha in the church-yard at Dhervizhana, where he usually wintered. Aravandinos asserts that he flourished under Ali Pasha, was the successor of Yeorghakis Zhakas of Mavronoro as capitan of Ghrevena and was killed at Kipurio in 1809. Yeorghakis Zhakas of Mavronoro was the founder of the best known brigand family. He served under Deli Dhimos whom he succeeded as capitan of Ghrevena, but later is said to have quarrelled with Ali Pasha and joined forces with Vlakhavas who in 1808 made an unsuccessful revolt in Thessaly. Yeorghakis who died in 1814, was succeeded by his two sons Yiannulas and Theodhoros, who by their activity as brigands compelled the authorities to recognise them as armatoli. In 1826 the two brothers were betrayed and attacked in their house at Mavronoro by Mehmed Agha, the energetic Mutesellim of Ghrevena. Yiannulas was killed, but Theodhoros escaped to Greece. Two years later he returned and his first act was to revenge himself on the Makri family who had betrayed him. He is said to have killed them on his brother's grave. About the same time he conducted a very successful raid against the rich Greek village of Neghadhes in the Zaghori. In 1831 he invaded Ghrevena and burnt many houses both christian and Turkish. The next year he with two companions was attacked by Mehmed Agha at Spileo, but escaped. In 1832 he took part with other brigand chiefs in the sacking and burning of Kastania in Phthiotis. Up till 1835 he remained in the Zaghori or near Ghrevena as the terror of the country, but in that year he retired into Greece. In 1852 he surrendered to the authorities at Yannina, but quickly returned to his old trade again. In 1854 he joined in the abortive rising in Epirus, Thessaly and Macedonia. He is said to have rescued some Samarina families when attacked in camp by Turkish troops, and was later blockaded by Abdi Pasha in the monastery at Spileo. When Zhakas was actively pursuing his trade as brigand in the Zaghori he made his head-quarters in the Vale Kaldă (warm valley) near Baieasa, the great hiding-place at all periods for robbers. To-day a craggy height near Valea Kaldă is known as Zhakas' fort and is so marked on the Austrian staff map. In 1878 in his old age he took part in the rising in Thessaly, and on its failure retired to his estate at Akhladhi near Lamia in Greece where he died about 1882 full of years and honour. On the Turkish side Mehmed Agha was the most prominent character at Ghrevena in those stormy times. His grandfather Husseyn Agha was one of three brothers who left Bana Luka in Bosnia in the eighteenth century. One settled at Avlona in Southern Albania, one somewhere in Anatolia, and the third at Ghrevena. His son

Veli Agha was ruler of Ghrevena in the days of Ali Pasha,
and after the death of the Lion of Yannina is said to have
taken part in the siege of Mesolongi. His son Mehmed Agha
was for some time at Yannina with Ali Pasha and was smuggled
out of the town across the lake in a coffin by Duda, one of the
Pasha's couriers. He then rode for his life to Ghrevena.
Afterwards he made Duda's two sons devrentji's, one at the
Bridge of the Pasha over the Haliakmon on the road between
Ghrevena and Shatishta, and the other at Mavranei. Mehmed
Agha on his death was succeeded by his son Veli Bey who
died in 1880. The latter's two sons Rif'at and Fu'ád live in
their grandfather's great fortified house in Ghrevena to-day
(1912). The house or rather fort (Plate IV 1) stands in the
middle of the town and covers an area of between two and
three acres. From outside one sees a high loopholed wall
built in an oblong space. At each angle is a square tower
and in the middle of each of the long sides there is another.
The gate is in the middle of the southern short wall facing
towards the river of Ghrevena and the two corner towers on
this side are larger than the others. The entrance goes
obliquely through the thick wall and one is in the midst of a
large courtyard in the centre of which a big, strongly built,
Turkish house stands like a keep. The whole place was
constructed for refuge and defence. Sheep and horses could
be pastured within the walls which enclose four springs and a
cistern. On the north side of the house was an isolated
tower standing in the court, which was the powder magazine.
The dates still visible in two places on the outside wall are
1829 and 1830 which show that the dates given in the tales
about the career of Mehmed Agha are probably fairly accurate.
He was exceedingly active in attempting to suppress brigandage and is frequently mentioned in the klephtic ballads. He
was constantly skirmishing with Zhakas and his friends, one
of whom Yeorghakis Bisovitis he compelled to surrender and
shortly after murdered in the market-place at Ghrevena,
according to Aravandinos. In December 1832 he besieged
the band of Suleyman Beltsopulos in the church at Subeno,
and setting fire to it destroyed both brigands and church

PLATE IV

1. GHREVENA: CORNER TOWERS OF THE HOUSE OF MEHMED AGHA
ON THE LEFT

2. SAMARINA: THE DANCE AT THE FESTIVAL OF THE ASSUMPTION

together. In 1844 he is said to have abducted a maiden
of Ghrevena called Sula, who had refused to become his wife.
His grandchildren say that his first wife was a christian maiden
from Phili and that on her death he married her sister Midhala
by whom he had one son and three daughters. He died
in 1864 not far short of eighty years of age.

Scanty as our information is it gives us some idea of the
state of the district during the first half of the nineteenth
century. The Turkish government frightened by the Greek
revolution had determined to extinguish the armatoli, between
whom and the brigands there was little difference. In Ghrevona
was a Turkish garrison and some Albanian irregulars. Their
duty was to suppress brigandage, and keep the main roads
safe. The brigands would protect their own country against
other bands, and support themselves by raiding neighbouring
districts, christian or Turkish. But as we have seen in the
case of the brothers Zhakas, there were feuds amongst the
brigands themselves. If pursuit was too hot the robbers
would retire into Greece, or surrender to the authorities and
keep quiet for a time till they found a favourable opportunity
to resume their profession.

Ghrevena itself consists of two quarters. One is the town
proper called Kasabas, really the Turkish word for town
(Qasaba), where are the market, shops, government offices,
prison and so on. The other is called Varoshi and lies to the
west beyond a small stream. It is an exclusively christian
quarter standing on a low hill, and comprises the bishop's
palace, the metropolis, and some houses clustering round
them. In Leake's day there were twenty, but now there are
many more. Pouqueville states that the town was founded
by colonists from a place he calls Castron-Bouchalistas, but
he does not say where this latter place was. It is possible
that it may be the Valakhadhes village of Kastro which lies
about three hours west of Ghrevena and contains the ruins of
a medieval fort. Locally it is said that the first inhabitants
of Ghrevena came from a place called Ghrevian Rakhiotis
a ridge on the hill towards the village of Kira Kale about
an hour north-west of the town. But with the information

at present at our disposal it seems impossible to decide how
or when the town was founded. Meletios, bishop of Athens,
who lived from 1661 to 1714, says the town was commonly
known as Avles, a statement doubted by Pouqueville. Leake
says, " The Turkish makhala (quarter) of Greveno . . . is the
chief place of Grevena, which in the plural number compre-
hends a great number of small Turkish villages and tjiftliks."
Locally it is said that the town was once known as Avles,
and that the particular quarter known by this name was inhabited by christians near the Turkish posting station and
stood, where there are now fields, near the centre of the town
on the bank of the river. Opposite this on the south side of
the river was another quarter called Tshakalia which was the
part burnt by Zhakas. This Avles quarter was still in existence about a hundred and thirty years ago and was the
Varoshi of those days. After the freedom of Greece Turks
from Lala in the Peloponnese unable to live under a christian
government came and settled in Ghrevena and occupied the
centre of the town. Then the movement of the christians
to the present Varoshi began. The Metropolis was built about
1837, and is dedicated to St George, St Demetrius and St
Akhillios. Before then there was only a small church of St
George on the hill top in the midst of a wood, and houses were
first built round it about 1780. The principal mosque by the
Turkish cemetery on the west of the town was once the church
of St Akhillios, and the other mosque to the east the church
of Ayia Paraskevi. These were taken over by the Turks from
Lala and about the same time they destroyed, so it is said,
three other churches in the town, St Demetrius, St Nicholas
and St Athanasius. The bishop did not always live at
Ghrevena, but at Kipurio, so they say locally, and he used
to be known as ὁ Ἅγιος Ἀυλῶν, a name which never occurs in
any of the documents relating to the bishopric referred to above.
Still the little stream that comes down from Kira Kale and
flows through the middle of the town is called Avliotis, and
consequently the tale about the name Avles may possibly
have some foundation and not be derived merely from a study
of Meletios' geography.

Ghrevena though situated in the valley and having no good water supply is a pleasant little town, but in summer is very hot. Above the town to the east is a large Turkish school and in a similar position to the west are the barracks. There are Greek and Vlach schools, several mosques, seven Greek churches and a Vlach chapel. A market well attended by the inhabitants of the neighbouring villages is held every Monday. The population cannot be estimated because so much of it is floating. The christians consist of Greeks from the Hashiot and Kupatshar villages, and Vlachs from Samarina, Smiksi, Perivoli, and Avdhela who are always more numerous in the winter. The Mohammedans consist of Albanians, Valakhadhes, and Turks from here, there and everywhere. Of course since the war of 1912 in which it was partly burnt, Ghrevena has probably changed considerably in every way.

Tuesday, May 31st, the second day of the fair.—Shortly after dawn we crossed the river on a diminutive donkey hired from a venerable Turk at a halfpenny a journey, and went at once to the fair. The crowd amounted to several thousands, and the majority were Vlachs. Vlach was the language most commonly in use, and no one who has heard the babble of a Vlach crowd can doubt the origin of the name Tsintsar. There were Vlachs from nearly every part of Southern Macedonia, and Thessaly: most were in the national costume. Vlach costume is a complicated and extensive subject, and for a full account of the various garments and their names the reader must turn to a later chapter. Besides Vlachs, there were Greeks mostly Hashiots, a few Turks not counting gendarmes and other officials, some gipsies dressed as usual in gaudy rags, and a number of Valakhadhes, and Kupatshari. The Valakhadhes are a mysterious people, Mohammedan by religion, but Greek by language, who principally inhabit the districts of Ghrevena, and Lapsíshta where they occupy many villages. The Vlachs call them Vláhadzĭ and say that they are Vlachs who became Mohammedans, deriving the name from Vlach Agha, but this etymology is hardly convincing. According to a more probable tale they are Greeks converted to Islam and are called Valakhadhes because the only Turkish they know is V'alláhi, By God. As an analogous case one may perhaps quote the Pomaks or Mohammedan Bulgarians of the Salonica province who after the Turkish revolution of 1908 were sedulously taught by the Young Turks as part of their programme of Ottomanisation to say *V'alláhi* instead of *Boga mi*. Nicolaidy who wrote in 1859 says that two hundred years before two Greek boys from a village near Lapsishta were taken as slaves to Constantinople and were there converted to Islam. Later they returned to their native land and began to preach the doctrines of their new faith. They made many converts among the christians anxious to escape from their inferior position and to obtain the right to bear arms, and were eventually rewarded with the title of Bey. Pouqueville seems to have thought that they were the descendants of the Vardariot Turks of Byzantine times, a theory which hardly seems possible. Weigand says that their racial type is Greek rather than Slavonic and that they have dark hair and aquiline noses. On the other hand many of those we have seen were tall and fair. But if the name Valakhadhes merely means that they are converts to Mahommedanism, it need have no racial significance.

The Kupatshari are hellenized or semi-hellenized Vlachs. That is to say that through intermarriage and the influence of the church and Greek education they have abandoned their native language. They still however retain the Vlach national costume, and many Vlach words occur in their dialect as well as many non-Greek sounds such as *sh, zh, tsh*, and *dzh*. They inhabit the district between Ghrevena and the pure Vlach villages of Pindus. At one of their villages, Labanitsa, which is only half hellenized we obtained some insight as to the process by which denationalisation occurs. In the school and church Greek is the only language used. All the older men in the village know Vlach and so do many of the women. But owing to the fact that the males outnumber the females the men are obliged to take brides from other villages. Pure Vlach villages like Turia and Perivoli are too proud to give their daughters in marriage to Kupatshari and so the bachelors of Labanitsa take brides from villages like Zalovo which are more or less completely hellenized. The children of these mixed marriages talk only Greek, the language they learn from their mothers, and so the younger generation for the most part knows only Greek. The name Kupatshari is derived by the Vlachs from the word *kupatshu*, oak tree, because the district inhabited by them is covered with oak woods. Lower down in the Haliakmon valley there are no woods, and higher up in the country from Turia to Samarina is the region of pines and beeches. This plausible explanation is rejected by Weigand, who says the word is of Slavonic origin and means digger or agriculturist. This would well apply to these people, for they are a settled folk and till the soil, and do not migrate like the mountain villages. Weigand further says that the Kupatshari district extends as far as Shátishta and into North Thessaly, but we have never heard the name applied to any other district except the lower hill country reaching from Ghrevena to Philippei and Kipurio.

The main business of the fair was concerned with the buying and selling of mules. These are brought from all parts, but the best according to experts are those from Kassándra and Xánthi. A young Kassandra mule half broken and not in condition to carry a heavy load for several months was selling at anything between eighteen and twenty-two Turkish pounds, a price slightly dearer than the year before. Mules that had already been worked were also being sold, and had branches stuck in the pack saddles to indicate that they were for sale. Horses were less in evidence. A few animals, small according to English ideas, but useful enough, were being cantered recklessly through the crowd, and shewn off to some Turkish beys and a group of gendarmes looking for fresh mounts. Each sale had to be confirmed by a document giving the description and price of the animal sold, which was written out and stamped by a local official. The rows of booths filled a large space : food stalls where bread, wine, and lamb in all forms were on sale did the greatest trade, and after them came saddlemakers, and the sweet shops. At one end of the fair was an open court with small stone built shops around it, where jewellery, knives, cottons, silks, woollen goods, and watches and clocks were sold. But all except the jewellery, which was mostly silver filigree work, some of the watches, and the knives, were of European manufacture. In another part Gipsy coppersmiths squatting on the ground were offering for sale water pots and jugs of all shapes and sizes. Near them were many Vlach women with cast-off clothes which were finding a ready market with Hashiots, and cloaks and heavy woollen rugs and blankets of their own manufacture.

Shortly after midday it began to rain in Pindus, and late in the afternoon the storm reached Ghrevena. The fair quickly became a scene of confusion, and there was a rush from all sides to cross the river to regain the shelter of the tents. Only a few had crossed when a bore was seen coming rapidly down, and what a few minutes before had been a clear stream of not more than a foot deep, was quickly turned into a muddy, impassable torrent. Some seeing what was happening ran down stream, and cutting off a corner owing to a bend in the river crossed just in front of the flood. Most however cut off from their tents had to wait in the rain and mud till an hour later when the river regained its normal size. Our tent was pitched on the hill side, and the rain soon began to trickle in at the bottom, and flow in streams across the floor. No trench that could be dug with a *baltáki*, that typical Balkan weapon, which is used for all things and does nothing well, proved of the slightest use. A *baltaki* in shape is like a broad bladed adze on a short haft, but in use is a cross between a hammer, a chisel, a spade, a carving knife and a can-opener. When bed-time came the women went out and cut branches from the thorn bushes round about. These they strewed on the ground and covered with rugs, and so made a couch which, if not absolutely dry, was not wet enough to be noticed.

These sudden storms and floods are a common feature in certain parts of Northwestern Greece, and Macedonia, and at times do considerable damage as happened at Trikkala in June 1907 when many houses were destroyed. In most generalisations on Greek climate the year is divided into a dry season, summer, and a wet season, winter. But this is by no means always the case. In 1910 there was practically no winter at all, except on the hills, until March, when snow fell in the Thessalian plain. In 1911 there was severe cold in January and February, and as late as the beginning of May snow fell on the lower hills. Throughout the summer violent thunderstorms are not uncommon in the Samarina district, and the Thessalian hills. They begin usually shortly after noon and last only for an hour or two, and Leake records the same phenomena as existing also in Aetolia and Epirus. The fact is that there are two separate climates in Greece, and the southern part of the Balkan peninsula. In the plains towards the east and south from Seres as far as Messenia there is a dry, warm southern climate. In the hills to the north-west and in Upper Macedonia there is a climate which may be called Central European, with short summers and winters, but with long springs and autumns. The effect of this on the country is most important, for it enables what may be conventionally called a northern race to flourish to some extent in latitudes suitable to mediterranean man. A careful examination of the flora and fauna of the regions referred to would possibly lead to the same conclusion.

Wednesday, June 1st.—Though we awoke soon after sunrise, several hours elapsed before the mules were collected, and it was 9 a.m. when we started from Ghrevena in a long line that was a good four miles from end to end. Our own party had been increased by the addition of a new mule, a purchase at the fair, which was said to be nervous, and had an uncertain temper. Just beyond the outskirts of Ghrevena we left the metalled road that goes towards Yannina, and turned up a muddy track over low hills covered with thick woods of stunted oaks towards Mavronoro. Mavronoro is a Kupatshar village, and to judge by appearances prosperous. The houses are strongly built of stone, and have few windows on the ground floor so as to be capable of defence. Round the village are vineyards, and orchards of plums, pears, apples, cherries and walnuts. The inhabitants live by agriculture or in bad seasons brigandage, though of late the younger men have begun to emigrate to America mainly owing to the conscription

3

of christians for the army instituted by the constitutional regime in Turkey. Passing through the middle of this village we soon after reached Vriashteno, a village of a similar type, but dirtier and inhabited by Valakhadhes. Thence we descended to the river of Vriashteno as the highter waters of the Venetiko are commonly called. Owing to the recent rain the river was well above its normal height, and even at the ford the water was up to the girths. The mules that were being ridden gave little or no trouble. But it was a different matter with the others which were laden only with baggage, or rather with baggage plus a few children tied round their middles or chickens tied by the legs. These mules, waiting till they were about half-way across, would then begin to wander aimlessly up stream, stumbling and slipping over the smooth round boulders in the bed of the river. The baggage would roll from side to side, first one pack and then the other would dip in the water, and the whole would threaten to fall. This had to be avoided at all costs, since if a laden mule falls in a river there is some danger of its being drowned. Sticks, stones and curses hurled indiscriminately from both banks had little effect. Finally several muleteers waded into the river and forming a line across the ford drove the stubborn animals through with their *furtutire*, which are light poles with a fork at the top. They are used as their name implies (*furtusesku*, I load, from Gk. φορτώνω) in loading mules to support the baggage already on one side and so prevent the pack saddle from turning over while the muleteer loads up the other side. All however crossed safely, except two which fell in midstream, but as they had no livestock on board no damage was done. At 2 p.m. we stopped in a grassy meadow on the further bank for a short rest and a meal. The sun had now come out and dried our rugs and coats wet with the drizzling rain that had been falling all the morning. Three hours later a start was made up a long gradual ascent broken by a few steep pitches, all now being on foot except a few old women and the smallest children. In parts the track was wellnigh impassable owing to the mud which in places was almost knee deep. Mules slipped and fell in all directions;

there were frequently two on the ground at the same time.
Grandmothers crossed themselves with fervour, and muttered
in Vlach : muleteers loudly made reflections on the parentage
of their much tried animals, and *Andíhriste*, " Antichrist,"
became the common form of address. *Andíhristu* is the Vlach
substitute for the Greek κερατάς, and like it has an endless
variety of meanings depending on the facial expression at the
time. Finally we emerged from the muddy track in the oak
woods, on to the bare top of the ridge near the little chapel
of Ayia Paraskevi. Below us about twenty minutes to our
left was the Kupatshar village of Vodhendzko, and beyond rose
the craggy ridge of Spileo with the villages of Sharganei,
Lavdha and Tishta nestling at its foot. To our right to the
north in a rift in the ridge on which we were, lay the little
hamlet of Tuzhi. Here for a short space the track was drier,
but soon after night and rain began to fall, and the path became
rapidly worse. The climax came when we slid for about half
an hour down a muddy slope in the dark. The long procession
was thrown into confusion, and on reaching the bottom where
we were to camp, several families had become mixed up, and
some units were separated from their main body. Our own
party, more by luck than skill, arrived at the bottom together,
and we had little to do but collect the mules and unload them,
and then struggle to put up the tent in the wind and rain, first
choosing a patch of ground that seemed less wet than the
average. Leaving the women to make things straight we
strolled over to another family that had arrived before nightfall and succeeded in lighting a fire. Comforted by the
warmth we crept into our own tent, and after a hasty meal of
bread, cheese and wine got to sleep as best we could. Other
families fared far worse than ourselves, many were unable to
erect their tents, others were separated into two or three
little parties and had to spend the night in the open with next
to nothing to eat, and only a rug to cover them. When we
awoke the next morning in this spot which is known as La
Valkó we seemed to be in another country. The night before
we had been amongst low hills covered with oak woods, but
now we were in mountain country sprinkled with pines, and

still rather bleak in appearance, for here spring had only just begun. This small valley is a most picturesque spot. On either side rise steep pine-clad hills, and down the centre runs a small stream that rises immediately below the Morminde ridge, of which more anon, joins another flowing from Smiksi, and hurries down to the river of Vriashteno. Just below the meadow where we camped this valley comes to an abrupt end and the stream pours forth between two huge crags that stand on either side like sentinels. There another road from Ghrevena to Samarina, known as the Kutsokale (The Lame Road), passes over the shoulder of the northernmost of the Doauă K'etri, The Two Rocks, as these two crags are called. But this involves a steep ascent over rough ground in order to reach Valkó, and so is impossible when travelling with families. Pouqueville refers to these two crags as " Les Deux Frères " : this name sounds possible, but we have not heard it used.

Thursday, June 2nd.—The morning, when we started soon after 6 a.m., was damp and chilly. We immediately cross the river opposite the small hamlet of Tshuriaka, and follow up the river westwards. After about half an hour we pass the khan of Philippei, where the Smiksi families turn off up a small valley to the left. Philippei which stands on the hill side about half an hour above the khan is a Kupatshar village, and in costume the inhabitants approach nearer to Samarina than the other Kupatshar villages. The principal occupation is sheep rearing. Proceeding up the valley we pass a small wayside chapel in a clump of trees in the river bed, and some clusters of wild plum trees, which in early autumn are yellow with their pleasantly acrid fruit. Another hour or more brings us to a long zigzag ascent up to the ridge of Morminde, which marks the eastern boundary of Samarina territory. We pass the Pade Mushată (Fair Mead), a favourite place for families to encamp, and in days gone by the scene of more than one brigandage, of which more is said in a later chapter. The Pade Mushată deserves its name ; it is a fine level space on the mountain slope, cut through here and there by rivulets of icy cold water, carpeted with good green turf, and in spring and early summer bright with flowers, primroses, cowslips, meadowsweet, gentian and cypripedium. Arriving at the top we find ourselves on a small saddle that joins Ghumara, a large conical mountain covered with pine and beech on our left, to the Morminde proper, a long, grassy ridge also partially wooded. Immediately before us is Gorgul'u, a fine, rocky arête, still covered with patches of snow, and wooded on its lower slopes. Behind Gorgul'u and half hidden in cloud is the triple massif of Zmolku, of which only two peaks, Zmolku and Moasha (The Old Woman), are visible. Directly in front of us deep down in the valley under the summit of Gorgul'u is the junction of two small streams, one rising at our feet on the Morminde and separating that from Ghumara, the other rising on the col called La Greklu near the village of Furka, on the direct road leading from Ghrevena to Konitsa, and separating the western extension of the Morminde from Gorgul'u. Just above this confluence and on the slope below the pine woods of Gorgul'u is Samarina itself (Plate V). All eyes were at once turned towards the village. Our field glasses were hastily requisitioned, as all wanted to see the famous church on which grows a pine tree, and also their own homes, the more so since several houses collapse every year owing to the heavy snows, and the infiltration of water under the foundations. The small col of Morminde marks the watershed of North Pindus, for the stream by the khan of Philippei flows into the Venetiko, and so in time joins the Haliakmon which empties into the gulf of Salonica. The river of Samarina formed by the two streams just mentioned joins the Aous a few miles further down, and eventually reaches the Adriatic. Half an hour beyond the col we camp for a short time, and make a hasty lunch. But rain coming on again we hurry on over a cobbled track, made by the inhabitants of Samarina from their boundary by the wayside shrine on the col of Morminde into the village. Here almost every stone and clump of trees has its name, for instance a small ravine where there is a saw mill is known as La Skordhei, further on below the road is a boulder called K'atra N'agră (The Black Stone), one in the river bed is K'atra a Buflui (The Owl's Stone), and a riven mass of stone on the hill side is known as K'atra Aspartă (The Riven Stone).   We soon pass a small shrine with a heap of horse-shoes by it, where the pious leave coins, and then crossing a bridge over the stream from the Greklu ridge, now a torrent in full flood, enter Samarina in a deluge of rain.

A crowd of those who had come up earlier (few families had stayed through the winter) came out to meet the new arrivals, to hear the latest news from below, and to escort relations to their various homes.   The house belonging to our temporarily adopted family had stood the winter well, so we found a shelter waiting for us.   Others were less fortunate, and one family had to dwell in a house that had only three walls left.   That evening female relatives of the family with whom we were living, brought in as gifts to welcome their relations home several *pite*, a Vlach speciality of which more below.   The next morning we made our way to the *misohori* or village square, where the market is held, and the village meets and talks.

Such was our journey with Vlach families from Thessaly up to their homes in Macedonia.   In Samarina alone there are each summer over eight hundred families, which with few exceptions spend the winter elsewhere, and though all do not go so far afield as Tirnavos, still some go yet further, and most if not all twice every year in spring and autumn, set out with all their belongings on a journey of several days.   This semi-nomadic life has its effect on the national character, and there are some Vlach customs which can be attributed directly to it. One minor result which is of practical use, is that it has taught the Vlachs, alone of Balkan races, that absolute independence in travelling is synonymous with absolute comfort.

PLATE V

SAMARINA FROM THE EAST

CHAPTER III

LIFE AT SAMARINA

Sămărina hoară mare,
Kathe dzuă ka păzare.

Samarina's big and gay,
Every day a market day.

W E have already described the position of Samarina on the lower slopes of Gorgul'u. If we look at the village from a distance it appears not as a compact mass of houses, but as a collection of more or less isolated groups of houses scattered over a gentle slope (Plate V). This effect is heightened by the fact that almost every house has a garden attached to it. Though the lower part of the village round the market place is more or less homogeneous, yet in all the other parts there are many blank spaces where there are no houses nor even gardens. This is partly due to the conformation of the ground. The hill side on which Samarina is built is not firm ground, but consists of a loose shale and gravel through which rock crops out here and there. The whole of the soil is saturated in the spring by the melting snows and the water penetrating beneath the shallow foundations of the houses causes them to fall. Were there no woods above the village to protect it from the torrents formed by snow and rain there would be considerable danger that the whole slope on which the village stands might slide right into the valley below. Curiously enough the four churches are all situated on the edge of the village. This is probably due to an old Turkish regulation that no church might be built within a village. In the centre at the bottom is the church of Great St Mary's, Stămăria atsea mare; on a bluff at the northern extremity stands that of Little St Mary's, Stāmāria atsea n'ikă. To the south on a ridge cut off from the rest of the village by a deep ravine is the church of St Elijah, Aigl'a, below which on the other side of the ravine is that of St Athanasius, Ayiu Athanase.

Before proceeding to describe in detail anything connected with Samarina, let us first take a general view of the village. The most convenient place to begin is the *Pade* of the church of Great St Mary's (Plate XIV 1). The *Pade* is a large green on the south side of the church, opposite to which is the principal Greek school, where there is a small library of old editions of classical authors bequeathed by a former schoolmaster. In the centre of the green is a row of lofty poplars which in the summer afford a pleasant shade for the classes held out of doors. To the east the edge of the green is enclosed by a low stone wall covered on top with short rough planks, a favourite place to sit and talk in the evening or on Sunday morning after church. Looking down into the valley from the edge of the green we see several mills both for grinding corn and for washing the woollen fabrics made in the village. Above these, as also all round the outskirts, is a network of meadows, where hay or clover is grown. Above them are a few houses with gardens dotted with plum, cherry and apple trees. If we turn our eyes further afield we can survey the wooded height of Ghumara to our right, or to our left the Morminde and the long ridge that leads from it to Samarina. We can see on it our road from Ghrevena, and keen eyes will pick out what muleteers or families are coming up. But let us walk through the village. We turn to the west and make for the principal entrance to the green leaving on our right behind the campanile of the church the large tall house of the Besh family, one of the landmarks of the village. In the same corner is the Shoput di la Stāmāria, the conduit of St Mary. Samarina possesses some fifteen or more similar conduits in different quarters, so that the inhabitants never have to go far for water. To most of the conduits as with this one, the water is brought in wooden pipes carved out of pine trunks from springs on the hill side above. All along the course of the pipe line are wooden traps to facilitate repairs or cleaning. Only a few conduits are built over a spring on the spot, and the water of these is considered the best. We next pass a willow tree with a wooden platform built round it where there are benches for those who patronise the small café opposite. Then we enter a narrow road roughly paved with cobbles and having on one side a small artificial stream which is used to irrigate the gardens below. On our left we notice some ruins in a garden and more on our right ; these are the remains of houses burnt by Leonidha. Passing one on each side the shops of two blacksmiths and knife makers we cross by a wooden bridge the Valitshe, a small rivulet which runs through the middle of the village, supplies water for irrigation purposes, and is a receptacle for rubbish of all kinds. Above on our left are two tailor's shops, and beyond them a sweet shop with a crowd of small children about it. On our right we pass more shops including one of the general stores of Samarina, where one can buy any non-edible necessary of life, such as lead pencils, cottons, aniline dyes, mirrors, silks and soap. Beyond this our road narrows suddenly between two houses, we turn sharply to the left and find ourselves in the *Misohori*, usually known as *La Hani* This is the market and meeting place of Samarina (Plate VI). It is a roughly triangular space paved with cobbles, and not more than a hundred yards long. In the middle are a large willow and a small cherry tree. The earth round their stems is banked up with stones so as to form a narrow platform about three feet high which makes convenient show benches for the muleteers to display for sale the goods they have brought up. Here we shall find muleteers offering petroleum from the railway at Sorovitsh, olives from Avlona or Volos, red wine from Shatishta, vegetables such as onions, green peppers, vegetable marrows and beans from Tshotili, fruit, cherries, pears or apples from the Kupatshar villages, and wheat from Kozhani or Monastir. What is not sold is not removed at night, but covered up in case of a chance shower, and watched by two or three muleteers who sleep on the sacks of grain wrapped in their goat's hair capes. Round *La Hani* are the principal cafés and food shops, and also the one primitive inn where the stranger may stay if he wishes. But Samarina is so hospitable that it considers it disgraceful that any respectable stranger should be forced to lodge at the inn and not be invited to stay in a private house. In front of each food shop is a long wooden trough on four legs about three feet high. This is lined with tin and filled with glowing charcoal over which lambs are roasted whole on a wooden spit. The roast meat is afterwards cut up and sold in joints. Muleteers when they return to Samarina often collect in the evening at one of these shops and discuss together two or three pounds of roast meat and as much wine as they please. On the other smaller spits of iron the lamb's fry will be roasted and sold as a kind of *hors d'œuvre* to be consumed with a glass or two of raki. If it be evening we may find *K'ibăk'i* also roasting on an iron spit. Should any one wish to celebrate some occurrence he will invite his friends to join in *K'ibăk'i* one evening. *K'ibăk'i* are small portions of meat, and are made by hacking up two or three pounds of mutton with a *baltaki*. When they are ready roasted the party will take them to the back room of the shop and make merry with meat, bread and wine, finishing the evening with dancing. This is the usual way of spending any *penitadha* left by departing friends. The custom is that any one on his departure from Samarina should leave behind with the friends who come to see him off, a sum of money called *penitadha*, which may vary from a humble five piastres to one or two pounds, for them to make merry with as they please after his departure. Some will betake themselves to a sweet shop and consume a pound or two of Băklăvă, a favourite Turkish sweetmeat made of thin pastry strewn with almonds or walnuts and drenched with honey. Others will make a night of it in *La Hani* with *K'ibăk'i*, with music and with dancing. Between the food shops there are also several wooden cobbler's booths with a kind of veranda outside where the apprentices sit and work. Practically every young muleteer learns a trade, and often in the summer instead of going about with his father and the mules will sit at his trade in Samarina, cobbling, tailoring or carpentering as the case may be. *La Hani* as

PLATE VI

SAMARINA: THE MARKET PLACE

the centre of the village is naturally the place where all roads to it meet. From the north-east corner goes a road which leads over a wooden bridge across the Valitshe, past a couple of food shops and a row of booths where tailors and cobblers work, below a mill and so to the bridge over the stream from La Greklu and into the Ghrevena road. The Yannina road leaves at the northern corner by a café and then for a short distance runs between cafés, food shops and sweet shops. One of these cafés is kept by a deaf and dumb man reputed the best barber in Samarina. Curiously enough the keeper of a café often combines these two trades, and some will further undertake to cure toothache by the application of pitch. Next is a small open space by the Shoput al Bizha round which are several more shops including yet another general store. Leaving this on the left the road goes straight on, then turns to the right by another sweet shop, passes the conduit called La Penda not far from the house of the Hadzhi-bira family to which Leonidha belonged, crosses a small stream below a mill and ascends a steep pitch on the top of which is a small green called Mermishaklu, a favourite walk in the evening, where boys and young men collect to play games. The Yannina road runs below the topmost part of Mermishaklu, along some meadows enclosed by stone walls or wooden fences to the Shoput al Sakelariu whence it follows the valley leading up to the Greklu ridge.

From the southern corner another road leads off past two cafés to the Shoput al Papazisi (Plate XX 1) which derives its water from a spring on the spot and is reputed to yield the best and coldest water. Thence the road slants up the hill leaving the church of Ayiu Athanase below it, passes several mills, and runs round a deep ravine where is the Shoput di t Vale, and climbs the other side to where stands the church of Aigl'a in a grove of tall pines. The school attached to this church is that used by the Roumanian party. Hence the road runs along the hill side to the monastery for about half an hour through woods of pine and stunted beech, amongst which are open spaces carpeted with bracken and wild straw-berries. From the monastery the road goes on to Briaza and so through Baieasa to Yannina and Metsovo, or through Armata to Konitsa.

There is yet another road leaving on the western side and leading up the hill. It starts between a sweet shop and a food shop, and then zigzags up the hill side in a space bare of houses leaving some distance to the left the large house which served as a Turkish gendarmerie station. We next reach a level space on the top of the steep pitch just ascended which is called Gudrumitsa. On our left is a low wooden sweet shop which is a favourite place for young men to forgather in the evening. They sit at the shop front consuming sweets and looking at the view, especially observing the Ghrevena road to see who is coming up. Behind this shop is a large stone-built house with a courtyard in front surrounded by a high stone wall (Plate XVI 1) which was the scene of the treacherous seizure of the robber chieftains in 1881 described below. We turn round to the left by this house leaving on our right another road that leads north towards Little St Mary's. We go along a flat space for some little distance till we reach another conduit, below which on our left is a kind of natural amphitheatre containing a few houses and gardens and in its centre the small shrine of Ayios Kosmas, supposed to mark the spot where he preached. From the conduit just mentioned we bear away to the left towards the ravine that cuts off the ridge of Aigl'a from the rest of the village. On the bank of the ravine by the road is the Shoput al Dabura also fed by a spring which rises just by it and is considered by some to supply better water even than Papazisi. Directly beyond we cross the ravine by a well-built wooden bridge and reach the group of houses inhabited by the Dabura family. Hence the road goes slanting gradually up the bare side of Gorgul'u into the bottom of the pine wood, climbs over the shoulder of the ridge and dips sharply down into the Vale Kārnă where there are five saw mills. The Vale Kārnă (Snubnose Valley) is a deep rift cut into the central mass of Zmolku. Its head lies midway between the bases of the peaks known as Zmolku and Moasha, and the torrent that runs down it is fed by the few patches of perpetual snow that lie in deep clefts on the eastern

foot of Zmolku and by one or two springs that burst out of the
rocks at a great height and shooting down over the precipices
are appropriately called Apa Spindzurată, the Hanging Water.
On the far side of the Vale Kārnă is the boundary between the
territories of Samarina and Armata, towards which latter
village a difficult track leads from the saw mills.

Some thirty years ago the deep ravine which now separates
the ridge of Aigl'a from the rest of the village was a small, in-
significant stream and then the woods of Gorgul'u, known as
K'urista came right down to the upper edge of the village itself.
Then too the Morminde ridge and Ghumara were thick with
pines and saw mills worked near the monastery. But they
cut the trees recklessly and wastefully, and allowed sheep and
goats to be pastured in the cleared areas, so that young pines
had no chance of coming to maturity even in this hill country
so well adapted for their rapid growth. So the destruction
proceeded till the slope of Gorgul'u was bare, and then came
retribution. The trees being away the melting snow and the
heavy rains descended unchecked on Samarina, threatened to
sweep away the village, and carved out the deep ravine already
mentioned destroying houses and gardens. Not till then did
Samarina awake to its danger and so some fifteen or twenty
years ago it was decreed that no one should cut trees in K'urista
or pasture any beasts of any kind there under pain of heavy
fines. Since then the wood has grown up thick and strong, the
destruction has been averted and pines will in time reclothe
the slopes of Gorgul'u. From the upper edge of Samarina to
the bottom of the K'urista woods is about a quarter of an
hour's easy walk up a gentle slope, now scarred with gravelly
streamlets where formerly, before the cutting of the timber,
there were grassy meadows. Arriving at the lower edge of
the woods we climb a small bluff and dive into the pines where
we find in a little basin of verdure an icy cold spring. This
spring is known to Samarina as The Spring, Fāndāna, and is a
favourite place for picnics and merrymaking at festivals.
There is room to dance, the pines give shade for sleep, and
from the edge of the bluff one can survey the whole of Samarina
together with the Morminde and Ghumara.

Only a few families remain at Samarina throughout the winter. Some of these stay by arrangement to act as guards in the empty village, others especially those who own saw mills stop to look after their business. Recently owing to the general rise in the cost of living other families have taken to remaining in the village. This is done to save the cost of two long mule journeys in the autumn and spring, and to escape the necessity of paying rent for the house in the town where they winter. But in these cases the husband and the elder sons if they have trades which they practise, will go alone to the towns in the plains for the winter leaving their wives and families behind. The principal towns of Epirus, Thessaly and Macedonia and even of Southern Albania receive each winter detachments of Samarina folk. They may be found in Yannina, Dhelvino, Berat, Ghrevena, Hrupishta, Shatishta, Kozhani, Elassona, Kalabaka, Trikkala, Kardhitsa, Larissa and Tirnavos. Of the latter towns Kardhitsa has two hundred, Trikkala three hundred, Tirnavos one hundred, and Larissa a hundred and fifty families. But in addition to these many winter at Tsaritsani or in the villages of the Potamia district near Elassona such as Vlakhoyianni ; and in villages near Larissa such as Tatar or Makrikhori several are to be found. But this does not of course exhaust the towns whither the men of Samarina go to winter, for they may be seen at Philippiadha, Katerini, Salonica or even in Athens itself. It often happens that in the town, where they winter, many gradually settle down and in course of time intermarry with the lowland Greeks and so after one or two generations become completely hellenized. Such are to be found all over Thessaly in the towns mentioned, and also in Almiros and Volos. Elsewhere they are to be found in Yannina and Athens, and in Shatishta and Kozhani in which two latter towns the hellenized Vlachs form the strongest part of the Greek population. In times past emigration from Samarina on a large scale has taken place to Verria, Katerini and Niausta, but this is dealt with below.

As to the population of the village it is naturally exceedingly difficult to form an estimate, since it varies greatly from year to year. Pouqueville our earliest authority says it contained eight hundred families, but he does not seem to have ever been in the village. Aravandinos whose book was published in 1857 gives seven hundred families. Weigand an impartial authority says that in 1887 there were no more than three thousand present in the village. But as we shall see below there were special reasons just at that time why the Samarina families in Thessaly did not go up for the summer. The official Roumanian account of the Vlach communities in Macedonia says that the population varies from four thousand five hundred to six thousand. To-day the village numbers some eight hundred houses and during the three summers (1910–1912) that we spent there many houses were re-built and some new ones erected. Thus the population seemed likely to continue to increase provided no serious political disturbance occurred to check it, as has happened recently since the autumn of 1912. In 1911 some thirty houses were built, and all the eight hundred were inhabited, some by more than one family. Consequently we believe that in the height of the season in July and August there must have been at least five thousand souls in the village. Many do not reside for the whole summer, but come up for a month only. Against the natural increase of the population has to be set the loss continually caused by the settlement of families in the towns of the plains, the wandering of the young men in search of work in their trades and emigration to America. The recent increase in the population between 1908 and 1912 was perhaps due more to the improved political conditions, for in those years several families were beginning to come up for the summer, a thing which many of them had not done for long years together.

On the whole life at Samarina, as noted long ago by Pouqueville, is hardly taken in a serious spirit, and the four summer months during which the village is gathered together each year are looked upon by young and old alike as a time to be spent mainly in enjoyment. At the same time business and work are by no means neglected, for most bring up with them all the appliances for carrying on their trades, and those who abandon the shops or whatever their work may be, and come

up purely for a holiday can rarely afford to remain for the
whole time. The earliest day for families to start to go up
to Samarina is St George's day, April 23rd (May 6th N.S.),
when the shepherds first leave the plains on their way up to
their summer camping grounds near their native villages.
But the time when the bulk of the ordinary trading folk go
up is at the end of May, in time for the fair of St Akhillios
at Ghrevena, the first of the great festivals that mark the
full summer season. The end of the full season is marked by
the lesser festival of St Mary on September 8th (September
21st N.S.) after which the ordinary people begin to leave the
village. The shepherds stay on till the day of St Demetrius,
October 26th (November 8th N.S.) on which day they start
to go down to their winter quarters. From then till next
St George's day the village is all but deserted and inhabited
only by those who have made up their minds to spend the
winter there either as guards or for other reasons. The
course of the full summer season between the fair of
St Akhillios and St Mary the Less, as the festival is called,
is marked by three great feasts which divide it into four
sections of about equal length, and those who are unable to
come up for the whole summer, will arrange their work so
as to be able to spend one of these divisions between two
festivals in their native village. The first feast is that of the
Holy Apostles, St Peter and St Paul, on June 29th (July 12th
N.S.). Next comes the festival of St Elijah (Aigl'a or Sānd
Iliú) on July 20th (August 2nd N.S.). Then on August 15th
(August 28th N.S.) is the great annual festival of the Assumption, the festival of St Mary (Stāmārie) the patroness of Samarina. This all truly patriotic natives of Samarina endeavour
to attend, and if they can come up at no other time during
the summer they will come for a week at Stāmārie. At it
the year's weddings are celebrated, the village dances are
held on the green of the great church of Stāmāria (Plate IV 2)
and in the days succeeding it betrothals are made for next
year. Between this day and the lesser festival of St Mary
there is, as all Samarina folk boast, more merrymaking than
in the whole of the rest of summer put together. Apart from

these great festivals when all work is of course in abeyance and the whole village gives itself up to amusement there are several minor festivals detailed on a later page and various smaller social functions of everyday occurrence. Amongst them a system of paying calls seems especially characteristic of Vlach life. A call can be made at almost any hour either in the morning or afternoon, and on any day, but a Sunday or a holiday is more normal. One rarely goes alone to pay such calls, but four or more go together. On entering the house they are welcomed by the householder and his family, and leaving their shoes on the threshold, if they are dressed in the Vlach national costume, are invited to sit on the rugs laid either on the built wooden bench running round the wall of the living-room or on the floor in the place of honour on either side of the hearth. Recently, since Samarina has possessed an expert joiner, chairs have begun to take their place among household luxuries and as seats of honour especially for those dressed à la Franca, for it is asserted not without truth that those who wear trousers find it uncomfortable to sit with crossed legs tailorwise on the floor. When all are seated cigarettes are passed round and then the usual refreshments are brought in on a tray and handed round by the wife or elder daughter. They consist of a spoonful of jam or a lump of Turkish Delight, a glass of raki or some similar liqueur and a cup of Turkish coffee. No native of Samarina is so poor or so lacking in dignity as not to offer any stranger who calls on him at least a lump of Turkish Delight and a glass of wine. Hospitality is the keynote of Vlach life and the stranger is quickly made to feel at home, if he is prepared to enjoy simple comforts. A whole day is sometimes spent in such calls, and on arrival in a village the traveller is usually taken round from house to house to make the acquaintance of the chief inhabitants. The noticeable feature about these functions is the part played by women. Vlach women, unlike women in a Greek village, are treated by the men with far greater respect and in some cases almost as equals. The women pay calls like the men and both converse together freely. On the other hand the women rarely and apparently never as a regular habit eat with the

4

men of a family. This is probably mainly a matter of convenience, since the women do the cooking, and does not necessarily imply any idea of inferiority. To a certain extent girls are kept secluded in that fashion dictates that they should not be seen out of doors unaccompanied by a brother, first cousin, or some elderly relation such as an uncle, aunt or one of their parents. This rule does not apply when they go to the spring for water or to the river to wash clothes. Further at dances at weddings and festivals no young men are allowed to dance with girls other than their sisters or first cousins who are blood relations according to the canons of the Greek church. But whole families will go out for picnics together and in general both sexes meet as equals. The superior status of women, which strikes one forcibly on coming from a Greek to a Vlach village, is probably due to a difference in marriage customs. In Greece it is the common thing for a man to be at home on his name-day to all his friends and relations, and Greeks in the villages are sometimes in the habit of paying calls on Sundays. But the fully developed social system as regards calling which the Vlachs possess is, as far as our knowledge goes, totally unknown in Greece. Further the Vlach custom according to which a whole village or parish is at home to everybody else on the festival of the parish church is, we believe, peculiar to Vlachs. The freer social life of the Vlachs, partly due to frequent travels, gives them in this respect better manners and a broader outlook on life. Consequently the Vlach women never become what the Greek village women so often are, drudges in the houses of their husbands, who often deem them little better than cook-housekeepers.

A frequent form of entertaining is lunching in the pine woods, especially in K'urista at the Fāndānă. This is the favourite spot at Samarina for a picnic, but every Vlach village has its special place which must be provided with an ice cold spring, smooth green turf for dancing and a few pines to give shade. The food at such an outing is always supplied by a lamb which should be killed, roasted and eaten on the spot. The lamb is dressed and placed on a wooden spit to roast over a fire of pine branches, and by its side the fry is set to roast on an iron spit. The latter is naturally done first, and is eaten as a kind of *hors d'œuvre* accompanied by glasses of raki. Then the lamb itself is devoured with bread, garlic and wine. Next, perhaps, a large tin dish of some sweetmeat such as Bāklāvă will be divided amongst the company. Finally all will dance and sing accompanied by such musical instruments as it has been possible to collect. The dancers will only interrupt their wild gyrations to drink one another's health in the good red wine of Shatishta or to fire off rifles and revolvers by way of shewing that they are thoroughly enjoying themselves.

Vlach feeding as a whole differs so much from the usual fare to be obtained in the other villages of Macedonia, Epirus and Greece proper, that a short digression may here be allowed. In contrast to the Greeks who as a race live principally on bread, olives, cheese and garlic, and eat little meat and that highly seasoned and disguised with sauces, the Vlachs think plain roast meat, hot or cold, in large quantities essential to any meal worthy the name. Even the muleteer as he jogs along his weary road always has a snack of cold lamb, bread and cheese washed down by long pulls at his wooden flask or wine skin. It requires some little skill to drink gracefully from a full wine skin while ambling along on mule-back. The triumph of Vlach cooking however is *Pită*, which may be considered the Vlach national dish. A *pită* is a kind of pasty made in a wide, shallow, metal dish which has a hollow, conical metal lid of great importance for the proper baking of the *pită*. When the *pită* is made the dish is placed on an iron tripod over a wood fire on the open hearth and then the lid which has been previously heated and covered with a thick layer of ashes to retain the heat is placed over it so that both top and bottom may be baked equally. The *pită* itself is made by laying four or more thin leaves of pastry in the bottom of the dish, on which a thick central layer of vege- tables, cheese or finely chopped meat is placed. The whole is then covered over with about six more leaves of the thin pastry, all of which are generously anointed with butter and occasionally small lumps of cheese. All kinds of *pită* are good, but perhaps the best is that made with leeks, nettles or some similar vegetable. For some obscure reason this dish is practically confined to the Vlachs, and is rarely to be seen in any Greek village. A variety of *pită* is known in Roumania, but *pită* to be really good must be made of freshly rolled pastry and must be baked in its special dish and not in an oven. Other foods to be met with are various kinds of vegetables, and the usual kinds made from milk such as cheeses and *yiaurti* which the Vlachs call *mărcatŭ*. But these latter are not peculiarly Vlach, and are common to all Balkan peoples who are shepherds.

An invitation to dinner in a Vlach house always means that the guest is expected to stay the night. For instance one of the writers during a few days' stay at Elassona in the winter spent each night in a different house owing to the hospitable invitations of friends from Samarina who were wintering there. This system of sleeping where one dines has given rise to a custom peculiar to the women. On Saturday nights after the week's work is over—for the women of the family do all the household work—the mother or one of the daughters will often be invited to go and spend the night with a cousin, married sister or friend. Such invitations may also be given on Sunday nights, but in all cases the person so invited must return to her own home at dawn the next morning. This custom is commoner amongst the unmarried than the married women. It is perhaps due to the desire of the girls to see something of one another, for being kept in comparative seclusion and being engaged in the work of the house they have few opportunities of meeting on ordinary days. The custom is known as going *azborŭ*.

The Vlachs have a reputation for heavy drinking and of all Pindus villages Samarina is generally considered to drink more than the others. Our experience hardly bears this out, and as far as we could see a Vlach village as regards drinking is much like any other christian village in the Balkans. Apparently in recent years a succession of bad seasons has brought about a rise in the price of wine and with it a decrease in the amount drunk. It cannot however be denied that in the summer at Samarina a great quantity of wine is drunk, but there is really very little habitual drunkenness. On the whole one may say with a fair amount of truth that the Vlach drinks more than his neighbours, but since he loses his temper less and does not use a knife at the slightest excuse and in fact is often without one, the result is less obvious. As can be gathered from the description of the village given above Samarina possesses several cafés and these are on the whole well patronised. But among the Vlachs the confirmed café loafer, a common Levantine type, who possesses the art of sitting down from early morning to sunset with one interval at noon for a meal and sleep, is rarely if ever seen. The Vlach who has nothing to do will walk about or go outside the village and sit on the hill side. The Greek idea of happiness lies in town life, and the wealthy provincial Greek who can live where he pleases prefers a house in the main street near to the chief café. The idea of a country house does not as yet exist, and few owners of large farms will live for choice on their properties, and will only rarely visit them. In this case however fear of brigands, especially in Thessaly, the part of Greece where large estates are most common, has been largely responsible. Still the country Greek of any class, with very few exceptions, would always vote for town life with its cafés and theatres. The ideal of the Vlach on the other hand is the life of the open road or country, up in the hills away from the plains and towns. Pines and beeches, which in the Balkans only grow in the hills, mountains, plenty of cold water, but only for drinking purposes, a fine open view and large flocks of sheep play a very large part in the Vlach ideal. A difference in temperament between Vlach and Greek comes out in many minor points. A Vlach has the quieter manner of speech, a comparative absence of gesticulation, and a lack of that excessive curiosity which especially in financial matters is so typical of the Greeks. He is also less hot-tempered and takes the small inconveniences of life in a more calm and tranquil frame of mind ; there is a lack of self-assertion and no race perhaps in the Balkans is more easily absorbed by others.

A similar difference can be seen in forms of amusement. Games of a vigorous type are not really known in Greece though a few have recently been imported and football is attempted at certain schools. The great aim of the Greek schoolboy in the town is to acquire a slow and staid gait, and even in the country he shows no desire for exercise. In a Vlach village however vigorous games which men as well as boys can play, are a normal amusement. These games are indeed crude, but they contain the main idea that all concerned should do something violent and that frequently. The reader may perhaps think this distinction exaggerated seeing the gymnastic training given in Greek schools with a view to winning successes at the Panhellenic games. But Panhellenic games and gymnastics of all kinds are still an artificial revival in Modern Greece, and are not as yet really native. The authors after many years' travel in all parts of Greece have only once seen a village game in progress and there as it turned out the population was entirely Vlach. On another occasion the authors spent five days in an up-country quarantine station on the Græco-Turkish frontier where those undergoing quarantine consisted of Greeks, Vlachs and Turks. The Vlachs killed time by playing games, at which the Greeks looked on in the intervals of card playing and cigarette smoking. The five commonest Vlach games are the following. First comes that called *Muma ku Preftlu* (The Mother with the Priest). One of the players sits down on the ground in the middle and another stands up behind him holding tightly by his collar or some other portion of his garments. The other players circle round running in and out, and try to smack the one sitting down as hard as they can on the head or shoulders without getting hit by the watcher. The watcher jumps about round the seated person, of whom he must not let go, and tries to hit one of the others with his foot—before beginning the players slip off their shoes—anywhere, but on the hand which does not count. He who is hit must then take the post of the watcher who takes the place of the one sitting down. When this game is played by ten or a dozen young men the fun is fast and furious, and the great delight of all is to wait for a favourable opportunity to spring upon the watcher's back and bring him to the ground. He who does this is for the time being safe according to the rules and the others can rush in and buffet the seated player as they please, till the watcher can resume his station. Another favourite is that known as *ku Gāmila* (With the Camel). One player bends forward, another comes behind him and also bends down clutching the first round the waist, behind the second come two or three more in a similar position. Another is chosen as watcher and he, undoing his long sash, fastens one end to the waist of the last of the four bending down, and holds the other end himself driving this unwieldy camel about. The members of the other side dart in and out first on one side and then on the other, each attempting to elude the watcher and jump on the camel's back, a proceeding which most likely will bring all to the ground in inextricable confusion. The watcher in the meantime runs about as far on either side as the length of the sash allows and tries to hit one of the others with his foot. If he succeeds the other side have to make up a camel and the one hit becomes the watcher. In this game too hits upon the hand do not count. The third most popular game is that called *Stun Gutsó*, which will be recognised as a Greek name meaning At the Lame Man. The players divide into two parties and mark out with stones a space which in area is probably equal to about a quarter of a lawn-tennis court. At one point on the edge of this a sort of base is marked off. In the base the players of one side stand while the others move freely about the rest of the space marked off. Then those in the base each in turn come hopping about the rest of the area and try to hit one of the others with foot or hand anywhere, but on their hands. The hopper must not change the foot on which he hops nor must he put his foot to the ground. If he breaks this rule his innings is over and another member of the side takes his place and so on till all have had an innings or till all the other party have been caught. The side in the field may run and dodge where and how they please within the marked area, but if they move outside it they count as caught. When one side has finished its innings as the hopping side, the other goes in and the winning side is the one which has caught most of its opponents. If all one side are caught the winners say that they *bāgară samară* (have put a saddle) upon them, meaning thereby that their opponents are little better than mules or donkeys. This indignity the losers have to wash out by standing treat with sweets or some other refreshment. Other common games are leapfrog known as *skamnakia*, another Greek name meaning small stools, and a game consisting in a competition to see who can jump furthest after giving two hops from a marked starting-point. This which is called *Arsarire la Treil'a* (Leaping the Third) is a more energetic game than it sounds, and a short run is allowed. These are the games most usually played by the boys of Samarina, but of course not the only ones.

Of all forms of amusement dancing is the most usual. Apart from the big festivals when the great village dances take place and weddings which are marked by much rather ceremonial dancing, picnics and most entertainments end with a dance. To the unskilled eye the dances are of the usual South Balkan type, but a little study shows that Vlach dances, although probably none of them can be considered as peculiarly Vlach, may be divided into two classes. The first class are the ring dances at the great village festivals when the greater part of the population will join in (Plate IV 2). Some Vlach villages, for instance Turia, hold such dances every Sunday through the summer. These village dances consist of two or more rings in which all join hands and move round slowly in a circle. The leader of the ring, the man on the extreme right, is the only one who indulges in any elaborate or vigorous step, for the others merely follow him round imitating his steps in a slow and solemn manner. The first or inner ring consists only of men, and the second or outer ring consists of women. However many rings there may be they always come in this order, and the sexes are always kept apart. In such dances the number of performers is limited

only by the number of rings it is possible to make up in the
space available. On such occasions even the leader will
refrain from being too elaborate or energetic in his steps, for
the village dances are always to some extent of a ceremonial
nature. The only occasion on which the two sexes dance
together in the same ring is in the solemn dance at a wedding
in which the whole bridal party takes part when the newly
married pair come out of the church at the end of the service.
This dance which is always performed directly outside the
church door is fully described below. The other class of dances
are those in vogue at the feasting before and after a wedding
and at all other entertainments. Here too there is a formal
system to be followed. The bridegroom or host will invite
two men to dance, for only men dance with men and women
with women, except in the case of brothers and sisters and
first cousins, and at weddings when any of the men holding
official positions may invite the bride to dance. The two
men will stand up in the centre of the company opposite one
another and dance a *singasto*, which like most of the names of
Vlach dances is said to be a corruption of a Greek name.
At first the two dancers pace solemnly and slowly backwards
and forwards in front of one another, then as the music is
gradually played faster and faster they begin to twirl round
and jump about moving about the room, but always keeping
in front of one another. This being over the two hold hands
and dance a ring dance together, first one leading and then
another the other. Thus each pair that is invited to dance
goes in all through three separate dances. When they begin
the ring dances the leader can call upon the musicians to
play whatever kind of dance he prefers, as a rule the one he
thinks he can dance best. The skill of the leader in the ring
dances is not shewn by his following the regular steps accurately, but in the number and beauty of the variations he can
introduce. Since, as a mocker might say, these variations
usually consist in prancing about on one leg or in whirling
wildly round, it will be seen that to do this in time with the
music demands considerable adroitness. But the local critics
do not approve of wild dancing, even prancing and whirling

about must be done decently and in order. The quieter kinds of ring dances are the *Serba* and the *Vulghariko* (Bulgarian), and the more energetic dances are those known as the *Tshamb*, the *Arvanitovlakhiko* and the *Karabatatiko*, which are reputed to be of Albanian origin, and certainly the *Tshamb* takes its name from the part of Albania between Tepeleni and Yannina known to the Greeks as Tshamuriá. Women of course do not dance these energetic dances ; the ring dance usually performed by them is the *Sirtó*, supposed to be derived from the Ancient Greek dance of the same name. This is a slow and stately dance, but rather dreary. A ring of women dancing the *sirto* to the tune of a monotonous song sung slowly in their wailing voices always has an effect of weird melancholy. All the dances are of an elementary three-step type, and the variations introduced are mere adornments to suit individual taste, but the *sirto* has few if any variations. In Samarina and apparently in most large villages local talent is easily capable of providing music which is taught at the higher grade schools. At weddings and festivals and other important occasions itinerant musicians are employed (Plate XVII). It is worth noting that among the Vlachs such musicians whatever their race, and they are now usually Greeks, are invariably spoken of as Gipsies, just as the Greeks call all shepherds Vlachs. There do not seem ever to have been any local native musical instruments, at least if such were ever employed for producing dance music they have totally disappeared. The itinerant musicians and the local talent use European instruments. A band of itinerant musicians consists at least of three performers, the leader with a clarionet, a fiddler, and a boy with a drum or cymbal to accentuate the time for the guidance of the dancers. A band may consist of more, but the leader is always the one who has the clarionet and acts as conductor beating time for the others by waving about his head and clarionet as he plays. When music cannot be procured, singing takes its place and this probably was the original custom. The shepherds who are natural and good dancers always dance to songs and have no native instrument of their own except flutes, which they

do not use for dance music. The probability that there were
never any local musical instruments is strengthened by the
fact that as a rule at the big village dances all dance to certain
well-known songs only. The great annual dance at Samarina
at the festival of the Assumption is known as *Tsheatshlu* from
the song to which it is danced. Further at the ceremonial
dance performed by the bridal party, when the newly married
pair come out of the church, the musicians are driven away
for the time being and the party dance to songs only. The
music is of the usual Levantine type which is familiar to any
who have heard the droning folk songs of Greece and the
Balkans. As to how far any particular dance can be assigned
to any one race we cannot say, probably none are really
Vlach ; but there seems to be a consensus of opinion, at least
locally, that certain dances are Albanian.

CHAPTER IV

THE COSTUMES OF SAMARINA

Brānlu larg, tsipunea luñgă
Shi kātshula fără fundă.

His sash too wide, his coat too long, his fez without a tassel.

VLACH SONG

ALTHOUGH it may be said that the Vlachs of Samarina
have a national costume, yet even this has been subject
to changes of fashion, and curiously enough the men's
dress seems to have been more affected by this than the
women's. But bachelors perhaps are not well adapted for
understanding the mysteries of fashion in regard to the dress of
women. The typical dress of the Vlach is that regularly
worn by shepherds and muleteers, and as a rule by all the
men who have not adopted European costume. In the following account we will first describe a simple, everyday costume
such as is worn by the young muleteer in Plate VII 3, and
then shew how this may be made more elaborate and elegant
for Sundays and festivals. Over a thick flannel vest a man
will put on a long, full shirt reaching to the knees, called
kāmeashă. This is of printed cotton usually pale blue or
grey in colour, and has a square skirt fully pleated in front
and quite plain behind. The result of the pleating is that a
man, when fully dressed, seems to be wearing a variety of
kilt or fustanella which is really the skirt of his shirt. It is
quite likely that the Albanian fustanella, which was adopted
by the Greeks after their liberation in 1821 as their national
costume, is a development of this pleated shirt. The shirt
may have narrow sleeves buttoned at the wrist or full loose
sleeves, but this depends on whether a waistcoat with or

PLATE VII

1. OLD MAN WITH BREECHES AND SARKÄ   2. MAN WITH TĀLĀGANŬ

3. MULETEER WITH MALLIOTŬ   4. YOUNG MAN WITH PALTO

SAMARINA: MEN'S COSTUMES

without sleeves is to be worn. On his legs he puts a pair of homespun leggings reaching to the middle of the thighs and called *tshoaritsĭ*. These are tied round below the knees with garters, *kăltsuvetsĭ*, and bound at the bottom with braid. This braiding is a great feature of the Vlach garments and though in appearance like braid is really an embroidered edge made by needlework with a very narrow kind of silken braid. Consequently the better the clothes the more braiding there is, for to make it well requires much expenditure of time, money and skill. The great point of the leggings is that they should fit tightly to the calf so as to shew the leg to the best advantage, and neatly round the ankle rather like a spat. Next comes a double-breasted waistcoat of jean with or without sleeves according to the type of shirt worn. This, which is called *dzhibadane*, fits very tightly across the chest and is fastened with hooks and eyes. Over this is worn a garment of homespun like a frock-coat that reaches to the knees, but does not meet in front and has no sleeves. This is called *tsipune* and is girt round the waist with a leather belt over which is wound a long woollen sash known as *brănŭ*. This is the universal foundation of the Vlach male costume over which a variety of outer garments may be worn. In Plate VII 3 a muleteer is shewn wearing the ordinary week-day great-coat of his class. This is a thick coat known as *malliotŭ* and is a little longer than the *tsipune* which it hides. It has tasselled buttons and can be made to meet in front ; at the back of the neck is a small conical hood which can be drawn over the head in bad weather. It is trimmed round the edges with red or blue braid, and has sleeves which are slit half-way down on the inside, so that if the wearer does not want to put his arms in them he may thrust them through at the shoulder and then the sleeves will hang loose down the back. On his feet he has particoloured woollen socks (*lăpudzi*) knitted by the women from wool spun and dyed at home. The peculiarity of these socks is that they are usually knitted from the toe upwards with bent needles. His shoes are *tsăruh'i*, the usual peasant shoe of the Southern Balkans. These have rather thin soles well studded with nails, hardly any heel, and turned-up toes decorated with a large tassel. On his head he wears a white fez, *kātshulă*, without a tassel. If the weather be cold or wet the muleteer will slip on over all these garments a thick loose cape of goat's hair called *tāmbare* (Plate XI 1). This is so thick that it is rainproof and sticks out all round so as to throw the rain off the lower limbs, although it does not reach much lower than the knees. The sleeves are sewn up at the end, but are slit through at the shoulder like those of the *malliotŭ*. There is a conical hood attached to the back of the neck ready to be drawn over the head, and it does not require fastening in front for it overlaps well and keeps its place by its own weight. This is the ordinary week-day costume of a young man, but for high days and holidays he will naturally put on his best. Then he will change the coloured shirt for a white one of fine linen, and with an enormous number of pleats in front, for the more pleats a shirt has the smarter it is (Plate VII 4). In fact it takes something like six yards of linen to make one. The jean waistcoat will be replaced by one of velveteen, the woollen sash by one of silk, and the white fez by a red one with a tassel. Then the *malliotŭ* will be discarded for a *paltó* (Plate VII 4), a great-coat of thick homespun with a velvet collar, full skirts and a waist, cut more or less after the model of a European great-coat of which it is a local variation. The full skirts of the *paltó* are required in order to accommodate the pleats of the *tsipune* behind. Like the shirt the *tsipune* is smarter in proportion to the number of its pleats (*kline*) behind. The ordinary everyday *tsipune* will have only nine or ten pleats, and not much braiding. The Sunday *tsipune* will have as many as twenty pleats and very elaborate needlework braiding down the edges in front ; in these two points the great beauty of a really elegant garment lies. The *tsāruh'i* of week-days also will be replaced by a pair of slip-on black shoes with low heels made rather like European walking shoes, except that they do not lace up and have very pointed toes.

A man of middle age will wear a costume that is practically the same as that just described, but there are some garments which are thought to be more suited to an older man. This

PLATE VIII

3. MEN WITH BRIDEGROOM'S DRESS

2. MAN WITH SARKÀ :
THE SHEPHERDS' DRESS

SAMARINA : MEN'S COSTUMES

1. MEN WITH PISHLI

is partly due to the age of the man and his clothes. That is to say he wore such garments when he was younger because they were then in fashion, and has not changed them since or rather never worn them out, because these clothes of homespun are exceedingly durable. Such a man will almost always wear a white shirt, unless he happens to practise a trade which renders a coloured shirt more economical in the matter of washing. His waistcoat will be sleeveless and most probably of broadcloth, though of course the colour and material of a waistcoat is a matter of individual taste. Over his *tsipune* he will wear a short jacket with slit sleeves similar to those of the *malliotŭ* : this is of homespun and called either a *pishli* or a *kundushŭ* (Plate VIII 1). He need not wear anything above this unless the weather is cold or wet, when he can put on a *malliotŭ* and a *tămbare*. But for festivals he may wear a long coat of homespun cut like a *malliotŭ*, but not so long and with sleeves and hood quite the same. This which cannot meet in front is called *tălăganŭ* (Plate VII 2), and is really a more elegant kind of *malliotŭ*. Old men will wear instead of the *tălăganŭ* a garment known as *sarkă* which is now out of fashion and so confined to the old (Plate VII 1). This resembles the *tălăganŭ* in length, in the hood, and in the fact that it does not fasten in front, but the point of difference is the sleeve. In the *sarkă* the sleeves are loose and triangular, falling freely down over the arm. From their appearance they are known as ears, *urekl'e*. Sometimes too an old man, and occasionally a younger man in winter, will don a pair of full knee breeches tight at the knees, but loose round the thighs, called *shilivări*. These cover the kilting of the shirt and the upper part of the leggings (Plate VII 1). The universal colour for the national costume is now dark blue (indigo), but once it used to be white. The shepherds, who are always the last to retain old customs, and some old men, always wear leggings, *tsipune* and all of white homespun with a white shirt to match (Plate VIII 2), which in the case of shepherds is of coarse hand-made linen. The main reason for the change in the colour of the costume from white to blue is the expense entailed in keeping white clothes clean and good. White is naturally more picturesque, but not so practical a colour for those engaged in trade. Nowadays the only fashionable men who wear white clothes are bridegrooms. For his wedding every bridegroom is expected to get himself a full national costume of white homespun which for the rest of his life serves as his very best clothes (Plate VIII 3). The leggings, *tsipune* and *pishli* are the same as in the ordinary clothes, but more elaborate and with more braiding, and the skirts of the *tsipune* are as full as they can be. The bridegroom's white shirt is pleated down the front of the chest because he wears an open waistcoat. This is of velvet and embroidered with the fine narrow braid so heavily that the ground can hardly be seen. So much skill is expended on the making of such a waistcoat that in spite of the small amount of stuff used, for it is tight and is open in front, twenty shillings is quite a common price. It is noticeable that the Pindus Vlachs from Avdhela, Samarina and Perivoli now settled in the Verria district, have given up the use of the kilted shirt and the *tsipune* and have adopted instead the *paltó* and the breeches which they make of brown not blue homespun (Plate XXIII). Boys do not from the very beginning wear the full *tsipune* costume, but a far simpler kind of dress. Over their underclothes they put on a long robe of jean rather like a dressing-gown. This has sleeves and is lined and fastened in front with hooks and eyes or buttons. It reaches to the knees and is girt at the waist with a belt. On his legs the boy will wear stockings and not socks, and as a rule nothing on his head unless it be Sunday when he will have a red fez. Over this long robe known as *andri* he can wear either a *mallioti* or a *paltó* (Plate XI 2). When he reaches the age of twelve or fourteen the *andri* is considered too short for a growing lad and so on his legs he puts homespun leggings of the usual type. The next stage is reached when he is about seventeen and is promoted to the full *tsipune* dress. The *andri* costume was once the ordinary garment of the town Vlach or shopkeeper, though now it is only very occasionally worn by such. Probably they wore this costume, which is perhaps in origin Turkish or at least oriental, in the times when it was considered a privilege by the christians to be allowed to dress like Turks.

PLATE IX

1. GIRLS IN TSIKETTĂ

SAMARINA: WOMEN'S COSTUMES

2. GIRLS IN DULUMĂ

Owing to recent events in the Balkans the next stage in the development of Vlach costume will be the abandonment of the fez, hitherto universally worn. The Thessalian Vlachs have already created a variety of fez which is fairly popular. This is small and shaped like a cone with the peak cut off. It is white and heavily embroidered with yellow silk, and when worn cocked on the back of the head, gives its wearer a very jaunty look. It is called a *keliposhe* (Plate XI 1, 2). In Thessaly or Greek territory the Vlachs do not as a rule wear the fez, but a small round cap of astrachan with a flat top. This may become the national headgear when the fez ceases to be worn.

In women's clothes there is not so much variety and there is at present no change like that from the *malliotŭ* to the *paltó* If the women's dress changes at all in the future there is most likely to be a general abandonment of their own local costume in favour of one purely European in origin. A woman when working about her house usually goes barefoot, for stockings and shoes will be put on only for high days and holidays. The shoes are of a slip-on type and not very strongly made ; in fact on journeys when the families are moving in the spring the women will frequently take off their shoes and walk along barefoot, since they find this more comfortable. The main garment worn by all women, as the foundation of their costume, is a simple frock all in one piece and without much waist. It is made of various cloths, which we are unable to describe precisely, known under the generic name of *katfé*, and their patterns are those which were common in England some thirty or forty years ago. This is what we were told when we sent some samples of *katfé* to Manchester asking if such could be procured now. Probably the stuffs of this kind now used in Samarina and the other Vlach villages are of continental manufacture, and some may even be made at Salonica or elsewhere in the Balkans. A bride will wear a frock of white silk (Plate XVII) and every girl is supposed to have as part of her trousseau another silken frock of a dark colour for second best wear (Plate XVIII 2). The system is that every girl is given as part of her trousseau as many frocks as she is thought

5

likely to need for the rest of her married life. Only widows or elderly matrons will wear black frocks. Over her frock a young woman whether married or unmarried will wear a *tsikettă* which as its name implies is a short sleeveless jacket of a zouave type, not meeting in front (Plate IX 1). The *tsikettă* is of fine homespun and heavily decorated with gold braid and needlework. Round the waist will be a belt with two large silver buckles of filigree work. If she wears a *tsikettă* a girl should not wear any other outer garment, and in fact the *tsikettă* is usually worn only on Sundays and festivals by the younger women. The girl, who wears a *tsikettă* on such days, will on week days wear nothing but the ordinary frock with an apron. The apron is a most necessary part of a woman's costume and whatever else she wears an apron must be worn. There are of course week-day aprons and Sunday aprons. If the *tsikettă* be not worn the girl will put on a *dulumă* directly over her frock (Plate IX 2, X) and this garment is to the women what the *tsipune* is to the men. It has no sleeves, does not meet in front, and is exactly like a man's *tsipune* except in length, for it reaches to the ankles. It is decorated round the edge with needlework braiding and the upper edges on either side above the waist are ornamented with a row of oval silver buttons set very close together. But such elaboration is as a rule reserved for the best *dulumă* to be worn at festivals. Like the *tsipune* the *dulumă* is girt in at the waist by a belt with silver buckles below which hangs the apron. The *dulumă* is of dark blue homespun like the *tsipune* and is a garment for every day wear. But when the housewife on Sunday puts on her best *dulumă*, her stockings and her best apron she has two other garments which she may put on. She may wear either a *sarkă* or a *paltó* (Plate X). The latter is a long, loose coat of black broad-cloth reaching to the knees, but not meeting in front. It has sleeves and round the edges is trimmed with fur. The *sarkă* is a somewhat similar long, loose coat, sleeveless and not meeting in front. It is black and trimmed with broad red braid round the edges and has braided decoration on the shoulders and on the skirt behind. It is a striking garment, but the great effect of it is from behind, for in front practically nothing of it can be seen. It must be admitted that on the whole the clothes of the Vlach women show less good taste than those of the men, and as for headgear they have none except a black kerchief twisted round their heads. The women obtain more elegance, as they imagine, by piling garment on garment, for when they put on their best clothes for Sundays they put on as many petticoats as they can carry. This has the effect, which is much admired, of making their skirts and the *sarkǎ* from the waist downward stick out crinoline fashion. In reality in the full glory of their festal garb they seem more like ungainly bundles of clothes than ladies of fashion and since they never wear corsets the effect is clumsy in the extreme. On the other hand the simple character of the *tsikettǎ* costume is rather picturesque, but any Vlach girl who looks at all pretty in her native dress must be really rather good looking, even when allowance is made for the fact that a native dress from its very quaintness gives a certain charm to its wearer.

The Vlach costume makes no difference between summer and winter. Really these heavy garments of homespun are ideal for a rough winter climate, but the Vlach will wear them in July as well. The same clothes are also worn day and night, except that at night some of the heavier outer garments such as the *malliotǔ*, *paltó* and *sarkǎ* will be taken off. Otherwise, both men and women, when they go to bed, first shut all the windows—the night air is so dangerous—and then bury themselves in piles of heavy rugs and blankets strewn on the floor. Yet for all their avoidance of the chill night air these same people will sleep out in the open at any time of year in almost any weather with nothing more than a rug and a *tǎmbare*. Contrariness can go no further. The costume of the men is in some ways practical for a mountain folk. It is thick, durable and leaves the movements of the legs free, in fact it has all the advantages of the Highlander's kilt and plaid. On the other hand it has considerable disadvantages ; it is heavy especially in the folds hanging from the waist behind, it is tight about the body and the thickness of the stuff, which is useful in winter and in wet weather as being nearly rainproof, is a serious drawback in the summer. Further the number of the garments and the complicated method of wearing them with their fastenings of hooks and eyes make dressing and undressing not so easy.   Still for the mountain country, which is the Vlach's native land, it is a good costume granted that washing all over and undressing are not things to be done every day.

PLATE X

SAMARINA: WOMEN IN SARKÄ, DULUMĂ, PALTO AND SARKÄ

CHAPTER V

GOVERNMENT AND TRADE, CHURCHES AND HOUSES

Πέντε Βλάχοι ἕνα παζάρι.
Five Vlachs make a market.

GREEK PROVERB

THE Balkan Wars of 1912–13 and the subsequent division of the territories that composed Turkey in Europe, have altered the political status of Samarina for it is now included in Greece. Thus it seems worth while to record how it and similar Vlach villages were governed in Turkish times. The Vlachs scattered about the Balkan regions will eventually become assimilated to the dominant race of the country in which their homes are incorporated. Under the Turks however owing to the feuds of the rival political propagandas which endeavoured to absorb each for itself the bulk of the inhabitants of European Turkey, the Vlachs preserved at least the semblance of a separate national unit, and in their hill villages were in ordinary times almost autonomous. The system of the Turkish government, such as it was, does not seem to have been applied at any one particular time, but rather to have grown up gradually and to have been based to some extent on the old local custom.

Samarina formed part of the kaza of Ghrevena and thus, as a part of the sanjak of Serfije, was a minor unit of the vilayet of Monastir. It lay on the borders of two vilayets, for the two villages immediately to the north and south, Furka and Briaza, were under Yannina. Lying as it does off the track of any main route the village was little troubled by Turkish government officials. The immediate power of the Sublime Porte was represented by a sergeant or a corporal and four other gendarmes. Occasionally during the summer patrols

consisting of fifty or so infantry under a subaltern would visit
the village and stay a few days while on a fruitless brigand
hunt.   One Sunday we heard a Young Turk officer make a
speech in Greek to the assembled village after church on the
benefits and ideals of the Ottoman constitution.   Other
representatives of the government were confined to the occa-
sional visits of tax collectors to receive the tithes due on saw
mills, trade profits and the like.   Another government official
was the preventive man whose duty it was to stop the import
of illicit tobacco which comes from the Berat district.   This
latter official could be a native of Samarina, but the others
were all strangers and as a rule Albanians, Mohammedans of
course, or Valakhadhes, though after 1908 the appearance of
Turkophone christian gendarmes from Anatolia caused some
surprise.   In the village itself its own local government was
in the hands of the *mukhtars* or head men of whom there were
five.   Four of these were elected by the Greek party and
each represented one of the four parishes into which the village
is divided, St Mary the Great, St Mary the Less, St Elijah
and St Athanasius.   The fifth was the *mukhtar* of the Roumanian or nationalist party.   Although it was not till 1905
that the Vlachs of the Turkish Empire obtained their recognition as a separate nationality from the Sublime Porte, yet as
early as 1895 the Roumanian party in Samarina is said to
have succeeded in procuring from the provincial authorities
communal rights.   These five *mukhtars* acted together in the
name of the whole village and no transaction was valid unless
approved by all five.   It was their duty to appoint watchmen
(Plate XI 1), to attend to the water supply and to make local
byelaws.   But after all they had no funds at their disposal
except such as could be obtained by public subscription or
from the wardens of the churches who would make grants
for any work to be done in their own parish.   In 1910 the
bridge on the road to the saw mills over the ravine near the
Shoput al Dabura required rebuilding.   A committee took
the matter up and went round the village explaining the
object and asking for subscriptions.   When enough had been
collected, woodmen were hired to cut the necessary pines high

up on Gorgul'u. Then when these were ready the young men including schoolmasters, especially those of the parish of St Elijah, which was the one most concerned in the bridge, went out on Sundays and feast days and dragged the heavy timbers down to the bridge ready for the carpenters to begin their work. In this way public works of great utility have been carried through.

The watchmen, of whom there were usually four, had to see that people from other villages did not pasture their flocks or mules or cut timber in Samarina territory. They also watched the woods of K'urista in which nothing is allowed to pasture, and any other pasture ground which was reserved for the time being. For instance regularly every year the muleteers agree to set aside a considerable space of pasture ground near the village where no one is allowed to pasture sheep or mules till the 15th of August. The object of this is to ensure that there should be good pasture close to the village for the mules of those who come up for the festival of the Assumption. Another local village official was the crier who by crying *La Hani* and elsewhere about the village made known to the inhabitants the decrees of their rulers and also advertised property lost and found.

Another institution of Samarina that deserves mention is the Νεολαία Σαμαρίνης, a sort of society which on holidays and festivals indulges in merrymaking. But it has also a practical side and its members unite in carrying out something for the good of the community in general. For instance they constructed in 1911 a small bridge on the Ghrevena road a little distance outside the village over a small stream, and it was planning the restoration of some disused drinking fountains on the same road. This society consists only of members of the Greek party and so in 1912 another society was founded called Πρόοδος in which members of both political parties could join. This beyond electing its first officers and committee has had little opportunity of doing anything so far, except to state its aims and objects.

Like the majority of the Vlach villages in the mountains Samarina supports itself by trade and not by farming, though there was a time and that not so very long ago when Samarina did to some extent engage in agriculture. Of other trades there are few requiring technical skill which the Vlach does not consider it beneath his dignity to engage in. Of technical trades there are two which the Pindus Vlachs and their cousins around Verria do not practise. They are not tin or copper smiths, for these are gipsy trades, nor are they masons. In the Verria district houses are built by Bulgar masons who come from the villages in the plain between Verria and Vodhena, and agricultural labour is done by Koniari Turks from the villages in the plain of Kailar. In Pindus the masons are Greeks from villages such as Kerasova, Burbusko (in Vlach Brubiska), Zhupan and so on. For instance an inscription recording the building of the church of St Athanasius at Muskopol'e in 1724 says that the masons came from Krimini, a Greek village near Tshotili. Metsovo is the only Pindus village which we have visited whose inhabitants are masons.

Though at the monastery of Samarina, which lies lower than the village and is inhabited all the year through, maize and rye are grown, and the abbot has lately planted a vineyard, it is now some thirty years since agriculture was undertaken by the villagers of Samarina itself. But there are clear signs that the village was once agricultural to some extent. Near the church of Aigl'a is a grass-grown threshing floor, and near the place called Tshuka which lies on the Morminde ridge below the Ghrevena road near the K'atră N'agră there are also threshing floors and traces of enclosed spaces, which were once ploughed. At H'ilimodhi on the borders of Samarina territory towards Dusko Samarina possessed a chiftlik where some thirty to forty families remained year in and year out. There corn was grown, and from here Samarina was partly supplied with the agricultural products which it now has to import from the plains. Why they abandoned this chiftlik, which still is part of Samarina territory, and serves now only as a sheep run is inexplicable.

The land which comprises the territory of Samarina is owned by the whole village in common. Every member of the village has the right to pasture his stock except in the areas which the community has declared closed for the time being. Any inhabitant of the village can cut timber and fuel where he pleases in the forests except in the forbidden woods of K'urista. Those possessing sheep or saw mills had to pay the dues on sheep and cut timber enforced by the Turkish government, and every plank cut to be sold outside the village had to bear an official mark to show that the dues had been paid. The only privately owned lands in Samarina are the lots on the site of the village itself and consist of houses, gardens and meadows. These are all fenced in and can be bought and sold and are held with title deeds. All the rest of the land is common property and can neither be bought nor sold, but every villager has the right to enclose any piece of ground he likes for a meadow, and so long as he keeps up the fence it is reserved for him and he can call in the village watchmen to drive off intruders. When any stranger, shepherd or muleteer, camps for a night on Samarina territory on his way elsewhere, the watchmen demand a small payment for the right of pasturage for his mules or sheep, and are entitled to enforce their claim by impounding some of his stock.

The other trades we may divide into two classes, those practised locally in the village and those which they only work at in the towns in the plains. But some natives of Samarina, who engage in trades of this latter class, practise them in the summer in Samarina to supply their fellow-countrymen. The only trade, and that not a common one, for which there is no demand at Samarina, is the gunsmith's. Trades which can be practised in the village, but of course to a far greater extent in the towns in the plains are, boot and shoe making, tailoring, milling, the making of pack saddles for mules, the making of knives and blacksmith's work in general, the making of sweets and pastry, carpentering and chair making. Another fairly common trade, although from its nature it is practised more in the towns than in the village itself, is that of silversmith and watchmaker. They make the silver filigree work for the big buckles and buttons worn by the women and set the coins given for betrothal gifts as necklaces or earrings. The metal which they use is obtained by melting down gold or silver coin. A girl who wants a pair of earrings will take a Turkish pound to the goldsmith and he retaining some of the gold as his payment will work the rest into the ornament desired. With these trades we may include the keeping of cafés, and khans or food shops. The keeper of a food shop will sell meat raw and roasted, raki, wine, beer in bottles from Salonica, cheese, bread and petroleum. The only professional men in the village are the three or four doctors, and the schoolmasters who including both Hellenic and Roumanian amount to about a dozen. A trade of more recent introduction is that of photographer which is followed by two or three. The capitalists of the village are the general store keepers who sell anything from dyes and writing paper to draperies and scents. They also indulge in merchanting ; they will buy up woollen stuffs of local manufacture or sheepskins and cheese, and send them in big lots to towns such as Yannina or Monastir, or else sell them at the fairs mentioned below. But of all the trades that of muleteer is one of the most typical. One of the commonest sights on the roads in Macedonia or North Thessaly, and Epirus are the long trains of loaded mules and the Vlach muleteers. A muleteer will own from three or four to nine or ten animals, one of which will be a horse. The horse which is more lightly loaded than the mules, carries the muleteer and his own personal property, and the mules are trained to follow it, for the master as he rides along at the head of his caravan will treat the mules with broken scraps of bread. His property on the horse consists of a goat's hair cape, a leather bag, containing a hammer, horse-shoes and nails, and a pair of saddle-bags, one full of barley for the mules, and the other stuffed with bread, roast meat, and a wooden box containing cheese, and last but not least a wooden flask (*kofă*) filled with wine (Plate II 2). In addition each mule carries its nosebag on its saddle, and their master a small metal flask of raki. The muleteers are not always content to carry goods for hire, and in fact they cannot always find such business. In such cases they do a little merchanting on their own account. A muleteer will load up at Samarina with planks from the saw mills (the principal export of the village), and take them down to Greece to Larissa and Tirnavos. There he sells them and buys instead olives or olive oil which he takes to Kozhani or Shatishta, where he will sell his load again and replace it with corn or wine to bring up to Samarina. One muleteer alone can work unaided four or five mules, loading them with the aid of his fellows, for they nearly always travel in parties, or with his *furtutira*. If he has more than five mules he will have one of his sons to help him : for instance a man and a boy of fourteen can easily work eight or nine mules.

The most typical local trades of Samarina are those connected with the saw mills, sheep and wool. In days gone by the pine woods of Samarina were far more extensive than they are to-day. Formerly the whole of Ghumara, the Morminde ridge, the eastern slopes of Gurgul'u and the valley above H'ilimodhi were thick with pine woods. But now all the best trees have been cut, and though these parts are still wooded, yet goats and sheep are allowed to pasture at will amongst the woods and so no young trees have a chance of growing. To-day there is a saw mill by the Skordhei, but the centre of the timber trade is at the four or five saw mills in the Vale Kārnă. Timber is only exported in the form of cut planks, and there is a great deal of waste in cutting the trees. The tops and branches are not put to any use, and much good timber, which might have been utilised had nature been a little less prodigal in endowing these mountains with woods, is left to rot on the ground. In the village itself long beams made from the more slender trunks roughly shaped are used for roofing, and the convex pieces sawn from the outsides of logs, that are to be sawn into planks are used for fencing and roofing. The saw mills are worked by water power (Plate XIII 2). A mill leet is taken off the stream some way above the site of the mill and run in a shallow channel (*kănale*) to a pool situated on the hill side directly above the mill ; into this other streams may be collected from springs near by to secure a sufficient volume of water. Since the volume of water is small the fall must be greater in proportion in order to obtain enough power to work the water wheel. Consequently from the outlet of the pool, which is lined with rough planks and puddled with clay, a long enclosed shoot of wood (*kărută*) runs right down on to the wheel itself. The wheel is small and placed low down against the pile substructure of the mill proper, and is connected with the gear that runs the saws by a system of belting. The saw blades, of which there are two or three, project from the floor of the mill. Against them the log to be sawn is rolled into position on a sort of cradle which by an ingenious arrangement moves towards the saws which work vertically. Attached to each saw mill is also a wooden shed built of waste planks where the sawyers sleep. These are often closed with ingeniously constructed wooden locks. Down the mountain side near the mill are several shoots for rolling down the logs, and from the bottom of the shoots are inclined ways of pine trunks for rolling the logs easily into the mill.

Samarina also possesses several ordinary water mills for grinding corn and maize. These are either in the village itself on one of the small streams running through it, or in the valley below where the river of Samarina gives a plentiful supply of water. When the grain is bought from the muleteers who bring it up and sell it in the *misohori*, the women sift it and sort out all impurities and if necessary even wash it. It is left in the courtyard of the house in the sun to dry for three or four hours with a small child to watch it and drive off chickens, and then it is rebagged and sent to the mill. For this purpose every miller keeps a donkey which he sends round in charge of a small boy to bring in the grain. The mills both as regards the leet and the tall narrow shoot for the water resemble the saw mills in arrangement ; but the wheel is placed horizontally to avoid the difficulty of transferring the power from a vertical wheel to the horizontal mill stones. The gearing is mostly of wood and the mill stones are not one stone, but are composed of many small pieces ingeniously fitted together and bound with iron hoops. Most millers also possess a *bătal'e* and *drăshteala*, the special apparatus necessary for washing the woollen fabrics when they are woven.

Sheep rearing is still an important trade at Samarina, but not so important as formerly. Up to 1877 Samarina possessed about eighty thousand head of sheep, but to-day has some seventeen thousand only. The diminution has been due to two causes. The rising of 1878 seriously injured the Vlachs as the principal shepherds, and the people of Samarina amongst them. Then the division of the Vlach country by the cession of Thessaly to Greece erected a customs barrier between the summer and winter pastures of the Samarina shepherds. Further the proximity of the Samarina country to the Greek frontier till 1912 rendered it easily liable to raids from brigands who would have their base in Greek territory where they were careful to keep within the law. Owing to the difficulty of the country they could after an exploit committed in Turkish territory escape to Greece and immunity and vice versa. This brigandage naturally concerned the shepherds more than other people because the shepherd from his trade is obliged to live out on the hills with his flocks far away from gendarmes. Brigands would come to a sheepfold and demand milk, bread and a roast lamb for supper. The shepherd could not refuse, or the brigands would revenge themselves by robbing him and perhaps by killing two or three hundred ewes. Similarly should a patrol of gendarmerie appear in pursuit of brigands the shepherd would have to feed them, and to give information as to brigands anywhere near. Should he refuse he would be beaten within an inch of his life and perhaps cast into prison. If the brigands were to hear that he had betrayed their whereabouts, they would return at the first opportunity, and either kill the shepherd or his flocks. In this state of affairs it will be seen that it needs a bold and determined man to take up the peaceful and Arcadian existence of shepherd, and it is small cause for wonder if many shepherds have sold their flocks and adopted other pursuits, while others not having much choice live hand in glove with brigands.

About St George's Day which falls on the 23rd of April O.S., the shepherds who winter in the Thessalian plains round Trikkala, or between Larissa and Tirnavos or in the Potamia district near Elassona prepare for moving to the mountains for the summer. The lambs which have been born during the winter in December or January are by this time weaned and capable of standing the journey. The flock which consists of from five hundred to two thousand head is divided into detachments. The ewes are divided into two classes, barren (*stearpe*), and milch (*aplikatori*, or *mātritse*), and these again are subdivided according to colour into flocks of white and black. The lambs and rams are likewise drafted into separate flocks. When the mountain pastures are reached the head shepherd sets up his sheepfold more or less in the same spot as in former years, and while he remains in the village looking after the sale of the produce, but visiting his fold almost every day, the charge of the flocks and the butter and cheese making devolve on his subordinates. The fold (*kutarŭ*) proper (Plate XI 3) consists of a round enclosure fenced in with thorns, branches and rough planks. At one end is a wide entrance (*ushe*) which can easily be closed or watched. Not quite opposite this a narrow exit (*arugă*) with a post in the middle so that not more than two or three ewes can pass out at a time. In front of this exit are placed four milking stones arranged two and two as shown. The milkers sit on these and as the ewes pass out seize them by the hind legs and milk them into large tin pails (*gāleată*). This place, where the milking stones are, is roofed in with rough planks on rafters laid over forked sticks, and forms the porch of the *kashari* proper, where the mysteries of cheese making are carried on. This is a long oblong shed boarded in at the sides, but open at the ends. In one corner is a locked cupboard where made cheese can be kept, also bread and any implements not in use. Along one wall is a long, inclined wooden table where cheese can be laid to drain. In the centre is a rough hearth, under a hook hanging from the ceiling, and walled in with stones on which are propped the pails in which the milk is boiled. Along the other side will be a row of tall slender tubs in which the cream is kept ready to be made into cheese. From the roof beams are hanging several bags containing half-made cheese from which the water is being drained out. Most of the shepherds make but one kind of cheese, *kash kaval*, which is bought up by merchants, sent to Yannina and thence exported to Italy where it appears as

PLATE XI

| 1. WATCHMAN IN BRIGAND COSTUME WITH HIS PET LAMB | 2. BOY IN ANDRI AND MALLIOTŬ |

3. SAMARINA: MILKING TIME AT A SHEEPFOLD

Caccia Cavallo. The making of this cheese is roughly as follows. The milk is boiled with the addition of a little salt. The resulting cream (*alkă*) is collected (sheep's milk is richer in cream in proportion than cow's), and kept for some time in one of the tubs. Then through a further process of boiling and straining it is turned into ordinary white milk cheese. This is shredded and reboiled, and then pressed into low, round wooden moulds. It is again strained and dried, and when hard it is taken out of the mould and placed on a board under a weight to harden still further, and at the same time is liberally salted till it has absorbed as much as it can. Then it is ready for market : the heads (*kapite*) of cheese are packed in rouleaux in sacks and so make their way by mule to Yannina. The constant and profitable nature of the demand for this *kash kaval* has caused the shepherds to confine their attention to making this. The result is that ordinary white cheese and butter are dear and scarce in Samarina where there are so many sheep. A favourite kind of cheese sometimes made is that called *urdu* (Gk. μανούρι), which is produced by a different process. *Yiaurti* (*mărkatŭ*) is also made, and amongst the poor a dish called *giză* is popular which is made by boiling butter milk. But butter milk (*dală*) is not common since butter (*umtŭ*) is rarely made. From fresh milk a dish called *lapte grossŭ* (thick milk) is procured by slightly turning it, and boiling it till thick. As a rule when milk is boiled a little salt is added to it. The shepherds continue this life in the hills till about the day of St Demetrius, October 26th O.S. when they move down to the plains for the winter. The ewes are milked up to the end of July, and then gradually milk becomes scarcer, cheese making stops and active work at the sheep fold ceases. The fold does not serve as a shelter for the flock, but only as a method of bringing them together. At night they sleep in the open watched by savage dogs, which however are not taught to drive the flock, but only to watch. At midday the flocks and their attendant shepherds will be found asleep under some large tree which gives enough shade to protect them from the heat of the summer sun. The flock when it wanders is led by an elderly ram with a bell. Towards the end of

August Albanian dealers appear at Samarina to buy up worn out ewes and rams to sell to butchers in the Berat, and El-basan districts. Shearing takes place just before or just after the spring migration to the hills. The sheep are not washed before shearing, and they are never dipped, but on the whole they keep very healthy. In 1911 however both sheep and goats throughout Macedonia and Thessaly suffered severely from some disease which seemed to take the form of an acute foot rot, and many died, and those which survived were in very poor condition. Undoubtedly careful breeding and a greater attention to cleanliness would produce much better results. Yet all things considered the quality of the cheese and mutton is excellent.

The wool trade is the most important trade of the village and the one on which it mostly depends. Every spring when the sheep are shorn the heads of families buy up quantities of raw wool for their wives and daughters to work up during the summer (Plate XII). When the village is reached the first process is to pick over the wool by hand to remove the more prominent impurities such as burrs, and smooth out some of the tangles. Next the wool is washed and spread out in the sun to dry, and is also kept in two qualities long thread and short thread. When dry the wool is carded. The carder a girl sits on one end of a long low kind of stool, in the other end of which is fixed a carding comb (k'aptine). This is a rectangular piece of wood with one side studded with small nails, and it has a handle attached to one of the long sides. The wool to be carded is laid on this fixed comb and the operator draws it backwards and forwards with a similar comb held in the hands till the wool is loose and fluffy. Wool with short thread after carding is rolled up into loose lumps (pitrikă), and then spun on a spinning wheel (tshikrike) into spools (tsăyi) of thread (tramă) for weaving. The spools are wound off into large round balls, and this is the thread used for setting up the warp on the loom. Other spools are wound off again on to spindles and make the woof. Long thread wool after carding is kept in loose lumps (apală), and then spun on the spinning wheel into flock (flokŭ). The spools of

PLATE XII

SAMARINA: WOMEN WORKING WOOL

this are wound into skeins (*trănă*) on a winder (*lishkitoru*) and then dyed various colours. These skeins are used to make the flock which is woven into the patterns of blankets, rugs and mats. Other wool with long thread after being carded is made into small lumps (*sumă*) and placed in handfuls (*kairŭ*) on the distaff (*furkă*) and spun by hand into thread (*ustură*) for weaving flannels, and stuffs. The thread which is to be dyed for weaving varicoloured carpets and rugs is first wound into skeins on the winder, then after dyeing is placed on an instrument called an *anemi* and from this wound into spools to be placed in the shuttle (*zvallsă*) for weaving. The principal stuffs made are homespun (*adhimtă*) which is usually white, and two varieties of the same, one thin and fine called *garvanitshu* which is usually black, the other a thick homespun (*garvano*) with a heavy flock from which waterproof outer coats and capes are made. Flannel (*katasarkŭ*) is also made, and many varieties of rugs and blankets. The rugs are called *tende* or *vilendze*, and may be compared to heavy blankets or coarse travelling rugs. They are made in lengths not quite a yard wide and four to six lengths go to make one blanket. The tents used on journeys are made of similar material, but rather thicker, and are always composed of six lengths and almost without exception the pattern consists of black and white stripes. The patterns of the rugs fall into two main kinds, both of which are geometrical. The first class is bicoloured in black and white and consists of a series of white diamonds bordered with black. In the centre of each diamond is a double axe with a short shaft also in black. The other patterns are of miscellaneous geometric types, and multicoloured, red, yellow, green, blue, etc. The rugs of the first type of pattern are smoothly made with a thick flock, but those of the second are more coarsely made and ornamented with long tassel-like pieces of flock woven in here and there. Both these kinds of rugs are however no longer in fashion, for even Samarina has its fashions. To-day it is the custom to make a mat-like kind of rug called *tshorgă*. These are made in two sizes small for spreading on the floor to sit or sleep on, and large to cover oneself with at night. These are

6

like thick woollen hearthrugs, and have a long, thick even flock all over carefully woven into the fabric. They are dyed indigo, or if not may be made with flock ready dyed when they boast all the colours of the rainbow. One regrettable feature is that the introduction of aniline dyes has caused them to abandon the use of local vegetable dyes, which gave far more artistic effects in colouring. Pillow cases (*kāpitin'i*) are also made from the local wool, and in these again the fashion has changed. Formerly the patterns were simple and geometric and the fabric was of a blanket type. To-day they are made of a carpet-like fabric, and decorated with floral and bird designs of an early Victorian appearance and executed on a red ground in blue, yellow and green aniline colours. Further instead of the earlier rugs carpets are now made with patterns somewhat similar to those of the modern pillow cases. The carpets are made in lengths, borders and all and the pattern is carefully calculated so that all should join up properly when the whole is eventually put together. Of similar fabric are the mantel borders, and door hangings which are used to decorate the principal room on festivals and other great occasions. A variety of *garvano* is made of goat's hair and is used for making the capes used by shepherds and muleteers. When made all the various rugs and stuffs with the exception of the carpets are washed and shrunk. The homespun and similar fabrics are treated in a beetling mill (*batal'e*). This which is worked by water power (Plate XIII 1), is a low shed—occasionally it is in the open—on one side of which are swung four heavy wooden hammers (*tshokote*) so arranged on a notched wooden shaft that they work two and two alternately. Along the other side is a narrow wooden shelf sloping towards the hammer heads and on the same level with them. On the other side of this shelf is a stout wooden beam for the hammers to beat against. In this is cut a narrow rill into which runs a small stream of water taken off the mill leet. From this rill small holes are bored leading on to the upper edge of the sloping shelf so that a constant, but thin trickle of water can always be running on to it. On the shelf is placed the stuff which has first been thoroughly wetted, and when the water is turned on to the wheel the hammers swing to and fro two and two beating the stuff against the beam behind it. With the constant trickle of water the stuff is always kept wet. Thus it is beaten firm and thick and smooth and at the same time well shrunk. This ensures the essential quality of good homespun that the lines of the warp and woof shall not be distinguishable on the surface. The rugs and blankets and the coarse stuffs with goat's hair are washed and shrunk in a *drăshteală*. This is a large, open, wooden tub built in the ground, and narrowing towards the bottom. From a long wooden shoot above a strong stream of water pours down into it. In this the rugs are placed and are whirled round and round in the seething torrent of water.

This is a brief account of the manufacture in which the women of Samarina spend most of their time, and the profits of this go a long way towards supporting the families. The two qualities which in addition to beauty, modesty and good temper, are most highly prized in a girl are her ability to work wool and to cook. Every year the heads of families invest nearly all their floating capital in the purchase of raw wool. Consequently throughout the summer in every family there is a shortness of actual cash, and the marketing of the village in the summer is one vast credit system. All the tradesmen keep big ledgers and daybooks, and so also do the cafés and food shops. Children instead of begging a halfpenny from their mothers to buy sweets will beg a small handful of wool. This is exchanged by the sweet shop man for peppermints or the like, and the wool he collects in a large box under his counter and in due course hands over to his womenkind to work. Thus Samarina to a great extent lives by wool and thinks in wool, far more so than any other Vlach village we have visited. Any untoward event in the woollen trade of Upper Macedonia or Albania would spell disaster for Samarina. The woollen fabrics when made are sold at certain well recognised fairs. The first is the fair of St Akhillios at Ghrevena which we have already mentioned. The next is a fair at Monastir to which the merchants of Samarina send every year about a hundred mule loads of coarse fabrics. The caravan conveying these leaves Samarina about ten days after the festival of the Assumption on August 15th O.S. The next fair takes place at Serfije and begins on the 16th of September O.S. and lasts for four days. Returned from that, all Samarina prepares to go to the great fair of Konitsa which begins on September 22nd O.S. and lasts for eight days. This is the principal fair for the Samarina wool trade ; for this the better rugs and stuffs are reserved. To this fair merchants come from all parts of Albania, equally from Scutari and from Yannina. With the money obtained by the sale of their products at the fair of Konitsa every Samarina family pays the debts it has been running up during the summer. Any failure in the success of this fair would wreck the credit system and plunge many into desperate financial difficulties. This fair may be said to end the summer season at Samarina for soon after most of the families desert the village and by the time the day of St Demetrius dawns only those who have made up their minds to winter in the village remain. Two other fairs concern to some extent also the people of Samarina. One is held at Tirnavos a few days after Easter and is principally a mule fair. The other takes place at Trikkala towards the end of September, and is mainly concerned with sheep dealing. But both these fairs have lost their importance for the Vlachs of Northern Pindus, since the cession of Thessaly to Greece, for the Greek customs duties were very heavy and a serious bar to trade.

Ecclesiastically Samarina forms part of the diocese of Ghrevena and the bishop naturally has supreme control over the churches of the village and was in the eyes of the Turkish government the head of its Greek community. Each of the four churches is under the management of its own wardens and priests. They provide for the upkeep and repair of the church and from its funds may grant money for any public works in the parish. The funds are mainly derived from the offerings made on Sunday and especially from those given at the festival of the church. The only church that possesses any endowment is St Mary the Great which owns most of the

PLATE XIII

2. SAMARINA : A SAW MILL

1. SAMARINA : A BEETLING MILL

booths and shops round *La Hani*. Each church has two or
more priests attached to it. They are paid by their flock and
their womenkind work wool. On the first day of every month
they go round and bless each house in the parish and the householder in return makes a small offering. They also receive fees
for baptisms, weddings and burials, and for reading over sick
persons. The largest and most important parish is that of St
Mary the Great which includes some two hundred and fifty
houses. The interior although like all orthodox Greek churches
may be described here, as it is a good example of the churches
not only in Samarina, but in the other Vlach villages to the
south. From the outside (Plate XIV 1) it has the appearance of
a tall and broad barn, and in this it resembles the majority of
the churches in Northern Greece. On the south side and on
the west is a low cloister (*hāiate*), a constant feature of these
churches which always have one at the west end and another
either on the south or north. At the east end of the southern
cloister is a chapel, another constant feature in Samarina at
least, in this case dedicated to St Peter and St Paul. The
entrance in use is on the south side towards the west end, but
there is another entrance in the middle of the west end, which
as usual in such churches is rarely used. If we enter from this
western door we find ourselves at once in the narthex, above
which is the women's gallery built of wood. The narthex is
separated from the nave by a solid wall pierced by a narrow door
in its centre, from which is taken the view of the interior seen
in Plate XIV 2 looking eastwards. On the left of this door
as we enter the nave is a table on which is a dish for offerings
of money. Here one of the wardens stands with bundles of
candles and tapers for the congregation to buy and set up
before the ikons. There is one man in the village who is a
candle maker and he supplies all its churches. The nave itself
is separated from the aisles by rows of built columns, along
which on either side of the nave are the stalls where the more
important members of the congregation stand. In the middle
of the stalls on the right is the bishop's throne of carved wood
and gilt. At the west end of the stalls on the other side is a
pulpit of similar workmanship. Towards the east end of the

stalls on both sides are the two reading desks where the chanters take their stand.   The walls are painted with fresco representations of the saints and biblical subjects.   The painting of ikons and the decorating of churches with frescoes is another Samarina trade, and at the present time there are said to be about twelve natives of the village who follow it.   Naturally this craft cannot be practised in the village alone and therefore such artists travel about all over Northern Greece, Epirus and Macedonia in search of work.   The churches of Samarina all seem to have been decorated by local artists, a fact which in many cases is borne out by the inscriptions in them.   The ceiling is flat and of wood decorated with small ornamental panels and painted.   Amongst Vlach villages the people of Metsovo are said to have been particularly renowned for making such ceilings in days gone by, but there is no reason to believe that it is a Vlach speciality.   The nave is separated from the chancel by a tall screen of wood, most elaborately carved and gilt. In this are inserted the principal ikons and before them hang votive offerings of silver, beads, coins, cheap jewellery and the like.   Above in the screen is a row of niches filled with ikons representing the important festivals of the church in order from left to right.   The one that is appropriate to the festival of the day is taken out and placed on a stand in the body of the church and by it is put a metal stand for the tapers of the worshippers.   Two similar taper stands are placed in the nave one on either side of the central door of the screen and in front of the two principal ikons.   From the centre of the top of the screen rises a great gilt wooden cross flanked by two dragons. Often too from the overhanging cornice of the screen project wooden doves from which are suspended the small oil lamps that are lighted before the ikons.   Within the screen the arrangement of the chancel with the *prothesis* on one side and the *dhiakonikon* on the other is the same as in all orthodox churches.   It is to be noted that there is only one apse behind the altar, on the roof of which grows the pine tree the great wonder of Samarina.   The whole roof of the church consists of rough planks covered over with overlapping stone slabs, and it is in such soil that this marvellous pine is rooted.

PLATE XIV

1. EXTERIOR FROM THE EAST

2. INTERIOR FROM THE WEST

SAMARINA: GREAT ST. MARY'S

As to the date of the church that cannot be ascertained, although there is an inscription which states that the wall paintings were executed in 1829. This translated reads as follows :—

✝ Beautified was this holy and venerable temple of our very blessed and glorious Lady, Mary the Mother of God, in the high-priesthood of the all holy and reverend Metropolitan the Lord Anthimos and when there served in this church Mikhail the priest and arch-priest and Khristos, Zisi, Steryios, Yeoryios and Khristos the priests, and in the wardenship of Yerasios Triandaphilos and at the expense and under the care of the same and with the contribution of Adham Tshutra and other christians in this village as a memorial for ever, and by the hand of Khristos the priest and Andonios his brother the sons of the priest Ioannis out of the same village in the year of salvation 1829 in the month of July the thirtieth day.

One of the ikons dates from 1811 and others from 1830, 1831, 1832 and 1834. From this we may conclude that it was about that time that the church took its present form, but it probably was in existence before then. If the local tradition is right in asserting that this is the oldest in the village, a church must have stood on this site for some two or three hundred years. Outside the church and standing separate from it near the south-west corner is the campanile. This is later than the church, at least all agree in saying so, but its exact date is not known.

Next in importance to Great St Mary's is the church of St Elijah. The parish includes some hundred and eighty houses, but is cut in two by the deep ravine already mentioned which has wrought such havoc among its houses. The plan and arrangement of this church are similar to that of Great St Mary's. The chapel attached to it in the cloister on the north side is dedicated to the Ayii Anaryiri, that is to say to St Cosmas and St Damian. An inscription states that the wall paintings were done in 1828, and this translated reads :—

✝ Beautified was this holy and venerable temple of the holy and glorious Prophet Elijah, the messenger of God, in the high-priesthood of the all holy Metropolitan the Lord Anthimos, and in the priesthood of the most reverend Mikhail the priest and archdeacon and Yerasios the priest and Khristos the priest, in the wardenship of Adham Hondre also called Samaras, and by the hand of Khristos the priest the son of the priest Ioannis out of the same village, in the year of salvation 1828 February the twentieth. The end.

One of the ikons dates from 1786 and in a klephtic ballad relating to Totskas the church is referred to as being well known at the time between 1770 and 1800, and the present priest has assured us that it is at least two hundred years old.

The third largest parish is that belonging to the church of Little St Mary's, which stands in a group of tall poplars on a rise at the northern end of the village. This numbers about a hundred houses. The church is of the same general type as the others, and has cloisters with a chapel dedicated to the Ayii Anaryiri, and a school which is used by the Greek party since that of Great St Mary's is not large enough. Round the church on the west and south is a *pade* enclosed by a stone wall topped with wood which serves as a seat, and over the gateway entering this is a short campanile. The south door of the church is built of stone on which are carved many strange devices, men holding flowers, St George and the dragon, lizards, lions, cherubim, and birds pecking at flowers. Over the door to the right is this inscription :—

Holy Virgin, Mother of God, help thy servants dwelling in this village, in the high-priesthood of Ghavril the all holy and divinely protected exarch of our most holy Metropolis Ghrevena, at the expense of Steryioyiani, in the year 1799 May the 28th : the master mason Zisi.

and directly above the door is the following :—

This temple of the Holy Virgin of the city of Samarina was conspicuous of old, but was again built beautiful to the world to the glory of the God of all mankind when there served as high-priest in our province the renowned Yennadhios the follower of wisdom, and under the care of and with great zeal by Zisi Exarkhu of the house of Hadzhimikha. Approach ye old men, young men come up, women run, hither Oh maidens, and worship the God of Heaven in fear of soul and heart, in the year 1865 August the 2nd : the master mason Yiani.

Also outside in the wall of the apse is a stone dated 1855. From the evidence it appears that a church was built on this site in 1799 and afterwards enlarged to its present form between 1855 and 1865. This agrees well with the local tradition, but we cannot discover whether there was any church here before 1799.

The last and smallest parish is that of St Athanasius which includes about seventy houses only. The church is of the usual type, and has a side chapel in the cloister dedicated to the Ayii Anaryiri. Now it has no school, for this collapsed in the winter a few years ago, but for some time it was used by the Roumanian party. Over the door of the church which is in the north side is the date 1778, and three ikons within are dated 1792, 1793 and 1855. We may thus conclude that the church in its present form was, like the others, built towards the end of the eighteenth century. In its construction the only peculiarity is that the columns in the nave are of pine trunks and not built columns of stone.

This completes the list of the churches of the village proper, but there is the shrine reputed to be dedicated to Ayios Kosmas which deserves mention. This lies in a little hollow on the hill side above Gudrumitsa where the martyr is reported to have preached to the village, and in memory of his visit the shrine was erected on the spot where he had stood. In a later chapter will be found further details of this remarkable man, who seems to have visited Samarina in 1778, for on a rock a little below Mermishaklu is this inscription :—

$$\begin{array}{ll} 1778 & \text{ΑΠΟ ΤΟΝ ΑΓΙΟ} \\ 1861 & \text{ΚΟΖΜΑ} \end{array}$$

and below

$$— — — \text{ΤΒΒΦΟΜΑΡΛΟΣ} — — — \text{ΤΕ}$$
$$\text{ΛΟΣΘΕΣ ΤΕΑΤΟΣ} — — — \text{ΡΗΝΕ}$$

The latter part is unintelligible, but the first two lines, although they do not seem to have been inscribed till 1861, apparently shew that he visited Samarina in 1778, the year before his death.

The monastery of Samarina which is dedicated to Ayia Paraskevi (in Vlach Sāndă Vineri), St Friday, lies about half an hour south of the village on the road to Briaza and not far above the river of Samarina. The buildings are well sheltered from the north and in winter are not snowed up. The site faces south and is well favoured by nature (Plate XVI), for all around the hill side is thick with pines and beeches, and in summer the bare patches are green with waving bracken and spangled with wild flowers. Below the monastery towards the river are a few meadows where hay is made and near these and also on the slopes of Ghumara opposite are some fields where barley, rye and maize are grown. In front is a garden full of vegetables and dotted with fruit trees, plums, cherries and apples. Before the door is a paved court enclosed by a low stone wall, where there is a stable and some sheds, as well as a spring of clear cold water and a fine walnut tree. Access to the monastery proper is given by a low, narrow gate in the west side closed with a heavy wooden door studded with iron. High above this outside is a projecting stone niche containing an ikon of Ayia Paraskevi, and directly above the door is a look-out place with a hole in the floor so that the monks could survey visitors and, if they proved undesirable, give them a warm reception. By the side of the niche a wooden balcony has recently been built so that the oil lamp hanging before the ikon of the saint can be lighted easily. Within the plan is similar to that of most Levantine monasteries, that is to say the buildings are arranged round a court. In this case the court is oblong, with the longer sides on the north and south. The lower range of buildings on the north has an open cloister against the court on the ground level, and the first and second floors have similar cloisters now partly closed in with wood-work. On the ground floor are the stables and store-rooms; on the first floor are the kitchens and rooms for servants; and on the second floor is a row of cells, built of wood, for monks; and on the west the guest-chambers. The principal guest-room is very similar to the principal living-room in a Samarina house, and the walls are decorated with picture postcards and photographs. The stairs leading to the upper stories are

at the north-west corner just inside the door, and it is said
that somewhere among the labyrinth of dark chambers on the
second floor is a so-called prison where Leonidha of Samarina
lay concealed from the Turks. All the windows look into the
court, a sure sign that the building was constructed to stand
a siege if necessary. Only the recently built guest-chamber,
which is high up at the south-west corner, has windows that
look outwards. In this case owing to the slope of the ground
they are so high above the earth that no danger from the outside can affect them. The church of the monastery is built
into the south wall on the ground level, but has high sub-
structures below owing to the slope of the hill. In these
below the exo-narthex, which is open, is a large cellar-like
room from which a secret passage is said to lead down to the
river. By this Leonidha and Dhuka are believed to have
escaped. At all events it can only be entered from above by
a trapdoor and might easily not be noticed. The church,
which of course has no other stories above it, is small and
domed, unlike the churches in the village which have gable
roofs with wooden rafters. The dome is supported on four
central piers of which the two nearest the chancel are columnar.
There is a small narthex and the chancel is separated from the
nave by the usual gilt screen of carved wood-work, and the
walls are decorated with pictures of saints and biblical subjects
in fresco. At the back of the chancel is a single apse and in the
wall above is the following inscription which gives the date
of its building :—

This temple of the holy, glorious and blessed virgin martyr of
Christ Paraskevi was built in the year 1713 from the Incarnation.

How old the monastery really is it is impossible to say.
The people of Samarina assert that it is eight hundred years
old and quote in support of this statement a stone carved
with a date high up in the outside of the west wall. The date
they read as 1066, but on careful examination with field
glasses it appears to us to read 1866. In any case the cutting
is fresh and does not seem to be anything like as old as 1066.
The stone too does not seem to be in its original position and
was perhaps transferred from elsewhere and recut. In other

days the monastery was wealthy and had many monks. It owns much land and many vineyards at Armata and once held a chiftlik at Skutina near Kalabaka, near which is a place called Paleo-Samarina because several families from the village used to winter there. The chiftlik was sold by three or four prominent men of Samarina in whose names it was then registered and they divided the money among themselves. According to the common belief of the village neither those men nor their descendants have prospered since because of this sacrilege. Now the young men of Samarina who have emigrated to America have formed in the cities whither most of them go to work, a society which they call the Ἑλληνικὴ Ἀδελφότης Σαμαριναίων, ἡ Ἁγία Παρασκευή. Its main object is to collect funds to buy back the lost chiftlik for the monastery, for it is believed that the surplus funds of the monastery will be available to be devoted to public works in the village. For some time towards the end of the nineteenth century the monastery was deserted, but recently the villagers determined that it should be revived and looked about for a suitable man to make abbot. They found a native of Samarina who was a monk at the famous monastery of Zaburdo, and had some sheep and goats. They thought that with this capital and the pastures round the monastery he would be able to restore it to prosperity. Their expectations have been realised, for the sheep and goats have multiplied and the monastery does a good trade in *kash kaval*. The abbot is energetic in overseeing the lands at Armata, has cultivated the garden and fields near, and has rebuilt much of the upper story on the inside with wood. The new guest-chambers are his work, and he has recently planted a vineyard. The monastery now employs an old woman as cook, several men as shepherds and labourers, and two or three boys, all of them Vlachs of Samarina. There are two monks, natives too, but they are not always in residence, and in 1911 a Greek priest was imported for the services of the church, for the abbot is a man of business and not of learning.

In the fields near the monastery stands yet another church called St Saviour's (Ayios Sotir) which forms part of the monastery. This is larger than the church of the monastery itself and in plan resembles those in the village, although it has no cloisters. It is roofed by a series of small domes and yet has the divisions between the nave and the aisles formed by arcades. The walls are covered with frescoes and the inscription accompanying them says they were finished in 1819. Its text translated runs thus :—

✝ Beautified was this holy and venerable temple of the holy, glorious and blessed virgin martyr and champion of Christ Paraskevi in the high-priesthood of the all holy and divinely protected Metropolitan the holy bishop of Ghrevena the Lord Vartholomeos, by the care and contribution of the holy fathers present in this holy monastery, by the hand of the poor readers Dhimitrios and Mikhail the sons of the priest Ioannis out of the same village Samarina, in the year of salvation 1819 in the month of October the fifteenth day it was finished, glory to God the Holy.

Thus we see that though the church is now called Ayios Sotir it was originally dedicated, like the monastery itself, to Ayia Paraskevi and in consequence it has changed its festival from the day of that saint to the feast of the Transfiguration. It is quite possible that the fact that both churches had the same festival caused the name of this second church to be changed, so that its feast should fall on a different day. This involves two collections of offerings instead of one. The building of this and the churches in the village itself falls at the end of the eighteenth century after the treaty of Kainarji in 1774 between Russia and Turkey by which the christians in Turkey were not to be prevented from building or repairing churches. We may however also conclude that this was the most flourishing period of Samarina, when there was most money available for building churches, not only in the village, but also at the monastery. A parallel instance is to be seen in the case of Muskopol'e, mentioned in a later chapter.

The only other churches on Samarina territory are those at the abandoned chiftlik of H'ilimodhi where there are two. One is dedicated to St Athanasius and the other to St Saviour, but both are small and not in good condition. Round them are the ruins of houses and a few small huts and barns used by those who go to cut hay there.

The houses like the churches are all built by Greek masons, and so are only Vlach in a secondary sense. As in many other Vlach villages nearly every house at Samarina has its own patch of garden, divided off by a rough stone wall or a rude wooden fence (Plate XV 2). Here are grown French beans, broad beans, cabbages, lettuces, sorrel, cucumbers, marrows, tomatoes, parsley, mint, potatoes and Jerusalem artichokes, in fact any vegetable that can be grown in the summer. Besides vegetables most gardens will boast a cherry or plum tree, and perhaps also an apple or pear. Here and there too one may see roses, marigolds and stocks, but like nearly all Balkan christians the Vlachs care little for flowers. The houses are built of stones and nearly all stand two stories high ; in size they vary from large imposing buildings capable of holding four or more families to modest dwellings meant for one family only (Plates XV 2, XVI 1, XVII). The smaller houses are often semi-detached and are frequently grouped round a small paved yard. Excepting round the doors and windows and in the angles where squared blocks are sometimes employed, the stones used are left rough and since lime cannot be procured on the spot, mortar is expensive and is used sparingly. The stones in consequence are usually laid in mud, but pointed on the outside with mortar and plastered inside and then white-washed. Battens of juniper, a wood that does not easily perish, are laid lengthways in the walls at fairly frequent intervals to act as binding courses. The roofs are all of a low gable type, for a flat roof of course would not stand the winter snows, and are made either of stone slabs, or of rough hewn planks. The only attempt at external decoration consists of grotesque figures and rude patterns which are occasionally carved on one or two of the larger stones built into the walls. A stone inscribed with the date and the builder's name is also sometimes seen.

In many respects the type of house built has gradually been changing during recent years and house architecture in Samarina is at present in an interesting transitional stage. The

PLATE XV

1. SAMARINA: THE MONASTERY FROM THE SOUTH

2. SAMARINA: GROUP OF HOUSES SHOWING OVEN, GARDENS AND
K´IPENG´I

older houses in the village have few and only small windows on the ground floor, and all the living-rooms are in the upper story. In the newer houses the need for defence has been less pressing so that windows on the ground floor are larger and more frequent. The living-room is still upstairs, but the downstair rooms are beginning to be used. Contemporary with this development there has been a great increase in small comforts and European ideas. Window glass has come into use, but is still far from universal. Generally speaking it is only found in the newest houses and in those inhabited all the year round. Boarded floors are supplanting the old mud floors, chairs at Samarina have come into vogue with a rush and most houses now possess one or two. Wall decorations such as picture postcards and the like are also a sign of the times. It seems therefore worth while to describe a house and its contents in some detail, and as typical we may select a house of moderate size, of respectable antiquity and one belonging to a family that is tolerably well off.

The house will be entered by a low, but wide door on the ground floor. This opens directly into a long, low room paved with rough slabs. If the owner be a muleteer this will at times be used as a stable, and along one side there will be a manger. If not, the manger or a place for one may be there all the same, but the room in summer at least will be the work-room and contain the loom, spinning-wheel, skein-winder, and stool and comb for carding, all of which would otherwise be upstairs. For the greater part of the day we shall find the housewife in the work-room at her spinning-wheel, an elder daughter will be at the loom, and a younger perhaps carding wool, all probably will be near the open door for the windows if any are small. Outside in the paved courtyard spread on a rug in the sun to dry will be the wool that has recently been picked over and washed. On high days and holidays the loom will be covered over with a rug and the other implements for weaving put out of sight. The rest of the ground floor is taken up by a store-room, in which are kept wooden chests full of spare rugs and clothes, homespun not yet made up, tins of butter or lard, and other household properties. There will also be a bin for flour and a few skins of cheese will probably be hanging from the roof. From the work-room a short straight staircase with a simple hand rail leads directly to the principal room of the house. The top of the stairway is usually fenced in with lattice-work, above which is a cupboard where the rugs used for bedding are put away.

Either across one end of the room or round two or three of the walls there will be a low wooden dais or *mindārlik'i*. Woollen rugs woven by the mistress of the house are strewn over it, and a few cushions are placed in the corners by the wall. In the day-time it is the place to sit upon, and at night it becomes a bed. The newer the house the narrower the *mindārlik'i*, and in some of the newest houses where chairs are intended to be used it has almost become a bench round the wall. Again, where the *mindārlik'i* is large, the remaining part of the floor, whether of boards or beaten earth—earthen floors are to be found even in upstairs rooms—is often left uncovered as it is not used to sit upon ; but where the *mindārlik'i* is comparatively small the rest of the floor is usually covered with a piece of carpet or rug. On entering a house the shoes are usually removed as the floor is still the place on which to sit, but with the increase of chairs and boots, both European innovations, this custom is dying out.

Partly built into the wall on the side of the room where there is no *mindārlik'i* will be the *misandră*, a very typical piece of furniture which may be described as a cross between a wardrobe and sideboard. The centre part of it, which is set back, consists of a large double-doored cupboard where rugs and pillows can be stored. Immediately to either side are a few small shelves, and beyond these large cupboards for more rugs or clothes. Elsewhere in the room there will probably be one or two small shelved cupboards built into the walls. Directly opposite the *misandră* and so on the dais or *mindārlik'i* and right up against the wall is the fireplace or *vatră*, a square of flat slabs plastered over with mud. Above it is a wide chimney that partly projects into the room and is ornamented by a special hanging of carpet. The chimney above the roof ends in a short, square, stone shaft covered with a large slab, but with slits at the side for the smoke.   The places of honour in the house alike by day and night are in the corners to right and left of the hearth.

In all the better houses there is a flat, wooden ceiling below the roof beams, and in the centre of it in many cases a simple carved pattern.   Round each wall at about a foot or two below the ceiling is a plank shelf, which holds glasses, bottles and various small objects.   Here too always on the east side stands the family ikon before which a wick floating in olive oil is always kept burning.   A small table completes the furniture, but tables like chairs are of course recent introductions.   The most striking innovations of modern times are probably pictures, photographs and ornaments of various kinds, the result largely of emigration.   These are nailed on the walls or placed on available shelves.   Favourite pictures, excluding picture postcards, include a series of oleographs of the Geneviève legend that emanate from Athens ; highly coloured prints of the crowned heads of Europe, famous Macedonian bandits and other celebrities, and portraits of the Greek or Roumanian Royal Families give some indication of political feeling.   Amid this galaxy of modern art, which is thought of exceeding beauty, one occasionally finds a quaint wood block or painting of Jerusalem and the Holy Places made some hundred years ago ; and once the treasured possession of some pilgrim, whose name perhaps appears in the corner.

In most of the houses perhaps a few books may be found, but these nearly all belong to the younger members of the family.

All but the smallest houses possess at least a second room on the upper floor, which is normally used as a kitchen and as a bedroom for the women, and in no case is as fully furnished as the others.   In one of the upper rooms there is usually a *niruh'ite* or small sink built into the wall, at which the family wash.   A small outer door in the upper story is usual especially in the older houses ; and since the houses are often built on the side of a hill, this door sometimes opens on or near to the ground level, but if not it has a short sloping ladder on the outside.   Many of the older houses have also a wooden balcony

7

partly closed in by a carved wooden grill which forms one whole side of a room; others have a small projection over the main entrance (Plate XV 2). This somewhat resembles a bow window; it is closed in with planking and has a row of small square windows with sliding wooden shutters, and around the inside a low wooden seat. Both forms are known as *k'ipeng'i*. More modern houses have small wooden balconies with an iron rail.

Outside the house there will be a shed used as a kitchen, if there is little room available within, and somewhere near at hand there will be an oven which is usually shared by several families. The ovens are dome-shaped and of a very common type (Plate XV 2). The base is built of stones and the upper part of clay strengthened with potsherds; the floor is made of flat slabs and the door which is square and low is closed with a slab or piece of tin or iron. When the oven is first made the dome of clay is soft and is only kept in position by a framework of wood. Consequently it has to be hardened. Two or three ventilation holes are made in the top of the dome and a fire is lit inside. This consumes the wooden framework, but at the same time bakes the clay hard, and the oven is then ready for use. To bake bread a fire is lit inside the oven and allowed to burn through; the flat loaves of bread are then baked in the ashes.

The Vlachs as a whole take great pride in their homes, and the houses in Samarina and in most of the Pindus villages are clean and well kept. Leake and other travellers have noted the neat appearance that Vlach cottages often bear in contrast with those of their neighbours, and Sir Charles Eliot to illustrate the same feature records how he once saw a Vlach use glass to mend a broken window, instead of the usual scrap of newspaper. But though the interiors of the houses are usually neat and clean, the villages are often untidy. A Vlach villager has a rooted prejudice against making repairs, and when repairs become necessary will often prefer to build a new house altogether. Abandoned and ruined houses are therefore not uncommon, and a single family may possess more than one in the same village.

The people of Samarina have a lasting feeling for the hills round their native village, a strong pride in their homes for the time being, but no scruples about abandoning one house for another. They employ Greek workmen to build for them, but their own folk as carpenters. The words they use for the different parts of their houses are Greek or Turkish. Thus the ground floor is called *hambla*, the store-room *kātoyie*, and the window *pālāthiri*, all Greek words. The upper room is called *nudă*, the chimney *buhare*, and the cupboards *dulăk'i*, all Turkish. *Niruh'ite* is Greek and *mindārlik'i* is Turkish. But these all denote the various parts of a house as opposed to a hut ; for the words used for the simplest essentials of a home, *kasă* hut or house, *poartă* door, and *vatră* hearth, are all Vlach. This indicates that there was a time when permanent houses were unknown and a nomadic life prevailed.

CHAPTER VI

BIRTH, BAPTISM, BETROTHAL, MARRIAGE AND BURIAL CUSTOMS

Omlu ari zh bană sh moarti.

Man has both life and death.

VLACH PROVERB

IN the Southern Balkans where the different races live side by side in the same towns and villages it is very difficult to decide how far any custom is peculiar to any one of them. The Vlachs are no exception to this rule and owing to their small number and their dispersion amongst other races, they have borrowed and adapted from their neighbours to a great extent. This is especially true of all customs in which the church is concerned such as baptism, marriage and burial where the Greek influence is predominant. Of the songs sung at betrothals and weddings the great majority are in Greek, but what was their original language, is a different question. The account here given of some of their more important customs is based on our own observation at Samarina and completed with the aid of information, which was taken down on the spot and verified wherever possible. There is no means of determining whether any particular custom is old or recent, though we have mentioned any changes in this respect which came under our notice. Consequently this is to be taken as a record of what was the usual custom at Samarina when we were there. To aim at completeness would be impossible, for it would take a lifetime or longer to reach it. Those who have attempted to collect folk-lore in the Balkans will know how much time and patience are required to get information especially from the women.

BIRTH

It is said that when a woman is with child she is not allowed to go out at night, for it is supposed to be dangerous for her. When her labour begins, a boy is sent to fetch the old woman, who acts as midwife and is the only person who assists at the child's birth. After birth the child is wrapped up in swaddling clothes and placed in a cradle or in a corner. Then the members of the family come to see the baby, for up till then they are not allowed to be in the house. The small boys of the family run about to tell the news to the relations of the mother to receive *sihārik'e*, that is to get a small gift, a few halfpence or some sweets. The mother lies down in bed covered with a thick rug and her relations bring gifts called *bāghānitsle*, batter cakes, pilaf, a bottle of wine and a *kulakŭ*. A *kulakŭ* is a flat round loaf of bread baked in a tin and bought from a baker. It is made of wheaten flour mixed with pease, and is decorated on top with patterns in sesame. The boy who carries these gifts—it is considered undignified for a grown-up person to carry anything—is rewarded with one or two piastres. Three days after birth they make preparations for the visit of the fates, who come, so they say, at midnight. The child is carefully dressed and one or two gold pieces or some other kind of ornament is hung round its neck. It is believed that if the child is thus decorated the fates will " write a good fortune for it." If not, the fortune given will be bad, and when anyone is unlucky one often hears the phrase " so was it written for him." The mother is not allowed to go out of the house, even to go to church for forty days from the time of the birth. When the forty days are completed she is churched by the priest, a ceremony which takes place in the house. Then the mother sets to work and washes the whole house, and all the rugs, clothes and other properties in it. She whitewashes it, repairs and rolls the floors of beaten earth and repoints with clay the stone-work round the door. When all this is finished and the house is literally and metaphorically clean again, she can go out, go to church and pay calls.

The child may not be taken out of the house till it has been

christened. When children are quite young it may happen
that they fall ill. If they are unbaptized, it will be said that
they are ill ; but if they have already been christened it will
be said that they have been bewitched with the evil eye.
Curiously enough the evil eye can only affect those who have
been baptized. One often sees women and girls with a blot of
indigo in the middle of their foreheads, which is a charm against
the evil eye. On the other hand the short lines or circlets that
are painted in indigo or pitch on the neck, wrists or forearms
are charms against diphtheria and other dangerous diseases.

BAPTISM

Generally christening takes place about eight days after
birth, but may be put off for a week or two. Exceptional
cases occur in which baptism is delayed for as much as a year,
and then the custom which forbids the child to be taken out
before its christening is not observed. The child has only one
godfather who should be the same person who acted as best
man at the parents' wedding. In Vlach the term *nunŭ* is
used for both duties. Often it is not possible for the same
man to act on both occasions, and then another godfather
has to be chosen. When the parents have decided that the
child is to be baptized, they send a boy with a *kulakŭ* to the
godfather to tell him that his presence is required. The godfather provides the child with christening clothes, arms himself with two or three wax tapers, a kerchief, a metal jug with
warm water and another with cold and goes to meet the
priests at the church. The child is brought there by the
midwife and then baptized according to the rites of the Orthodox Eastern Church. Baptism takes place by immersion and
immediately after the child is confirmed and so made a full
member of the church. When the priest baptizes the child
the name is given him by the godfather who names the child
as he pleases. Small boys belonging to the family crowd
round and as soon as they hear the name given by the godfather run off to the parents' house and to relations to tell
the name and receive *sihārik'e*. The first to bring the news is

given a piastre, and the others halfpennies or sweets. After the ceremony in the church the company returns to the parents' house, the godfather carrying the child in his arms and holding in his hands two lighted tapers. As soon as they enter the house the mother takes a gold or silver ornament and a piece of bread and kneels before the godfather and kisses his hand, after which she takes the baby and puts it in the cradle. Then the godfather goes up to the child, kisses it and makes some gift, a gold piece, a dollar or whatever he likes. After that they all sit down, eat drink and make merry. When they begin to sing the following song is that considered most appropriate :—

Get up Demetrius and change your clothes and put on your golden dress and let us go to the Aghrapha, high up to Karpenisi that you may christen the child and give him his name. He has eyes like the priest and eyebrows like the bishop.

BETROTHAL

In Samarina there is no fixed age for betrothal which generally occurs about one year before marriage, but the girl is usually about twenty and the man between twenty-five and thirty or even older. In a large family the girls, unless some of them are much younger than their elder brothers, marry first and the elder sisters and brothers always take precedence of the younger. This is the reason why the bride is always younger than the bridegroom. In every case it is looked upon as a natural thing that one should marry. Owing to the fact that more boys are born than girls, old maids are unknown ; but old bachelors are despised. The social life of the Vlachs in which both sexes meet on almost equal terms and the fact that a Vlach girl has no dowry means that theoretically in both betrothal and marriage there is a certain freedom of choice on both sides. How much this is so in practice it is not possible for a stranger to say. Among the Greeks no girl can hope for marriage unless her parents can give a dowry large enough to attract some suitable young man, and the bridegroom's principal aim in choosing a bride is to obtain as much money as possible. This leads, as in all countries where the dowry system is the rule, to much wrangling. The dowry is paid in cash and is the absolute property of the husband, and is only repayable in the event of divorce or of the bride's death soon after marriage. The Vlachs all condemn this system alleging that it prevents free choice, but many of them will marry Greek girls for the sake of the dowry. But the position of women among the Vlachs is better than in Greek villages where a girl has no choice at all. Among the Vlachs no young man can hope to obtain a bride till he is in a position to support a wife. He on his part will look for a bride who works wool well and is a good cook. Her abilities as a housewife are important for she brings him nothing else except her trousseau, some rugs, and a few household properties. No wedding presents are ever given.

When a young man reaches a suitable age and thinks he can afford it, he takes the first step and applies for the hand of some girl on whom he has set his affections. He selects two older men, who should be married, of about forty or fifty years of age and generally respected in the village, as his ambassadors (*pruksinitsĭ*). They approach the parents and ask them if they are willing to give their daughter to the young man in question. The answer may be given the same day, but more often two or three days pass while the family consider the proposal. All the important members of the family are consulted and they enquire about the young man to see if he has a good character and is hard working and healthy. Often two or more young men will propose for the same girl at the same time. Then even more deliberation is required and it is necessary, perhaps, to find out if the girl has any preference. If she has, it is expressed in the most modest way through her parents. If the parents are not willing to give their daughter in marriage to a candidate, the saying goes that he has been beaten ; and the same phrase is applied to the unsuccessful ambassadors as well. When a favourable answer is given the ambassadors return to the would-be bridegroom and bid his family prepare for the formal betrothal and exchange of rings. This will take place on a festival or on a Sunday. A betrothal may take place at any time in the summer, but since all Samarina, if it can, comes up to the village for the festival of the Assumption, this is the time for the young men to propose for brides. The holidays which follow this festival are the days preferred for celebrating a betrothal, which takes place as soon as possible and always in the evening after work is done for the day.

On the appointed evening a party of friends and relations meets at the bridegroom's house, where they are joined by a priest. Then without the bridegroom they proceed in silence to the house of the bride. On their arrival they find the friends and relations of the bride's family collected together. The bride however does not appear, for she is hidden away in the back part of the house with some of her bosom friends. As they enter they say " *Bună seară* " or " καλή 'σπέρα," " Good evening," the language used indicating the political party to which they belong, Roumanian or Greek. No reference to the betrothal is made, but after they sit down and talk a little and are served with the usual refreshments, one of the older members of the bride's family addresses them. " We see that you have come with a large party some with sticks, some with rifles, but we do not know what your object is." Then one of the elders of the bridegroom's party or one of the ambassadors answers, " We have heard that you have a girl, good, beautiful and hard working, who is called So-and-so ; we also have a young man, good and hard working, if you are willing let us betroth your girl to the young man." " If it is for such business that you have come, then welcome. We are willing, and we betroth the girl." Then a table is brought in. A Vlach table is of the ordinary type used in peasant houses in the Balkan peninsula and in Anatolia. It is low not more than eight inches high, and circular being about three feet in diameter, and can easily be carried by one person even when loaded with dishes. On the table is the best table-cloth and three soup plates, two full of sweets and the third empty. In the empty plate the bridegroom's party place the betrothal gifts. These consist of one or more gold coins sometimes made into necklaces, a gold ring tied on to a piece of red or blue ribbon, and a silk head-kerchief. The betrothal necklaces of gold pieces worn by the older women at Samarina consist mainly of old Turkish gold pieces especially those struck by Sultan Abd-ul-Mejid, with occasionally one or two Venetian sequins or even Roman aurei or Byzantine solidi. In more recent times Napoleons and English sovereigns have been introduced, and earrings of half Napoleons or half sovereigns are common. But the modern coins that are most popular for betrothal necklaces are the big Austrian gold pieces known as " *Afstriakadzi*," which cost two and a half Turkish pounds and have the nominal value of twenty florins. At two betrothals, at which we were present, the betrothal gift instead of the necklace was a Turkish five pound piece. As soon as the bridegroom's party have put down the betrothal gifts the younger men of the bride's party demand that they should " whiten " the plate. To " whiten " the plate the bridegroom's party throw into it some silver coins never less than a dollar, so that two or three days later the bride's party may make merry with roast mutton and wine. Then the bride's party put the bride's ring in the plate. The priest says a short prayer, takes the rings in his hand and exchanges them three times. The bride's ring, after he has kissed it, he gives to the bridegroom's party for each to kiss in turn. So the bride's ring is kept by the bridegroom's party, who give it to him to wear when they return to his house. A similar ceremony is gone through with the bridegroom's ring which is kissed in turn by all the members of the bride's party who keep it, and give it to the bride, with the other betrothal gifts. The bride however does not wear any of these gifts as long as she is betrothed, but entrusts them to a sister, a cousin or a bosom friend to wear for her. When each kisses the ring he wishes " *Hāirlitka shi stefane bune !* " which means " Here's to the wedding, good luck (lit. good bridal crowns) ! " Immediately after the exchange of rings they begin to sing the three songs which are always sung on these occasions usually in the order here given. Never are more or fewer songs sung. Formerly this was the moment when it was the custom to fire off guns and rifles, and any one of either party, who possessed a firearm, would bring it with him and fire it off as often as he liked, as soon as the first song was begun. Latterly this has been put down by the Turkish government. The first song, which is Greek, is :—

The maiden from the east and the youth from Stamboul, the two strangers have met in a strange garden. You are a stranger and I am a stranger, let us two meet. I have a thousand gold pieces and five hundred piastres. Come maiden let us stay, let us spend the evening. I have three hundred and two gold pieces in a golden hand-kerchief. Take them maiden and count them, take them, reckon them.

The second song is in Vlach and is given below as the seventh in Appendix IV.

The third and last song is Greek :—

From rock to rock I walk, from stone to stone. Where am I to find a good mate, good and honourable, like a swift horse, like a fast plough ox, like a good wife who honours her husband, like two affectionate brothers who love one another ? And now an attempt is made to part them. And what cause can be found to part them ? You have vineyards and fields to divide. All that are in the middle and are good, take them master ; and all that are on the border and are bad give them to your brother. Find such cause against him that you may go and kill him.

Papayeoryiu, who has published an account of the Samarina betrothal and wedding ceremonies, gives a different song instead of this. We have never heard it sung ourselves at this point, but it is still known in the village and is sung during the merrymaking that follows the formal ceremony.

After the singing of these songs the bridegroom's party departs on its way back to his house. On their way back they sing loudly and joyfully this Greek song :—

Bright little moon light me on my road. I hasten to pass the streets and cross the bridges. Far away there on Olympus an aged stag pastures, and his eyes ever weep. He pours forth red tears, red and green, and tears all blue.

Each member of the party takes a handful of flour with him, and when they arrive at the house and are received by the bridegroom, they throw the flour over his head and face and say " May you grow white like the flour ! " by way of wishing him long life. The bride is treated in the same way by her friends and relations. After that both at the bride's and at the bridegroom's they sit down to a hearty supper, and the rest of the evening is spent in dancing and singing. If musicians can be procured they dance to music. Otherwise they sing songs to which they dance.

When the bridegroom's party leaves the bride's house they look about for something to steal, a pillow, photographs, or any other small object that can be taken unobserved. These are presented by them to the bridegroom on their return to his house and are given back the next day to the bride's family.

The next day about noon or soon after the friends and relations of the bridegroom collect again at his house and then go in a body to the bride's house together with the bridegroom who thus pays his first formal call on his future parents-in-law. They are entertained with batter cakes, roast lamb and other refreshments, but since batter cakes form the prominent dish this call is known technically as " going to eat batter cakes at the mother-in-law's." Again they dance, sing and make merry till the evening.

At the betrothal the two families usually also fix the time for the wedding, which usually takes place a year hence at the festival of the Assumption. During all this year the bridegroom never sees the bride. If he calls unexpectedly on her family in hopes of seeing her at the first alarm of his coming she will hide herself. Such modesty is highly prized, and any betrothed maiden who breaks through the established custom is thought no better than she should be. Thus the bridegroom during the year of betrothal can see the object of his affections only by accident. The future bride will not attend festivals where she is likely to meet her betrothed, except that of the Transfiguration which is especially a girls' festival and from which young men are supposed to keep away, though they rarely do so.

During the time of betrothal the relations of the bridegroom go from time to time to the bride's house with " *poamile*," the fruits. Each one of the bridegroom's family buys a ring, a

PLATE XVI

1. SAMARINA: THE HOUSE OF PĀGĀTSĀ

2. SAMARINA: TAKING THE BRIDE ON HORSEBACK FROM HER HOME

kerchief, and one or two pounds of sweets. They put them in a basket, which is given to a boy to carry on his head, the basket being covered with a white cloth, and they go in procession to the bride's house. First comes the boy with the basket, then the sisters and cousins of him who sends the fruits. The bride when she receives the gifts and takes them out of the basket puts in their place two or three pairs of home knitted socks, and a handkerchief for the boy who carries the basket. At lent again the bridegroom's relations send similar gifts, with the same formalities, but instead of sweets they put in *halva*, a Turkish sweetmeat made of honey, sugar and sesame, which is a favourite lenten food in the Orthodox Church. For Easter again the bridegroom sends the bride an Easter candle for her to use in church at the Easter service.

MARRIAGE

The earliest day in the summer for a wedding to be celebrated is the festival of St Elijah on July 20th ; but this does not often happen, and if the day of St Elijah comes in the middle of the week, the wedding will take place on the following Sunday. Most of the weddings at Samarina are celebrated at the festival of the Assumption whether it falls on a week day or a Sunday. Those which for one reason or another may have been delayed, will take place on one of the Sundays following the Assumption. The latest day for a wedding is the festival of St Mary the Less as the Vlachs call it, which is in reality the feast of the birth of the Virgin and falls on September 8th. Rarely is a wedding postponed beyond this day or the Sunday that follows it. In the account here given of the customs observed at a wedding at Samarina, we have assumed for the sake of convenience that it takes place on a Sunday.

When the year of betrothal is nearly complete, and both families are ready for the wedding they finally decide some five or six days beforehand when it shall actually be celebrated. The first sign of the imminence of the wedding is the " throwing down of the trousseau " at the bride's home. This is done

during the last week before the wedding, and means that the
trousseau is ready and is laid out for inspection by any relation
or friend who wishes to see it. The trousseau consists of
rugs, blankets, pillow-cases, kerchiefs, stockings, frocks and
garments of all kinds. Usually the bride's parents try to provide her with as many clothes as she is likely to need for the rest
of her life. If the wedding is to take place on a Sunday, on
the Saturday morning the invitations are sent out to all the
friends and relations of the families. Often as many as two
or three hundred invitations are sent out. They are written
on slips of paper in purified Vlach or Greek, but never in the
spoken language, and distributed by small boys. They
usually take the following or some similar form :—

Doamna shi Domnul ——— au haraua si Vă fakă kunuskut
mărtarea a featil'ei a lor   ———
                                    ku
                    Dl. ———
shi vă părăkălsesku ta si avets buna vrearea si tin'isitsĭ ku yinirea
avoastră ñgrunarea a lor tsi va s fakă tu 15 di Avgustu oara 8 a la
turka la bisearika Stămăria tsea Mare

Sămărina, 14 Avgustu 1910
Parintsăl'i

_____

'Αξιότιμε Κύριε,
Εὐαρεστεθίτε παρακαλῶ ἵνα τημήσετε αὔριον οἰκογενιακῶς τὴν στέψιν
τοῦ υἱοῦ μου   ———
μετὰ τῆς Δεσπινί'δος

_____   _____

Εὔχομε διὰ ὑμὺν καὶ κατὰ πόθον σας
ἐν Σαμμαρίνῃ τῇ 20ῃ 8/911
ὁ πατήρ

_____   _____

On Saturday afternoon the groomsmen and the bridesmaids meet at the bridegroom's house " to put on their aprons."
The groomsmen (furtatsĭ) are three or four or more unmarried
cousins, or friends of the bridegroom who act as stewards at
the wedding. They serve wine to the guests, lay the tables,

and clear them, and have to do anything the bridegroom orders. The bridesmaids (*surate*) are unmarried cousins of the bridegroom, and are always at least one less in number than the groomsmen. They are the servants of the bride and the women guests. They lead out the bride, they take her to kiss the hands of guests, they wait on her and see that she is given food to eat. The sign of office worn by groomsmen and bridesmaids alike is a plain white apron (Plate XVIII 2). The groomsmen fetch the musicians who have been hired beforehand by the bridegroom for the whole time that the wedding festivities last. The sums paid to these musicians vary according to their abilities, but a good party can command as much as two Turkish pounds for playing at a wedding during the three or four days the festivities last. In addition they are given gifts of money by the guests and spectators. The leader is summoned by a nod and the giver makes the gift by sticking the coins on to the musician's forehead. The custom is that the friends and relations of one who is dancing should thus " tip " the musicians. For instance the members of the bride's family will shower coins on them when the bride leads the dance. Similarly a young man will stick a humble gift of three or four piastres on the leader's forehead when his best friend is dancing. A favourite coin to give is the big bronze hundred-para piece.

When the groomsmen, bridesmaids and musicians are all assembled they go with the bridegroom's gifts to the bride, a ceremony which is called taking the *ghălĭkă* to the bride. The *ghălĭkă* is a low, broad basket in which are placed the gifts, a veil, tinsel strips for decorating the bride's hair, scents, henna, brooches, combs, mirrors, soap, a handkerchief and sweets. They go in procession, the musicians leading the way followed immediately by the boy who carries the basket on his head covered with a white cloth ; the rear is brought up by the groomsmen, and other male friends of the bridegroom. At the bride's house they are given refreshments, wine, raki, Turkish delight, or preserves, and they sit down for a short time while the musicians play for any of the female members of the bride's family to dance if they wish. The bride empties the basket and puts in socks for the bridegroom and his parents, and either socks or handkerchiefs for the groomsmen. When they have finished dancing they return to the bridegroom's and dance there again. In the evening the groomsmen with the musicians go again to the bride's house, where all dance till dawn especially the women folk of the bride's family. The groomsmen demand that the bride should come out and dance. She then makes her appearance dressed in one of the gowns forming part of her trousseau, and dances with the senior groomsman. The gown she wears is dark and usually of silk but may be of any dark coloured stuff, and she, though holding herself rather stiffly, does not clasp her hands in front of her or behave in the doll-like fashion she has to adopt on the morrow. Sometimes the bridegroom will come with the groomsmen, but he is required to sit in a corner and not make himself conspicuous or dance. The whole party sits down to eat at the bride's and many small tables are brought in, and after eating they dance till dawn with frequent refreshments of wine or raki. Towards dawn the groomsmen depart with the musicians to the bridegroom's. They send the musicians away to sleep, but without their instruments which the groomsmen hold as an earnest of the musicians' presence on the morrow. Then each retires to snatch a few hours' sleep before the real labours of the wedding begin. On the Saturday evening the women, but especially the girls of both families, put henna on the nails and palms of their hands, and this is also done to the bride.

On the Sunday morning a married sister or cousin of the bridegroom with a boy goes round to distribute one *kulakŭ* each to the *nunŭ*, groomsmen and bridesmaids. The *kulakŭ* is placed in a basket and covered with an embroidered cloth which the boy carries under his arm. This is the official invitation to the wedding. The receiver of the *kulakŭ* puts in the basket some rice or sweets, and gives refreshments to the bringers and one or two piastres apiece.

Towards midday the groomsmen summon the musicians to the bridegroom's house where all his relations and friends assemble for the ceremony of shaving the bridegroom. A barber is called to the house, and as soon as he begins his work the company present throw money, piastres or halfpence, into his basin, and sing this Greek song which has special reference to the shaving of the bridegroom :—

On the rock sits the bridegroom, and the rock gave forth water for them to shave the bridegroom. The hand which shaves him holds a piece of gold. Silver razor move gently, gently lest the hair be scattered.

When the bridegroom is shaved, he is made to stand upright in a shallow metal dish, and changes all his clothes from head to foot. Every garment has to be quite new, and if he wears the Vlach national costume, he has to put on the white clothes which are the distinguishing mark of a bridegroom. While he is dressing those present sing a special song which is usually that sung also at christening feasts and has been given above. Meanwhile at the bride's house the bride is prepared for her wedding with similar ceremonies. While she is being dressed they sing this Greek song :—

Upstairs, downstairs, in the lofty palaces, go mother fetch my hidden frocks. I would be a bride that I may worship the cross and kiss hands.

While her hair is being combed they sing this Greek song :—

My silver comb move gently, gently lest her hair be scattered, the hair of her head, and a stranger take it and make it a charm.

As in the case of the song referring to the shaving of the bridegroom, so in this song too the last lines refer to the idea that a charm to bind a person can be made from a lock of his hair. Consequently when hair is cut or shaved it must not be scattered, but carefully collected and burnt.

Soon after noon the wedding starts, as the phrase is, and before this the majority of those invited by the bridegroom's family will have assembled at the house. First of all the bridegroom attended only by the groomsmen and the male members of his party goes in procession with the musicians leading the way to the bride's home to kiss his mother-in-law's hand. After he has done this and they have amused them-

8

selves with songs and dancing there they return to the bridegroom's house.   After a short interval the bridegroom's party
forms in procession once more and moves off to the *nunŭ*.   The
procession is formed as before, but this time the women of the
bridegroom's family join and bring up the rear.   The *nunŭ* is
either a friend of the bridegroom, or some older man.   He acts
as a kind of godfather to the happy pair, and has the duty of
exchanging the rings and crowns during the wedding ceremony.
He also is supposed to act as godfather to the children.   At
the house of the *nunŭ* the party stop for a short time, and are
joined by his party, for the *nunŭ* too has the right of inviting
his friends and relations to the wedding.   He invites " with
the wooden flask " as the saying goes, sending round to all, he
wishes to invite, a boy with a wooden flask of wine.   The boy
offers the flask to the person to be invited saying " You are
invited by the *nunŭ*," and the one invited then takes the
flask and drinks saying " Here's to the wedding, and good
luck to us."   When the procession moves off from the house
of the *nunŭ* his party takes its place immediately after the
musicians.   In front of his party goes a boy carrying a tray
on which are five wax candles, the roll of stuff for a frock
which is his gift to the bride, the crowns if the *nunŭ* gives them,
and some sweets mixed with barley and rice.   The crowns are
metal circlets with two raised semi-circular bands crossing one
another on the top.   If the *nunŭ* does not give the crowns then
those belonging to the church are used, for each church has a
pair for use at weddings.   Then the whole procession returns
again to the bridegroom's house to pick up any guests who
may not have joined the procession hitherto, and then finally
starts for the bride's house.

Before the party reaches the bride's house one of the groomsmen mounted on a horse goes on ahead to receive *sihārik'e*, and
to give the news that the bridegroom is coming.   As soon as
the procession arrives the first groomsman goes in to put on the
bride's shoes, for he carries with him a kerchief in which are a
kulakŭ and a pair of shoes.   When he kneels to put on the
shoes he puts some small coins in them, and the girls around
the bride hit him with their fists and do not let him go till he

has thrown down some small coins for them to scramble for. They also sing the following Greek song :—

Put me on a pair of shoes, groomsman, and a ring, and put your hand in your silver purse, and if you have silver coins treat us. Do not grieve for the gold pieces, and if you have half piastres give to the gallant lads.

While the groomsman is putting on the bride's shoes her mother is " girding the bridegroom with his sash," for it is the custom that the mother-in-law should on this occasion give him a silken sash, which is carefully preserved and worn by the bridegroom on all great occasions in his after life. When the mother-in-law puts on the sash she places near the bridegroom's foot a glass full of water. When the fastening of the sash is done, the bridegroom throws a dollar into the glass, and then kicks it over. Then when the bridegroom and the groomsmen leave the house two male cousins of the bride refuse to let the groomsmen leave without giving the hundred and ten paras. The groomsmen pretend that they do not want to give anything and resist, but finally give the required coin, a bronze hundred para piece which was current in Samarina at a hundred and ten paras. The trousseau is then carried out and loaded on mules brought for the purpose. Meanwhile the *nunǔ* and his party have been singing and dancing in the courtyard outside with the other guests. They usually sing this Greek song, of which a Vlach version is known :—

Black-eyed maidens watch us, blue-eyed maidens address us ; two other maids have come as well. Which shall I take, which shall I leave ? Black Eyes wants fine clothes ; Blue Eyes wants gold pieces. You are better Black Eyes, for fine clothes become you.

After the bridegroom and his party have come out of the house and loaded the trousseau, they move off with the *nunǔ* and his party in the same order as before to the church. Then the bride is brought out of her home dressed in a white silk frock and wearing a veil ; her hair is decorated with tinsel. She carries herself very stiffly like a doll and moves very slowly. Her eyes are all but shut and she holds her hands clasped in front of her. She is supported on either side by a brother, a first cousin, or by one of the groomsmen, and is led gently forward. As soon as she comes out of the house she is given a glass of wine to drink, and when she has drunk she throws the glass backwards over her shoulder and breaks it. When she crosses the threshold she must do so with the right foot first. While all this is being done the bride's party sing this Vlach song :—

They have taken you, they have seized you, my beautiful one ! They have taken you to foreign lands, my darling, to foreign lands and distant. For what cause, mother, have you driven me from my home ? I have not driven you forth, my girl, for I send you to your home and to your household.

When the bride has come out into the courtyard these three songs are sung in Greek :—

In the centre of the courtyard a partridge stands and speaks, " Where are you brothers ? Come here that you may send me forth ! " " And do not fear tender one, we are all round about and all fire our muskets."

To this the bridegroom's party reply :—

Your village we have trodden, your maiden we have taken.

and the bride's party answer :—

Come good gossip, what great evil do I do that you should send the hawk to take my partridge away from me, and my parish is disgraced and yours is adorned.

As the last line of the first of these three songs shows it was at this point that the cousins and brothers of the bride used to fire off guns, rifles and revolvers. After this singing is done the whole procession moves off to the church the bride and her party bringing up the rear. Often the bride is mounted on horseback (Plate XVI 2) and accompanied by two young male relations also mounted. Sometimes she even stands upright on the saddle. As they make the way slowly to the church many songs are sung.

When at last they reach the church the *nunŭ* with the *nună*, who is his wife if he is married or his mother if he is a bachelor, accompanied by the boy carrying the tray with the crowns and other paraphernalia enter first. Next follows the bridegroom with the groomsmen and the bridesmaids, and lastly the bride with her two supporters crossing the threshold right foot first. All the rest of the guests remain outside and dance to the music provided, and with them will probably be one or two of the groomsmen. The dances are all ring-dances, those taking part in them joining hands and only the leader executing any movement at all elaborately. The members of the different parties keep together and do not intermingle, and are arranged thus : first come the men of all the parties, who do not always keep apart, next the women of the party of the *nunŭ*, next the women of the bridegroom's party, and lastly the women of the bride's party. Thus a dance consisting of from five to seven rings is formed, the inner ring being the leading one.

The wedding service is done according to the liturgy of the Orthodox Eastern Church and is read in Greek, as far as Samarina is concerned, though the priests are of course Vlachs and natives of Samarina. As a rule two priests officiate at a wedding especially on days when there are three or four weddings at the same church. When the bridal party enter the church they stand in front of a table placed in the middle of the nave. On the table is a New Testament, and by it are placed the crowns and the *kulakŭ* brought by the *nunŭ* from which three small pieces are cut, the rings, and a glass of wine. On the west side of the table stands the bridegroom on the right with the bride on his left. Immediately behind them is the *nunŭ* ; the *nună* stands on the bride's left and by them is the boy with the tray. Around them where they please stand the groomsmen, the bridesmaids, and any other friends or relations who have come into the church. As soon as the priest begins the first prayer each groomsman has to put on his book one or two halfpennies. When the priest has finished the prayer he takes the four candles and lights them, and gives one each to the bride and bridegroom, and two to the *nunŭ*. Then he takes the rings, makes the sign of the cross with them three times, and puts the bride's ring on the bridegroom, and the bridegroom's ring on the bride's hand. Then the *nunŭ* changes the rings three times and finally the priest joins their hands by linking their little fingers together. After some prayers the priest takes the crowns, and having made the sign of the cross with them to both bride and bridegroom, places them on their heads. In the meantime the *nună* has spread on their shoulders the roll of stuff fastening it with pins. Then the *nunŭ* with arms crossed changes the crowns three times. At the end of the service the priest takes the bridegroom by the right hand, and he in his turn holds the bride by the hand, while the *nunŭ* supports them from behind. In this manner all four circle three times round the table stopping to make a reverence at each side in turn. During this the company present take handfuls of sweets and rice from the tray carried by the boy, and pelt the bridegroom, bride and *nunŭ*. The small boys, who have managed to elude the verger and squeeze into the church, go scrambling for the sweets about the floor. This done the father-in-law and mother-in-law go up to the bridegroom and bride and kiss them first on the forehead, then on the cheeks. The bride kisses their right hands and as she does so they give her a small coin. After them the groomsmen and bridesmaids and any near relation present come and salute them in the same way. As soon as they have kissed the bride the others, who stand round, thump them heartily on the shoulders. With this the wedding ceremony ends and all go out of the church. If, as is sometimes done, the service takes place in the bridegroom's house everything is done in exactly the same manner.

The first to come out of the church is the *nunŭ*, next the bridegroom, and last the bride again crossing the threshold right foot first. If while the service has been going on another wedding party has entered, the other members of it crowd round the bride so that the bride who has just been married shall not see the other as she goes out. This is done because it is believed that if the newly married bride sees one or more other brides in the church her husband will have just so many wives besides herself, or in other words that she will not live long and that her husband will marry again. As soon as they have come out of the church they drive the musicians away from the dance, and form one large dancing ring. This is lead by the *nunŭ*, and in the middle between the women and men the bridegroom is placed with his mother-in-law on his left hand. On the other side of the bridegroom are the grooms-men. The bride stands apart attended by the *nună* and bridesmaids. But after the dance has gone round once or twice the *nunŭ* goes up to the bride, takes her and places her in the ring on the bridegroom's left so that she is between her husband and her mother. They dance to this Greek song :—

Come out youths and dance, come out maidens and sing, that you may see and learn how love is caught. It is caught by the eye, it descends to the lips and from the lips to the heart; there it takes root and does not move, but only sends out roots and fibres, and green flowers.

After they have danced a little they break up the ring and the procession is re-formed in the same order which was observed on the road to the church. Then they move off to the bridegroom's house singing songs of different kinds. As soon as they reach the house the party of the *nunŭ* and the women begin to dance in the court, while the bridegroom's party sing this Greek song till the bride approaches the door :—

Come out mother and mother-in-law to see your son who is coming ; he is bringing a partridge dressed with gold coins and she is hidden by them. Enter, enter little partridge into the bridegroom's house ; here build your nest and here nestle.

At the door stands the mother-in-law waiting for the bride. She has in her hands an apron, a pair of buckles for a belt, or a chain of steel or silver to which a knife is attached, a plate with butter, a lump of carded white wool off the distaff, and a *kulakŭ*. As the bride crosses the threshold right foot foremost, she takes with three fingers a little butter, and anoints the lintel above her head three times with it. Then the mother-in-law breaks over the bride's head the *kulakŭ*, the fragments of which are snatched by the boys and youths standing round to the great discomfort of the bride who cannot see what is being done above her head. Next the mother-in-law pulls the handful of wool to pieces over the bride's head saying, " Long life to you, and prosperity, and may you grow white like this wool!" and kisses her on the forehead, when the bride bends to kiss her hand. Finally the bride is invested with the apron, and the buckles or chain as signifying that she is now mistress of the house. The whole party, bridegroom, bride, *nunŭ*, groomsmen and bridesmaids, then go upstairs and sit down for a short time. Then they come out into the courtyard or some suitable open space near the house and dance (Plate XVII). The bridegroom dances with the men, and the bride with the women of the bridegroom's family. But if the *nunŭ* dances and leads the first dance as is usual on these occasions, he dances in the men's ring, the bridegroom in that of the women of his family, and the bride with the women of her family. The dances are all ring-dances, and as a rule at the request of the *nunŭ* when he is leading the dance the bridegroom and bride dance together, each in turn leading the ring. In olden days the *nunŭ* acted as master of the ceremonies at the festivities on the evening of the wedding and his orders were supposed to be obeyed without question, but now this is nearly obsolete. The dancing continues till dusk and then the guests begin to depart. First to go are the relations and friends of the bride. The bridegroom and bride see them off walking a little way with them, and they and their companions sing in Greek :—

If you are bent on departing farewell to you. If you pass by my mother's house greetings to her.

As each says good-bye he shakes hands with the bridegroom, and kisses the bride on the forehead when she stoops to kiss his hand, and he at the same moment " tips " her by slipping a small coin into her hand. Men say good-bye first, then women and lastly the girls, and as they go they sing in Greek :—

We started with the sun, we depart late with the moon. I am coming and you are sleeping, come wake up that you may enjoy life. Wretched Platamona what are the maidens within your walls ? Grecian maidens, Turkish maidens and chieftains' little daughters. High up in a kiosk they sit and watch for the ships that come from Egypt laden with rouge.

PLATE XVII

SAMARINA: BRIDE AND BRIDEGROOM DANCING OUTSIDE THE BRIDEGROOM'S HOUSE

As soon as they reach the house of the bride's parents they dance in the courtyard there singing :—

From the courtyard a maid is missing, and from the parish one is missing, and from her mother one is missing, and from her brothers one is missing.

After this they separate and each returns to his home.

After the bride's family has gone the bridegroom and bride see the *nunŭ* off with similar ceremonies and sing this song in Greek :—

Stay *nunŭ* to-night as well ; I have five lambs ready roasted, and another five ready spitted and a stewed hare.

The *nunŭ* however is not to be tempted by such good cheer and departs with all his company. Occasionally the bridegroom will see him home.

As it is by now dusk the bridal party and the guests go upstairs into the bridegroom's house and dance till dinner is ready. As the company is numerous three or four tables are required. The bridegroom sits at one table with the elders, and the rest of the male guests as they please at the others. The bride sits on a stool on one side and rises whenever the men drink wine. When they have finished eating they sing songs while still sitting at table, and they tease the bride and make jests at her expense in the hope of making her laugh and so lose for a moment her modest composure. Later in the evening they begin to dance again and then many young men, relations or friends of the bridegroom, bride or of one of the groomsmen, will come in to make merry. When the guests arrive and sit down the bride is led by two bridesmaids, one on each side of her, to kiss their hands, and they, when the bride takes their hands in hers, slip into her palm a small coin never less than a halfpenny. On days when there are several weddings the young men of Samarina who are not closely connected with any family that has a wedding will form bands about six or eight strong, and go visiting the various houses where there are weddings in the evening and join in the dancing. At the bridegroom's home the dancing, and other festivities are continued till shortly before dawn. Many of course retire to sleep at an earlier hour, but the bridal party does not cease merrymaking till just before dawn. Then they send away the musicians again without their instruments, and each tries to enjoy a few hours' sleep, before the festivities of the Monday are begun.

Early on the Monday morning the bridegroom's mother, the bridesmaids, and other female relations of the family are astir and set about preparing food, for soon after midday the bride's relatives will come with *bubghala*. A boy with a wooden flask of wine in his hand is sent round to all the relations of the bride to bid them prepare, for soon after noon they are to go to the bridegroom's with the *bubghala*. Presently from all parts of the village where relations of the bride live women and girls are to be seen hastening to the home of the bride's parents. Each carries under her arm a broad, shallow basket covered with an embroidered cloth (Plate XVIII 1). All assemble at the bride's home and anxiously await the coming of the groomsmen with the musicians. Soon after their arrival, a procession is formed and they go to the bridegroom's. In front of all go two groomsmen, carrying a long wooden spit on which is a lamb roasted whole ; they are followed by the musicians, the other groomsmen, the male members of the bride's family, and the female relatives of the bride each with her basket. At the door of the bridegroom's house a groomsman awaits them with a jug of wine and several glasses. They go up-stairs where the groomsmen serve refreshments. Presently the tables are spread and they eat the dishes prepared by the bridegroom's family. When these are finished, each female relative of the bride brings out from her basket the dishes she has prepared and distributes them round the tables. This meal is called *bubghala* because together with the batter cakes and other sweets which are made for it, it is the custom that each should also make one dish of *bubghdla*, which consists of breadcrumb crumbled up and fried with sugar. After eating they sit at table and sing songs for a short time and then go out and dance in the courtyard till dusk when the bride's relations depart with the same ceremonies that were observed on the first day.   The other guests stay at the bridegroom's and dance and merrymake till midnight or later.

As said above all the trousseau is taken to the bridegroom's on the Sunday when the bride is taken from her home to the church.   But one dress, the second best, is left behind at the bride's home.   This is brought to her by her relations on the Monday when they come with *bubghala* and those who bring this frock, dress the bride in it there and then, and she wears it throughout the rest of the festivities.

On the Tuesday after lunch the bridegroom's family, the groomsmen, and the bridesmaids meet together again at the bridegroom's.   They put a jug in the bride's hand and take her out to draw water.   First in the procession go the musicians, next follows the bridegroom with the groomsmen and other men, and the bride conducted by the bridesmaids and escorted by women brings up the rear.   Three conduits are visited in turn, and as they near each they sing this in Greek :—

If Anthitsa comes for water, do not give her water, but only ask her, " Anthitsa whom do you love ?   Yianni the merchant."

When they reach the conduit the bride fills the jug with water and empties it, she refills it and empties it again, and does so yet a third time.   When she fills the jug for the third time the bridegroom throws a few halfpennies into it, and these are emptied out with the water into the mud and eagerly scrambled for by the small boys who crowd round.   While the bride does this the rest sing in Vlach :—

Fill sister, empty brother, to cause our sister anger.

The first conduit visited is that nearest to the house and that to which the bride will have to go to draw water for daily use.   The other two are chosen according to fancy, and exactly the same things are done at both of them.   From the third conduit they return to the bridegroom's and dance till the evening.   As they reach the house they sing in Greek :—

Let my mother-in-law know that I come from the spring cold and frozen to find the fire alight and the pasty in the oven.

Early on the Wednesday morning the groomsmen rise and go about to find a rolling-pin, for on this day they set the bride to make a *pită*. As they approach the bride they bring out from under their great-coats one hand which holds a rose twig with as many thorns as possible. This they show to the bride and ask, " Do you see bride, what a fine rolling-pin I have brought you ? " She smiles in a sickly manner. When all are assembled they choose out the rolling-pin which has most thorns, and is most crooked. Then some ashes are put into a flat tin dish and the bride is set to stir in the yeast. She pours water on the ashes and the groomsmen, the bridesmaids, and the others throw halfpennies into the ashes. As soon as the bride puts out a hand to mix in the yeast the groomsmen flick her hands with the stinging nettles which they have in their other hands hidden under their coats. Next a pastry board is brought and the bride takes a handful of the wet ashes and begins to roll out the leaves of pastry. When she very timidly lays her hands on the thorny rolling-pin to roll out the ashes, they sting her again with the nettles and so the play is carried on till the bridegroom intervenes and takes the bride away.

The same day in the afternoon the bridegroom, bride, groomsmen, and bridesmaids and other women go to the bride's mother to eat batter cakes. There they eat, sing, and dance till the evening. With the ceremonies of this day the duties of the groomsmen and bridesmaids come to an end, and when they leave the bridegroom's house on this evening after escorting the bridal pair home, they take off their aprons, which hitherto they have worn continually, as a sign that their duties are done, and give them to the bride.

On the Thursday, Sunday and Tuesday evenings following the bride and bridegroom go to dine and sleep at the home of the parents, which is known as going *azborŭ*.

Some time after the wedding the bridal pair invite both the families and entertain them. What is done on such occasions depends on the pleasure of the hosts and guests. On the Sundays and other feast-days succeeding the wedding-day the bride accompanied by her mother-in-law and one or

PLATE XVIII

1. BRINGING THE BUEGHALA

2. BRIDE AND BRIDEGROOM WITH THE BRIDESMAIDS AND GROOMSMEN

SAMARINA: WEDDING CEREMONIES

two other women goes to visit the *nunŭ*, the groomsmen and the bridesmaids, and make gifts to them. To the *nunŭ* " she throws a shirt and socks " as the saying goes, and he " tips " her with a dollar. To the groomsmen she gives a pair of socks, and if she pleases to their mothers a pair of stockings, and they give in return five piastre pieces. The bridesmaids and their mothers are given stockings, and they also are expected to give five piastres. This ceremony is the last observance directly connected with the wedding according to the modern custom of Samarina, though very probably in days gone by the festivities were much more protracted. For instance Papayeoryiu has noted many observances which are no longer used to-day. He says that at the betrothal the rings were put into a glass of wine when the bridegroom's party produced the betrothal gifts. Afterwards before the formal exchange of the rings they were crossed three times in the glass by a young man whose father and mother were both alive.

As to the wedding customs he says that the preparations began on the Thursday before. On this day the bridegroom sent the *ghalikă* to the bride. On the same day too the groomsmen and bridesmaids, who were chosen from those whose fathers and mothers were still alive, met at the bridegroom's house to make the bread for the wedding. The yeast was mixed in by the first bridesmaid who carried a knife and pistol while the others sang this Greek song :—

Your first leavening a maiden leavens for you, a maiden with mother, with father, with brothers, with cousins.

On the Friday the trousseau was laid out for inspection at the bride's home, and on the Saturday the groomsmen went round with a wooden flask of wine to invite the guests. Most of the changes seem to have been made with a view to shortening the wedding festivities and making them simpler and so less costly. Throughout the wedding customs there are many indications both in the songs and the various observances which seem to point to the fact that marriage by capture was recently the Vlach custom, but we have found no other evidence of this.

BURIAL

When any person is dead an old man or woman is called in to lay out the body and put on it new clothes. Then the body is laid out in the centre of the room with an oil light burning at its head and with an ikon laid on its breast. The women of the family then come and weep round the body and sing dirges. The Vlach women are noted for these dirges, and often improvise them. At Samarina the dirges may be either in Greek or Vlach, and it is noticeable that the typical instance of this custom given by Fauriel refers to a woman of the Vlach village of Metsovo. If death occurs in the morning, the funeral takes place the same afternoon ; but if it occurs in the afternoon, the funeral is postponed till the next morning. When the appointed hour arrives word is sent to the priests who put on their vestments, and come to the house. After the priest has said a prayer four men raise the body and put it in the coffin. On the spot where the body was laid out they break a glass. Then the funeral procession is formed. In front of all goes a boy carrying the coffin lid ; next come two women with broad, shallow baskets under their arms, covered with cloths. One of the baskets contains the collyva which is blessed by the priest and distributed to those present after the funeral, and the other some dishes of meat, which are also eaten after the funeral. Following them come two or more boys carrying the long poles on which are fixed representations of cherubim. On each pole a handkerchief is tied by the family of the dead man. Then follows the priest chanting with two chanters. Following him four men come carrying the body in the open coffin. Under the coffin at each end are fixed short poles which project on either side and serve as handles. To these also handkerchiefs are tied by the family of the dead. Last come the mourners, the men first and the women behind with black kerchiefs thrown over their heads or shoulders. On the way to the church the priest halts several times and turning round says a prayer while the others stand still. As soon as the church is reached two men stand on either side of the door and distribute wax tapers to all the mourners. The body is placed in the middle of the church, the women assemble round it, and at the head stands one of the immediate relations of the dead, the mother, a sister, or a cousin. Round the coffin lighted candles or tapers are placed and the mourners also light the tapers that have been distributed to them. When the service is finished the mourners kiss the dead for the last time on the forehead. Then the coffin is lifted and they go to the grave in the church-yard. When the coffin has been laid in the grave the pillow is removed from it and in its place is put a stone or a pillow-case filled with earth. After the priest has said another prayer and thrown a little wine and earth on the face of the dead, the lid is laid on the coffin and the grave is filled in. Three or four days after the funeral the family of the dead place a monument on the grave. This takes the form of a long oblong box of planks inverted. At the head is a small box-like cupboard in which they light tapers or small oil lights. Again on the top of this a wooden cross is placed, on which they usually write the name and age of the dead.

After the boiled wheat and the food that has been brought are distributed and eaten the mourners return to the house of the dead man's family. At the door stands a man with a vessel of water, and a shovel with some lumps of charcoal that have been lighted and put out. He pours water over the hands of the mourners who thus wash their hands, and as each enters the house a piece of the charcoal is thrown after him. They stay a short time in the house and condole with the family, and each goes home, though some stay to eat there. At a funeral the only refreshment offered is coffee, preserves are never offered, and when the mourners receive the refreshments the only wish uttered is, " Long life to your excellencies ! " On the second day after the death the women of the family go to the grave and wail by it, and distribute boiled wheat again. This is called " giving the third." On the ninth day they " give the ninth " in a similar way and on the fortieth day the fortieth, and after a year they give the year. For a year from the death the family of the dead gives as refreshment to guests or visitors nothing but coffee, and never preserves or sweets. They take no part in merrymaking of any kind, and the women wear a black kerchief on their heads for the whole year. After five or seven years the grave is opened and the bones are collected and placed in a small wooden box or in a bag and put in the bone-house which is attached to every churchyard. Often too on Sundays or festivals after church the women of the family will go to the churchyard and sit and wail over the graves of their dead. At Whitsuntide they celebrate the special festival of the dead as usual in the Orthodox Church. None of these funeral customs can be described as peculiarly Vlach. For instance in the Greek villages of the Zaghori when the body is carried out of the house a glass or jug is broken in the gate of the courtyard to prevent the dead taking anything else with him from the house and to break the power of Charon. There too the bones must not be dug from the grave in the even years after the burial, but in the odd years, three, five and so on.

PLATE XIX

SAMARINA: A PRIEST AND HIS FAMILY AT A FESTIVAL

CHAPTER VII

FESTIVALS AND FOLKLORE

Ναπ᾿ωη σ᾿σαρμπατȣ᾿αρε σσναπο᾿η παναγγ᾿ηρρȣ
Σ᾿αρμπατȣ᾿αρε ν᾿ȣ κὰ σαρμπατȣ᾿αρηα τηα᾿ερη.

Then a holiday and then a festival,
A holiday not like the holiday of yesterday.

Codex Demonic, f. 91

THIS chapter is only a fragment for it deals primarily with the festivals and folklore of Samarina as far as we came in contact with them, and we record them here to complete our picture of Vlach life as illustrated by that village. To this we have added notes on folk customs elsewhere which we have seen or enquired about on the spot.

The fair of Ayios Akhillios at Ghrevena can hardly be considered as a festival for it serves mainly as a meeting-place for the families on their way up to their villages, Samarina, Avdhela, Perivoli and Smiksi. The first true festival occurs about a month after this. It takes place on the day of St Peter and St Paul, one of the great feasts of the Orthodox Eastern Church, and the two following days. All the muleteers come back to the village for it, and the families, which cannot get up in time for the fair of Ghrevena, will try to reach the village by Mavronoro, which is the special name for this festival at Samarina and its three nomad neighbours. The Vlachs of Verria, who are colonists from these four villages, also still preserve this name for the festival. It is derived from the Kupatshar village of Mavronoro near Ghrevena, where in days gone by they used to hold a fair on the day of St Peter and St Paul which was very well attended. Pouqueville refers to the fair, and on the flyleaf of a book in the monastery of St Barlaam at Meteora some manuscript notes mention the price silk fetched at this fair in 1786. It

9

was held at Mavronoro till about 1860 and was then transferred to Ghrevena as the fair of Ayios Akhillios, when that
town became the seat of a kaimmakam. The exact date of
the transference is unknown, but natives of Samarina at
Verria who left their village after 1854 have assured us that
they remember the fair being held at Mavronoro. In Samarina
itself the origin of the name Mavronoro for the day of St Peter
and St Paul is unknown, a fact which shews how soon in
countries which have no written history the origins of things
become obscured. Apparently just as all the Vlachs of Samarina and its neighbours attend the fair of Ghrevcna to-day,
so in days gone by they all flocked to Mavronoro. To-day at
Samarina Mavronoro as a festival is not marked by any special
festivities. After the church service which takes place at
Great St Mary's, because the side chapel of that church is
dedicated to these saints, it is the custom to pay calls. The
other two holidays if the weather is fine and warm are devoted
to picnics at the monastery or at the spring in the woods of
K'urista. The comparative unimportance of this festival is
due to the fact that it comes early in the summer.

A few days before Mavronoro is the day of St John the
Baptist, on June 24th. This is celebrated merely as a holiday and is not of any great consequence as a church festival,
but at Samarina it is notable for the customs observed by the
girls. On the eve of St John's Day the girls collect together
in bands of between fifteen and twenty and select one as their
leader who is called Arumana. They then dress her as a
bride with any scraps of finery they can procure (Plate XX 1).
They take a metal jug into which each member of the band
throws a flower to which she has tied some trinket of white
metal belonging to her which she can easily recognise. Then
they start in a kind of bridal procession, all who can holding
umbrellas over their heads especially over the bride who is led
along by two of their number at the head of the procession.
As they start they sing this Vlach song :—

Look how beautiful she is, white and rosy like a Turkish woman.
Look at her chest how she seems like a chosen ram. Look at her
apron how it seems like cheese out of the skin.

They make their way to three conduits in turn singing any songs they please on the way, but the majority are in Vlach, though Greek songs are heard.   As they approach the first conduit they sing in Greek :—

Little spring fenced with stones give us water to drink that you may see how we sing.

Then the bride takes the jug and fills and empties it three times exactly as is done in the wedding custom while the others sing :—

Fill sister, empty brother, to cause our sister anger.

As they move on to the next conduit they sing in Vlach :—

Where shall we stay to-night ?   Beyond the sea a caravan passes loaded with salt and a big lad mounted on a mule with his forelock combed and his moustache twisted.

At each of the other two conduits the same performance is gone through, but when they leave the last they keep the metal jug filled with water.   They then take the jug and hide it for the night in some secret place known to them alone.   Usually they choose a place in the meadows on the outskirts of the village, for the boys and young men are on the watch to try to find it and play tricks with it.   The next evening on the day of St John the Baptist they collect together again, fetch the jug, and go in procession with the bride and repeat the performance of the evening before in all its details except that they go to seven conduits instead of three.   Then they retire to some quiet spot and take their trinkets out of the jug of water singing suitable songs as they do so.   They draw their trinkets one by one and each as she does so looks at it carefully and tells her fortune by it.   She can thus decide whether she will have good luck or bad, and—this is a subject of the greatest interest to all girls—find out whether she will marry

Tinker, tailor,
Soldier, sailor,
Apothecary, ploughboy, thief.

The trinkets they call *klidhone* which is Greek, and this custom of telling fortunes on St John's Day by means of *klidhone* is well known in Modern Greek folklore. The custom however has been borrowed by the Vlachs and is well known in all the Vlach villages of the south and centre. At Klisura and Neveska for example the girls go out to the meadows on the eve of St John's Day and pick a special flower to which they tie their trinkets. They have a procession in much the same way as at Samarina and as they pass through the streets people put money in the jug. At Samarina however they do not regard the custom merely as that of the *klidhone*, but as a rain-charm. There seems little doubt that we have here two observances blended into one, the *klidhone* and the other well-known custom of *Pirpirună*. The *Pirpirună* custom is used as a rain-charm throughout the Balkans in times of drought in the summer, but here at Samarina it seems to have been made annual. We have never heard of the *Pirpirună* observances, as such, being done at Samarina, but the word is well known in the village. For instance, " *Mi adrai Pirpirună dip*," " I became a regular *Pirpirună*," is a slang phrase for " I was wet through."

The *Pirpirună* custom amongst the Vlachs is in brief as follows. If after the day of St Thomas, April 21st, it does not rain for three weeks it is very serious for the crops and meadows, because the early summer rains are most important for their proper development. Then a girl, usually a poor girl or a gipsy, is taken and stripped and then dressed in leaves and flowers and made to walk in procession through the village. The girls with her sing suitable songs and she herself dances. As she passes the houses people throw water over her and wet her thoroughly. The song usually sung is the following or some variant of it :—

Pirpirună, Sarandună, give rain, give, that the fields may grow, the fields and the vineyards, the grass and the meadows.

We have heard of this being done at Turia where the girl is now not naked, but lightly clad and decked with leaves and flowers. Wherever there are Vlachs this custom is known and the girl who takes the principal part is called *Pirpirună*, *Perpună*, or *Păparună*. In Northern Greece, but not south of Epirus and Thessaly, it is known as *Perperuna*, *Perperia*, *Papparuna* and *Porpatira*. It flourishes in Bulgaria in the east as *Peperuda* and in the north as *Pemperuga*. In Roumania it is called *Paparudă* or *Păpălugă*, and in Servia and Dalmatia *Dodole* or *Dudule*. The origin of the custom has been claimed by all these races. The Roumanians and Vlachs point out that *Păparună* and *Pirpirună* are words that occur in their language, and mean " poppy " and " butterfly," but they fail to explain what poppies and butterflies have to do with rain-charms. Those who claim a Hellenic origin overlook the point that it only occurs in North Greece, where there is so much mixed blood, and not in Crete and the south, and they provide a Greek derivation for *Perperia* and *Porpatira* and say it means merely procession, but it is hard to see why any procession should be a rain-charm. In Bulgarian too the word *Peperuda* means butterfly, and it seems that the custom, if its name is any criterion, is really Slavonic. One of the few old Slavonic pagan gods, whose names are known, was Perun the Thunder-God, whose name at once suggests *Pirpirună*, and it is perfectly natural that he should have to do with rain especially in the summer-time. Sir Arthur Evans has recorded that near Uskub he found that the inhabitants of a village Moslem and christian alike were in the habit of pouring libations of wine over a Latin inscription to Juppiter in order to produce rain, though they had no knowledge as to what the stone said. We were shewn a spot near Monastir where an inscription lies buried, but no one can dig it up, for it would never stop raining if they did. When ancient inscribed stones still have such power, it is not hard to believe that Perun is still invoked to-day to send the summer showers.

The next festival after Mavronoro is that of the Ayii Anar-yiri, St Cosmas and St Damian, whose day falls on the 1st of July. This day is observed as a holiday and a service is held in the church of St Athanasius because its side chapel is dedicated to them. Next on July 20th follows the much more important festival of St Elijah for which all muleteers will try to return. They have time between Mavronoro and St Elijah to make one journey down into Thessaly and back, since it takes them from eight to ten days each way allowing for halts and the selling and buying of their merchandise. This is the day when the whole parish of St Elijah wears its best clothes and is at home to receive callers (Plate XIX). All the village first attends the service in the church, and the rest of the day will be spent in social entertainments such as calls and picnics. On July 26th follows the festival of Ayia Paraskevi to whom the monastery is dedicated, and the whole village spends the day there. Family parties are made up consisting of men, women, boys and girls, all mixing together on equal terms, and soon after dawn they start for the monastery laden with bread, wine, sweetmeats and a lamb ready to be roasted and any other provisions they need to enable them to pass the day in the most enjoyable manner. Each family selects some shady spot in the meadows round the monastery and after attending the service in the church roasts its lamb and consumes its eatables. The day ends with a general dance of all those present and they return home in the evening.

On August the 6th the other church at the monastery that called Ayios Sotir celebrates the day of the Transfiguration, which is a women's festival, for it is the day when the unmarried girls communicate. They have duly fasted for the previous week and early in the morning start for the monastery to attend service in the church. The boys and young men, who are expected to keep away, will sit on the hill of the church of St Elijah to see what girls are going, and then if they think it worth while, will follow them to the monastery. The only other men who go on such days will be the fathers or husbands of the women going to communicate and any men who have been invited by the abbot to stay the night with him and sample the good cheer of the monastery. From this day up till the day of the Assumption the whole village gives its mind towards preparing for that great festival, and everyone is occupied with thoughts of marriage and giving in marriage. The only break is provided by the festival of St Athanasius which is held in the church of that name on a

PLATE XX

1. SAMARINA: ST. JOHN'S DAY, ARUMANA AT THE CONDUIT OF PAPAZISI

2. ELASSONA: VLACH QUARTER ON THE LEFT WITH THE MONASTERY ON THE HILL ABOVE

Sunday about a week before the Assumption. This is not the proper day of St Athanasius, for that falls on January 18th. But it is the rule that every church at Samarina should have a festival during the summer in order to collect money through the offerings of those who attend. The church of St Athanasius can have no proper festival in the summer except the unimportant one of the Ayii Anaryiri, and so it celebrates the day of St Athanasius out of due season with the pious object of obtaining money for church expenses.

About three days before the day of the Assumption shepherds from all the country round appear in the village with the pick of their lambs, for it is the custom that every paterfamilias at Samarina should roast and eat his own lamb on this day just as at Easter. The green before Great St Mary's resembles a sheep fair and there is much animated haggling, the deceitful Vlach of Samarina attempting to outwit his subtle Greek and Kupatshar neighbours. In the evenings the gipsy musicians are to be heard in the wineshops round the *misohori*, and much drinking and dancing goes on in order to welcome friends and relations who have come up for the annual festival. It is probably highly necessary to drink good luck and long life to these new arrivals, for most of them will either be about to be married or will be thinking of proposing for the hand of some girl. When August 15th dawns the whole village flocks to the service at Great St Mary's, and it often happens that the bishop of Ghrevena comes up specially to officiate on this occasion. After the service all go home to eat their lambs and to prepare for the weddings which take place soon after noon. Since sixteen or more weddings may take place on this day, it will easily be understood that for the rest of this day the whole village is given up to singing and dancing, eating and drinking and all kinds of amusements. The festival of the Assumption continues with gradually decreasing vigour for a week, and on the two days that immediately follow the 15th of August after the service in the church a great combined dance of the whole village takes place. They dance to songs on the green of Great St Mary's. Two long rings are formed, the inner of men and the outer of women, and these reach all round the green from one extremity to the other (Plate IV 2). The men are all in their best white clothes and the women conspicuous with the bright red braid on their *sarkă's*. Towards the end of the week as the wedding ceremonies come to an end the news runs through the village first that one and then that another has become betrothed, and so the feasting that accompanies betrothals is substituted for the weddings. One form of amusement is replaced by another, and the old men and women, who can no longer dance, sit at their doors in the sun and gossip and discuss how often the would-be bridegroom had been " beaten " in his previous efforts to secure a bride. In the evenings bands of boys and young men will be seen strolling round the village and visiting first one conduit and then another. They do this in order to see the girls, who will be drawing water shortly before dusk, and the attentions of the young men naturally cause much giggling and blushing amongst them. Thus they pass the time till the feast of St Mary the Less on September 8th which marks the end of the wedding season, and the day of the Beheading of St John the Baptist, a strict fast which comes in the middle of this period, is a welcome relief to the feasting. After St Mary the Less, which is a minor edition of the festival of the Assumption, people begin to leave the village and the families get ready for the fair at Konitsa and begin to think of paying their bills for the summer. When the fair of Konitsa is over and the day of reckoning is done, they pack up and caravans of families go down through the gathering rains to spend the dark days of winter in foreign towns.

The winter has its festivals no less than the summer, there is St Demetrius on October 26th, St Michael on November 8th, and St Nicholas on December 6th. But these for the Vlachs in general are merely church festivals and holidays. It is with the approach of Christmas that they celebrate a great festival that marks the middle of their winter, for then they know that every day brings them nearer to the time when they will go out up to their native hills again. On Christmas Eve in each house a big fire is made to keep Christ warm. A shovel is put into it and the ashes are not removed till Epiphany and the fire must be kept continually alight. The boys form bands and go wandering about and knock at door after door with a big stick and sing in Vlach :—

Kolinda, melinda, give me the cake mother for Christ is born in the stable of the oxen for fear of the Jews.

or in Greek :—

Give me a cake mother that we may go further; as this year my lads, as this year, so next year too.

They sing till the door is opened and they are given fruit such as currants, chestnuts and walnuts. The leader of the band carries a long thread at his waist with a small piece of stick at the end. On this they thread the cakes given them, which are like doughnuts, with a hole in the centre. In other days when the boys entered the house they sat down a little, and after a time the householder threw currants and peas on the floor. The boys then went down on hands and knees and picked them up with their mouths baaing like sheep. Sometimes each house made a kind of Christmas cake nicely decorated on top with sesame seed and currants which was kept till Epiphany. Then it was sprinkled with a few drops of the newly blessed water, broken into pieces and given to sheep, goats, horses, mules and cattle to keep them well and healthy. On Christmas Day when he comes out of church each person takes a leaf of the holm oak or a pinch of salt and throws it into the fire saying :—" With brides, with sons-in-law, with children, with lambs, with kids. For many years ! " If what is put in the fire crackles all will be well for the year and vice versa.

During the twelve days that elapse between Christmas and Epiphany the Vlachs believe that the mysterious beings called *Karkandzal'i* or *Karkalanzā* wander about the earth from dark till cockcrow. They especially haunt the springs and defile the water, and it is very dangerous to meet them. They are finally driven away by the blessing of the waters at Epiphany. Between the Day of St Basil, New Year's Day, and

Epiphany a curious mumming performance takes place which is well known throughout Thessaly, Macedonia and Thrace. The object of this mumming is to drive away *Karkandzal'i*. Who these mysterious beings are no one can tell, they appear in Greek folklore wherever there are Greeks, Turks believe in them and so do the Vlachs, but we have not yet information as to whether they appear in Bulgarian folklore. The name varies between *Kallikandzaros* and *Karkandzalu* and every place which believes in them has some different form. Their origin and the meaning of the name are equally obscure and the recent ingenious attempt to trace their ancestry to the Centaurs does not seem satisfactory. The Samariniats call the mummers *Ligutshari* and the young men delight to make up such bands. In other times they would make up the band on New Year's Day and after performing in their own village spend the days before Epiphany in wandering round other villages in the neighbourhood always returning home for Epiphany. It sometimes happened that two bands met on the road and then there was a struggle to see which was the better. Neither would wish to yield except to force, for the weaker band had to salute the leader of the stronger. Thus it has been known to end in bloodshed, so they say, and near Verria they will point out places in the hills called *La Ligutshari* where a struggle between two bands ended in some one being killed. A band may consist of any number up to twenty, but there are really only seven essential characters, the bride, the bridegroom, the old woman who nurses a puppet in her arms pretending it is her child, the old man or Arab, the doctor and two men dressed in skins to represent bears or sheep or wolves or devils. These latter characters always have masks of skin and wear on their heads a piece of board in which is inserted a kind of plume made of the tail of a fox, wolf or goat. They are always heavily loaded with rows and rows of mule and sheep bells to make more impression when they dance. The Arab too usually wears a similar costume. If more than seven people compose a band, the extra persons will duplicate other characters such as the bride and bridegroom, of whom there can be any number up to six, and the devils or bears, or they may introduce fresh characters such as the doctor's wife or a priest. The brides are invariably young men dressed in girls' clothes, and no women ever take part in such mumming; it would be improper. The plot of the play which the mummers performed was very simple. The Arab or old man would annoy the bride with his attentions. The bridegroom would naturally intervene and a lively quarrel would ensue, which ended eventually in the death of one of them. He was duly mourned either by the bride or by the old woman and the doctor was called in. Through the doctor's skill the dead was restored to life and the play ended with a general dance of all the characters and the sending round of the hat. In other days the play seems to have included something in the nature of an obscene pantomime, of which traces still survive. Nowadays the play varies much from place to place, for instance at times the Arab will attempt to steal the old woman's puppet baby and this provokes the bridegroom's interference. The mumming used to begin after church on New Year's Day, but now in some places it is done only at Epiphany. The Greeks of Pelion have transferred the festival to May Day, the Thracian mumming among Greeks and Bulgarians alike occurs at the beginning of Lent, and within the memory of man the bishop of Ghrevena has forbidden the Vlachs of that town to do their mumming at the New Year and compelled them to transfer it to Carnival. Wherever there are Vlachs the custom is known. It still flourishes in the glens of Pindus at Turia and Baieasa and at Briaza where they call the mummers *Arugutshari*. They are known by this name at Klisura, at Neveska as *Ishk'inari* and at Krushevo as *Arak'i*. In the Meglen at L'umnitsa and Oshini they appear as *Dzhamalari*. The Samariniats at Verria, Elassona and Vlakhoyianni still observe the custom. At Verria where we have seen it on New Year's Day, it is much curtailed, for only one character appears, the Arab masked and dressed in skins and loaded with bells (Plate I). Boys in groups of four or five will don this dress and wander about the town from quarter to quarter where the Vlachs dwell. They waylay any one they meet and demand money to drink his health and wish him good luck for the year. Each

member of the band carries a large knife of some kind and they
threaten the victim's life till he pays. At Elassona Vlachs
and Greeks unite in the mumming (Plate XXI), but the former
seem to be in the majority, and all the usual characters appear
though the Arab here is an Albanian armed with a blunderbuss
to shoot the bridegroom with ashes and the typical two-
stringed Albanian guitar. Similarly wherever there are Greeks
in Thrace and Macedonia the custom is still observed. We
have heard of it at Stenimachos in East Bulgaria and in Adrianople, at Boghatsko near Kastoria and throughout Thessaly.
From the obvious similarity between this mumming and some
of the ancient Dionysiac rites some would hail this as a Hellenic custom come down from remote antiquity. However
since in Greece itself it is not known anywhere south of
Thessaly, but only in regions where Greeks live side by side
with other races, the Hellenic origin does not seem proved.
All that we can say is that it seems common to all the races in
the centre of the Balkan peninsula for the Bulgars and Albanians too know it, but we cannot on the present evidence
decide which race had the honour of inventing it. It is remarkable that belief in the *Kallikandzari* is universal in Greece,
but the mumming in their honour is not. As for its supposed
Dionysiac connection that still remains to be proved, and after
all even Dionysus himself was not in origin a Hellene, but a
stranger from the north. The mumming apparently reached
its height on the eve of Epiphany when the bands would visit
the houses after dark and levy contributions on the occupier
willy-nilly. On such occasions they seem to have had full
licence to steal chickens and any similar trifles they could
lay their hands on. Then on the day of Epiphany after the
usual Orthodox service of blessing the waters the bands re-
appeared to take toll from all who had eluded them before.
Sometimes the bands collect money for the church of their
parish, but as a rule the contributions they levy are spent for
their own pleasure. The last possible day for them to linger
is the feast of St John the Baptist which immediately follows
Epiphany, but by then their services are no longer required,
for *Karkandzal'i* flee as soon as the waters are blessed. To

PLATE XXI

ELASSONA: VLACH AND GREEK MASQUERADERS AT EPIPHANY

prevent any chance of harm from any *Karkandza* who may have remained the wise Samariniat housewife will take the ashes that she has been collecting on her hearth ever since Christmas and sprinkle them all round her house outside, which will effectively drive away *Karkandzal'i* who are left.

After Epiphany there are no great festivals till Easter, or at least such festivals as occur are not particularly Vlach. Pious craftsmen for the sake of a holiday will in January duly keep the days of St Antony and St Athanasius. The latter day is for some Vlachs an important festival as marking the middle of winter. In some of the Meglen villages one or two oxen are killed at the church and the meat boiled. Each house sends a boy for a dish of the meat, paying money for it which goes to the church. All Vlachs who are Greeks in politics will duly observe Lady Day because that is now the national festival of Greece. Lent and Easter they keep as all orthodox christians, and their observances do not differ from those of the Greeks. But Easter since it is a moveable feast cannot be depended on by the nomad Vlachs, for they may have to spend it on the road. No true Vlach would put off attending the fair of Ghrevena merely because he wanted to spend Easter in his winter quarters in some town, and they say that Easter was spent on the road in 1854 when the Samarina families were attacked by Turkish troops while in camp. Only for the day of Lazarus, the Saturday before Palm Sunday, have the Vlachs any peculiar observances. On this day the young girls collect in groups of five or more (they call themselves *Lazarine*), and make a doll representing a boy. One of them is chosen as leader to carry the doll, and then decorated with flowers they wander from house to house singing songs either in Vlach or Greek. Sometimes two of them, either girls or boys, unite to carry the doll, and this seems to be done to avoid the possibility that the people, they visit, should make jokes at the expense of the girl carrying the boy doll. On the last day of February the boys run about the streets with bells in their hands and cry, " Away mice, away snakes ! " This custom however is observed amongst many peoples at this time of the year.

After Easter come the feast of St George, which is a great day for the Vlachs, for then the shepherds break up their winter camps and move off to their native hills, Ascension Day and the feast of the Trinity which are kept as feasts of the church. At Whitsuntide they keep the feast of the dead which they call *Rusal'e*. On these days they decorate the graves with flowers and take to the churchyard dishes of collyva and other food which are blessed by the priest after which they are distributed amongst those present. This is done, as the old women say, that the dead may eat and also for the repose of their souls. The custom is known in Greece and elsewhere, and it is interesting that the Greeks too keep the *Rusalia*, which like the Vlach is derived from the Latin *rosalia*.

The Vlachs are faithful sons of the Orthodox Church and very religious, if to be religious is to observe the superstitions which the church encourages. We have seen the famous miracle working ikon of the monastery of Zaburdo brought up to Samarina by pious muleteers to cure a dangerous infectious disease, which was attacking the mules of the village. At Elassona in the middle of January the famous ikon of the Virgin is brought down in solemn procession from its monastery on the hill above (Plate XX 2) to the church in the centre of the Vlach quarter mainly inhabited by Samariniats. After the service a spirited auction is conducted in the church for the honour of keeping the ikon for a night in one's house. The bids are made in oil to be given to the monastery. The first bid is made by the priest who as he comes down the steps from the altar at the close of the service shouts out " Thirty okes of oil for the ikon ! " which indicates the reserve price. On the occasion when we saw the auction the ikon was secured by a syndicate of Samarina muleteers, who combined to bid a hundred and twenty okes of oil, and carried off the ikon in triumph. Naturally the entertainment of this miraculous ikon attributed to St Luke brings the best possible luck for the successful bidders.

Other examples of superstitions common among the Vlachs and known at Samarina are the belief that every deep glen or ravine is the home of demons or devils who delight to leap about the rocks, and the idea that springs are the homes of beings called *Albile shi Mushatile*, the Fair and Beautiful Maidens. These mysterious maidens live in small springs especially those closely surrounded by bushes or overgrown with ivy. As they are naturally jealous of any pretty girl it is wise to leave by the springs where they live a piece of money or a rag torn off a garment and tied on to one of the bushes. If any girl or boy is ill, it is due to the jealousy of these beings. Then the relations with white aprons and white kerchiefs on their heads on which they carry loaves of bread and with a sprig of basil in their hands will go early in the morning to the nearest spring where *Albile shi Mushatile* dwell. The springs are usually a little way outside the village. They cut the bread and sing a song like the following :—

Fair and Beautiful Maidens have pity on us. What you have given us, do not take from us. What you have taken from us, give us back.

On one occasion an old woman of Samarina hearing that we were in search of antiquities said, " I suppose they must have candles of human fat." Her belief was, that, if one had such a candle and lighted it, either the light would guide us straight to what we were seeking, or else the antiquities would spring up from the ground automatically. Another time during a thunderstorm on the mountains we were directed to sit under a special kind of pine where we should be sheltered from the rain and safe from the lightning. Pines of this kind have a small cruciform branch on their tops and so no lightning will ever strike them. The pine on the roof of Great St Mary's was once cut down by an impious priest ; but the next morning the priest was found dead in his bed and the tree was back in its old position where it flourishes to this day.

The Vlach folk-beliefs are endless and as will be seen from the examples that have come under our notice are of mixed origin and it is impossible to say how many are genuinely Vlach.

CHAPTER VIII

THE HISTORY OF SAMARINA

Shi eara tsi nu shi eara.

And there was what was not.

Preface to *Vlach Folktale*

SAMARINA from its position in Pindus on the borders of Upper Macedonia and Southeastern Albania is little likely to be visited by European travellers unless they go there with some set purpose. Further the fact that it lies just off the main road from Ghrevena to Konitsa helps to keep it in obscurity, and even this road is not often used by European travellers who usually cross the chain of Pindus by Metsovo or by Kortsha (in Greek Koritsa, in Vlach Kortsheaua). Leake and Pouqueville, our earliest authorities, mention the village, but never visited it. Since their time the only European who has been there and given any account of it is Weigand. The Italian botanist Baldacci was in the district in 1896, but not in Samarina itself. Apart from these the only European who has been there recently according to the accounts given us in Samarina was a German, who stayed one night when travelling through from Albania back to Salonica. The villagers are never tired of telling how geologists have been there to look at the mines reported to exist on Zmolku, but do not know their names. The mere fact that none of the earlier European travellers ever passed anywhere near the village means that for its history before the time of Leake we are entirely dependent on local tradition. Even for the various events connected with Samarina in the nineteenth century the main source of information is oral tradition again. There are however a few scattered references to Samarina in some modern Greek books. From the statements of the travellers and the modern Greek references we have been able to obtain a few points the dates of which can be fixed approximately. On to this skeleton we have attempted in the following history of the village to fit what we have learnt from various natives of Samarina. The result can make no claim to be accurate, for the local traditions are often very inconsistent. Perhaps the history of Samarina makes up for its lack of accuracy by picturesqueness and the fact that it is probably typical of what the Vlach villages went through in Turkish times.

All the local traditions agree in saying that the village was not always where it is now. Formerly there were three or four little hamlets which in the course of time coalesced into Samarina. But exactly where these hamlets were no one quite knows, but all are quite sure that one was at the monastery of Samarina. This was not a healthy site and the inhabitants had to migrate elsewhere, because the place was full of snakes which bit the children. Another settlement is said to have been at a place called La Pālita about ten minutes to the south of Samarina on the road to the monastery. Here the slope of the hill is gentler than elsewhere and covered with grass and dotted with pear trees, so that it seems quite possible that it was once inhabited. Another hamlet is said to have been on the ridge opposite Samarina, but opinions differ as to where it was. One would place it at the Tshukă a rocky bluff below the Ghrevena road and near the K'atrăN'agră; another would put it by a spring called the Fāndānă al Ahuri (the spring of Ahuri) higher up on the same ridge above the Ghrevena road; and yet a third would place it at the Shoput al Kodru further along the ridge on the road to Tshotili. The tale is that Ahuri was a shepherd and wished to build the village by his spring. A hot dispute took place between him and other shepherds who wanted to build the village by the willows in what is now the *misohori* and a fight ended in his being killed there by his spring. The most likely of these three sites is the Tshukă where there are disused threshing floors and other signs of cultivation to say nothing of a large number of pear trees. Another hamlet stood somewhere on the

10

present site of the village, probably near the site of Great St Mary's Church. To these settlements others will add one supposed to have existed on the slopes of Gurgul'u above the woods of K'urista at a spot called La Koasta. This hardly seems likely in view of the roughness of the ground and the height of the mountain. No permanent settlement can have existed here, though it is quite likely that shepherds camped here for the summer. Probably the tradition that one of the original hamlets stood on Gurgul'u is due to a confusion with the tale that the ridge of Gurgul'u was used as a refuge by the people of Samarina during Albanian raids. At all events it does not much matter where these isolated hamlets were, it is enough that there is a consensus of local tradition that Samarina first came into being through their union.

Four families are said to have taken the initiative as regards the foundation of the village. These were the families, Honia, Dadal'ari, Nikuta and Barbaramu. Of these the Dadal'ari family is still well known in the village, but for a widely different reason. Once upon a time this clan was rich and powerful, but latterly through the decline of the sheep-rearing industry has fallen on evil days. It is now a bye-word for pride and poverty. As a rule every bachelor from elsewhere, who visits Samarina, is advised to take a wife from the village, and he, if he be well posted in the local traditions, will admit that he is willing, but that he would prefer as his bride one of the daughters of Dadal'ari. Any stranger who makes such a remark will at once achieve a great reputation as a wit, in Samarina at least. The heads of these families are said to have been *tshelnikadzĭ*, head shepherds, and it is highly probable that the scattered settlements, which were united to found the village, were not permanent hamlets, but merely the hut encampments of large groups of shepherds, who return year after year to encamp in the same spot for the summer among their native hills. Nowadays such camps are small, but in earlier times they were of a patriarchal character. In addition to his own family the Tshelnikŭ had under his control many shepherds who watched his flocks and their families as well. Thus in the flourishing days of the Vlach pastoral life as many as fifty families might be united under the leadership of one Tshelnikŭ. Some local authorities assert that the founding of Samarina took place in the fifteenth century, others more wisely profess complete ignorance on this point. Although it is probably true that Vlach shepherds were camping for the summer round about the present site of Samarina in the fifteenth century and for many a long year before then, yet it seems to us that in placing the foundation of the village in the fifteenth century, tradition is giving a date at least a century too early. After the first permanent settlement other families came from time to time and so increased the size of the village. In the sixteenth century the families Hutsha, Tsan'ara, and Hoti or Karadashu settled in Samarina and in the seventeenth century they were followed by the family of Hadzhimati. These are the facts that local tradition loves to retail, and it is impossible to check them. To follow back for any period of years the history of any one of the families of Samarina with their ever-changing surnames and continual inconsistencies is beyond the patience of any ordinary mortal. From the time of its foundation till the end of the eighteenth century when we have the first written records of the village and its inhabitants, Samarina was increasing in size and prosperity. The accounts given by Leake and Pouqueville indicate that it was then in a flourishing condition, and we know from the inscriptions given above that about this time the churches were built.

Probably the wealth and prosperity of the village attracted the attention of the Albanians. As noted by Leake in South-eastern Albania the Albanians have for a long time past been encroaching on the neighbouring peoples, whether Greek, Vlach or Bulgarian. At the same time they were continually raiding beyond the limits of the lands in which they were settling. For instance the Greek districts of Poghoni and the Zaghori suffered severely. Prominent amongst these raiders were the people of Tepeleni, the home of Ali Pasha, and Kolonia the wild hill country lying between Konitsa and Kortsha. It is said that during the eighteenth and early nineteenth century Albanians from the districts mentioned

were continually attempting to plunder Samarina. However the boast of Samarina is that it has never been robbed
by Albanians, although they admit that on one occasion the
whole population went up and camped on Gurgul'u. There
the women and children were placed in safety on the peak
and the men lying behind hastily constructed breastworks of
stones successfully defended the honour of Samarina. Local
pride apparently overlooks the fact that if the whole population were on the heights of Gurgul'u the village must have
been at the mercy of the Albanians who could have plundered
it unhindered. It is in connection with these raids that we
hear of the first hero of Samarina. The great defender and
leader of the village against the Albanians was one Yanni al
Preftŭ. In 1743 he is believed to have chased home to Tepeleni
from Samarina and Kerasova Veli Pasha the father of Ali
Pasha, the Lion of Yannina. So great was the terror which
he caused among the Albanians that even to-day, so Samarina
boasts, Albanian mothers quiet their naughty children by
saying that Yanni Prift is coming. In this respect Yanni
al Preftŭ can be ranked with heroes like Hannibal, Richard
Cœur de Lion, and Napoleon whose names are used to stop
babies crying. On one occasion he led out the men of
Samarina, and met and defeated Arslan Bey of Kolonia who
was coming with innumerable Albanians to set his foot on the
village, as the local phrase goes. Aravandinos says that
he attacked a band of Albanians returning from the south
with the plunder of Thessaly, and robbed them of most of
their booty. Possibly, like Totskas, he harried Albanians on
their way home after subduing the Peloponnesian revolt of
1770. Yanni al Preftŭ, who is said to have belonged to the
great house of Dadal'ari, fell fighting as befitted so valiant a
man. The accounts of his death vary. Some believe that
he was basely deserted and left alone to fight against hopeless
odds by three men of Samarina who were jealous of his renown.
The three traitors are said to have been Nak'i al Kosa,
Dzima al Nikuta and Dzima al Kututriñga. Others
say that the Albanians treacherously attacked and killed
him and this is the account that is celebrated in the local

ballad. The version of this which we were told in the village runs thus :—

"What are these banners that come from the ridge of Greklu ? " And Yiannis smiled, he tosses his head, "My girdle holds my sword, it holds my musket too." And he mounts the slope like a splendid pigeon, and his mother near at hand shouts to him and wails, "Where are you going Yianni all alone, with no one at your side ? " "Why do I want many men, I go alone." He begins to cry aloud like a stallion. "Where are you going Albanian dogs ; and you, men of Kolonia ? I am Yiannis the priest's son, Yiannis the son of priest Nikolas. This is not Ghrevena, this is not the Zaghori, this is not Laista and all the Vlach villages. Here are mountain heights, the heights of Samarina, where boys and women and girls know how to fight."

The published versions which differ slightly in that they specify the place of his death, Hassan Kopatsi a spring on the road from the top of the Greklu ridge to Kerasova, add three lines at the end emphasising the fact that he fell by treachery :—

He did not finish his speech, and he groans heavily. The fatal lead comes through his shoulder. They slew the Captain Yiannakis by treachery.

About this same time, 1775, an Albanian called Ismail Dhamsis is said to have been warden of the roads of Furka and Samarina. He seems to have been very energetic, and was in consequence waylaid and murdered by brigands at a place called Skurdzha in Samarina territory on the top of the ridge to the east of H'ilimodhi. This place is not far from the pass known as La Lupŭ Spindzuratŭ (the Hanged Wolf) on the road from Dusko to Furka. His death is celebrated in the following song :—

Were you not content, Ismail Agha, with Furka and with Samarina ? Yet you were anxious to have Dusko as armatolik as well, and evil induced them to lay an ambush for you. "Ismail, throw down your arms, Ismail surrender ! " "Am I to throw down my arms, am I to submit ? I am Ismail Agha, the whole world fears me." They fire one volley and he remained on the ground. Albania wept for him, wept for Dhamsis.

At this time too according to the tradition there were coiners at Samarina who practised their trade at a place called

La Kāzăni (the Cauldrons) on Zmolku above the Vale Kārnă. The spot is well known and it is said that the ruins of the factory can still be seen and that false money is often found about there. One of the coiners was the father of Adham Tshutra, the *tshelnikŭ* who was the principal subscriber towards the cost of the wall paintings in Great St Mary's. When he was denounced to the authorities and the Turks came to arrest him, he hid under a large pile of unworked wool lying in his house and so escaped. One of the klephtic ballads relates to Miha of Samarina who is said to have been a companion in arms of Yanni al Preftŭ. Miha denounced to the authorities as a coiner one Itrizis who is said to have been a native of Samarina. Itrizis was sent to Constantinople and remained a long time there in prison. On his release he avenged himself as told in the song and then went into Thessaly and joined Vlakhavas. The date according to Aravandinos is 1785. It hardly seems probable that a native of Samarina should have been called Itrizis, which seems far more likely to have been an Albanian name. The ballad tells the story thus :—

Mikhos was going down from Samarina with his musket at his side, with his sword in his girdle, to go to his winter quarters, to Sikia and to Pertori. A bird went and sat on his right shoulder, and it did not speak like a bird nor like a swallow, but it spoke and talked the speech of man. "Mikho, tread that path, pass along it, and another time you will not tread it nor will you pass along it." He lowered his eyes and tears came into them. "My little bird, where did you learn this, where did you hear this, my bird?" "Yesterday I was in heaven with the angels and I heard them number you with the dead." He did not finish his speech, his speech was not complete, a volley was heard in the midst of the ravine. Itrizis was lying in ambush for him high up in the pass ; Mikhos of Samarina fell down dead on the earth, he who was armatole at Furka and klepht at Samarina.

There are frequent references to Samarina and its inhabitants during the rule of Ali Pasha in Yannina from 1788 to 1822. He was supreme in Epirus, Southern Albania, Thessaly, and Southwestern Macedonia, and consequently the great majority of the Vlachs fell within his sphere. Two natives of Samarina are said to have been in his service as secretaries—he used Greek as his official language—and their names are given as Zhogu al Lala al Hadzhik'iriu and Miha al K'irianŭ. They seem to have made good use of their opportunities. They say that a Greek of Vradheto, Ioannis Tsigharas, and his three cousins from Tshepelovo returned to their native land from Wallachia with money which they had made abroad. They were denounced to Ali Pasha by these two men of Samarina who alleged that they had robbed their caravan. The four Greeks were thrown into prison and condemned to death. They were rescued by a relation of theirs, Ioannis Kapas, but lost all their money, and were obliged immediately to go back to Wallachia to make more. Another native of Samarina called Adham is said to have served as mudir of Dhomeniko under Ali Pasha. He died suddenly and it is believed that he was poisoned, of course by the Turks to whom the christians attribute all the evil that takes place in the Balkans. Ali Pasha is also reported to have attempted to abduct a girl from Samarina, but tradition is not sure whether he wished her for his own bride or for some one else. The name and parentage of the girl also differ. Some will say he was enamoured of a girl of the family of Hadzhik'iriu who was hurriedly married to Adham Tshutra. Others say that he attempted to abduct a girl called Haidha of the great house of Dadal'ari in order to send her to Napoleon for his bride. Yanni al Preftŭ is believed to have rescued the girl from having this greatness thrust upon her. In any case Samarina and the neighbouring villages of Avdhela and Perivoli boast that they always stoutly resisted all attempts of Ali Pasha to encroach on their liberties. He was notorious for reducing villages of peasant proprietors to the status of chiftliks and so obtaining all the produce of the village, the inhabitants of which were thus little better than serfs. It was under his rule that Samarina obtained possession of the chiftlik of H'ilimodhi, which is said to have been a Bulgarian village of peasant small-holders. It happened that a man of Samarina was killed at H'ilimodhi and his fellow-countrymen applied for redress to Ali Pasha, who answered that they could do as they liked. Consequently the men of Samarina descended in force upon

H'ilimodhi, drove out the Bulgarians, and annexed the village and its lands to Samarina. Local tradition says that Ali Pasha especially favoured Samarina, and many families assert that they possessed rescripts issued by him till recently. Most of these are said to have perished when Leonidha burnt some of the best houses ; at all events we have never been shown any such rescript. To-day on a rock in the grove of pines on the slope of the bluff, where stands the church of St Elijah, the following inscription is to be read :—

1821

ΑΠΟ ΑΛΗ

ΠΑΣΙΑ

What this means it is hard to say. Barth found in the Elassona district the words " Ali Pasha 1823 " in Greek on a small fort at Selos, which although a chiftlik did not belong to him. Heuzey however says that he built a small fort at Selos to guard the pass through Olympus to Katerini. Ali Pasha was killed in 1822 ; but the inscription may have been put up later in order to record that the fort was built by him. Thus the inscription at Samarina may refer to the establishment of an armatolik there by him, or it may have been cut at a later date and be of no significance whatsoever.

Another native of Samarina, a monk called Demetrius, fared badly at the hands of Ali Pasha. After the failure of the insurrection of the armatoli under Vlakhavas in 1808 Demetrius went about Thessaly advising the christians to be patient and submit. He was denounced as preaching sedition and brought before Ali Pasha loaded with chains. Pouqueville, who is our sole authority for the story and at his best not a sober historian, says that the following conversation took place between the tyrant and the monk :—

Ali. You have preached the kingdom of Christ and consequently the fall of our faith and our prince.

Dem. My God reigns from all eternity and for all eternity, and I reverence the masters whom He has given us.

Ali. What is that you carry on your breast ?

Dem. The precious image of His mother.

Ali. I wish to see it.

Dem. It may not be profaned. Order one of my hands to be cut off and I will give it to you.

Ali. Is it thus that you mislead men's minds : that we are profaners ? I recognise in this speech the agent of the bishops who call in the Russians to reduce us to slavery. Name your accomplices.

Dem. My accomplices are my conscience, and my duty, which oblige me to console the christians and make them submissive to your laws.

Ali. Say to your laws, christian dog !

Dem. I am proud of that name.

Ali. You carry an image of the Virgin which they say is valuable ?

Dem. Say rather miraculous. The mother of Our Saviour is our advocate with her Immortal Son and with God. Her miracles for us occur daily, and every day I invoke them.

Ali. Let us see if she will protect you. Executioners apply the torture !

Then the executioners threw him down at the feet of the Pasha who spat in his face. They thrust thorns under the nails of his hands and feet, they pierced his arms, but in spite of his pain the only words he uttered were " Lord have mercy on thy servant ! Queen of heaven pray for us ! " They placed round his head a string of knuckle-bones and drew it tight, but it broke without producing a confession from him. Then the tired executioners asked that the torture be postponed till the morrow. Demetrius was removed and thrown into a damp cell. The next day they hanged him head downwards and lit a fire of resinous wood under his head. Fearing that he might die and so escape them, they released him and placed him on the ground with planks over him on which they danced to break his bones. Finally Demetrius, triumphant over all these tortures, was imprisoned in a wall only his head being left free. They fed him in order to pro- long his agony, and he did not die till the tenth day. So great was the admiration of his firmness under torture that a Mohammedan of Kastoria even asked to be baptized. For this he also afterwards suffered martyrdom. As a matter of fact after the death of Demetrius Ali Pasha is said to have stopped the persecution of the christians in Thessaly which he had begun to revenge himself for the rising of Vlakhavas.

Though on the whole Samarina fared well under Ali Pasha, yet the troubles in Epirus and the destruction of Muskopol'e and other flourishing Vlach villages after 1770 had their effect on Samarina as well. Its population, which then numbered fifteen thousand souls according to local estimates, began to scatter and many families wandered forth towards the east to find new homes away from the storm centre at Yannina. Many settled at Shatishta ; between one hundred and fifty and two hundred families are said to have gone to Niausta where their descendants are almost entirely hellenized ; others settled in the Pierian plain at Katerini, and others joined their cousins from Avdhela and Perivoli in the movement to the hills of Verria which later received larger contingents from the same villages. This cannot be anything like a complete list of the places whither families from Samarina wandered, and probably few towns in Southeastern Macedonia did not receive a detachment of Pindus Vlachs at the beginning of the nineteenth century.

The next historical mention of Samarina is in connection with a certain Yeoryios Dhervenas, a native of the village of Dherveni near Konitsa, who from 1821 onwards was a noted robber in the districts of Ghrevena and Konitsa and the Zaghori. In order to check his raids he was made capitan of the armatoli of Konitsa and Samarina, but since he still continued to devote himself to his favourite profession, he was ambushed and killed. His death which is said to have occurred in 1826 is celebrated in the following song :—

Three little birds were sitting high up at Radhotovi : from the evening they wail, and at dawn they say, " Yiorghodhervenas has gone out on to the mountains of Samarina, he demands taxes, he demands payment. He starts to write letters, to send them to Konitsa. To you Suleyman Bey and the headmen ! Send me the taxes, send me the payment lest I burn the villages and lay them waste." He did not finish his letter and he hears a volley, twelve bullets pierce him and he utters no word.

Shortly after this in 1845 we hear that the principal power at Samarina was in the hands of one man Yannuli al Miha al Hadzhi, who was apparently recognised by the government as the headman of the village. He was an active and intelligent man, a good speaker and possessed of considerable wealth and influence. His great faults are said to have been his love of power and money and his objection to any form of opposition. He had such authority that his seal or signature was necessary to legalise documents and deeds relating to the sale of houses and land. He is said to have used the following phrase :—Ὁ τῆς Σαμαρίνης Προεστὼς Γιαννούλης Μίχου βεβαιῶ διὰ τὴν κοινότητα . . . The immediate cause of his fall was that he attempted to induce the people of Samarina to raise the standard of revolt, probably about the time of the Crimean war. He was resisted by Dzhoga al Hadhzik'iria and Dzhima al Papayeoryi of the house of Tshutra, who taunted him publicly that he treated Samarina as though it was his chiftlik. The proposed revolt fell through, and shortly after Yannuli al Miha was denounced to the Turkish authorities at Yannina by his enemies who alleged that he had embezzled money which he had collected on behalf of the state. The intervention of the Turks secured his complete fall from power and he died not long afterwards. Then the chief of the opposition Dzhoga al Hadzhik'iria became the principal man in Samarina with the assistance of Dzhima al Papayeoryi.

In 1854 the Crimean war broke out and this event naturally affected Samarina. The Greeks taking advantage of the embarrassments of the Ottoman Empire brought about a rising in Thessaly, Epirus and Southern Macedonia. Few natives of these regions actually joined the insurgents except brigands, and the revolutionary bands were mainly composed of volunteers from Greece including men who deserted from the army for the purpose and gaolbirds liberated especially with this object. Many of the volunteers were true patriots, natives of the country who were living in Greece, and other Greeks from all Greek-speaking lands. But on the whole the conduct of the insurgents towards the christian population of the country they wished to free was disgraceful and they plundered right and left.   Large numbers of cattle and sheep were seized and driven down into Greece where meat was cheaper than it had ever been before as Finlay bears witness.   The Mohammedans were robbed as well, but since the christians far and away outnumber the Turks in the region concerned they naturally suffered most loss, especially since one way to hurt a rich bey was to plunder his chiftliks which would be inhabited by christians alone.   Amongst those who lost heavily were the shepherds of Samarina, and this was one circumstance which gave the prosperity of the village a severe check.   Further in the spring or early summer—May 20th 1854 is said to have been the day when the families were on their way up to Samarina going by the usual route through Dhiskata they were attacked in camp by Turkish troops and suffered severely.   Exactly how this came about is not clear, but as far as we can gather from some of those present it occurred in the following manner.   The insurgent movement was in progress and a large band under the leadership of Zhakas was in the neighbourhood of Ghrevena.   He had told the families not to move till he could come and protect them on their way up to the hills.   They however had gone on by themselves and were in camp one evening not very far from Dhiminitsa when Mehmed Agha of Ghrevena appeared with an escort of Kurdish cavalry and demanded the dues payable on the sheep, four piastres a head.   The men of Samarina protested that they had no money to pay with then because it was the beginning of the season, but they would pay in the autumn.   One old man, Hadzhiziku by name, encouraged them to resist Mehmed Agha's demands by force if necessary, and he suspecting that they were taking up the attitude of insurgents, which was partly true, ordered his troops to charge.   The Kurds accordingly rushed the encampment killing and plundering, and the Samarina people fled in terror to the shelter of the trees where they were comparatively safe from the cavalry.   They also resisted, as they could, for some of them had arms, and one Yanni al Taha is said to have killed the leader of the troops and so checked their attack.   About eighty people are said to have been killed and among them Hadzhiziku himself.

The rest of the folk were saved by the trees and nightfall. The next day Zhakas came up with his band about three hundred strong and a slight engagement took place between him and the Turks in which he lost a few men. On this occasion the women of Samarina put white kerchiefs on their heads and shouldered poles, so that the Turks at a distance might take them for armed men and not attack. Mehmed Agha retired to Ghrevena and the families under the escort of Zhakas reached their villages without any further adventures. After this Zhakas was pursued by Turkish troops and besieged by them in the monastery at Spileo where the caves in the cliffs have always been the traditional refuge for outlaws. He succeeded in breaking out of Spileo and made his way to Kalabaka where he united with Ghrivas who had been driven from Metsovo. They and other insurgent bands were finally routed by the Turks on June 17th 1854 at Kalabaka. In subduing the insurrection the Ottoman government employed as usual Albanian irregulars who were attracted by the prospects of plunder. On their way home some of these irregulars under the command of Mudum Bey of Trikkala wished to pass through Samarina territory and camp for one night in the village. Yanni al Taha at the head of the men of Samarina met them at the Doauă K'etri and offered them meat and bread, but refused to allow them to pass through the village. According to another account the people of Samarina waylaid some Albanians at the Lupŭ Spindzuratŭ and robbed them of most of their booty, but this seems to us an imaginative version inspired by the memories of past history. To this period the following song probably refers. The man who told us the song said it was an old song, but he did not know its date ; others said that its hero flourished under Ali Pasha ; and others again that the events related took place in 1854.

What is the evil that takes place this week ? My blood brothers, the dogs, have deceived me, have betrayed me, and they said to me, " Come, Dhuka, come up to Samarina, that we may become blood brothers on the twelve gospels." He was holding the cross in his hands, he was kissing the gospels, and patrols entrapped them round about the monastery. Listen, they summon Dhukas ! Listen, they call to Dhukas ! " Come out, come out, Dhuka, come out and submit ! "

" I am not a bride to submit, and to kiss hands.   I am the famous
Dhukas, famous throughout the world : the Sultan knows me and the
Grand Vizier knows me too."

Dhukas was a well-known brigand, and this song refers to his
betrayal and death.   Some of his friends invited him to come
to the monastery of Samarina that they might there go through
the ceremony of blood brotherhood.   He came, but they had
given information to the Turkish troops who came and surrounded it while Dhukas and his friends were swearing brotherhood.   When summoned to surrender Dhukas refused and
escaped from the monastery, probably by the cellar-like room
under the exo-narthex of its church.   He ran down to the
river, crossed it and was making his way up the slope of
Ghumara opposite.   The troops pursued and shot him on the
top of the ridge opposite to the monastery, which in consequence is still known as La Dhuka.

In 1856 when peace reigned again party strife broke out
once more at Samarina.   Dzhoga al Hadzhik'iria who as leader
of the opposition had succeeded to the power and place of
Yannuli al Miha began in the course of time to abuse his
authority very much as his predecessor had done, and to act in
the same high-handed manner.   He quarrelled with Dzhima al
Papayeoryi by sending the *mukhtars* and a gendarme to the
house of Miha Dzhima's brother, then a newly married young
man, to arrest him for failing to pay a debt which he was
alleged to have owed to the state.   The Turkish authorities
at Yannina were appealed to by both sides, for the opposition
now asserted that Dzhoga al Hadzhik'iria had embezzled the
proceeds of some taxes he should have collected for the government.   Miha al Papayeoryi was imprisoned at Ghrevena for
some time, but was liberated by bribery.   Then the Vali of
Yannina sent up an officer to Samarina to see which was the
stronger party in the village.   All the inhabitants were
summoned by the ringing of the bells to the *pade* of Great
St Mary's, and the officer put forward Miha to make his
defence to the people.   Then he ordered Dzhoga to stand on
one side and Miha on the other and the inhabitants to shew their
preference for one or the other by dividing there and then.

The division shewed that the party of Miha was much the stronger, and he became in his turn the principal man in the village, but he never seems to have enjoyed as much power as had been held by his predecessors. Another version of these party quarrels says that they were not so much personal affairs between the leaders, but that a great question of policy underlay the quarrel. One party, presumably that of Dzhoga, wished the inhabitants to sell Samarina and its territory wholesale as a chiftlik and that the folk should then go and settle elsewhere. This proposal was strenuously resisted and finally utterly defeated. The beaten party were so unpopular that they were obliged to withdraw from the village and seek new homes elsewhere. Consequently they went and joined those of their fellow-countrymen who had some time previously begun to make their homes on the hills of Verria, and others went to Katerini. About a hundred families in all settled round Verria and about the same number at Katerini. These are still referred to at Samarina as the beaten party (*bătutsi*). These events took place between 1854 and 1860 according to tradition, which is notoriously uncertain about dates.

In the years of peace that followed the stirring events of 1854 Samarina seems to have gradually increased in prosperity. In 1877 the village is said to have numbered twelve hundred houses and each year many more were being built. The part of the parish of St Elijah which is beyond the deep ravine was then full of houses, and there were many on the slope below Great St Mary's. On the other side houses stretched along the road from the village to the bridge on the Ghrevena road over the stream coming down from the Greklu. They even, so it is said, talked of building beyond this bridge. Then too the shepherds were very prosperous, for Samarina possessed 81,000 head of sheep. But the outbreak of the Russo-Turkish war seriously injured the village, and the political changes that ensued have had a permanent evil effect on it. As in 1854, so in 1878, the Greeks stirred up an insurrection in Thessaly, Epirus and Southern Macedonia, and as before volunteers from Greece and deserters from the Greek army composed the bulk of the insurgent forces. But in Thessaly, especially on Pelion, a large number of natives took up arms and local brigands joined them in the hope of plunder. The rising, which except on Pelion and Olympus had little local support, was soon stamped out by the Turks and the Albanian irregulars they called in to assist them. In April 1878 the insurrection, which had begun in January, was brought to an end mainly through British intervention. Following the established precedent the insurgents plundered christians and Mohammedans impartially, and the Samarina shepherds suffered severe losses. A native of Burbusko has told us that during the rising he and his companions in arms drove down into Greece many head of sheep and cattle from the Hashia district and the country round Elassona and Larissa, which is the very region where many Vlach shepherds winter. Then after the rising was over the Albanian irregulars robbed and plundered with fire and sword in Thessaly and the Elassona district. So great was the terror caused by these licensed marauders that ninety-four families wintered in Samarina, preferring to risk the cold and lack of food in the mountains rather than face the dangers of the plains.

On the failure of the insurrection the brigands who had joined it returned to their former occupation and the years that followed up to 1881 were full of danger for Samarina. Amongst the brigands who had taken part with the insurgents was a native of Samarina, Leonidha al Hadzhibira, a member of a well-known and wealthy family. He had been a brigand since 1875 at first as the lieutenant of Zhurkas and later as an independent leader. He had gladly taken part in the insurrection as a means of legalising his own robberies, and because he was apparently really eager to free the christians of his native land from the Turkish domination. His compatriots like to believe that for his services to the Greek cause he was decorated with the order of the Redeemer. But for many years he was the terror of the country and his native village suffered heavily from him, for he invaded it many times and burnt many houses including some of the best and richest. To this day the Vlach villages of the Zaghori say that Leonidha and Davelis

MAP I

NORTHERN PINDUS

Scale about 1:600.000

Vlach Villages thus ▲ SMIKSI
Kupatshari " " ◆ Mavranei
Valakhadhes · · ▲ Vriashteno

Former Greco-Turkish Frontier thus ·—··—·

THE TERRITORY OF SAMARINA, SKETCH MAP.

Scale about 1:200.000

were the causes of their ruin. The following song refers to one of his exploits in that region : —

When he was at Baieasa, Ho, Captain Leonidha ! he did a deed of daring with eleven men. Leonidha in the village, the Turk outside. He seizes a musket, Ho, Captain Leonidha ! he seizes a musket. O, for three long hours all the old men shout : " Ho Captain Leonidha, see that the Turkish braves do not burn our village ! " " Come my lads, let us depart, let us attack the Turk, let us take him alive, and let us attack him."

We have heard many accounts of his daring from his brothers and nephews and from an ex-brigand who served under him. In the continual skirmishes which he had with the pursuing detachments of Turkish troops he is said to have had a charmed life. Some attribute this to the fact that he carried upon him a piece of the True Cross. He never took cover, but walked proudly up and down the line of his men, and encouraged first one and then another, displaying his person to the Turks just as the Scots displayed theirs to King Edward I at Berwick. He even did not hesitate to raid towns where troops were stationed, as is evidenced by his attack on Hrupishta. His career closed in 1880 in the following manner. The Turks had arrested his mother and sister and taken them to Ghrevena where they held them as hostages hoping that Leonidha would submit. In the meantime the pursuit of his band continued and at last he was engaged in a life-and-death struggle on the hills between Blatsă and Shatishta. In the engagement Leonidha was mortally wounded and hidden by his men who could not take him with them. On their retreat he was found by the Turks and after a desperate resistance in which he cut down several of the enemy, he took his own life. His head was cut off, taken to Ghrevena and exposed in the market-place, and then his mother was brought to identify it. She to the general surprise denied that it was her son's head in order to hide her grief, but when she returned to her home she gave way to uncontrollable weeping. According to custom the Turkish authorities sent Leonidha's head to the Bishop of Ghrevena asking him to bury it. He however refused on the ground that he could not give christian burial

11

to a suicide. His death is celebrated by the following
song :—

> I need no mourning mother, I need no dirges. The mountains
> mourn for me ; the Vlach villages mourn for me ; night and dawn
> mourn for me, the stars and the moon ; the brides of the Hadzhi,
> the brides of Hadzhibira mourn for me. They were sitting at the
> window and were gently singing. They were asking all the travellers
> that passed by, " Perhaps you have seen our gallant son, Leonidhas
> himself ? " " Yesterday evening we saw him in the haunts of the
> klephts. They had lambs roasted, rams on the spit. They have
> slain Leonidhas, the first of the captains, who was the standard of the
> mountains and the banner of the klephts."

The Turkish version of the death of Leonidha has been
preserved by Sir Valentine Chirol. After six days' ceaseless
tracking a strong detachment of gendarmerie surrounded him
and his band in their lair and killed them to a man.

In almost every village throughout the country, which they
made their playground, the brigands had some friend or
relation who acted as their guide, philosopher and friend
and supplied them with food and information. This man
who is known as a *kulauz* (the Turkish *qilaghuz* guide) would
act as negotiator between the brigands and the authorities
if they wished to submit and obtain a free pardon. On the
other hand, if the authorities were determined to extirpate
the brigands, they would first attempt to arrest every such
kulauz, so that the brigands should have no means of obtaining
food and shelter. The following song relates to the death of
one Dhimitraki al Pazaiiti who acted as *kulauz* for Leonidha
near Dhiminitsa :—

> Have you heard what happens this week ? This week they slew
> Dhimitrakis. The poor fellow had gone to the village, high up to
> Dhiminitsa to fetch the musicians to go to Leonidhas. On the road
> where he was going, on the road where he goes he met three Turks
> at the church behind the trees. They give him three shots with their
> Martinis, the three in order. One grazes his skin, and the second hits
> him in the foot, and the third the fatal one takes him in the heart.

Leonidha was not of course the only brigand who infested
Southwestern Macedonia in those times. In October 1880
when some families from Samarina were going down to their

winter quarters near Elassona a dramatic incident took place, which is recorded in the following song :—

Birds of Ghrevena and nightingales of Komati when you go down to the Aghrapha and down into Greece, give the news to the klephts and to all the captains ; they have slain Karadzhas at desert Komati. He came out in front of the families to lay a tax upon them. He demanded a heavy tax, a dollar a mule. At first they speak him fair, so that he may let them go. " Sit down quietly Yiorghaki, sit down. The wine is drunk. Yesterday that dog Zhurkas stripped us, he took a hundred pounds and seventy capes." " Well did he treat you, and how shall I treat you ? " He demanded a heavy tax, a dollar a mule. When Dili Zisis heard this, he was very angry, and he seizes an axe, and buries it in his skull. Like a tree he splits, and like a cypress he falls : black birds wept for him, and white birds surrounded him.

The incidents to which this song refers are briefly as follows. One night when in camp on the road between Ghrevena and Dhiskata the families had been held up by a brigand called Zhurkas who was the leader of a large band. As the Samarina families were then on their way to their winter quarters at the end of the summer season after the fair at Konitsa they were well off for ready money. Zhurkas took all he could extract from them and seventy goat's-hair capes as well for his men. The next morning the families broke camp early as they were anxious to get through a difficult pass called Skara (the ladder) leading to Dhiskata, before any other brigands heard of their whereabouts. They had not gone far when they were again held up by Yeorghakis Karadzhas, a well-known and desperate brigand. He had only two men with him. He and one other came out into the narrow road and held up the long procession of mules, while the third stopped on the ridge above as though ready to signal to a large body in hiding. Karadzhas demanded that they should pay a dollar (according to another account five piastres) for each mule. In vain they entreated him to let them go in peace for Zhurkas had robbed them only the night before. Then a muleteer Zisi al Tshopa who had lost heavily the night before was seized with ungovernable rage, snatched up an axe and rushed against Karadzhas who was sitting with his rifle on his knees watching that none should pass without paying. With one blow he laid Karadzha low, and then backed by several others, who were fired by his example and snatched up knives and *furtutire* and any other weapon that was handy, attacked Karadzhas' companion Vasili. He attempted to escape, but was soon overtaken and hacked to pieces. The third who was watching on the ridge when he saw the fate of his comrades, made off with all speed. This tale which is actually true gives an excellent illustration of the state of the country in those years. It shows the daring impudence of the brigands, and the patience of the people till goaded to desperation. Karadzhas is said by some to have been a Kupatshar, by others to have been a Greek from Greece. A week or ten days before his death he had held up an earlier caravan of Samarina families in the Pade Mushată on the Morminde. This we have on the authority of a man who was present as a boy. He and other boys as usual when nearing a camping-place were going on ahead of the families, and running down from the col of Morminde to the Pade Mushată, and with them was a man with a rifle, to see if all was safe for the families. Suddenly Karadzhas and his two companions looked out from behind some trees and ordered hands up. The man was disarmed, bound and thrown into a ravine near by. The boy spectators of the scene were too frightened to give warning. Then as the families came down the narrow track in Indian file Karadzhas ordered them to halt and pay a dollar a mule. When the families at first refused he left his two men to watch, and went alone amongst the mules and began cutting the ropes and letting the loads fall. The families were then obliged to pay : our informant's family which had seven mules thus paid seven dollars. The families however too frightened to camp in the Pade Mushată after this, went down to the khan of Philippei. There they found a detachment of Turkish troops who immediately went in search of Karadzhas. They surprised him, as he and his companions were sitting round a fire dividing their spoil. Though they had no sentinel, yet the three brigands escaped, but with the loss of all their booty. A few days later Karadzhas and one of his comrades met their fate in holding up

a second caravan of Samarina families as related. They say
that when Karadzhas was killed he had his pet lamb with him—
the Vlachs in the summer delight in keeping pet lambs (Plate
XI 1), which they kill for the festival of the Assumption.
Karadzhas' lamb was captured, killed and eaten by the
triumphant Samariniats.

Another brigand Yeoryios Yioldhasis who haunted the
mountains of Samarina, was caught and shot by the Turks
near the village. His head was brought into Samarina and
hanged on the willow tree in the middle of *misohori*. His
death, which is alleged to have been brought about by
treachery, is recorded in this local song :—

Three little partridges were sitting on the crest of Zmolku. One
looks at Yannina, and another down towards Konitsa, and the third
the smallest looks at Samarina. Yeoryi get up from there, away with
you high up to the look-out post. The patrols have entrapped us,
they have taken our heads. In front they bring us bread, and behind
is the patrol.

In the summer of 1881 the Turkish government took active
measures against the brigands who were still at large. Eventually a major called Mukhtar Agha succeeded in inducing most
of them to submit. The principal brigands who agreed to
come in on the promise of a free pardon were Ghushu al Dhispuli,
nicknamed Makriyeni, because his beard reached to his knees,
and his lieutenant Simika, both of Samarina ; Makri of Perivoli,
the brothers Garelia of Briaza, and Gika an Albanian. In all
forty-seven are said to have submitted, and on hearing the
news the commandant of Yannina came up to Samarina with
a large force to receive their formal submission and to issue
the pardons. The events that followed are related in the two
following songs :—

Have you heard what happens this summer ? The klephts and all
the captains have submitted. The treacherous commandant deceived
them and misled them : he said to them, " Come here that I may
give you pardons." And they poor fellows were deceived, and were
shut up in his courtyard. The hour was six or seven about midday.
When Mukhtar Agha heard of it he was very angry.

The three Vlach villages have deceived me and betrayed me,
Avdhela, and Perivoli, and treacherous Samarina. My friends, my
fellow-countrymen, have betrayed me, the dogs, and said to me,

"Come leader, come and submit!" and they said to me, "Come, Ghushu, come and submit, submit to the Pasha in the house of Pāgātsā. They took us and they bound us, Albanian dogs! About evening they take us along the mountains, at dawn they bring us to Furka, they take us to Yannina. The Albanian dogs took us and hanged us.

What happened on the coming of the commandant to Samarina was this. All the brigands who had agreed to surrender were called into the village and formally submitted. They were in Samarina three days; then the commandant told them to come to his house after midday when the trumpet sounded. He was stopping in the big house of Pāgātsā on the ridge of Gudrumitsa which has a large courtyard in front of it (Plate XVI 1). He promised that he would then have their pardons ready so that they could go to their homes. The trumpet sounded soon after midday when nearly everybody was taking his midday siesta. Further as it was a festival, the day of St Elijah, the event was not likely to attract much notice in the village. When the unarmed brigands entered the courtyard of the house, troops entered from the other side, seized and bound them. Then for the next two days the forty-seven brigands bound were paraded about Samarina under escort as an object-lesson to the inhabitants. After that the commandant departed for Yannina taking the brigands with him. On the way at Furka he shot three of them, the brothers Garelia, and Gika. The rest were thrown into prison at Yannina where Makri of Perivoli and ten others died. After nineteen years the survivors were released on June 20th 1900 O.S., and came up to Samarina for the summer. In the autumn they went down into Greece. Dhispuli now (1911) serves as watchman at a chiftlik near Trikkala. His lieutenant Simika came to the Samarina district in 1903 as a brigand, was sentenced to ten years' penal servitude in Greece in 1904, and died in prison.

Other brigands of Samarina who flourished at the same time were Nak'i Pala, Nak'i Katărah'ia, and the three brothers Shkraku named Dzhima, Yeoryi and Zisi. These three latter together with Davelis, and the brothers Garelia plundered the village of Vísiani in the Zaghori on April 25th 1881 O.S., and took away five mule-loads of booty, and thirteen captives including a priest and eight women. The damage they did is said to have amounted to 5500 pounds Turkish. Some of the exploits of Katărah′ia have been chronicled by Sir Valentine Chirol. He was one of those who raided Hrupishta : he seems to have delighted in fiendish cruelty, and was for some time the terror of Upper Macedonia.

At the congress of Berlin and in the subsequent treaty in 1878 after the close of the Russo-Turkish war it was proposed that Thessaly and Epirus should be ceded to Greece. The Porte obstinately refused to hand over the provinces in question, and a conference was summoned at Constantinople in 1881 which finally persuaded the Ottoman government to cede the greater part of Thessaly, and the province of Arta. In the interval the Vlachs of Pindus disturbed by the proposed partition of their country sent in a petition to the Great Powers asking that either less or more territory should be ceded to Greece, so that whatever happened they would not be divided between two states. Samarina joined in this petition which is said to have contained fourteen thousand signatures. The prospect of the division of the country inhabited in winter and summer by the people of Samarina was of course a matter of the greatest moment.

If we consider for a moment the distribution of the Samarina families in the winter it will easily appear how the eventual cession of Thessaly to the kingdom of Greece in 1881 affected the fortunes of Samarina. For all those who were accustomed to winter round about Larissa, Tirnavos, Trikkala, Kalabaka and Kardhitsa it meant the erection of a customs barrier between their winter quarters and their summer homes. Many decided to settle permanently in the towns of Thessaly, and become Hellenic subjects. Others, while still remaining Turkish subjects, were afraid to go up to Samarina for the summer. The houses of those who no longer came up for the summer remained tenantless year in and year out. In course of time the severity of the winters and the lack of repairs caused many of them to fall into ruin. Thus we may say that the political events of 1881 coupled

with the lack of public safety in Southwest Macedonia produced what we may call a dispersion of Samarina, from which
it only recently began to recover. At this time many of
the shepherds gave up sheep rearing and took to other trades,
and many others too wandered away in search of work and
never returned to their native village. In 1886 troubles
between Greece and Turkey broke out again and there was
great danger of war. As Samarina was close to the new
frontier, war was likely to affect the village seriously. Consequently most of those who were wintering in Thessaly decided at the suggestion of Zisi al Dzhimuzhoga, the principal
sheep owner of Samarina, not to go up to their home for the
summer, but to stay in Thessaly or go up into the Thessalian
hills. As a result the village was almost deserted that year, and
the next summer too not many families went up for the season.
Like other historical events this was celebrated by a song :—

Firs of Zmolku, pines of Samarina, do not open your buds this
year ; wither up this year. The Vlachs have not appeared to us from
the midst of Greece. Some have gone to the Aghrapha, and some to
Renda, most have gone to Slitshani, none will remain, and some have
stayed in the plains, down in the plains. Curse on the cause, Zisis
Dzhimuzhogas ; he is the cause, he was the reason. He brought misery
on the people and all the Vlach villages. Girls still remain unmarried
and young men betrothed.

The last line refers to a Vlach custom, peculiar to the
nomad villages about which more is said above. As a rule
betrothals take place about the festival of the Assumption,
when most folk are in Samarina, and the weddings take place
the following year at the same time. If the families for any
reason did not come up to their native village for the summer,
no weddings could be celebrated, for the would-be brides and
bridegrooms would be widely separated.

Similarly the war of 1897 between Greece and Turkey
which took place in the spring affected Samarina. Many
families fled southwards before the Turkish advance, and
consequently either went up to Samarina late or else did not
go up at all. This of course only applies to families in the
habit of wintering in Greek territory. One shepherd told us

that when the Turks advanced into Thessaly he retired before
them with his flocks into the hills round Rendina. As the
war was not over by the time he wanted to go up to the mountains for the summer he took his flocks for that season into
the Peloponnese where he pastured on Mt. Khelmos in Achaia.
But as the war was soon over and the Turkish troops were not
followed by Albanian irregulars to the same extent as on
former occasions, the effect of the war on Samarina was slight
compared with the damage wrought by the risings of 1854
and 1878. This war is also recorded by a local song :—

Bitter has the spring come upon us, black the summer. Do you
not mourn villages, and hamlets, and provinces ? What is the evil that
happens this summer ? This year there will be war, Greece with Turkey.
It was one Friday evening, Saturday was the day of Lazarus. And the
Turks conquered, they took Thessaly. Edem Pasha came down from
the midst of the Meluna, he awakes at Tirnavos, he lunches in Larissa.
It happened that the day was Easter with the cry of " Christ is risen ! "
He finds the eggs all red, and the rams ready spitted, and he sweeps
the villages as far as Velestinos.

It is said that during the war some Vlachs offered their
services as volunteers to the Turkish authorities, but they
were not accepted. Any native of Samarina who took part
in the war fought on the Greek side. During the negotiations
for peace a petition was presented to the Great Powers asking
that the northern part of Thessaly at least should be given
back to the Ottoman Empire, but this time Samarina had no
concern with such petitions. The bulk of the population of
Samarina, then as now, is in politics Greek. But it is possible
that some adherents of the Roumanian party in the village
signed the petition. In Samarina as in most Vlach villages
there are two political parties the Greeks and the Roumanians,
though all are by nationality Vlachs. In Samarina from time
immemorial the Greek party has been dominant from its close
connection with the church, the language of which is Greek.
Similarly the earliest schools founded in Samarina were those
started under the auspices of the church. Consequently the
natural political tendency of the inhabitants was towards
Greece, and this was greatly strengthened by the cession of

Thessaly. Samarina was brought nearer the Græco-Turkish frontier, and about half the population of the village were wintering in what became Greek territory. To this must be added the natural attraction of christian subjects of the Ottoman Empire towards the nearest christian state.

Although it was not till 1905 that the Sublime Porte officially recognised the Vlachs as a separate nationality and thus placed them on an equal footing with the Greeks, Bulgarians and Servians, the Roumanian community at Samarina had been recognised by the Turkish provincial authorities in 1895. The Roumanian school in the village was started in 1879 and has continued to exist ever since. When it was first opened it was exceedingly popular and is said to have reached an attendance of about two hundred. However the intervention of the Bishop of Ghrevena in the interests of Greek soon checked this promising beginning and since then the numbers attending the Roumanian school do not seem ever to have exceeded fifty, while the Greek school can count on two hundred or more. During the years when Greek bands were sent into Macedonia to destroy the Roumanian propaganda by burning schools and killing schoolmasters, many of the Roumanian party at Samarina went over to the Greek side, but no murders occurred in the village as happened elsewhere. On one occasion after the Avdhela murders in July 1905 O.S. the Greek band that had committed them proposed to go on to Samarina to kill some of the prominent Roumanians. A strong detachment of Turkish troops happened to visit Samarina at the time, and the band could not enter the village until they had departed. On their eventual entrance however the Greek party at Samarina took up a determined attitude and greatly to their lasting credit declared they would have no killing.

From the proclamation of the Ottoman constitution in 1908 till 1912 Samarina enjoyed peace, and once again commenced to grow larger. The improved political conditions induced many who had not seen their native village for many a long year to go up again for the summer. One result of this was that many new houses were built and several ruinous ones restored. Then too there was a growing movement visible in the village in favour of families wintering there, while the fathers and young men went down to work in the towns of the plains. Emigration to America, which first began about 1900, was also responsible for an increase in prosperity. It is said that there are as many as five hundred young men of Samarina working in America and most of them send regular remittances home. They go to work for the most part in the cotton and boot factories in Lowell, Mass., and in Manchester and Nashua, N.H. After 1908 the emigration of the young men was unconsciously encouraged by the Ottoman constitution under which all christians were liable to serve in the Turkish army. Consequently the young men of Samarina would get away to America before the time came when they were liable to be called up for military service for the benefit of the Turk.

The events in the Balkans in 1912–13 have of necessity affected the future of Samarina and what time may bring forth one cannot tell. But no one who has visited the village can fail to wish that it may flourish and prosper.

CHAPTER IX

THE VLACH VILLAGES NEAR SAMARINA

Νισεῖς βουνὰ ἀπ' τὰ Γριβινὰ κὶ πεῦκα ἀπ' τοῦ Μιτσόβου !

Ye Mountains of Ghrevena and Ye Pines of Metsovo !

The Ballad of Zhakas

SAMARINA is the largest and to-day the most flourishing of a group of Vlach villages along the range of Pindus and a brief account of these will help the reader to realise the position of the Pindus Vlachs as a whole. From Samarina to Smiksi the next village to the south on the eastern slope of the range is a journey of three hours. We follow the Ghrevena road as far as the Morminde and thence diverge along the side of Ghumara past the Pade Mushată. Then after crossing the crest of a small ridge running out at right angles to the east from the base of Ghumara we descend into the head of a small valley. Smiksi is a picturesque village of about a hundred houses and, as it lies in the hollow at the head of the valley, is not seen till close at hand. It is less exposed than Samarina and so is reported to be airless and relaxing, but despite this its inhabitants invariably winter in the plains about Elassona and Larissa. Smiksi was not always an entirely nomad village, for as at Samarina some of the inhabitants once lived there permanently and devoted themselves to agriculture. They say that lower down in the valley at a place called Biga, there was once an agricultural village. The people of this joined with others from elsewhere and founded Smiksi which was at first rather higher up the hill side than it is to-day. The small stream by which the site of Biga lies eventually joins the main river by the khan of Philippei. It is a wide, grassy valley and the slopes are dotted with pines, but there stands alone in the bottom of the valley one tall pine, which is called the tree of Ayios Kosmas.   They say that when he visited Smiksi the tree was small and that he blessed it and fastened a wooden cross to its top.   The tree in the years that have passed since then has grown very tall, but the cross is still there, fastened to its top, to bear witness to the truth of the tale.   The houses in Smiksi are neatly kept, but small in size except a few which are as so often happens the product of emigration or successful brigandage.   The village as a whole when compared with its neighbours is somewhat lacking in character and is over-shadowed by Samarina and Avdhela, largely through its small size and consequent lack of any prominent industry. In one respect however it is to be envied, for it has kept clear of political quarrels.   Vlach is the only spoken language except in the church, but the dialect contains many Greek words for the inhabitants nearly all winter in Greek districts. As to trade it may be said that the people of Smiksi practise the same as Samarina, but to a less extent ; the two principal trades are those of shepherd and muleteer.   From the village a difficult track leads over the shoulder of Ghumara to Briaza and the Aous valley, and another following the eastern side of the main range of Pindus leads to Avdhela, which is about two and a half hours away.

If Smiksi tends to be small and featureless, Avdhela is the reverse and has a definite character of its own.   It has large forests, chiefly of pine and most of its wealth in conse-quence depends on the trade in timber.   Planks from the Avdhela saw mills are taken down regularly by Vlach mule-teers to the districts of Ghrevena and Kozhani, and North Thessaly.   The lack of historical documents of any kind and the vagueness of local tradition makes a detailed history of the village quite impossible, but the following perhaps may be taken as including the main points in its development. Its origin is attributed to several Vlach shepherds who for the sake of greater security joined their various family camps into one.   No one pretends to know the date when this hap-pened, but there is a general idea that it was some two hundred years ago. The positions occupied by the hut encampments of the different groups of shepherd families, before their union into one village, are still pointed out in the immediate neighbourhood and are known by the following names, Boboania, Sardhimiu, G'oni, Broti and Guguleka, which are said to have been those of the original founders. As far as we know however such family names do not exist in Avdhela to-day. By the beginning of the nineteenth century the village must have been of some size, for about that time thanks to Albanian raids and the government of Ali Pasha a group of Avdheliat shepherd families under the leadership of Badraleksi migrated to the hills above Verria and settled there. Besides these other families left their homes in Pindus and settled elsewhere and apparently about the same period the practice of the whole village leaving their home for winter, instead of only the shepherds and a few families, began to increase. Lack of safety in the first instance probably induced whole families to move and the same reason would make many of them settle more or less permanently in the towns of the plains. This in fact can be seen to-day, when many brigands are known to be out the number of families which venture up to their summer homes is appreciably fewer, and as soon as conditions become better the number increases and some will begin to stay in the hills the whole year through. In Macedonia and Epirus the hills are a refuge and protection against the government, but the plains and towns against private and political brigands. The principal places whither the Avdheliat families go to winter are Ghrevena, Elassona and Dhamasi, and Tshoti, Zarkos and Ghrizhano in the Peneus valley between Trikkala and Larissa. But compared with Samarina and Perivoli the number of Avdheliat families in Thessaly is small, for most of the Avdhela emigrants have gone to the hills of Verria. Consequently except for the timber trade the cession of Thessaly to Greece in 1881 affected Avdhela less than Samarina. Latterly the political troubles between 1903 and 1908 have done serious harm to the village, for Avdhela like its colonists in the hills of Verria is strongly nationalist. In 1905 a party of nationalist families on their way from Ghrevena to Avdhela for the summer was attacked on the road by Greek bands and, in spite of a strong escort of Turkish soldiers, was scattered and plundered, several of the troops and Avdheliats being killed.   Later in the same year a political band from Greece raided the village, killed some of the nationalist leaders and fired some of the houses.   In the conflagration the principal church then used by the nationalists was burnt, whether intentionally is not known for certain.   After 1908 when affairs were for a time quieter many families returned and the village began to increase, a circumstance which was especially due to the inflow of money from America, but by 1911 only a portion of the destruction wrought by the Greeks had been repaired.

In appearance Avdhela is a typical Vlach village standing on the side of a hill, and contains about three hundred and fifty houses, most of which stand in a small garden.   There are several churches in the village, but none are of any great age or of any interest except the big church that was burnt.   The oldest is dated to 1751 or perhaps 1721, for the lettering is not clear, and a slab on the wall of the burnt one records its erection by Greek masons from Zhupan.   There are two schools in the village, one Greek and one Roumanian, and at the time of our last visit in 1911 the latter had by far the best attendance.   The boast of Avdhela in recent years has been its great success in education, for in this point the Roumanian schools have an advantage over the Greek in using a script which is of more than strictly local use.   Further not so much time is wasted in teaching ancient history which is the great curse of nearly all Greek village education.

Not much over an hour from Avdhela is Perivoli, situated like its neighbour on the slope of Pindus, but in a more exposed position.   In situation, appearance and history the two villages are very similar.   Perivoli according to tradition was founded some two hundred years ago by the union of three villages, Bithultsi, Karitsa and Baietan.   At first the united village was not on the site of the modern Perivoli, but lower down the valley by the monastery of Ayiu Nikola where the inhabitants cultivated corn fields and vineyards.   When the village was moved up the hill is apparently not known. Like Avdhela and Samarina it was formerly more prosperous than it is now. It suffered from the rule of Ali Pasha, and the cession of Thessaly made a great difference to it because a large number of Perivoliats winter in Thessaly. After the cession of Thessaly in 1881 many of these settled permanently in the towns, but apparently a little time before this there had been some emigration from Perivoli. One of the great trades of the village was that of shepherd and the number of sheep owned by the village increased enormously up to 1877, so much so that the pasture land of Perivoli could carry no more sheep. Then some of the shepherds had to find fresh pasture grounds for the summer, and in consequence of this a large number of Perivoli people, who wintered at Toivash and in the plain to the east of Larissa, started a summer village of their own at Istok on the hills between Resna and Okhridha. This Toivash-Istok colony of Perivoli numbers about two hundred families, and another hundred families are settled at Alli Meria and elsewhere near Ano-Volos. But the great wintering-place for Perivoli folk is Velestinos and the villages near it such as Taktalasmán, Dedhéryianni and Khatsóbasi where there are said to be at least about four hundred families some of which are permanently settled there. Trikkala, which might be called the Vlach metropolis, contains about two hundred Perivoli families and these go for the summer to a place called Koromilia in the hills above Kalabaka. Thus it will be seen that the village was once much larger than it is to-day. Tradition says that the upper part of the village where the ruins of houses can be seen was thick with habitations which reached as far as the edge of the *pade* on the top of the slope above. This open green which possesses a fine spring of cold water is the place where the great village dances are held every year at the festival of Sāndă Vineri as the Perivoliats usually call their patron saint. The feature of the village is its *misohori* or square which like the pine tree on the church at Samarina is the envy of its neighbours. It is a wide terrace partly natural and partly built up on the sloping hill side and on three sides has shops or houses, the latter tower-like buildings several stories high. On the fourth side the ground falls away sharply and leaves an unbroken view over the lower part of Perivoli and line after line of wooded hills rising above the valley, at the head of which the village stands. A few large plane trees for shade, a spring near at hand and a seat along the terrace edge make this *misohori* the obvious centre for Perivoliat rank and fashion. On an extension of the *misohori* to the north-west stands the principal church, at the east end of which there is another small terrace well shaded with plane trees and affording good opportunities for quiet talk on hot days. Beyond the church are the two schools, Greek and Roumanian which divide the juvenile population of the village between them. The territories of Perivoli which exceed those of any other Pindus village, are mostly covered with thick forests of pines. Timber and wood cutting coupled with sheep-rearing are the chief trades, but in recent years emigration has increased and it is on money made in America that Perivoli now mainly depends. On the far side of Mount Ou or Mount Egg, which takes its name from the peculiarly shaped rock on its summit, is a deep wooded ravine rejoicing in a trout stream that runs down to join the Aous near Baieasa. This is the famous Vale Kaldă the sure refuge of brigands and the pride of the whole land of Perivoli. Tradition records that the metal workings here are those of the Romans who also fought a battle in this valley in days gone by. That fighting occurred here is probable from the modern reputation of the valley which affords a short cut across the mountain of Perivoli and might be of strategic importance, but we know of no reason for assigning either the fighting or the metal workings to the Romans. The Vale Kaldă, which the state of the country did not allow us to visit, would certainly be worth investigation, for even if the tales about its history are inaccurate, its scenery and its trout would repay the traveller. The costume of Perivoli is the same as at Samarina and the national dress is more worn than at Avdhela. But the Perivoli type is shorter in the skirts, for the *tsipune* and the kilted shirt stop above the knees, and the whole costume is less ornate.

12

Samarina, Smiksi, Avdhela and Perivoli are the only villages in Pindus where nearly all the population migrates each winter to the plains, and for this very reason form a group by themselves and have many points in common. The effects of their annual migrations are various. They promote a wider outlook on life in general in contrast to the utter stagnation normal in remote villages, and they also do much towards keeping alive a strong local patriotism. On the other hand the yearly changes are a serious financial drain, for they involve the upkeep of two houses apart from the expenses of transit ; but what is lost in cash is perhaps gained in health by a summer in the hills. The mode of life is affected chiefly in the following ways. Agriculture is almost impossible and is in consequence despised. Home comforts to be of any use must be portable and so an abundance of rugs, blankets, carpets and cushions is a sign of wealth. Local opinion in valuing the four villages always places Samarina first, as it is by far the largest having eight hundred houses to about four hundred at Perivoli. Though all have good water that of Samarina is the coldest, and the climate in summer is cooler and so better. Then it has an annual festival that lasts for a week, it has more pastry-cooks, it consumes more wine and finally there is the famous pine tree growing on the roof of Great St Mary's to prove the truth of the local proverb "*Dumnidzeu easte Sărmăn'atŭ.*" "God is a Samariniat" and so bestows his favours on his native village. As to which village ranks next there is some dispute ; Avdhela would plead education, Perivoli its forests, its village square, and its mountain. Smiksi—happy is the place that has no politics and no ambitions—is content to come last among the four villages all of which consider themselves vastly superior to their neighbours. They carry this attitude so far that they will very rarely marry outside themselves, and not often with one another. Of the four, intermarriage between Avdhela and Perivoli is the commoner ; Smiksi, which used to go more with Avdhela, has latterly owing to its political sympathies inclined more towards Samarina. Samarina as regards intermarriage makes an exception in favour of Furka, and the only other villages admitted into the circle are Turia and Baieasa. As to the morals of the four local cynics give their verdict thus. Smiksiats kill through hatred; Avdheliats rob by guile—is this the result of education?—; Perivoliats rob by force; Samariniats are skilful and successful liars. This estimate is probably libellous, but need not for that reason be entirely untrue.

Between Perivoli and Turia the next important village to the south there is little to be noticed. We leave Perivoli by the main track to Ghrevena which we follow down the valley as far as the monastery of St Nicholas. Here according to several accounts services in Roumanian instead of Greek were held as far back as 1867, but the building is now in ruins and was used some few years ago by a band of brigands lying in wait for the Perivoliat families on their way home in the spring. Just beyond the monastery we turn southwards through some of the finest of the Perivoli woods and passing a few saw mills after some two hours' walking cross a steep ridge and emerge by the poverty-stricken hamlet of Labanitsa. Labanitsa possesses some vineyards and a few fields of hay and maize is situated in an open valley which under more favourable circumstances should be capable of successful cultivation. The soil is good and deep, there is abundance of water and the hills around are well timbered. Despite these natural advantages the village is in a poor condition; the houses are in a state of decay and its inhabitants exist rather than live. The people of Labanitsa are Kupatshari, who have been described in an earlier chapter.

Hence up the valley to Turia is a short three hours through country very pleasant to look upon. Turia or as the Greeks call it Krania is a good-looking and prosperous village considering its position near the old Græco-Turkish frontier and on the high road between Yannina and Ghrevena. It lies at the foot of a group of hills adjoining the Pindus range to the northeast of Metsovo and the stream that runs through it is a tributary of the Venetiko. The meaning of Turia the Vlach name of the village is, as far as we can tell, unknown. Krania the Greek name means cornel tree, and arose from the following circumstance. A large cornel tree used to stand just outside the village by the khan on the Ghrevena-Metsovo road, and, as this was a favourite halting-place for muleteers, it became widely known and eventually gave its name to the village. Being considerably lower than either Perivoli or Avdhela Turia is inhabited all the year round.   It owns several cornfields and vineyards, although some of them have been abandoned through the political troubles of recent years.   Near the village are one or two mills ; the hills give good pasturage for sheep ; and on the south side of Mount Ou there are several saw mills. The Turia Vlachs, unlike those in most of the higher villages, cultivate their fields themselves instead of employing Greek, Turkish or Bulgar labourers.   Nearly every house stands in its own garden which is full of vegetables and flowers ; thus the village, which is divided into several parishes, covers a large area for its population of about two thousand souls. There are seven churches, the largest of which built in 1790 stands in the centre of the village close to a huge plane tree. The other six are on the outskirts of the village or else a short distance outside it.   This is the usual position for churches in Macedonian villages and is probably due to a law in force at least in the vilayets of Yannina and Monastir as late as the middle of the nineteenth century, which enacted that no church might be built within the village area.   Local tradition how-ever has a more romantic explanation for the position of the Turia churches.   All so they say, stand on the original village boundary which was marked out some two hundred years ago by a pair of black oxen yoked to a plough.   When the boundary was thus determined they were buried alive with the plough on the spot where the church of St Elijah now stands.   This tale is highly suspicious, the more so since it comes from a village which would delight in proving a Roman ancestry. Still suspicious though the tale is, it does not however seem to be an invention of the last few years, for it is known better by the older generation than by the younger.   Pouqueville, who gives no authority for his statement, says that the village was founded in 1507.   Local tradition says that round about where Turia now stands were four hamlets, Nturia, Akornu—*kornu* is the Vlach for a cornel—Kāldǎroshǎ and Kodru Mare which about two hundred years ago came together to found the existing village. Leake in the early years of the nineteenth century stayed a night at Turia and describes it as consisting of fifty neat cottages, and having an appearance of comfort and successful industry seldom seen in Greek or Turkish villages ; " unhappily " for these poor Vlakhiotes " he adds, " their village has lately become one of Aly Pasha's tjiftliks." Since then Turia has increased and prospered and is now a free village. Its recent history is the tale of the struggle of rival propagandas. In 1884 a Roumanian school was started—there had previously been only a Greek school—owing to local enterprise and the nationalist Vlach party grew rapidly in numbers. The strength of the nationalists was principally due to the fact that they found an efficient leader in Dimitri Tshikmă, a man of energy and organising ability. In the dark years between 1905 and 1908 his life was more than once attempted by Greek bands, but he always escaped though once severely wounded. In the autumn of 1912 he was killed when the Greeks occupied the district. When force was employed to stop the nationalist movement he saw to it that the bands that came against his home got more than they gave. He enlisted the services of the Skumbra family, three brothers, Farsherot Vlachs and skilled brigands who settled at Turia. Just before the war of 1912 six out of the seven churches were in the hands of the nationalist party and their school was flourishing. This proportion of six to one, although the Greek party was small, exaggerates the difference in size between the two sides, and at Turia the Greek propaganda and schools have suffered at the hands of the nationalists. Elsewhere almost without exception, the reverse is the case, which shows what a great difference one energetic leader makes in spreading a propaganda. Amongst the neighbouring villages Turia has acquired some reputation for its dances which in summer are held nearly every Sunday as well as on festivals. They even go so far as to keep gipsy musicians in the village most of the summer. To the stranger however the dances show no peculiar characteristics and have no features that cannot be seen as well or better elsewhere.

A short distance to the west of Turia the road from Ghrevena to Metsovo and Yannina enters the foothills of Pindus by the narrow and wooded gorge of the river of Milia. An hour and a half from Turia and some four hours short of Metsovo the pass opens out into a small upland valley. Here on a knoll above a few well-watered meadows is the small Vlach village of Ameru, which the Greeks call Milia, locally known to fame for the excellence of its roast lamb and its yiaurti. Although it is situated half-way between Turia and Metsovo the centres of rival propagandas, Ameru inclines towards the wealth and strength of Metsovo. Vlach is the language of the village, and the men all know Greek as well, but how far this language is known by the women we cannot say. It is quite probable that some of the older women know no word of Greek. In the village itself there is little or nothing of interest ; the church is a large barn-like building dating from 1754 and so somewhat older than most. The neighbourhood is too un-settled for trade, except the inevitable ones of timber cutting, wool working, sheep rearing and muleteering. The village is too small to do much business and many have emigrated to find work in Constantinople, America, Australia, Roumania and New Zealand. From Turia to Ameru the road is good, but from Ameru to Metsovo it is little more than a rough track, although in places it shews signs of having once been a cobbled way.

The position of Metsovo or Amintshu, as its inhabitants the Vlachs call it, on the great pass through Pindus over the ridge of the Zighos, has been described so often that we may pass on at once to some account of the village itself. Under the Turks Metsovo was the seat of a kaimmakam and had a small permanent garrison lodged in a tumbledown castle of no great size that stood on a knoll in the centre of the town. The town or rather village, for its present cóndition scarcely warrants the former title, consists of two parts one on either side of a deep ravine. The larger and more important portion which faces south is called Serinu (Sunny, the Latin *serenus*) or in Greek Prosilion, and the smaller which is situated on the lower slopes of Peristeri and has a northern aspect is known as

Nkiare, Sunset, or in Greek Anilion.   Though both parts are included under the name of Metsovo or Amintshu, yet the latter names are as a rule restricted to Serinu, and Nkiare is regarded as a separate village.   In many old accounts of the size of Metsovo it is often left uncertain whether Nkiare is included or not.   At present both divisions in all probability do not contain more than six hundred houses in all, of which the large majority and all the important public buildings are in Serinu.   Metsovo presents the curious anomaly of a worn-out village which is still or at least up to the war of 1912 was still decaying, but which nevertheless possesses a group of public buildings far and away superior to those of any of its more prosperous neighbours.   These are all due to the generosity of a number of its sons and in particular to George Averoff. Averoff, by birth a Vlach, by name a Slav and by education and preference a Greek, was a native of Metsovo.   Leaving his native village in early youth he had a brilliant business career and amassed a large fortune.   Having been born at a time when all local education was entirely Greek and due to Greek initiative and progress, Greece naturally became his adopted country.   He rebuilt the stadium at Athens in marble and together with some other natives of Metsovo the Historical and Ethnological Museum at Athens.   The Greek cruiser that bears his name, the only modern ship in the Greek navy, was bought through his munificence.   In his gifts to Greece his native village was not forgotten.   A large school was erected and endowed ; a public garden was laid out ; and a large sum of money was left on trust that its income should be used for the improvement of Metsovo.   One result of the Averoff benefactions has been to make Metsovo more Greek than Vlach.   At the present day Vlach though still the mother tongue is looked upon with disfavour and vigorous efforts were made to suppress a small Vlach school which was patronised by a few families.   Whenever a stranger appears Metsovo does its best to disguise its Vlach origin, and pretends to be purely Greek.   An interesting paper by a Greek doctor, Mr. Spiridhon Sokolis, who practised there in 1861 shews how great a change has taken place in this respect in recent years.

At that time with only a few exceptions none of the women or the boys up to the age of ten knew Greek at all, so that Mr. Sokolis had to employ an interpreter. The men however could speak Greek freely as it was an essential language for commerce.

Despite its school, its buildings and the Averoff trust Metsovo is far from being a flourishing town. It has little trade, there is no prosperous local industry and its flocks and herds are few. The women work wool to some extent and recently were learning to weave carpets. The majority of the men go to find work abroad and many of them are prosperous merchants in Greece or in other parts of the Levant, but they have mostly severed all connection with their original homes. The rest, nearly all in fact who keep up any connection with Metsovo, are small shopkeepers, smiths or wandering masons, carpenters or wood carvers. We have already commented on the fact that the Vlachs of Metsovo are masons, this is probably due to its having been a settled town when most of the other villages were still collections of temporary huts. Vlach carpenters considering how much of the timber trade is in Vlach hands are few in number and deficient in skill. Wood carving as a craft seems peculiar to Metsovo and is only practised by a few who wander from place to place in search of work. The strong similarity that exists between the carved screens in the churches of Pindus—some are almost identical —suggests that all are due to the same school of carvers. It is just possible therefore that they may be largely of Metsovite origin, but this is mere conjecture and as far as we know is unsupported by local tradition, although they say that the elaborate ceilings still to be seen in some of the older houses in Yaninna, that date from the times of Ali Pasha, are the work of craftsmen from Metsovo.

The early history and origin of Metsovo is most obscure and no connected account is possible, but we give the following notes and anecdotes for what they are worth. In 1380 Thomas, despot of Epirus, seized and extorted money from a certain Isaiah of Metsovo whom the Chronicle of Epirus describes as ὁ Τιμιώτατος ἐν ἱερομονάχοις and Καθηγούμενος τοῦ Μετζόβου. The same document has many references to the Vlachs of Pindus, especially the Malakasians, a name which then seems to have extended as far as the Zaghori and perhaps included Metsovo as well, though there is no other mention of the town itself. It is not clear whether Metsovo was then in existence as a permanent settlement or not, but by the fifteenth century it was occupied by a group of Vlach families who were in the habit of wintering in Thessaly at Neokhori or Ghrizhano. The following explanation as to how this nomad village came to obtain privileges from the Sublime Porte and so prospered and grew, is given by Aravandinos and Lambridhis, whose accounts differ slightly in details.   If the tale is true, then it fully exemplifies the proverb that sober truth is stranger than fiction.   In the year 1656 a Vizier fell under the displeasure of Sultan Mohammed the fourth and was in consequence banished to Kastoria.   Even there the wrath of his master pursued him and he was sentenced to death.   However the Vizier heard of his master's intentions in good time and so took to flight.   In his wanderings he took refuge in the house of a priest at Ghrizhano and there he met a certain Vlach of Metsovo, Steryiu or K'iriu Floka.   Floka dressed the Vizier in Vlach clothes, befriended him and concealed him at Metsovo. In the due course of time it came to pass that the Sultan repented and pardoned the Vizier who returned to Con-stantinople and became Grand Vizier.   He did not forget Floka and sending for him asked what he desired for himself and his native village which had sheltered him in his distress. Whereupon Floka asked for various privileges for Metsovo, to wit, a partial remission of taxation, special grazing rights and the wardenship of the pass.   All these were granted and extended also to the adjacent Vlach villages of Malakasi, Kutsufliani, Ameru and Vutunoshi.   In this way Metsovo from being a group of huts became a privileged town and as such attracted Vlachs from all parts, for it offered them safety and through its position on the pass excellent opportunities for trade.   Whatever the truth of the tale of Floka it is a fact that special privileges were enjoyed by Metsovo up to the time of Ali Pasha, but they seem to have been due to the fact that the district was directly under the Valide Sultan and so not subject to the various extortions of each local pasha in turn. Moreover towns on passes often receive preferential treatment, especially when they are largely composed of muleteers, a class which it is to no one's interest to oppress.

Though we cannot accept the romantic history of Aravandinos and Lambridhis, for it seems that the Vlach districts had been under the protection of the Valide Sultan ever since the Turkish conquest in the sixteenth century, yet it does seem to be true that it was in the seventeenth century that Metsovo first began to prosper. Lambridhis says that in 1735 it had 379 houses, early in the nineteenth century 700, and by 1880 about 835 houses. Leake who was twice here in 1805 says that on the second occasion he was lodged at Anilio " in a neat Vlahkiote cottage which has a plastered floor and walls and an air of comfort unknown in the houses of the Greek peasants." Holland who travelled in 1812 and 1813 estimates the number of houses at fifteen hundred, which is probably an exaggeration, and Bowen in 1850 speaks of it as a large Wallachian village with about a thousand houses. Local tradition gives an estimate of nine hundred to a thousand houses up to 1854 ; since then the village has steadily declined, and in 1911 the total number of houses both in Serinu and Nkiare did not exceed eight hundred. It was in the eighteenth and the early part of the nineteenth century that Metsovo flourished and possessed an important foreign trade. It is said that from 1719 there was a French commercial agency at Metsovo concerned mainly with the export trade. Metsovo merchants had business houses in Venice, Naples, Trieste, Marseilles, Vienna, Moscow, Odessa, Constantinople, Salonica, Seres and Alexandria. Woollen goods and thick goat's-hair capes or cloaks were the principal objects of this export trade, though cheese also played a considerable part. The cheese trade alone still continues, and *kash kaval* is manufactured near Metsovo and exported to Italy. Local accounts confirm the existence of this extensive foreign trade, but add little or nothing to our knowledge of its details. Native industries and home trade prospered at the same time. Pewter plates and dishes were a local manufacture and a few are still to be seen to-day in the village. Woollen rugs and carpets with ornate designs were in demand locally and this weaving industry has recently been revived. A large carrying trade over the Zighos and along the Ghrevena road added to the importance of the town, and in return for giving hospitality to officials and distinguished strangers Metsovo was excused all taxes but the poll tax. This arrangement did not necessarily mean that the village gained much, because the inhabitants had to support a detachment of armatoli to safeguard the pass. The decline of Metsovo began in the time of Ali Pasha of Yannina who succeeded in getting the town into his hands and in setting its privileges at naught. Leake, Pouqueville and others writing about this time describe the rapid increase in brigandage and taxation which seriously injured all trade. Then came the Greek revolution of 1821 which laid all wealthy christian villages open to suspicion and plunder, and about the same time the invention of the power-loom in the west of Europe fatally injured the woollen trade.

Any prosperity that remained was finally extinguished by the so-called revolution or un-official war of 1854. The Russian attack on the northern provinces of Turkey in Europe had provoked the most sanguine hopes in Greece, and it was generally believed that with the appearance of Greek forces across the frontier, Epirus and Thessaly would rise at once against the Turks. Officially the Greek government kept the peace, but unofficially it encouraged the sending of bands over the frontier to stir up insurrection. As happened in the case of Samarina and its neighbours the main result of this movement, which was a curious mixture of patriotism and plunder, was that those who were to be freed from Turkish tyranny found themselves pillaged by both sides. During the few months, for which this rising lasted, Metsovo like other towns and villages in Epirus, and Thessaly suffered heavy losses. The town had been incited to revolt by the Greek consul at Yannina and became the prey of both sides in turn. Ghrivas the most prominent of the Greek leaders occupied it and levied 150,000 piastres from the inhabitants. On the approach of

the Turkish troops he assembled the women and children in a
church on the pretext of defending them, but, when he once had
them safely inside, stripped them of all their jewellery and
valuables. He then retired to the most easily defensible
part of the town, but when the Turks began to attack, retired
burning some thirty houses to cover his retreat. Abdi Pasha
entered Metsovo and what had been left by Ghrivas was taken
by the Albanian irregulars. In all about a third of the village
was destroyed and the rest reduced to a condition of the utmost
misery. To this account taken almost word for word from the
Parliamentary Papers we may add an extract from a letter of
Ghrivas himself which may to some extent shift the blame from
the leader to his followers.

" After a battle of historic fame at Metsovo, of which I sent
you the description and plan to-day, seeing the greatest con-
spiracies and treacheries existing against me on the part of my
companions in arms I was compelled to retreat thence and to
take the direction of Thessaly. . . . Whilst in Epirus I beheld so
many of our soldiers indulging in every sort of violence, I was
compelled to dismiss them and now I have about four hundred
chosen men. Were I to tell you all the atrocities which had
been committed against the property and honour of the
christian population by our soldiers both in Epirus and Thessaly
you would be struck with horror and would curse the hour in
which this new struggle had first begun."

Even before the district had been cleared of Greek troops
Metsovo and other christian villages were appealing to the
Turks for aid. The troubles of 1878 and 1881 did not affect
Metsovo so much except that the brigandage that followed the
rising made the country generally unhealthy for trade. But
after the cession of Thessaly to Greece in the latter year and the
advance of the Græco-Turkish frontier to a line between Metsovo
and Malakasi the resulting customs barrier on the Zighos killed
what hopes there were of a revival of trade in this direction.
The last Balkan war of 1912–13 and the consequent cession of
Epirus to Greece may revive the trade between Yannina and
Thessaly along this route, and in this case Metsovo may once
again prosper, but it is at present too early to judge how great

a drain this last war has been on the resources of the country. To the south of Metsovo along the southern part of the Pindus chain the Vlach villages continue. This large group of villages is known as the Aspropotamos district mainly because many of them lie about the upper waters of that river. But geographically and to some extent too dialectically they form a separate division of the Vlachs, and since their recent history has been so different from that of their northern neighbours and we have not been able to visit any of their villages ourselves we omit them here. They will be briefly discussed in a later chapter.

From Metsovo therefore we go northwards and following the western slope of Pindus instead of the east we come to Baieasa and the other Vlach villages of the Zaghori. The Zaghori is a rough and hilly district in upper Epirus lying between Pindus and the mountains usually known as Papiñgu and Mitsikeli. The main road from Metsovo to Yannina which follows the course of the river of Metsovo may be said to form the southern boundary of the Zaghori and the upper waters of the Aous from its source to Konitsa the northern limit. The main route from Metsovo into the Zaghori runs northward following up the course of the river of Metsovo and then turning to the west by the khan called Pantalonia on the Austrian Staff map comes to Floro the first of the Vlach villages of the Zaghori. The khan of Pandalonia, which being interpreted means " The Trousers Inn," owes its name on the maps to a mistake, for its proper name is Pende Alonia, the Five Threshing Floors. Many reasons made it impossible for us to visit all the Zaghori villages and therefore we made directly for Baieasa by a little used route which follows the course of the Aous. This track is rather inaccurately marked on the maps and since it passes several places of interest it seems worth while to describe it in detail.

We ascend the hill slope to the north behind Metsovo and following the course of the river upwards reach in about forty minutes a fine, well watered plain on the eastern side of which the Aous rises. This particular plain has given rise to some discussion owing to the existence in connection with it of several names supposed to be survivals from antiquity.   Leake who was the first to call attention to them, says that the whole plain is called Politzía and that on a slope near it is a place known as Beratori which is thought to be a corruption of Imperatoria.   Here wrought stones are said to be found as well as coins and traces of metal working.   On the opposite side to Beratori stood a beech tree called " Fago Scripto."   The name of the plain is said to be derived from the Greek πολιτεία and to indicate that a city once stood here.   The Vlachs to-day call it Pulitshaii or if they talk Greek Pulitsa or Pulitses which is probably merely the Slavonic Politsa, plain.   Likewise the name Fagŭ Skriptu is of no importance, although, in spite of the fact that there is no " written beech tree " there to-day, the name still survives applied to a small wood.

A name like this is not nearly so remarkable as has been thought.   We have seen in the case of Samarina that it is a Vlach characteristic to name each prominent rock, tree, hill or wood, and many similar place names could be quoted. Imperatoria or as we were told Peritore is a spot on the stony slope at the bottom of the south-western side of Mount Ou.   It lies on the east bank of the Aous just opposite to the point where the road to Floro turns away due west.   We could see nothing of the ruins which are tentatively marked on the Austrian map and are mentioned by Leake and Weigand, but about the plain opposite to Imperatoria on the west bank of the Aous we saw indications that seem to show that metal working had once been carried on here.   If however Peritore or whatever the correct local form of the name may be, does stand for Imperatoria, which we are inclined to doubt, it would seem to show that a military camp of Roman times had stood here.   That there had been a military camp here would not be remarkable because this plain lies at the junction of so many important routes.   To-day it is covered with grassy and well watered meadows.   In spring and early summer the edges of the rivulets are bright with wild flowers and the scent of the new mown hay is heavy in the air.

From the supposed site of Imperatoria to Baieasa the Aous instead of flowing almost straight as the Austrian map implies makes a large bend to the west, and the track that is marked as following the river bank is also unknown. On enquiring at a shepherd's camp the best way to Baieasa we learnt that there was a path over the stony ridge on the east bank cutting across the bend and rejoining the river about two hours further north. The man in charge of the cheese making in the camp turned out to be a Vlach from Siraku who was busy making *kash kaval* for export to Italy.

After crossing the ridge mentioned we came down to the river again by some saw mills belonging to Baieasa. From this point to the village our route followed the course of the river through a rough and well wooded gorge passable only on foot. The timber from the saw mills is not taken into Baieasa, but direct to Yannina by way of Floro, and the men at the saw mills are only able to find the path to the village by blazing trees at intervals to serve as guides. About an hour before reaching Baieasa we came to the point where the Vale Kaldă joins the Aous, and from there onwards the valley widens out and the path is easy. The gorge through which we came was full of splendid timber, and the scenery is good, but the place has a bad name, for brigandage is not unknown and the sawyers are not left to follow their trade in peace.

Baieasa called by the Greeks Vovusa which is also the modern name of the Aous is the most eastern of the villages of Zaghori. The extent of this district has already been indicated, but since it is one of the best known parts of Epirus a brief digression will not be out of place here. The Roumanian propaganda claims that the whole region once spoke Vlach, but that in the course of time it has been largely hellenized. This is inaccurate for really only the eastern part of the Zaghori has been and still is Vlach, while the whole of the western portion has always been Greek as far as our knowledge goes. From the time of Leake to the present day there has been no great diminution of the Vlach speaking area which comprises the following villages :—

Leshnitsa, Dobrinovo, Paliohori, Laka called by the Greeks Laista, Baieasa, Tsherneshi, Seshǐ, Floro called by the Greeks Phlamburari, Grebenitsǐ, Makrini, Dragari, Doliani and Dreshtenikŭ.

Of these the last four are at least semi-hellenized, and all the others are Greek in politics though there is a Roumanian party in Baieasa and a few adherents of it in Laka and Tsherneshi and one or two other places.   Apart from these the remainder of the forty-two villages which are reckoned as belonging to the Zaghori are inhabited by Greeks alone and in spite of rumours to the contrary it does not seem that villages like Neghadhes, Thsepolovo and Phrangadhes ever spoke any other language within the memory of man.   It will be noticed that the name Zaghori itself and many of the village names are of Slavonic origin, and this feature is common both to the Greek and Vlach villages.   A few Slavonic words are to be found in the local dialect of Greek and the Vlach as always contains Slavonic traces, but in all other respects no Slavonic influence can be detected to-day, although the names indicate that there was once a Slavonic domination and probably also settlement in the region concerned.

The advance and increase of Hellenism in the Zaghori is due almost entirely to its close contact with Yannina.   In Turkish times it was directly dependent on the Vali of Yannina and it was one of the ancestral dominions of Ali Pasha.   Yannina like Metsovo was and still is to some extent a great centre of commerce and at the same time of Hellenic education. The Greek schools at Yannina in the eighteenth and early nineteenth centuries had considerable influence not only in the city itself, but in the country subject to it.   The spread of Greek at that time can be seen in various ways.   Ali Pasha used Greek almost as his official language, and over the gate of his castle at Yannina is an inscription in Greek in which he claims descent from Pyrrhus king of Epirus.   The great epic of more than ten thousand lines relating all his exploits which it was his great delight to have read to him by its author Hajji Sekhret a Moslem Albanian from Dhelvino is written entirely in Greek. A Moslem Albanian who claims in modern Greek to be a descendant of Pyrrhus and delights in a Greek epic of his own deeds recited to him by his own Homer is a most remarkable phenomenon.   Important however though the Greek schools at Yannina were, the view that they caused a revival of learning

cannot be held unless the term learning is degraded to its
lowest level.   Education then as now meant first and foremost
reading and writing, and because all letters then were Greek
it meant the spread of Hellenism.   The part played by such
education in the racial questions of the Nearer East can hardly
be appreciated in Western Europe.

One man beyond all others helped to spread Greek education among the villages of the Zaghori ; this was a Greek
priest known since his martyrdom as Ayios Kosmas.   The
Vlach tales about this interesting man are many and various,
and most are highly coloured by political propaganda that
only originated many years after his death.

Now this is the story that the Greeks tell.   In the year
1714 in the village of Meghalo Dhendri in the district of Naupactus there was born a boy to whom the name Konstas was
given.   From his earliest youth upwards he was filled with a
great desire for all kinds of learning and having passed through
many schools with great distinction he withdrew in the year
1758 to the Holy Mountain to the monastery called Philotheu,
where he changed his name to Kosmas.   After two years at
Athos he repaired to Constantinople and entered on his life's
work by preaching in the churches ;   thence he journeyed to
Naupactus, Mesolongi and Vrakhori preaching there likewise.
In 1775 he was at Athos once again before setting forth on a
long missionary journey through Albania, Epirus, Acarnania
and Macedonia.   It was on this journey that he visited the
Zaghori.   His fiery zeal for religion was only equalled by his
passion for education ;   he founded many schools ;   his elo-
quence wherever he went attracted great crowds, and Turk
and christian alike regarded him as a prophet.   He foretold
to Ali Pasha, so the legend runs, his future power and greatness, and after his death Ali Pasha contributed towards
building a church to his memory near Berat.   The end of this
holy man came on August 24th 1779 when he was hanged at
Berat by the Turks at the instigation of the Jews of Yannina.
Among some of the Vlachs, especially the nationalists, a
different tale is current.   They record his journeys among
the Vlach villages ; at Samarina the place where he preached

13

is still shown and the date of his visit is recorded on a rock ; he is said to have passed through Baieasa in 1777. But so far from being regarded as a saint he is spoken of with the utmost hatred as a Greek political agent. He taught so it is said that Greek was the language of God and Vlach that of the devil. His prophecies and miracles too, it is said, were due to trickery and he is accused of using torture against all who would not believe in him.

There is probably more truth in both these versions and less discrepancy between them than at first sight appears. To attribute his zeal for Greek schools to political propaganda to reclaim " Vlachophone Hellenes " is to antedate a movement by about a century, since it was not until recent times that the theory of Hellenes and Vlachs being racially the same was ever perpetrated. Kosmas encouraged Hellenism merely because he encouraged reading and writing, for the two were then almost identical, and for the rest he was probably a fanatical priest. Persecution is a common fault in such characters, if they are intolerant of opposition, and trickery is little thought of especially in such surroundings. For example there is prevalent in Macedonia a legend of a priest, who by the aid of a gramophone concealed in a tree produced a political speech from God Almighty. The nationality of the priest differs according to the teller of the tale, but the device is thought clever and Odyssean rather than disgraceful. That Kosmas at times exceeded the limits of peaceful persuasion seems probable from one of his own letters in which he says, " Ten thousand christians love me and one hates me ; a thousand Turks love me and one not so much ; a thousand Hebrews desire my death and only one does not." The greatest tribute to his personality is the fact recorded by Leake and confirmed by local tradition, that at his orders the fair sex of the Zaghori did their hair after a new fashion and adopted a new form of headdress. The spread of the Greek language in which Kosmas helped both by his teaching and by his martyrdom has brought with it the spread of Greek customs and ideals. And now intermarriage between Greek and Vlach will help to weld the two races into one.

The past history of the Zaghori which is mainly a list of acts of brigandage and oppression can be found in a detailed, but muddled form in Lambridhis. Each village seems to have gone through very similar experiences, so that a few details of the past of Baieasa will suffice for an example. From the middle of the sixteenth century up to the time of Ali Pasha at the beginning of the nineteenth the villages of the Zaghori possessed special privileges and many of them were under the Valide Sultan. But to regard them, as is sometimes done, as forming a semi-independent republic is to go beyond the evidence. The independence such as it was, was presumably more illegal than legal, and the Capitans little different from those that existed in every part of the peninsula.

Baieasa itself according to local tradition was formed by an amalgamation of four hamlets, Baietan, Stă Vineră, Bistritsi and Sānd Dumetru. The first of these Baietan it is said helped to found Perivoli and since the dialects of Baieasa and Perivoli belong to the same group it may be true that they have a common origin. The last of the four hamlets Sānd Dumetru is now the upper quarter of Baieasa around the church of Saint Demetrius. Apparently these hamlets were not permanent habitations, for they say that the people of Baieasa once used to winter at Doliani the Vlach village lower down in the Zaghori. So it is possible that Baieasa was at first only the summer resort of the shepherds of Doliani who eventually made a permanent settlement in the hills. Outside the village in a small side valley on the other bank of the river a group of Farsherot Vlachs have recently encamped each summer. So far they have lived in wooden huts and booths, but this annual camp if it continues will in time probably join up with the existing village.

During the eighteenth century, this is the boast of Baieasa, the three most famous Capitans of the Zaghori were natives of this village and their names and exploits are still recalled. They were Yoti Blatshola 1710–1750, Nikolak'i Davli 1750–1780 and Badzhu Bairaktari 1780–1800. The dates of these three chieftains were told us in Baieasa, but are too simple to be accurate and are probably only approximate. Lambridhis gives the same three names thus, Γιώτη Μπαλτσιόρα, Δούβλη, and Μπάτζιος; and he assigns the first to 1700–1710, but does not date the other two. Blatshola's chief claim to fame is the following exploit. He was once captured by his enemies, and handed over to the Turks at Yannina and sentenced to be immersed in boiling pitch. When brought to the pot he dipped his hands in the boiling liquid and flinging it over executioners, troops and crowd made good his escape. He was afterwards killed near Metsovo. The courage of Davli is proverbial, but examples of his bravery do not survive. Badzhu whose name Bairaktari means standard-bearer, is usually connected with Ali Pasha whose standard-bearer he is believed to have been. As far as the traditional dates go this is quite possible, but the title Bairaktari has, especially in Albania, the meaning tribal chief and so the tale that he carried Ali Pasha's banner is probably only a pious local fiction.

Brigandage which has always been one of the great pastimes of the Southern Balkans seems to have reached its height in the Zaghori. During the eighteenth century only six cases on a large scale and all due to Moslem Albanians are recorded, but between the fall of Ali Pasha and 1878 there were twenty-one. In this period Greek and Vlach brigands played a prominent part, especially Zhakas, and according to Aravandinos whose accounts are fully confirmed by local tradition, the christian bands surpassed the Moslem in their fiendish cruelty. One reason for the increase of these raids was the existence in the neighbourhood of a political frontier after the freedom of Greece. A frontier is in fact a necessity for brigandage on a large scale; during the winter the bands live in peace; in the summer they cross the frontier and return in the autumn with their plunder and perhaps with prisoners for ransom. This well known system has continued up to the present day and a brigand on one side of the frontier was a national hero the other, as in the cases of the brothers Skumbra and of Davelis. Between 1878 and 1883 brigandage as the aftermath of the rising of 1878 seems to have been incessant. In these five years £T60,000 were levied from the Zaghori, out of which Baieasa paid two thousand pounds. Whole villages were sacked and many of the deeds done cannot be described here. Among the more notorious leaders were Davelis, Leonidha of Samarina whose exploit at Baieasa has been referred to above, Manekas a Bulgarian, Gika an Albanian, the brothers Garelia of Briaza, Ghushu al Dhispuli of Samarina and Takos from Eurytania, and they on several occasions are said to have disregarded the rules of the code of klephtic honour. The system of ransom usually respected was often abused. One band seized a newly married couple, who thus spent their short honeymoon with the brigands. The bridegroom was ransomed and released ; then a ransom was demanded for the bride which was duly paid. But the brigands killed her and returned her dead body to the expectant bridegroom. Boiling oil and the practice of toasting women in ovens were among the methods employed for extorting money. Davelis whom we have met at his Thessalian home, where he ranks as a national hero, has the worst local reputation. Takos of Eurytania retired to his native land in Greece, but could not discontinue his habits and attracted the attention of the government. However he was protected by a fellow countryman then minister of justice. In 1883 after strenuous efforts on the part of the Turkish authorities this carnival of brigandage ceased and since then similar atrocities have not been committed, although brigandage on a small scale has continued and children have from time to time been seized and held for ransom. On the top of the steep and wooded ridge opposite Baieasa on the west bank of the river is a spot known as La Fezlu, where is the grave of a Turkish officer who was killed in the pursuit of the brigands. His death is celebrated in the following Vlach song :—

Has not Filureaoa satisfied you, Turk, Warden of the Passes ? Have not the Hashia satisfied you, that you have gone out by night on the mountains up to the Vlach villages and that you were going to Tsherneshi to the Vlach huts ? And the shepherds were saying to you and the shepherds tell you, " To Baieasa Turk do not go, do not go to Baieasa for there all the brigands are assembled, for there are all the capitans. There is the dog Gika, and Ghushu al Dhispuli, Ghushu al Dhispuli the old man, the one with the long beard, there is Capitan

Makri, Makri the Perivoliat, and Turk, there are the Garelia's, the
brothers Garelia of Briaza." The Turk he would not hear, the Turk
he would not listen. The Turk fought at Baieasa with those Vlach
brigands and the famous Turk was killed, the poor fellow was killed.

Apart from acts of brigandage Baieasa suffered on other
occasions. In 1814 it was plundered by the orders of Ali
Pasha and in 1829 during the Greek revolution was sacked
by the Turks. In consequence of this the inhabitants left
their home and took refuge in Greece at Vudhonitsa near
Thermopylæ, but the natural attraction of the mountains for
the Vlachs made them come back in 1835. But one result of
its past history and sufferings is that from time to time, especially at the beginning of the eighteenth century, many families
left the village and wandered forth to find fresh homes elsewhere. Most of them went to Western Thrace, where they
settled in Seres itself, at Dzhumaia which has three hundred
families from Baieasa, Poroi, Nigrita, Melenik, Nevrekop and
at Peshtera on Rhodope. In recent years emigration to
America has robbed the village of the young men.

Few if any villages in Pindus have a more beautiful situation than Baieasa. The river already a considerable stream,
which is not easy to ford in summer and in winter is a raging
torrent, divides the village into two parts, joined by a bridge
of the usual Turkish type, a high narrow arch with low parapets
so that loaded mules can pass with ease (Plate XXII 1).
The houses in the village are usually several stories high and
carefully built for defence with few or no windows on the
ground floor. The main part of the village is on the east
bank of the river and the bridge mentioned affords the sole
means of access to it. In the small quarter on the west bank
the church of St Athanasius stands close to the bridge head
which it serves to guard, for it is built entirely of stone with
a solid domed roof and loopholed. All the inhabitants are
Vlachs, but the men know Greek. There is a Greek school
and a Roumanian, though the building was destroyed by a
Greek band in 1905 and has not since been rebuilt. The
chief trade is in timber, for Baieasa boasts that it possesses
more saw mills than any other Vlach village. The other

PLATE XXII

1. BAIEASA: BRIDGE OVER THE AOUS

2. VERRIA: THE GHETTO

common Vlach trades of sheep rearing, wool working and muleteering are also practised, but none to any very great extent, for many of the muleteers employed in carrying Baieasa timber to Yannina are Samariniats. The costume originally worn was very similar to that at Samarina ; but this is now mostly replaced by European or rather à la Franca coats and trousers. Many of the Zaghori villages, Vlach and Greek alike, wear a costume like that in vogue in Epirus with white stockings and short blue trousers. This though a native costume seems to be an innovation in the Vlach villages, and is perhaps due to the influence of Ayios Kosmas.

The great feature of Baieasa which distinguishes it from all its neighbours is the possession of a wooden clock made on a novel plan by a native who died only recently at a great age and has already become the centre of a group of legends. Apparently quite unlettered he devised a number of mechanical improvements chiefly connected with water mills and smithies. Stories are told of his wonderful power of making calculations in his head which even the European enquirer could only do on paper. Locally he was regarded as being almost uncanny. Examples of unusual ability are often found among the Balkan villagers quite irrespective of race, but the faculty for invention other than verbal, is exceedingly rare. Implements and tools of everyday use even among the Greeks— the sharpest-witted in a way of the Balkan peoples—are of a primitive type or else copies of European models.

Three hours north-west of Baieasa—the first half up a hilly slope and the second a gradual descent along a narrow, but fertile valley—brought us to Laka or Laista as the Greeks call it. An hour and a half farther north on a bluff between the Aous and one of its tributaries is Paliohori. Both are Vlach villages and have had a typical history similar to that of other Zaghori villages. Laka was in Leake's day one of the most prosperous, but since then it has suffered much from brigandage and the lack of security. Most of its four hundred houses are still in good repair and it has a good Greek school and a well-paved misohori shaded by a large plane tree. Trade however is bad, the fields and vineyards are not sufficient to support the population and most have to emigrate. Emigration has for many years been the main support of the villages of the Zaghori, Greek and Vlach alike. The men often go to work in Constantinople or at Drama, Kavala or other towns of the Thracian littoral, but the majority have in times past gone to seek their fortunes in Roumania especially the Greeks. In some villages to-day there is hardly an able-bodied man to be seen, for all have gone abroad to make money. It was quite a common thing for a young couple to marry, and then for the bridegroom to go off to try his luck in foreign parts. He might never return, or he might come back after many years to a wife who had almost forgotten him and to a child he had never seen. In the folk-songs of the Zaghori there are a great number which refer to this state of affairs. Many of them are in the form of laments by brides or deserted sweethearts invoking curses on Roumania for detaining their men. To-day the same class of song continues, but with the substitution of America for Roumania. Laka if asked would declare itself to be of pure Hellenic stock, but in private all its inhabitants talk Vlach glibly. We were told with pride that the women all know Greek, which probably means that some still know only Vlach. The knowledge of Vlach songs was also denied, but one which was recited to us is given on a later page. Paliohori which claims to be the mother village of Laka—a claim that Laka disputes—was sacked by Leonidha and Davelis and has never recovered. Most of its houses are in ruins and the twenty-five that stand are not in good condition ; the fields are neglected and its few inhabitants poverty-stricken. It is less hellenized than Laka, for some of the inhabitants display an affection for their mother tongue. Here an older type of costume is preserved especially amongst the women, which resembles that of Laka illustrated by Weigand.

An hour and a half west of Paliohori and close under the precipices of the highest part of Papiṅgu which is here known as Gamila, Mount Camel, is Dobrinovo, a village in size and appearance very similar to Laka. The whole village talks Vlach as its native tongue, but our enquiries into its history and dialect did not meet with approval.   North of Dobrinovo is the last Vlach village of the Zaghori, Leshnitsa, a small village, but outwardly more prosperous than either Laka or Dobrinovo.   By race and language it is Vlach, but in politics and religion Greek.

It will be seen that of the Vlach villages in the Zaghori we can speak of five only from our own personal knowledge, Baieasa, Laka, Paliohori, Dobrinovo, and Leshnitsa.   All these are entirely Vlach by race and in all of them Vlach is the mother tongue, yet in four cases out of the five the great majority of the people are Greek in feeling.   Corresponding with this political division is a division in the mode of life.   The most hellenized villages are those that have been agricultural or non-nomadic for a long time.   Baieasa on the other hand to judge by its history has not long ceased to be nomadic and from its timber trade and muleteering has remained more typically Vlach.   Generally this distinction holds good in the southern part of Pindus too, the hill villages which depend on trade and muleteering, two professions more closely connected in the past than now, retain their sense of nationality and even when hellenized still consider themselves Vlachs.   The agricultural villages on the other hand tend to deny any Vlach origin at all.   The fundamental cause is historical and religious and goes back far beyond any modern political propaganda.   The agricultural villages have always had a precarious existence, and oppression from their rulers and their fellow-countrymen has reduced the sense of independence to a very low ebb. They have also intermarried more freely with the Greek, Albanian or Bulgarian villages round them.   The hill villages such as Samarina or Avdhela are proud of their nationality and their independence, and rarely marry outside their own special group.   If they do marry outside it is the men who do so, and then usually for the sake of the cash dowry which the Greeks give, but Vlachs do not.   Such men after marriage settle in the plains and towns, and so in the hill villages themselves there is little or no intermixture of Greek blood.

To the north of Aous, high up on the slopes of Zmolku and so overlooking the Zaghori is a line of Vlach villages, Palioseli,

Pădză, and Armata. These all stand on a track that leads from Konitsa along the south side of Zmolku and over Ghumara by way of Briaza and Smiksi to Ghrevena. Though now of little importance this track in places shews signs of having once been cobbled and so was probably in earlier times a much used through route. Of the first two villages Palioseli and Pădză which both contain over two hundred houses we can say little, for we arrived at an ill-omened hour when the annual examination at the Greek school was taking place. Both villages were eager to prove their pure Hellenic origin, and so all our enquiries about their history and dialect were out of place. They are both Vlach by race and language and resemble Laka and Dobrinovo in many ways. Neither of them seems particularly flourishing, as trade is bad in consequence of brigandage ; they are agricultural and so mainly supported by the men who all go abroad to make money.

From the track between Palioseli and Pădză a wonderful view can be obtained. Behind us to the north is the triple mass of Zmolku, the highest peak of Pindus ; in front and immediately below us is the Aous hurrying down to the Adriatic ; beyond to the south is the Zaghori which from here seems to consist of parallel ranges of hills running north and south. On the east rise the lower peaks of Pindus, Ghumara, Vasilitsa and Ou with their lower slopes covered with thick pine woods. In strong contrast to the gravelly hills of the Zaghori and the woods of Pindus is the western boundary with the bare and craggy sierra of Papiñgu which rises in height towards the north where it ends in a vast wall of limestone cliffs. Between this and the southwestern end of Zmolku is a narrow, deep and precipitous cañon through which the Aous forces its way into the plain of Konitsa.

The position of Papiñgu and Zmolku frowning at one another across the Aous has caused the Vlachs to localise here a folktale of which many versions are found in the Balkans and particularly amongst the Vlachs. It probably belongs to the class of tales that are native to a district rather than to any one race. In Vlach folklore the mountain personified as a demon plays a leading part, and this is especially true of any mountain that has a small lake near its summit. It is in this lake that the demon has his home and in Vlach folklore as a rule he was originally a shepherd who being crossed in love drowned himself and his flock. On Zmolku there is such a lake known as the Lakŭ Vinitŭ, the Blue Pool, and this is inhabited by an evil spirit who was in earlier life a shepherd broken-hearted through unrequited love. The tale referring to Zmolku and Papiñgu says that the demons of these two mountains fought by hurling great rocks at each other, a veritable war of giants. Eventually the demon of Zmolku conquered by a trick worthy of Odysseus. Each demon would catch in his mouth the boulders the other hurled, and swallow them like peas. The demon of Zmolku, deceitful like all Samariniats, compounded boulders of salt, and so made his adversary terribly thirsty. The demon of Papiñgu lay down to drink, and drank and drank and drank till he burst. Thus they explain the presence of white boulders round the Lakŭ Vinitŭ, because though there is no white stone on Zmolku, there is on Papiñgu, and so these white stones are some of those which the demon of Papiñgu hurled across at his enemy.

Of the past history of the three Vlach villages north of the Aous we must plead complete ignorance. Lambridhis seems to imply that they produced their full quota of brigands, but latterly they have been more sinned against than sinning. Armata the last of the three a poor hamlet of less than a hundred houses is connected with the monastery of Samarina which owns land, especially vineyards, in the village. Locally it is famous for the mythical beauty of its maidens. It is mainly an agricultural village, does little trade and anyone, who can, leaves it. We have met men of Armata settled at Verria and others who have made money in America. Under a good government and with security it might prosper, but the men and women of Armata who live there will always have to wring a hard living from the ungrateful soil by the sweat of their brows.

The last Vlach village on Pindus to the south of Samarina is Briaza, which lies on the east bank of the Aous at the point where the river flowing north from Baieasa turns westwards to Konitsa. The country round is well wooded and the village lies in the midst of vineyards and cherry orchards. It is mainly agricultural, though there are several saw mills and its people are noted for the excellence of the pitch they make. Despite apparent natural advantages Briaza is at a low ebb, and in prosperity must rank with Pădză, Palioseli and the Zaghori villages generally rather than with Samarina or Perivoli. Much of its present state is due to lack of public safety, for it has suffered both recently and in the past from bands political and otherwise. Lambridhis describes it as a shameless nest of robbers and names a certain Efthimiu who flourished about 1837 as the most notorious offender. There are two schools in the village, Greek and Roumanian, and no friction exists between them as long as they are left to themselves. This is the case in most villages and most of the Macedonian feuds about religion and education have been organised from outside. Vlach is the tongue commonly spoken and some of the women know no other. A costume similar to that of Samarina except in detail is still worn, but is rapidly being given up for European clothes.

A short three hours north of Samarina is the Vlach village of Furka. The road to it leaves Samarina by the place called Mermishaklu and thence follows up the river of Samarina to its source on the ridge known as La Greklu. This is covered with thick beech woods where the Samarina folk come to cut fuel, and owing to the woods and the narrowness and difficulty of the road on the summit it has always been a favourite place for brigands to hold up caravans of Samarina muleteers on the way from Yannina. A little beyond the spring called La Greklu the Yannina road goes straight down the valley of a small stream through pleasant upland meadows to Kerasova. They say that the spring owes its name to a Greek, who was in bad health and came up to Samarina for the summer to be cured by its fine climate and good water. After a few days he was so much better that he could venture a walk as far as this spring. He drank of its water, reputed to be the coldest on Zmolku, and at once dropped down dead. Baieasa has a similar tale and the Vlachs are never tired of telling such stories about the excellence and coldness of their mountain springs. From La Greklu the path to Furka bears away to the north following the top of a low line of hills on which the village stands. Unlike Samarina Furka is not a nomad village, for its inhabitants, at least the womenfolk, stay there all the year. In days gone by it supported itself by sheep rearing and agriculture. To-day agriculture is still carried on, but in a feeble manner; and the numbers of its flocks have declined. The troubles of 1878 affected Furka shepherds very severely, and, though the majority of the resident men make their living by sheep, yet the village as a whole lives on money from abroad. All the able-bodied young men are in America or elsewhere making money to support parents and sisters or wives and children. Brigandage as elsewhere has been the curse of the village and the tall tower-like houses of the big shepherd families still standing are silent witnesses to the fact that in Furka no man of means was safe unless his house was his castle. A few years ago too political bands troubled them, and the small Roumanian party was extinguished. In costume the people resemble Samarina very closely and with Furka the Samariniats have more intercourse than with any other village except Smiksi. They will give their daughters in marriage to Furka, an honour which they rarely or never do to any other village. Perhaps it hardly deserves this honour, for its houses, not two hundred in number, are mean and dirty, and this collection of ruinous dwellings makes a very poor appearance on the top of a treeless, windswept slope. Of its history we know little. It once had over three thousand inhabitants, but fell into the hands of Ali Pasha as a chiftlik. In consequence of their sufferings the people began to emigrate, and all were about to go forth in a body to find a new home, when the Turkish government intervened and forbade emigration fearing the country would be depopulated.

CHAPTER X

THE DISTRIBUTION OF THE VLACHS

Ἡμεῖς οἱ Βλάχοι ὅπως λάχῃ.

We Vlachs are the Children of Chance.

GREEK PROVERB

BESIDE the Vlachs in the northern part of Pindus who have already been described, there are numerous other groups in various parts of the Balkan peninsula, which can often be distinguished by differences in dialect and in some instances by a difference in costume. The members of some of these isolated groups are often known collectively by certain names ; for example all who live in the villages on Mount Gramos are called Gramosteani, the Vlachs of Albania also are known as Farsherots or by the Greeks as Arvanito-vlakhi, Albanian Vlachs. These names which are for the most part geographical, have remained unchanged by migrations and so denote the place of origin which is often not the present place of residence. The Farsherots, who have wandered more than most, are often to be found far away from the borders of Albania. The chief Vlach districts to-day are distributed as follows.

In Acarnania there is a group of six Farsherot villages which are fully inhabited during the winter ; in the summer the people go up into the southern part of Pindus with their flocks. The largest village which according to Weigand has about seven hundred and fifty inhabitants is Kutsobina, but the best known and most accessible is the hamlet of Suroveli which occupies part of the site of Stratos close to the Aspro-potamos. These Acarnanian Vlachs are by profession mostly shepherds and still live in groups of families under the patriarchal rule of a head shepherd. In one case, where the head shepherd was dead, Weigand found them living under a matriarchy exercised by his widow. The chief point of interest about them is that excluding a few isolated families who have settled in the towns they mark the southern limit of the Vlach communities. It might be thought that since Acarnania was known in medieval times as Little Vlachia in contrast to Great Vlachia or Thessaly, that these Vlachs are the descendants of the medieval population. But this is not so, for Weigand has shown by the study of their language and folk songs that they are Farsherots and must have wandered south from Albania. Further Lambridhis records that they came from the village of Bitsikopulo in the district of Paleopoghoni in Northern Epirus about the year 1840.

Far to the north of Suroveli and about the sources of the Aspropotamos is another group of villages inhabited by Vlachs. These, the most southern of the Pindus Vlachs, are distinct in origin and dialect from their Farsherot kinsfolk lower down the river and are commonly known as the Aspropotamos Vlachs. The villages actually situated in the Aspropotamos valley are neither large nor numerous, but they join an extensive group that reaches northward to Metsovo and spreads widely to east and west over the higher slopes of Pindus. At present there seems to be no real distinction between the villages in the river valley and those outside it, but it is not impossible that some distinction once existed. The name " Aspropotamite " is often used as if it denoted a definite class and Leake has recorded that for purposes of grazing there was a well-defined boundary between the Aspropotamos valley and the pastures towards Yannina. Treating however the district as one, the chief villages are, in the valley itself Gardista or Gardhiki and Halik'i, the latter at the source of the river ; Kalarites or Kalarl'i and Siraku on a tributary of the river of Arta, and towards the Thessalian side Malakasi, Kastania and Kornu or in Greek Krania. Gardista and Halik'i are primarily shepherd villages and have little or no history, but Kalarites and Siraku have in their day been places of considerable importance. The position of the two villages is alone sufficiently striking to attract attention. They stand facing each other, one on either side of a narrow mountain valley in the midst of country as wild and desolate as any to be found in Greece ; their narrow streets are zigzag paths worn out of the hill side and the topmost houses in Kalarites rise several hundred feet above the lower quarters of the village. Leake and Pouqueville, who both travelled in this district in the early years of the nineteenth century, have left much valuable information as to its past history as well as its condition at that time. According to a tradition prevalent in Kalarites at the time of Leake's visit, the Vlachs had only been settled in that part of Pindus up to that time for a space of two hundred and fifty years. This if true would place the date of their first settlements in the sixteenth century. Since the adjacent country is not rich this date may perhaps be defended on the theory that they were not driven to live in the less fertile parts until after the Turkish conquest. On the other hand since it is known that Vlachs were at Metsovo, which is only a few hours off, at a considerably earlier date, it seems far more probable that this tradition only refers to the beginning of permanent villages. A local saying quoted by Leake gives an idea of the early state of the district : " Velitsa is a fortress, Matsuki a town, Kalarites an outlying quarter of the town and Siraku five houses."

By the nineteenth century however this saying no longer held good ; Matsuki had only twenty-five houses and Siraku and Kalarites with five hundred houses each had a total population of some five or six thousand, besides several hundreds engaged in business elsewhere. This striking change, as in the case of Metsovo, was due to the rise of a large foreign trade which was mainly carried on through Yannina ; and as an example of commercial enterprise at this time it may be mentioned that merchants of Kalarites were employing Greek boats from Ghalaxidhi to ship their goods to avoid being dependent on foreign craft. Besides the advantages of a large trade Kalarites like many of the neighbouring villages was spared the extortions of a local governor by paying dues direct to the Valide Sultan. After 1800 however both these advantages soon disappeared, the trade failed and Ali Pasha of Yannina felt himself strong enough to extort money impartially from all villages alike. The annual fees from Kalarites were gradually increased from 14,000 up to 45,000 piastres, and for permission to have church bells a sum of 15,000 was exacted. At the independence of Greece several of the inhabitants moved into the new kingdom, and the population decreased. The new Græco-Turkish frontier in 1881 followed the line of the river and Kalarites became Greek, but Siraku remained Turkish. This caused a further decline in prosperity as it interfered with such trade as still remained. Many families from both villages have now settled in various towns in Greece, and have severed all connection with their former homes. The recent change in the frontier however may increase the prosperity of both villages. Zalakostas one of the best-known poets of Modern Greece was a native of Siraku. Malakasi, which is on the main route leading from Epiruo into Thessaly, is perhaps one of the oldest of the Vlach villages on Pindus ; it occurs in the legend of the founding of Metsovo by Floka, and the Malakasians are mentioned several times in the Chronicle of Epirus. This need not however imply the existence of a proper village. As might be guessed from its position Malakasi has undergone experiences similar to Kalarites, but always on a smaller scale. Pouqueville estimates its population at about five hundred families, but in recent years it has sunk to nearly half that number. Kastania and Kornu are largely shepherd villages, and like all in the hill districts near the frontier have had ample experience of brigandage.

In the Thessalian plains there are large Vlach colonies in many of the towns and villages, but only a few small hamlets in which the population is exclusively Vlach. All the Vlachs in the Thessalian plains, whether now permanently settled or not, seem to have been until recent times only winter visitants ; most come from Samarina, Avdhela, Perivoli and the other villages on Northern Pindus and so need no further description. In Southern Thessaly however in Almiros and in a few hamlets not far away the Vlachs are Farsherots. Their home village

14

is Pleasa, and until 1881 when the frontier was changed most
used to return there each summer, but after that date some
settled permanently in Thessaly and others found new winter
quarters farther north at Vlakhoyianni.

To the north of Thessaly and in what was till recently
Turkish territory, the next Vlach district is on the slopes of
Mt. Olympus. Here there are three villages Vlaho-Livadhi,
Kokinoplo and Fteri. Vlaho-Livadhi the largest, though half
its former size, has still in summer some three thousand
inhabitants. The Olympus Vlachs, as their dialect shows,
have mixed with Greeks for longer than most of the Vlachs on
Pindus ; many have left their mountain homes and have
settled in Elassona, Katerini and Serfije ; others have moved
northwards to Salonica and in fact of the Hellenic population
in Salonica to-day many in origin are from the Vlach villages
on Olympus.

To the north of the Haliakmon and on the hills that form
the watershed between it and Lake Ostrovo are two separate
groups of Vlachs ; one in the east around Verria and one to
west that includes Vlaho-Klisura on the hills to the east of
Kastoria. To the north of this second group is a third containing Neveska, Belkamen, and Pisoderi.

It has already been noticed in connection with Avdhela
and Samarina that early in the nineteenth century a number
of Avdheliats led by Badraleksi abandoned their homes on
Pindus and settled on the hills by Verria (Plate XXIII).
They were joined by detachments from Perivoli and Samarina,
especially by the *Bātutsĭ* from the latter village and their
numbers were increased by a small band of Farsherots. This
movement was the beginning of all the Vlach settlements in
the hill district south of Verria, where the chief villages are
Selia and Ksirolivadi. Selia is divided into an upper village,
which is the Farsherot settlement, and a lower one the site of
Badraleksi's original encampment. This and the fact that
the village is still rented as a chiftlik and is not freehold
are obvious indications that the Vlachs are newcomers to the
hills of this region. They say that Selia was first colonised
in 1815, but that in 1821 the upper village was sacked and

PLATE XXIII

VERRIA: VLACHS FROM SAMARINA AND AVDHELA

thereupon the Samarina families migrated to Niausta. Ksiro-livadi, unlike Selia, is an old inhabited site, though it is comparatively recent as a Vlach village. Formerly it was inhabited by Greeks who grew flax and rye, but about 1819 it was totally destroyed in a raid of Albanians or Turks. This date, which we were given in the village, may be too late, since none of the tombstones in the old Greek churchyard bear a later date than 1780. At all events its position on the old paved Turkish high road from Verria to Kozhani and Yannina must have rendered it very accessible to marauders. The present village is also rented by its Vlach inhabitants as a chiftlik and like Selia is inhabited only in the summer. A third village Doliani is more recent than either and was started by a number of nationalist Vlachs not so long ago as a permanent village to avoid intercourse with Hellenism and Greek education. They first purchased the land which was a chiftlik and then procured an architect to draw up plans for a model village. A large school has been built and a church, and the land of the village site divided into plots each large enough for a house and a small garden. The village lives by sheep rearing, timber cutting and agriculture, for which Turks from the Koniari villages in the plains of Kozhani and Kailar were being employed. All the land belongs to the community which receives the rent for pasture and arable land and lets out the right of cutting timber. When the timber in one area has been cut, the community takes care that it shall be replanted or else shut up and the trees allowed to grow again naturally. Thus the village was gradually forming a fund for its own general purposes aided by gifts of money from natives working in America. They were thinking, if their scheme succeeded, of buying yet another chiftlik and founding a similar Vlach colony. In addition to this the community was hoping that some day it would be able to maintain its school and church by itself without any help from the Roumanian propaganda. The only condition laid down for an inhabitant of the village was that he should be a Vlach of the right political faith. By 1911 the village had made an excellent start and was increasing in size and prosperity, but its future is now most problematical. But, whatever happens, it has the unique distinction of having been designed according to a plan and on a kind of communistic scheme.   The only other Vlach village in these hills is Gramatikova which is a Farsherot settlement. Verria itself besides being the winter home of most of the Vlachs of Selia and Ksirolivadi, has a small permanent Vlach population mainly engaged in trade especially in the merchanting of the cheeses made in the hill villages. Besides Vlachs the town contains a large Greek population, a ghetto of Spanish Jews (Plate XXII 2), many Turks and some Bulgarians. Its chief feature is perhaps its excessive number of churches of which there are said to be seventy-two. Many of the smaller houses are grouped together in walled compounds, in most of which there is a small church. It is in these compounds that the nomad Vlach families from Selia and Ksirolivadi spend the winter, hiring them *en bloc* from the Turkish landlords.

To the west of the hills of Verria and beyond the plain of Kailar we come to another big range of hills which gives shelter to several Vlach villages.   These which we may call the Klisura group lie on the ethnological boundary of Greek and Bulgarian. This group contains four villages, Klisura or Vlaho-Klisura, Blatsă, Pipilishte and Shishani, and in addition there are several Vlach families at Selitsa and in the town of Shatishta which contains many Samariniats. Shishani and Blatsă are now almost entirely hellenized and both these villages seem from the first to have been partly Greek. Pipilishte is said to be purely Vlach, but in politics is Greek. Shishani, though now small, must once have been an important place because the full title of the Bishop of Shatishta is " His Holiness of Shishani and Shatishta." At present Klisura with some three thousand inhabitants has been for a long time the largest purely Vlach village in this district. It stands perched on the steep hill side at the top of the pass on the high road from Kailar to Kastoria. The road is one of the best in Macedonia and this is of great importance for Klisura which makes its livelihood mainly by trade. The houses are large and indicate considerable prosperity in the past, though as usual there has been a decline in recent years. There is another group round Neveska a large and prosperous Vlach village four hours north of Klisura and situated at a higher elevation and commanding a more extensive view. The position of Neveska (Plate XXIV) amongst the mountain meadows and woods coupled with its magnificent outlook over the plains of Kailar and Monastir with their lakes has a wide reputation and is popularly supposed to rank second to Samarina alone. The inhabitants of this group of villages are not nomadic, although many go abroad to make their fortunes as merchants in Egypt and Servia. The houses though large and roomy are built more closely together, and gardens are not as common as in the Pindus villages. In the better houses in both Klisura and Neveska a curious local method of wall decoration can be seen. The upper part of the walls, which are as a rule covered with plain white-wash, are ornamented with a friese of Greek gods and god-desses about three feet high painted in monochrome blue. The designs and execution are rude and of no artistic merit, but merely interesting. North of Neveska lie three more villages Pisoderi, Belkamen and Negovani which have all been settled in the last hundred years by Farsherots. Only the first is purely Vlach, for the others also contain a considerable Albanian population.

To the west of these again and beyond the upper waters of the Haliakmon come the villages of northern Pindus between Samarina and Metsovo and the Zaghori which have been described in a previous chapter. But at the extreme northern end of Pindus there are a few Vlach villages on the slopes of Mount Gramos which lie near the point where the ethnographic boundaries between Greeks, Bulgarians and Albanians meet. The most important of these are Gramosti and Densko which is about six hours north of Furka. These villages are mainly inhabited by shepherds and muleteers and also do some trade in timber. They are nomadic and many of them spend the winter at Hrupishta. With them we might group the villages like Nikolitsa and Linotopi which are no longer inhabited by

Vlachs. They were however in the eighteenth century before their ruin at the hands of the Albanians very flourishing and widely famous. Their inhabitants are now scattered far and wide ; for instance there are Gramosteani to be found amongst the glens of Rhodope in Thrace and families from Densko may be met at Aliphaklar in the plain of Ayia in Thessaly. Adjoining the Gramos group to the north comes another block of Vlachs who centre about the large Albanian town of Kortsha. This block falls into two divisions. One lies to the east of Kortsha and contains the villages such as Pleasa, Morava and Stropan mainly inhabited by Farsherots who are shepherds and muleteers, and in addition the few families settled in the mixed Bulgar-Albanian town of Biklishta. These Farsherots are apparently newcomers and do not seem to have been settled in this district for more than two hundred years. Still as we have seen Pleasa itself has sent forth colonies, as instanced by the Pleasa Farsherots at Almiros in South Thessaly. This shows how ineradicable the spirit of wandering is in the Vlachs. In Kortsha itself there is a considerable Vlach colony mainly composed of Farsherots from Pleasa and its neighbourhood, but there are several families from Muskopol'e who are very much under Greek influence and a few from the Gramos district. The other division of the Vlachs in this region lies about Muskopol'e and Shipiska which in the seventeenth and eighteenth centuries were large and flourishing towns. Of the two Muskopol'e, the Plain of Musk, was the larger and the most renowned, for it was the great commercial centre for Central Albania and Upper Macedonia and its merchants had branch houses in Venice, Vienna and Buda-Pest, and like their kinsfolk beyond the Danube frequented the great fair of Leipzig. The wealthy Greek colony in Vienna was largely composed of Vlachs from Muskopol'e and elsewhere, for example Leake remarks that at Shatishta and Selitsa German was commonly known because of trade connections. Locally it is believed that the town once contained eight or ten thousand houses and a population of about sixty thousand souls. These figures Weigand is inclined to credit, but Leake was more sceptical. As the traveller to-day can see from the extensive ruins amidst the meadows

PLATE XXIV

NEVESKA FROM THE SOUTH-EAST

that surround the present village on all sides it was once much larger and in size easily surpassed any other Vlach town. So if we assume that the local estimates of its former population are thrice as great as they should be, we can put its inhabitants at twenty thousand without any danger of being unduly credulous. Leake who passed through the place in 1805 says its prosperity which was at its height about a hundred years before, had then been declining for the last seventy years. This statement seems to be on the whole correct. Muskopol'e possesses many churches most of which now stand isolated among the stone strewn hayfields that once were busy parishes, and on the slope of the hills about half an hour to the north lies the monastery of Muskopol'e dedicated to St John the Baptist. The monastery church was built in 1632 and the majority of the churches in the town date between 1700 and 1760. So if the building of churches is a sign of prosperity then Muskopol'e flourished most between 1650 and 1750. In the monastery there is a historical note book, locally known as a codex. It was begun in 1772, and written in the same hand as this date are notes of various events from the great rain of ash all over Rumeli in 1631 down to 1754. The unknown historian dates the flourishing period of Muskopol'e to the seventeenth century, and then gives several rescripts relating to the monastery issued by the Patriarchs of Achrida Ignatios, Gregory, Raphael, and Philotheos between 1693 and 1718. The latest patriarch mentioned is Joseph (1746–1749). The next date is 1780 and by a different hand, and on the flyleaf is written in an attempt at classical Greek, " Muskopol'e, Muskopol'e, where is thy beauty ? Where is the fair form that thou hadst in the seventeenth century ? The most accursed of men have wrought my destruction. May the Lord give thee back thy former beauty through the intercession of the Holy Baptist."

These dates all agree with tradition which places the first sack of Muskopol'e by Albanians in 1769 and the second in 1788. Finally the harsh rule of Ali Pasha brought about its complete ruin and its inhabitants were dispersed throughout the Balkans. To-day it is a small village occupying the kernel of the old town and inhabited partly by Albanians and partly by Vlachs, some of whom are true natives and others Farsherots. Even in the days of its greatness there was probably a considerable Farsherot element in the population, which is recorded in local tradition and accepted by Weigand on philological grounds. The Geography of the Thessalian monks Daniel and Gregory published at Vienna in 1791 says that it had much wealth, twelve kinds of trades, a good and famous school, a printing press and was in a word adorned with all the beauties of a European city. The printing press was managed by a monk called Gregory who published religious books, of which ten are known, and was renowned as one of the earliest presses in European Turkey. To-day no sign of the press, either of type or machinery survives, and it might reasonably be doubted whether the press ever existed there at all, since no European traveller ever saw it, for it is possible that the books were printed in Constantinople, Venice, Vienna or some similar place for Muskopol'e. Local tradition is not always to be trusted and the point can only be decided by an examination of all the books bearing the imprint Muskopol'e. But the town was justly famous as a seat of Greek learning and education. Ioasaph a well known patriarch of Achrida, to whom the wealthy Vlach merchants gave the golden mitre made in Venice and now preserved in the Cathedral of St Clement at Okhridha, was a native of the town, and so also Kavalliotis, Daniel, and Boyadzhi who compiled Vlach and Albanian lexicons and grammars to further the spread of Hellenism.

The history of Shipiska is in every respect similar to that of its neighbour Muskopol'e. These two towns with Nikolitsa and Linotopi were companions in prosperity and in misfortune, and one may safely say that no Vlach villages ever before or since have reached such a pitch of material greatness. Their wealth and fame are known all over the Balkans, and their ruin is proverbial, for Vlach songs still tell how neither their riches nor their education could save them from the Albanians when they marched to set their foot upon them.

To the north of the plain of Kortsha is the well known town of Okhridha, to use the Greek name, built on a rocky peninsula jutting out into the north-east corner of the lake of the same name. The lake is renowned through the whole region ; local statisticians say it is twenty hours in circumference, over two hundred metres deep and possesses eighteen kinds of fish of which the salmon trout are known throughout Macedonia. In summer too the country produces three kinds of cherries, yellow, red and black, the last being most excellent. All round the lake stand steep limestone mountains and these naturally are the haunts of Vlachs. Hidden among the wild Albanian mountains to the south-west of the lake is a small group of Vlach villages of which Lunka and Grabovo are the largest. To-day they are very small and miserable, but in days gone by were much larger till they fell under the same curse as Muskopol'e, and so their inhabitants are to be found almost everywhere, but at home. At the north end of the lake where the Black Drin starts on its course to the Adriatic in Struga and Beala are Vlach colonies principally composed of Farsherots living amongst Albanians and Bulgars. In Okhridha too there is a large Vlach element all of whom with the exception of two families are said to be nationalists. The Okhridha Vlachs came from Lunka, Nikolitsa and Linotopi at the time of their ruin, and now many of them have wandered still further afield and their places in the Vlach colony have been filled by Farsherots. To the east of Okhridha on the hills that cut it off from Resna and the basin of Lake Presba is Istok where the Perivoliats of Toivash and Suphlari have their summer homes. Near them on the same hills is a large Farsherot colony at the village of Ilino. In Resna itself there are a hundred or more Vlach families from Muskopol'e and in the neighbouring village of Yankovets are forty more ; all these came after the destruction of their mountain home. About the neighbourhood too there are small colonies of Farsherots to be found as for instance at Levareka a little to the north. But like Okhridha the population of Resna is overwhelmingly Bulgarian with a certain Turkish and Albanian element.

East of Resna and between it and Monastir, which the Vlachs call Bitule, lies another large group of Vlach villages to which we may add Krushevo and the Vlach colony in Monastir. This group can be divided into two, one containing the two westernmost villages of Molovishte and Gopesh, and the other Măgarova, Tărnova, Nizhopoli, Krushevo and Monastir. The latter may be dealt with first. Măgarova, Tărnova and Niz-hopoli are pure Vlach villages with very few Bulgarian or Albanian families living among them. They are all three of quite modern origin for their first inhabitants were refugees from Gramosti, Muskopol'e, Linotopi, Nikolitsa, and Biskuki, and in Nizhopoli are some Farsherots. Since each family still remembers from what village their ancestors came it is clear that these Vlach colonies are not much over a century old. It is the same with Krushevo which was at first a purely Vlach town founded by refugees from Metsovo, Linotopi, and Niko-litsa who bought a small chiftlik and by their industry and keenness in trade have made it a large town. To-day there is a considerable Bulgar element in its population and in consequence it suffered in the rising of 1903. It is also the seat of the Greek bishop of Okhridha and Presba, who now that his proper diocese has almost entirely gone over to the Exarchate, resides here among the hellenist Vlachs. Similarly the Vlachs of Monastir are descendants of former inhabitants of Muskopol'e, Linotopi and Nikolitsa who fled east to escape the Albanian terror. They are no inconsiderable part of the population of Monastir, and form with patriarchist Bulgars and Albanians the main strength of the Greek party for pure Greeks are few and far between. Monastir also contains a large colony of Spanish Jews, and a considerable number of Albanians and Turks. If the Albanians are Mohammedans it is very difficult to separate them, for the Turk like the Greek always confuses religion and nationality.

In contrast to this division of the Vlach inhabitants of the district are the villages of Molovishte and Gopesh. The latter is perched in a fine open situation on a wooded hill side on the route of the old road from Elbasan through Okhridha to Perlepe. Molovishte on the other hand is hidden in a ravine at the foot of Mount Peristeri. Both villages admit that they received detachments of refugees from Furka, Nikolitsa, Neveska and Muskopol'e, but both alike assert that they have been in existence for at least three hundred years. Molovishte says it was once lower down the ravine near Kazhani on the Monastir-Okhridha road, and Gopesh believes that its first founders came from Nunte in the Meglen long before Muskopol'e suffered for its pride. The dialect spoken by them confirms in a way their traditions. Both villages have dialectic peculiarities which separate them from Măgarova or Monastir and these peculiarities they share with the Meglen Vlachs. This does not necessarily mean that they have the same origin as the Meglen folk, though this is possible. The Meglen villages have some linguistic traits in common with the Roumanians from beyond the Danube and like them have come more in contact with Slavs. On the other hand the Vlachs of Pindus and the south live on the borders of three races, Albanians, Bulgars and Greeks, and so one would naturally expect the Slav influence on their pronunciation to be less strongly marked than in the case of the people of Gopesh, Molovishte or the Meglen who live as isolated units in a Slavonic sea. Thus the peculiarities of the dialect of these two villages may only indicate that they have occupied their present habitations for a very long time, and so naturally Slavonic influence has made itself felt, for the men in this region all talk Bulgarian as well as their mother tongue. All the Vlach villages just mentioned are now declining in numbers, for political troubles and the consequent injury to trade have made many emigrate to Bulgaria, America or elsewhere in search of work and a good livelihood.

To the north and north-east of Monastir there are no purely Vlach villages, but every town of importance such as Perlepe, Veles, Prizrend, Ipek, or Uskub contains a Vlach colony composed of immigrants from the west and south-west.

To the north-west of Salonica and west of the town of G'evg'eli which is on the Salonica-Nish railway, the small hill district now known as the Meglen, but formerly called Moglenia, lies among the Karadhzova mountains. It divides into two halves, Bulgar-Meglen to the west, and Vlacho-Meglen to the east. The Meglen Vlachs are in several ways quite distinct from all others in the Balkans. They alone of all the Vlachs use the term Vlach of themselves or their language, for the others without exception call themselves by the proud name of Arumāni or Romans. The dialect of the Meglen is so different that when first heard it is almost unintelligible ; some of them belong to the Moslem faith, and nearly all, unlike their kinsfolk of the south-west, are devoted to agriculture and are not traders or craftsmen. The population of Vlacho-Meglen amounts to just over fourteen thousand, and is distributed among eleven villages of which L'umnitsa is the largest. The westernmost village Nunte is Mohammedan, though till about a hundred years ago it was christian, and a church and a ruined monastery still exist to show that they have changed their faith. The tale goes that the people tired of Turkish oppression decided with the bishop—Nunte boasts that it was once the seat of a bishop—and priests at their head to embrace the religion of the Turks their masters in hopes of better treatment. Besides the eleven villages of the true Meglen Vlachs, there is one Livadhi which serves as a summer residence for shepherd Vlachs from Gramosti who spend the winter in the plains between Yenija and Salonica. They however keep themselves aloof from the Meglen folk, for they consider themselves far superior to agriculturists. As might be expected from their environment the Meglen Vlachs are strongly under Bulgarian influence, and when Weigand visited the district in 1889 two villages in particular, Barovitsa and Koinsko, were rapidly changing from Vlach to Bulgarian. Greek influence, which had been decreasing, was confined to the schools and churches. Recently many of the nationalists, who are said to be in the majority in this region, have placed themselves under the Exarch. The Meglen Vlachs more than many others seem to retain their national costume ; the men wear a form of *tsipune*, and the women's dress, though it has become rather Bulgarian in appearance, has been little affected by European stuffs and fashions. Thus at the village dances the fair sex of the Meglen make a brave show with

their quaintly decorated aprons and large silver buckles of
local manufacture.

To the east and north-east of Salonica there are many
Vlachs to be found, but there are few if any villages inhabited
by them alone. All these Vlachs are refugees from Vlaho-
Livadhi, Neveska, Klisura, Pindus, Gramosti, or the Muskopol'e district, and have settled amongst a population that is
in the main Slav, for, where there is any Greek element at all,
it is the Vlachs themselves who form no inconsiderable portion
of it. Seres is the most southerly town in this region which
has a Vlach colony, and this is said to number as many as
two thousand souls, although there may be many more, for
they are nearly all almost completely hellenized. The progress
of hellenization with the consequent absorption of the Vlachs
among the Greeks makes it excessively difficult to distinguish
those of Vlach origin and those who are not. Nevrekop,
Demir Hissar, Melenik and Poroi are other towns in this
district where Vlachs are to be found and like their fellows
in Seres they are subject to hellenization, and are mainly
refugees from the south-west and Pindus, for some of them came
originally from Baieasa. As purely Vlach villages Weigand
quotes Ramna to the north of Lake Butkovo, Buzhdova and
Lopova north of Melenik, and the summer village of Baba
Ali to the north of Seres. Yet farther to the north is Upper
Dzhumaia with a considerable Vlach colony many of whom
are nationalists. In this neighbourhood all about the ravines
and ridges of Rhodope and its outlying ranges many encampments of Vlach shepherds exist. Weigand reckons
the total number of such hamlets of huts at forty-two and
according to him they have all wandered eastwards from
Gramosti. It is interesting to note that these shepherds and
their womenfolk have still preserved the Vlach national dress
so characteristic of their homeland. They are of course
nomads and many of them winter in the plains about Kum-
anovo and Egri Palanka. In Bulgaria the most important
colony is in Sofia itself where half the trade is said to be in
Vlach hands, the other half being in the hands of Spanish
Jews. There are also Vlach colonies in other Bulgarian towns

such as Tatar Bazarjik and Philippopolis and it is noticeable that Bulgarian commercial establishments, such as the
Bulgarian National Bank, recruit their staff among the boys
who have been trained in the Roumanian Commercial School
at Salonica. The main point of the interest of the Vlach
colony in Sofia is that it is the result of what might be called
secondary migration. The Vlachs of Sofia have mostly come
from Monastir, Krushevo and Măgarova during the last thirty
years, and as we have seen the bulk of the Vlachs of the
Monastir district were refugees from Pindus, Gramos or
Muskopol'e. The most easterly Vlach colony of which we
have heard, apart from that at Constantinople, is at Sufli on
the railway a little to the south of Dimotika where a band of
wanderers from Laka have settled. In Servia there are Vlachs
in Nish, Belgrade, Vrania and other towns and in summer a
number of shepherd families are to be found close to Nish.
The total number of Vlachs in Bulgaria and Servia is not
great and at present at least there is a clear distinction between
the Vlachs of the south and the Roumanians proper, some
of whom live south of the Danube in the districts of Timok
and Viddin. The two divisions overlap a little, but speaking
generally one may say that north of Nish and Sofia are
Roumanians and south of it are Vlachs.

From the Vlachs in Servia, Bulgaria, East Macedonia and
Thrace we may turn to those in the west of the peninsula, in
Epirus, Albania and Dalmatia on the Adriatic slope. A few
of these have already been noted, since the Zaghori villages are
strictly speaking in Epirus, and Kortsha and Muskopol'e are
more in Albania than not. All of these however are on the
central line of mountains that divides the peninsula, rather
than definitely west of it like the settlements that now concern
us. There are some Vlachs permanently settled in Yannina,
and a large part of the Greek population there is almost
certainly of Vlach origin; there are also a few families in Preveza
and other towns; but apart from these and the Zaghori villages
there are no Vlachs in Epirus except the families who come
there only in winter from Siraku and other Pindus villages.
In Albania however there are two definite groups. A

southern one due west of Mount Gramos on the hills which
lie to the north of Premeti between the rivers Aous and Osum,
and a northern group just to the west of Berat.   The southern
one contains only four or five small villages, including Frasheri
from which the Farsherots take their name.   By Berat there
are thirty-eight villages or hamlets, all of small size, with a
total population in winter of perhaps ten thousand, but in
summer considerably less. In the towns such as Avlona, Elbasan
and Durazzo there is also a Vlach population.   Conditions of
life in Albania are more primitive than elsewhere, the villages
are smaller and more scattered, and the nomadic population
larger.   In many parts of the hills therefore there are probably
shepherd Vlachs who are not included in either of these two
groups of villages.   To the north of Albania along the Adriatic
coast a Vlach population once existed ; several Vlach place
names are recorded in Sir Arthur Evans' papers on Illyria,
an invaluable work for Dalmatian ethnology.   Ragusa itself
contained a large Vlach element and Dalmatia was the home
of the Morlachs or Black Vlachs.   In Istria at the present
day a Vlach dialect is spoken, but between Istria and Albania
it has now ceased, and the Istrian Vlachs, who like the Meglen
call themselves Vlachs, are widely separated from those in
Balkan peninsular proper.

The present distribution and condition of the Vlachs
suggest numerous points of interest.   In the first place
it becomes clear that though many are now settled in the
towns and villages on the plains as traders, yet as a distinct
race the Vlachs still belong to the hills.   The exclusively
Vlach villages are all situated in or near the hills, and the
Vlachs elsewhere are colonists fast losing their nationality.
Usually, if not always, it is the upper village that is regarded
as the home of those who migrate, and, while their houses in
the hills and the land that surrounds them are usually their
own, their houses in the plains are normally rented.   Few of
the hill villages in the present form are however of any antiquity
and some like Doliani, Krushevo, Belkamen and Dzhumaia
are the result of quite modern migrations ; most like the
Pindus village lay claim to having been founded by the union

of several shepherd encampments about two hundred years ago. The few villages that are definitely older are like Gopesh, Metsovo, Kalarites and Muskopol'e are situated on or near natural trade routes. The recent date of the Vlach villages is not only guaranteed by tradition, it can be proved in several ways by the lack of any old buildings and by the deeply rooted prejudice against the builder's trade. We may say then with fair certainty that the Vlachs belong to the hills, though their villages there are with some exceptions of recent origin. The recent history of the Vlachs as a whole is like that of the Pindus villages ; there has been a continual change throughout from nomadism in the hills to a settled life in trading villages near the passes in the plains. From time to time this change has been accentuated ; in the eighteenth century there was a great increase in trade ; Vlach merchants were settled at Yannina, Metsovo and Kalarites were com-mercial centres, Muskopol'e was at its most flourishing stage and at the close of this period comes the formation of the bulk of the Vlach colonies round Monastir and Seres. The trade of the eighteenth century produced a great increase in settled life ; it also had other effects, it brought the Vlachs into prominence, but at the same time it helped towards denationalisation. The Vlach on becoming a trader and a permanent dweller in the towns came into close contact with other races ; and a knowledge of Greek became essential instead of a luxury, especially to those who settled in the Greek towns. Hellenism was also helped by the power of the Patriarchate which was at its height in the latter half of the eighteenth century. In 1767 the Greek Patriarch with the aid of the Turks had succeeded in suppressing Bulgarian, Serb and Roumanian churches ; this too was the period of elementary Greek reading books for the instruction of Albanians, Vlachs and other. The closing years of the eighteenth century were a period of storm and stress, trade declined generally not merely in the south, and the prosperous Vlach villages such as Metsovo, Vlaho-Livadhi, and Klisura all dwindled. The families that left these villages, which were Vlach trading centres in the hills, settled in the towns on the plains and became merged into the other races. Thus the decline like the rise of commerce has helped towards the disappearance of the Vlach race, and Hellenism in the Balkans which in every other race has rapidly decreased of late, among the Vlachs alone has made progress.

The fortunes of the Vlachs from the time of the Turkish conquest, when they submitted and in many places secured the privilege of being under the Valide Sultan, up to the eighteenth century are almost impossible to ascertain in detail. Local tradition does not really begin till later, and outside tradition there are few or no surviving records. The fifteenth, sixteenth, and seventeenth centuries are therefore almost a complete blank, and the history of the Vlachs before that period forms a separate subject. It may however be safely assumed that the change from a wandering to a fixed life was a continuous process, and that the early tales of Metsovo and Samarina, if not in detail true, are so in their main outlines.

CHAPTER XI

THE VLACH LANGUAGE

Ἡ γλῶσσα μᾶς εἶναι μία μεγάλη σαλάτα.

Our language is one great salad.

CRETAN SAYING

VLACH is a Latin language and a dialect of Roumanian, but naturally owing to the isolation and dispersion of those who speak it, it has remained in an undeveloped condition and from time to time adopted many foreign words. But although the adoption of foreign words may obscure the language for those who have only a slight acquaintance with it, for all that the grammar, which is the essential base of any tongue, retains its true Latin character. Roumanian dialects fall into the following groups :—the Roumanian of the kingdom and Transilvania with many subdivisions, the Istrian dialect, Meglen and lastly Vlach with its own subdivisions. Some Roumanian philologists say that Vlach is in the condition in which Roumanian proper probably was several hundred years ago. Its isolation and the fact that it was not reduced to writing have kept its syntax in a very simple state. Like all Roumanian dialects Vlach has one great peculiarity which marks it off from all other Romance languages. The article instead of being placed in front of the noun is attached as a kind of suffix at the end, and it is through the declension of the suffixed article that the nouns themselves are declined. The article is of course derived from the Latin *ille*, for example the Latin *illum vicinum* becomes in French and Italian *le voisin* and *il vicino*, but in Vlach *vitsinlu*. This peculiarity in the position of the article the Roumanian dialects have in common with two neighbouring

languages, Albanian and Bulgarian, and it also occurs in some
South Russian dialects, but elsewhere among Indo-European
tongues is found only in Scandinavian languages.

Owing to the fact that Vlach has never been written till
recently there is no literary language which can be said to be
generally known in all Vlach districts. Nor of course is there
any recognised convention of spelling as in other languages.
These circumstances make it very difficult to give any account
of the tongue without straying into digressions about dialectic
tricks. In the following brief account of the structure of Vlach
we have attempted to set down the common forms which cannot be described as peculiar to any one dialect, but the base
of our knowledge of the language is the dialect of Samarina.
At the end we have tried to show how the pronunciation and
vocabulary vary in the separate dialects where such can be
distinguished. In every case, for the sake of brevity, we
have not troubled to indicate all the exceptions and irregu-
larities, for Vlach grammar like every other has plenty of
these.

PHONETIC CHANGES

As regards the vowel sounds it is necessary to bear in mind
that the general tendency of Vlach is in favour of the following
changes :

Unaccented *o* (*oa*) and *e* (*ea*) become *u* and *i*,
Unaccented *u* and *i* are dropped,
Unaccented *a* becomes *ǎ* or *ā*, except when initial,
Unaccented *ǎ* or *ā* are dropped.

This is well illustrated in the following verbs :

Infin. *mkáre,*	Pres. *mǎkǔ,*	Pret. *mkai* ;
Infin. *kripáre,*	Pres. *krépǔ,*	Imper. *kreápǎ* ;
Infin. *skuteáre,*	Pres. *skótǔ,*	Pret. *skoáshu* ;
Infin. *bāteáre,*	Pres. *bátǔ,*	Pret. *bātúi* ;
Infin. *p(u)teáre,*	Pres. *pótu,*	Pret. *ptúi.*

These changes naturally affect spoken Vlach very much.
The final *i* in conjunctions such as *shi* and *si*, in verbs and in

pronouns like *tsi*, *mi* and *l'i* drops, and this in turn produces other changes. Thus :

> *s* becomes *z* before *b* as *voi z beau*, I want to drink,
> before *d* as *voi z dormu*, I want to sleep,
> before *v* as *vine z veadă*, he came to see,
> before *y* as *l'i dzăse z yină*, he told him to come,
> *sh* becomes *zh* before the same consonants,
> *z duse la hani zh biu*, he went to the inn and drank,
> *kădzu zh d aklo*, he fell from there too,
> *vin'u zh vidzui*, I came and saw,
> *si skoală zh yine*, he gets up and comes,
> *ts* becomes *z* before the same as,
> *z băgai measa*, I set the table for you,
> *z dedu lăna*, I gave you the wool,
> *tsez vă*, go (for *dutsets vă*).
> *z yine tată ts*, your father is coming to you,

Also *f* before *d* becomes *v*, thus we get *vdzi* for *fudzi*, he went, and when the *i* and *u* of *l'i*, *li* and *lu* drop before a consonant a sound varying between *ā* and *ă* is introduced before the *l*, e.g.

> *āl' dzăse*, he told him,

but before vowels *ā* is not inserted and only the *i* drops, e.g.

> *l' adră kartea*, he wrote the letter for him.

As to final *i̯* and *ŭ*, they are not pronounced when the word is in the middle of a sentence, but only if it is at the end, e.g.

> *ved kā easte glarŭ*, I see he is mad,
> but *easte glar, u vedŭ*, he is mad, I see it ; and
> *tora h'im fratsĭ*, now we are brothers,
> but *vai h'im frats tora*, we will be brothers now.

But final *ŭ* and *u* are often retained after two consonants.

Before plunging into Vlach grammar it will be advisable to give a short list of the principal phonetic changes that the original Latin sounds have undergone. We have the change of

> *l* to *r*, *kare* for *qualem*,
> *ll* to *u*, *steauă* for *stellam*,
> *rv* to *rb*, *korbŭ*, for *corvum*,
> *nct* to *mt*, *umtŭ* for *unctum*,
> *pi*, *pe* to *k'i*, *k'e*, *k'inŭ* for *pinum*, *k'ale* for *pellem*,
> *bi*, *be* to *g'i*, *g'ine* for *bene*,

intervocalic *b* to *v*, *avemŭ* for *habemus*,
vi to *yi*, *yinŭ* for *vinum*,
intervocalic *v* being dropped, *nou* for *novum*,
fi, *fe* to *h'i*, *h'e*, *h'il'e* for *filiam*, *h'erbu* for *ferveo*,
ti, *te* to *ts*, *tutsĭ* for *toti*, *tsară* for *terram*,
tionem to *tshune*, *rugatshune* for *rogationem*,
di, *de* to *dz*, *dzăkŭ* for *dico*, *dzatse* for *decem*,
s to *sh*, *shedŭ* for *sedeo*, but not always,
ski to *shti*, *shtiu* for *scio*,
ki, *ke* to *ts*, *fatsă* for *faciem*, *dzatse* for *decem*, *tseară* for *ceram*,
kt to *pt*, *optŭ* for *octo*,
ks to *ps*, *h'ipse* for *fixit*, *frapsinŭ* for *fraxinum*,
qua to *pa*, *eapă* for *equam*, except in relatives, *kăndu* and
　　kătŭ for *quando* and *quantum*,
qui, *que* to *tsi*, *tsi* for *quid*, *tsintsĭ* for *quinque*,
gua to *ba*, *limbă* for *linguam*,
gi, *ge* to *dzi*, *dze*, *mardzine* for *marginem*, *dzeană* for *genam*,
gn to *mn*, *lemnu* for *lignum*,
j to *dzh*, *dzhone* for *juvenem*.

Genders

There are three genders,—Masculine, Feminine and Neuter as in Latin. As in the case of other Romance languages it would perhaps be more correct to say that there is no Neuter as a direct survival of Latin. The neuter nouns in the singular have become assimilated to the masculine and in the plural to the feminine. However in Vlach as in Italian a large number of original neuter plurals have survived. Consequently for the sake of simplicity we have preferred to treat the neuter as a separate gender, though this inevitably leads to some inconsistency.

The Formation of the Plural

All Masculine Nouns end in *u*, *ŭ* or *e* according to their Latin originals, and foreign words may end in *u*, *i*, *a* or *o*, e.g. *omŭ* (man) from *homo*, *kăne* (dog) from *canis*, *udă* (room) from the Turkish *oda*, *pitrupŭ* (warden) the Greek ἐπίτροπος, *pampordzhi* (steamer captain) from the Italian *vapore* with the Turkish termination *ji* (e.g. *áraba*, a cab ; *árabaji*, a cabman and *marañgo* (carpenter) from the Greek μαραγγός.

The plural invariably ends in *i* ; even the plurals of foreign words which usually form it by adding *adzĭ* to the stem end in *i*. We have *lupŭ* (wolf) *luk'i*, *tramvaidzhi* (tram conductor) *tramvaidzhadzĭ* (from the English *tramway* through the Italian with the Turkish termination *ji* and the plural ending *adzĭ* adopted from Modern Greek which delights to use this, e.g. ἑορτή ἑορτάδες, βασιλιάς βασιλιάδες), *udă udadzĭ*, *pitrupŭ pitrupadzĭ*, *marango marangadzĭ*.

All Feminine Nouns end in *ă* or *e* according to their Latin derivation, *measă* (table) *mensa*, *fatsă* (face) *facies*, and foreign words that are of the same gender, e.g. *tin'ie* (price) from the Greek τιμή, *zanate* (trade) from the Turkish *sanat*.

Nouns in *ă* form the plural in *e*, e.g. *kasă* (house) *kăse*, and those in *e* in *i*, e.g. *parte* (part) *părtsi*, *politie* (town) *politii* (Greek πολιτεία), *kunak'e* (camp) *kunăk'i* (Turkish *qonaq*).

In words ending in *auă*, if they are of Latin origin, the *ll* of the stem reappears in the plural, e.g. *steauă* (star) *stealle* from *stella*, but if they are foreign words, the plural is formed in *ei*, e.g. *kukuveauă* (owl) *kukuvei* from the Greek κουκουβαΐα ; but the two classes are sometimes confused and we get *kukuveale*, and *măsei* (jaws) instead of *măsealle* from *maxillae*.

Feminine nouns ending in *mă*, which are really Greek neuters, form their plurals as in Greek with a slight alteration, e.g. *mathimă* (lesson) *mathimate* for the Greek μάθημα μαθήματα.

Dzuă (day) *dzăle* (Latin *dies*) is quite irregular.

All Neuter Nouns end in *u* and make their plural in *e*, e.g. *lemnu* (wood) *leamne* from *lignum ligna* ; but those of the Latin third declension make the plural in *ure*, e.g. *k'eptu* (breast) *k'eplure* for *pectus pectora*. This latter termination by false analogy has become the usual form for the neuter plural, e.g. *lokŭ lokure* for *locum loca* (place) and *yinŭ yinure* for *vinum vina* (wine). It thus occurs in borrowed words, which are made neuter,

> as *nomu nomure* (Greek νόμος), law ;
> and *gustu gusture* (Italian *gusto*), taste.

In some cases it even occurs in masculine and feminine words, e.g. *lapte lapture* (masc. from *lac* milk) and *kale kăl'ure* (fem. from *callis* road).

A few words still retain the true Latin form in their plurals :

omŭ oamin'ĭ for *homo homines,*
soră surăre for *soror sorores,*
oaspe oaspitsĭ for *hospes hospites,* and
kapŭ kapite for *caput capita.*

Then certain nouns implying relationship form the plural in *an'i* or *ān'i* :

mumă mother, *mumān'i,*
tată father, *tātān'i,*
papŭ grandfather, *pāpān'i,*
lală uncle, *lālān'i,* and
aushŭ old man, *aushān'i,* though *aushi* also occurs.

This termination occurs as a plural form in some family names :

Paka Pak'anl'i, the Paka's,
Yaka Yak'anl'i, the Yaka's,
Tsaknak'i Tsaknak'anl'i, the Tsaknaki's, and
Dudul'uri Dudul'uranl'i, the Dadal'arı's,

while the other usual form for the plural in family names is *adzĭ* :

Lighura Lighuradzl'i, the Lighura's,
Fole Ful'adzl'i, the Fole's.

These plurals in *ān'i* apparently correspond to the Old French acc. sing. and nom. and acc. plur. in *ain* or *ains,* e.g. *ante antain* aunt, *Eve Evain,* which is perhaps the Vulgar Latin termination *anes.* This also occurs in Italian and Romansch and in all three languages in exactly the same class of words as in Vlach.

One peculiarity of Vlach is that the final *i* of the plural often affects the preceding consonant and changes it. This of course applies to all masculine nouns except those which make their plural with *adzĭ* or *an'i.* It also affects most feminine nouns, but not all. The majority of the feminine nouns end in *ă* and so make the plural in *e,* but since the general tendency in Vlach is to change unaccented *e* into *i,* for most practical purposes the plural for them also ends in *i.* The only words which this does not affect are those ending with *shă,* e.g. *moashă,* the plural of which is always *moashe,* old women. The consonants affected are many and we have the change of

> n to n', mănă măn'i (hand), anŭ an'i (year),
> m to n', lăkrimă lăkrin'i (tear), yermu yern'i (worm),
> l to l', poală pol'i (apron), kalŭ kal'i (horse),
> g to dz, tshorgă tshordzi (rug), largu lărdzi (broad),
> k to ts, bisearikă biseritsi (church), shoariku shoaritsi (mouse),
> t to ts, poartă portsi (door), bărbatŭ bărbatsi (man), but niveastă niveaste (bride),
> d to dz, grendă grendzi (tree trunk), but pravdă pravde (beast of burden),
> b to g', iarbă ierg'i (grass), albu alg'i (white), but limbă limbe (tongue),
> p to k', groapă grok'i (grave), lupŭ luk'i (wolf), but tseapă tseape (onion),
> f to h', bufu buh'i (owl),
> v to y, gavŭ gayi (blind),

and even foreign words are not exempt, for we have

> adete adetsi, the Turkish ádet, custom,
> kărklikŭ kărklitsi, the Turkish qirqliq, a forty para piece,
> k'ibape k'ibăk'i, for the Turkish kebab, roast meat,
> lukume lukun'i, for the Turkish loqma, piece, lump,
> psofu psoh'i, the Greek ψόφιος, dead (of animals),
> sklavu sklayi, the Greek σκλάβος, slave or prisoner, and in the singular
> prukuk'ie, for the Greek προκοπή, progress.

Another characteristic feature of Vlach is that the radical vowel of the stem can be affected by the following vowel of the termination. Thus :

> o becomes oa, and
> e becomes ea,

when followed by a, ă or e, but they appear as simple vowels if i or u follow. If final e has changed to i, the rule given is observed.

This rule affects feminine nouns in the singular, e.g.

> oară ori, hour ; oaie oi, sheep ;
> seară seri, evening ; ml'eare ml'eri, woman ;

and neuter nouns in the plural, e.g.

> kornu koarne, horn,
> meru meare, apple.

Also *a* becomes *ă* if the next vowel was or is *i*, e.g.

karte kărtsi, letter,
măkare, măkări, food,
adunare adunări, meeting.

These last two words are of course infinitives used as nouns.
Foreign words too have to bow to this rule, and we have

livadhe livădzi, meadow, from the Greek λειβάδι,
kunak'e kunăk'i, camp, from the Turkish *qonaq*.

These phonetic changes of vowels and consonants do not affect nouns alone, but of course verbs as well, which will be illustrated when we come to consider the conjugations.

THE ARTICLE

The masculine article is *lu* for words in *u, ŭ, i, o* and *ă*, and *le* for those in *e*, and the plural in all cases is *l'i*.

The feminine article is *a* with the plural *le*.

The neuter article is *lu* with the plural *le*.

The suffixed article affects to some extent the final vowel of the word to which it is attached. Before *a ă* drops, and *e* is retained except when it follows

sh as *kămeashe kămeasha* (*camiciam*), shirt,
l' as *fumeal'e fumeal'a* (*familiam*), family,
or a vowel as *kleaie kleaia* (*clavem*), key.

Before *lu* final *u* and *ŭ* disappear except after a vowel as

boulu (*bovem illum*), the ox,

or two consonants as

okl'u okl'ulu (*oculum illum*), the eye.

Before *l'i i* drops, *omlu* (*homo illum*) *oamin'l'i homines illi*) ; and before *le i* is retained and *e* becomes *i*, as

părtsile (*partes illae*) and *measile* (*mensae illae*).

Foreign words follow the same rules, *e.g.*

pitrupŭ pitruplu (Greek, warden), *yatru yatrulu* (Greek, doctor),

and the final vowel, if accented, is retained before *lu*, as

paltolu (Italian, greatcoat),
k'iradzhilu (Turkish, muleteer), and
tsăruhălu (Greek, cobbler).

The suffixed article is declined and thus the cases of the nouns are formed, e.g.

		mensam illam	*dominum illum*	*fratrem illum*	*lignum illum*
S.	Nom. Acc.	*measa*	*domnulu*	*fratile*	*lemnulu*
	Gen. Dat.	*a measil'ei*	*a domnulu*	*a fratilui*	*a lemnulu*
P.	Nom. Acc.	*measile*	*domn'l'i*	*fratsl'i*	*leamnile*
	Gen. Dat.	*a measilor*	*a domnilor*	*a fratslor*	*a leamnilor*

It will be noticed that the genitive singular is formed from the original dative. In the singular there is an alternative form of the genitive and dative in which the article is suffixed to the preposition *a* and not to the noun, and this also was a dative form originally, e.g.

illi puellae	*illi domino*	*illi fratri*	*illi loco*
ale feate	*alŭ domnu*	*alŭ frate*	*alŭ lokŭ*

But this form is hardly ever used in the case of words expressing inanimate objects, and when used as a genitive is nearly always personal, e.g.

> *dulumălu ale feate*, the girl's coat,
> *kutsutlu alŭ furŭ*, the robber's knife;

but we have rare cases such as :

> *koada ale steauă*, the star's tail (of a comet),
> *patlu ale yilie*, the bottom of the glass.

Other cases if required are formed with the aid of prepositions, e.g.

> *di* to make a genitive, *gură di asime*, a mouth of silver ;
> *di la* to make an ablative, *di la pălăthiri*, from the window ;
> *pri* to make an emphatic accusative, *mi mundri pri mine*, he looked at me ;

but this last is probably due to Roumanian influence.

The Vocative is always the same as the unarticulated nominative, e.g.

> *feată* girl, *frate* brother, *tată* father, *fitshorŭ* boy ;

but certain words implying relationship make the vocative in *o*, e.g.

> *lalo* uncle, *teto* aunt, *maiko* mother ;

and this has been adopted from Bulgarian.

Only a few words still preserve the true Latin vocative form, e.g.

> *vitsine* neighbour, *bǎrbate* husband, *furtate* blood brother, *krishtine* christian, *kusurine* cousin.

Exceptions to any rule are the vocatives of

> *Dumnidzeu Dumnidzale* God, *Hristo Hristoase* Christ.

DIMINUTIVES

These may be formed by the addition of the following terminations :

> *ikǔ, ikǎ* as *fitshorǔ fitshorikǔ,* little boy ; *featǎ fitikǎ,* little girl ;
> *ushu, ushǎ* as *Kola Kulushu,* little Nicholas ; *kurkubetǎ kurkubitushǎ,* a lit'le vegetable marrow ;
> *itshǎ* apparently only feminine, as *gurǎ guritshǎ,* a pretty little mouth ; *yilie yilitshǎ,* a pretty little glass ;
> *shorǔ* apparently masculine only, *k'inǔ h'inshorǔ,* a nice little pine ; *bunǔ bunshorǔ,* rather good ; *lokǔ lokshorǔ,* a nice little place.

Fitshorǔ boy, is itself really a diminutive of this last class and is derived from the obsolete *fetǔ,* which would of course be the masculine form of *featǎ* girl.

An Albanian diminutive is *zǎ, nǎtheamǎzǎ* a very little.

ADJECTIVES.

Adjectives are declined in all cases like the nouns. Those in *u* decline thus :

> S. M. *bunǔ*　　F. *bunǎ*　　N. *bunǔ*
> P. M. *buni*　　F. *bune*　　N. *bune*

The adjective is of course not articulated unless it comes before the noun or is turned into a noun itself by the addition of the article, for instance one can say :

> *eu mundriam bunlu a indreagǎl'ei fumeal'e*

or

> *eu mundriam bunlu a fumeal'il'ei indreagǎ*

> I was considering the good of the whole family.

As a rule the adjective comes after the noun which it qualifies, e.g.

un kal bunŭ, a good horse ; *ună kasă mare*, a big house.

Adjectives in *e* have the same forms for all genders :

M. F. N.	S. *vearde*		P. *verdzi*	green	
	mare		*mări*	great, big	
	dultse		*dultsi*	sweet	

Adjectives in *esku* form thus :

S. M. *yiftesku*   F. *yifteaskă*   N. *yiftesku* gipsy
P. M. *yifteshti*   F. *yifteshti*   N. *yifteshti*

Those that end in diphthongs are exceptions, for in the feminine they are assimilated to the nouns in *auă*, e.g.

S.	M. *arău*	F. *araua*	N. *arău*	wrong
	greu	*greauă*	*greu*	heavy
	nou	*noauă*	*nou*	new
P.	M. *arăi*	F. *arale*	N. *arale*	
	grei	*greale*	*greale*	
	noi	*nale*	*nale*	

Laiŭ, black, follows the ordinary rule.
Adjectives of foreign origin decline thus :

S. M. *hazo, fukara*   F. *hazoan'e, fukaroan'e* mad, poor
P. M. *hazadzĭ, fukaradzĭ*   F. *hazoan'e, fukaroan'e*

and this termination can also be used to form feminine nouns in the case of foreign words, e.g.

vāsil'e king,   *vāsiloan'e* queen ;
tshelnikŭ shepherd,   *tshelnikoan'e* shepherdess.

The Comparison of Adjectives

The comparative is formed by placing *ma* more before the positive, and the superlative by putting *ma* before the articulated positive, e.g.

bunŭ good, *ma bunŭ* better, *ma bunlu* the best.

An intensive comparative may be formed by the use of *ka* or *ninkă*, e.g.

ka ma slabŭ or *ninka ma slabŭ*, much worse.

ADVERBS

The only true adverbial form is *g'ine* well, the adverb of *bunŭ* ; otherwise those formed from adjectives have the same form as the unarticulated masculine singular.

The principal adverbs of time and place are :

> *aoa, aoatse* here,
> *aklo* there,
> *di supra, susŭ* above,
> *năundru* within,
> *iñg'os* below,
> *năfoară* out of doors,
> *aproape* near,
> *napoi* after,
> *ninkă* still, again,
> *atumtsea* then,
> *tora* now,
> *asăns* to-day,
> *măne* to-morrow,
> *paimăne* the day after to-morrow,
> *aieri* yesterday,
> *aoaltari* the other day,
> *dineavra* just now.

AFFIRMATIVES AND NEGATIVES

Vlach has no proper words for yes and no. In the south where Greek influence is strong *ne* and *oh'i* are used. In the north *nu* is used for no, and *ashitsi* or *ashi* (lit. so) is used for yes, though occasionally the Slavonic *da* is employed through Roumanian influence.

Negatives and affirmatives can be qualified with *fără di altă* certainly, and *nakă* or *poate si h'ibă* perhaps.

NUMERALS

The numerals from one to ten are :

> *unŭ, doi, trei, patru, tsintsĭ, shasse, shapte, optŭ, noauă, dzatse.*
> Eleven and twelve are *usprădzatse* and *dosprădzatse*, fifteen *tsisprădzatse* and so on.

Twenty is *yiñgitsĭ* ; thirty, forty and the other tens up to a hundred are *tredzătse, patrudzătse* and so on, with *sheidzătse* for sixty and *obdzătse* for eighty.

A hundred is *ună sută* and a thousand is *ună n'ile*.

Twenty-one is *usprăyiñgitsĭ* and so on, but thirty-one is *tredzătse unŭ* and so with forty-one, etc.

All numerals above ten take after them the preposition *di*, e.g.

shapte oamin'i but *tredzătse di oi* ; the only exception is *yiñgitsĭ*.

Pronouns

Personal Pronouns

		ABSOLUTE.		WITH VERBS.		
		Nom. Acc.	Gen. Dat.	Nom.	Acc.	Gen. Dat.
First Pers. S.		*eu, io, mine*	*a n'ia*	*eu*	*mi*	*n'i*
P.		*noi*	*a noauă*	*noi*	*noi*	*nă, nā*
Second Pers. S.		*tine*	*a tsăia*	*tine*	*ti*	*tsi, tsă, tsā*
P.		*voi*	*a voauă*	*voi*	*voi*	*vă, vā*
Third Pers. S.	M.	*elu*	*a lui*	*elu*	*lu*	*l'i*
	F.	*ea*	*a l'ei*	*ea*	*o, u*	*l'i*
P.	M.	*el'i*	*a lor*	*el'i*	*l'i*	*lă, lā*
	F.	*eale*	*a lor*	*eale*	*li*	*lă, lā*

For the third personal pronoun one can also use :

S. M. *năsŭ*   S. F. *năsă*   P. M. *năshĭ*   P. F. *năse*

Possessive Pronouns

The possessive pronouns and pronominal adjectives can either be independent or suffixed :

The independent forms are—

		S. Nom. Acc.	Gen. Dat.	P. Nom. Acc.	Gen. Dat.
First Pers.	M.	*ameu, amelu*	*amilui*	*amel'i*	*amilor*
	F.	*amea*	*amil'ei*	*ameale*	*amilor*
Second Pers.	M.	*atău*	*atălui*	*atăi*	*atălor*
	F.	*ata*	*atăl'ei*	*atale*	*atălor*
Third Pers.	M.	*a lui*		*a lui*	
	F.	*a l'ei*		*a l'ei*	
First Pers.	M.	*anostru*	*anostrui*	*anoshtri*	*anostror*
	F.	*anoastră*	*anostrei*	*anoastre*	*anostror*
Second Pers.	M.	*avostru*	*avostrui*	*avoshtri*	*avostror*
	F.	*avoastră*	*avostrei*	*avoastre*	*avostror*
Third Pers.	M. F.	*a lor*		*a lor*	

If a neuter is required the masculine form is used in the singular and the feminine in the plural, e.g.

> *loklu atău, leamnile atale,*

and so throughout.

The suffixed forms are as follows :

		Nom. Acc.	Gen. Dat.
First Pers.	M.	*n'u, tatăn'u* my father	*n'ui, a tatăn'ui*
	F.	*n'i, maikă n'i* my mother	*n'i, ale maikă n'i*

An enclitic *mŭ* is also used with vocatives, e.g. *maiko m* ; this is the Modern Greek enclitic possessive *μου*.

Second Pers.	M.	*tu* or *ts, kaplu ts* your head	*tui, a fratitui*
	F.	*ta* or *ts, kasă ts* your house	*tai* or *ts, a maikătai*
Third Pers.	M.	*su* or *l'i, tată l'i* his father	*sui* or *l'i, a fratisui*
	F.	*sa* or *l'i, kasă l'i* his house	*sai* or *l'i, a sorsai*
First Pers.	M. F.	*nă* or *nā* indeclinable	
Second Pers.	M. F.	*vă* or *vā* indeclinable	
Third Pers.	M. F.	*lă* or *lā* indeclinable	

Demonstrative Pronouns

		S. Nom. Acc.	Gen. Dat.	P. Nom. Acc.	Gen. Dat.
This.	M.	*aestu*	*aestui*	*aesti*	*aestor*
	F.	*aestă*	*aestei*	*aeste*	*aestor*
That.	M.	*atseu, atsel*	*atselui*	*atsei, atsel'i*	*atselor*
	F.	*atsea*	*atsel'ei*	*atseale*	*atselor*

Relative Pronouns

		Nom. Acc.	Gen. Dat.
Sing.	M. F.	*kare*	*a kui*
Plur.	M. F.	*kari*	

Indeclinable, all genders and all cases, *tsi*.

For the genitive and dative plural of *kare* a periphrasis with *tsi* is used, e.g.

> *oamin'l'i atsel'i tsi lā ded kartea vdziră,*
> those men to whom I gave the letter have gone.

Both *kare* and *tsi* are used as interrogatives as well :

> *kare easte* who is it ?

Relative Adverbs

Of these we have *kăndu* when, *kumŭ* how, *kătsé* why, *iu* where or whither and *di iu* whence, all of which are used interrogatively as well.

To these we may perhaps add :

> *iuva* nowhere,
> *aliura* somewhere else, and
> *pute* (Greek ποτέ) or *vără oară* never.

Indefinite Pronouns

		S. Nom. Acc.	Gen. Dat.	P. Nom. Acc.	Gen. Dat.
One, some.	M.	*unŭ*	*a unui*	*năskăntsĭ*	*a năskăntor*
	F.	*ună*	*a unei*	*năskănte*	*a năskăntor*

In the plural *a unor* is sometimes heard.

One, some.	M.	*vărŭ, vrănŭ*	*a vrănui*
	F.	*vără, vrănă*	*a vrănei*

This is nearly always negative, e.g.

> *nu vidzui vrănŭ*, I saw no one ;

but it can occasionally be positive :

> *am vără sută di kal'i*, I have about a hundred horses.

Kanŭ which is probably Greek in origin is similar in meaning and declension.

Other.	M.	*altŭ*	*a altui*	*altsĭ*	*a altor*
	F.	*altă*	*a altei*	*alte*	*a altor*
The other.	M.	*alantu*	*alantui*	*alantsi*	*alantor*
	F.	*alantă*	*alantei*	*alante*	*alantor*

Kătŭ (*quantum*) how many, *tutŭ* (*totum*) all, *multu* (*multum*) many and *ahăntŭ* (*atque* or *eccum tantum*) as many as, all follow the ordinary rules for adjectives.

Kathe each, and *kăte* one apiece, are indeclinable, e.g.

> *la kathe fitshor dedu kăte ună mishkătură di păne*,
> I gave each boy one scrap of bread apiece.

We may also add here *tsiva* nothing, *dipŭ* altogether and *nătheamă* a little, e.g.

> *Nu am tsiva paradz dip*, I have no money whatsoever,
> *Voi nătheamă păne*, I want a little bread.

PREPOSITIONS

In Vlach the prepositions may be either simple or compound. The commonest simple prepositions are :

a at, *a kasa,* at home ;
tra for, *atseu easte tră noi,* that is for us ;
di of, *kasă di sare,* a house of salt ;
la to, at, *si duse la hani,* he went to the inn ; *easte la hani,* he is at the inn ;
ku with, *steaua ku koadă,* the star with a tail ;
in in, *in kasa,* in the house ;
pri on, *pri measa,* on the table ;
sum under, *kădzu sum kinŭ,* he fell under a pine tree ;
kătră towards, *kătră seară,* towards evening ;
fără without, *fără minte,* without sense ;
pănă as far as, *pănă muntile,* as far as the hill ;
după behind, after, *vine după mine,* he came after me ;
niñgă near, *u băgă niñgă mine,* he put it near me.

Compound prepositions in ordinary use are :

di la from, *kuskri di la ghambrolu,* wedding guests from the bridegroom ;
di pri out of, *u arkă di pri pălăthiri,* he threw it out of window ;
di tu out of, *noi vinim di tu Añglie,* we came from England.

CONJUNCTIONS

The commonest are :

shi, di and,
ma but,
i . . . i either . . . or,
ni . . . ni, nekă . . . nekă neither . . . nor,
kă because, as, since, that,
kăndu, kara when,
după tse after
ku tute kă or *molonoti* (Greek) for all that,
ka si, makă if,
taha as if,
tă si or *tră si* in order that,
ka, kanda as, like ;

and where Greek influence is strong *omos* however, *lipon* well and similar words will be used, and we have heard the Persian *hem* (also) used as meaning and.

VERBS

The conjugation of the Vlach verb follows the Latin very closely in many respects. We will begin with the auxiliary verbs *h'ire* to be and *aveare* to have.

H'ire to be (Latin *fieri*).

Ind. Pres.	Imperf.	Pret.	Subj. Pres.	Imper.
esku, h'iu, h'im	eará'm	fui	si esku, si h'iu, si h'im	
eshti, h'iĭ	earai	fushĭ	si eshti, si h'iĭ	h'iĭ
easte, i	eará	fu	si h'ibă	si h'ibă
h'imŭ	earám	fumŭ	si h'imŭ	
h'itsĭ	earátsĭ	futŭ	si h'itsĭ	h'itsĭ
suntu	eará	fură	si h'ibă	si h'ibă

The future is formed by using *va si*, *vai* or *va* with the forms of the present subjunctive, e.g.

vai h'iu, vai h'ii, vai h'iba, etc.

The difference between *va si* and *vai* is dialectic, the former being used in the north and the latter in the south. *Va*, as a rule, is only used when a pronoun intervenes between it and verb, e.g.

va n' h'ibă arkoare,
I shall be cold (lit. there will be cold for me).

The conditional is made by using *vrea* in the same way, e.g.

ka si yineai tine vrea h'ibă ună mare hărauă tră noi,
if you came it would be a great pleasure for us.

We have heard a perfect in use at Muskopol'e, *am fută* I have been, and so it is possible that a past participle *futŭ* does exist.

In the south a perfect subjunctive still survives, *si furim*, but is used as an imperfect.

Aveare to have (Latin *habere*).

Ind. Pres.	Imperf.	Pret.	Subj. Pres.	Imper.
am	aveám	avúi	si am	
ai	aveái	avúshĭ	si ai	ai
are	aveá	avú	si aibă	si aibă
avémŭ	aveámŭ	avúmŭ	si avemŭ	
avétsĭ	aveátsĭ	avútŭ	si avetsĭ	avetsĭ
au	aveá	avúră	si aibă	si aibă

The future is formed with *va si, vai* or *va*, e.g.

vai am, vai ai, vai aibă, etc.,

like the present subjunctive.

The conditional is formed with *vrea* in the same way as the future. The present participle is *avāndălui* (really a Latin gerundive) and the past participle is *avutŭ*.

From the latter a compound pefect and pluperfect can be formed, *e.g.*

am avută I have had, *aveam avută* I had had.

In the south a perfect subjunctive with an imperfect meaning still survives, *si avearim*, otherwise if an imperfect or other tenses of the subjunctive are wanted they can be formed by using *si* with the corresponding tenses of the indicative, e.g.

si aveam, si am avută, si aveam avută ;

but in a simple language like Vlach such tenses are very rarely if ever required.

A future perfect can be made by using *vai* or *va si* with the preterite :

vai avushĭ you will have had, or *vai ai avută.*

Similarly a past conditional can be made by using *vrea* with the preterite :

vrea avu he would have had.

The other verbs may be divided into four conjugations on the basis of Latin.

THE FIRST CONJUGATION contains most verbs of the Latin first conjugation, verbs in *edzu* and *zburăsku* to speak.

Kăftare to ask for (Latin *captare*).

Ind. Pres.	Imperf.	Pret.	Subj. Pres.	Imper.	Part. Pres.
kăftu	*kăftám*	*kăftai*	*si kaftu*		*kăftāndălui*
kăftsĭ	*kăftai*	*kăftáshĭ*	*si kaftsĭ*	*kaftă*	Part. Past.
káftă	*kăftá*	*kăftă*	*si kaftă*	*si kaftă*	*kăftatŭ*
kăftămŭ	*kăftámŭ*	*kăftămŭ*	*si kăftămŭ*		
kăftátsĭ	*kăftátsĭ*	*kăftátŭ*	*si kăftatsĭ*	*kăftatsĭ*	
káftă, káftu	*kăftá*	*kăftáră*	*si kaftă*	*si kaftă*	

Future, *va si, vai* or *va kaftu*, etc.   Conditional, *vrea kaftu*, etc.
Compound perfect and pluperfect, *am kăftată, aveam kăftată*, etc.

Other extra tenses can be formed if needed as in the case of *aveare*. It is to be noticed how the change of accent affects the vowel in the first syllable ; as another example we can take—

    skulare to raise (Latin *excollocare* or *excolare* for *exlocare*).

Ind. Pres.	Imperf.	Pret.	Subj. Pres. Third Pers.	Imper.	Part. Past.
skolŭ	*skulám*	*sk(u)laí*	*si skoálă*	*skoálă*	*skulátŭ*

Verbs in *edzu* form the present thus :

    Lukrare to work, *lukredzu, lukredzi, lukreadze, lukrămŭ, lukratsĭ, lukredzu,*

but are otherwise regular.   The third person of the subjunctive is *si lukreadză*.

Zburăre to speak, makes its present thus :

    zburăsku, zburăshti, zburashte, zburămŭ, zburatsĭ, zburăsku,

but in all its other tenses is quite regular.   The third person of the subjunctive is *si zburaskŭ*.

THE SECOND CONJUGATION makes the infinitive in *eare* and the preterite in *ui* ; it contains verbs of the second and third Latin conjugations, a few of the fourth, and the few verbs in *sku* which are of Latin origin like *pasku păshteare* to pasture.

    videare to see (Latin *videre*).

Ind. Pres.	Imperf.	Pret.	Subj. Pres.	Imper.	Part. Pres.
védŭ	*videám*	*vidzúi*	*si vedŭ*		*vidzăndălui*
védzĭ	*videaí*	*vidzúshĭ*	*si vedzĭ*	*vedzi*	Part. Past.
veáde	*videá*	*vidzú*	*si veadă*	*si veadă*	*vidzutŭ*
vidémŭ	*videámŭ*	*vidzúmŭ*	*si videmŭ*		
vidétsĭ	*videátsĭ*	*vidzútŭ*	*si videtsĭ*	*videtsĭ*	
védŭ	*videá*	*vidzúră*	*si veadă*	*si veadă*	

    Future, *va si, vai* or *va vedŭ*, etc.   Conditional, *vrea vedu*, etc.
    Compound perfect and pluperfect, *am vidzută, aveam vidzută.*

Other compound tenses can be formed for the subjunctive, etc., as in the case of *aveare*.

As another example we can take the common verb—

    tritseare to pass by (Latin *traicere*).

Ind. Pres.	Imperf.	Pret.	Subj. Pres. Third Pers.	Imper.	Part. Past.
trékŭ	*tritseám*	*trikúi*	*si treakă*	*tretsĭ*	*trikutŭ*

The principal verbs in *sku* of this conjugation are—

> *kunosku* I know, *mesku* I treat, *pasku* I pasture, *akresku* I grow, *hasku* I gape, *invesku* I clothe.

They conjugate thus :

mishteare to treat.

Ind. Pres.	Imperf.	Pret.	Subj. Pres. Third Pers.	Imper.	Part. Past.
mésku	*mishteám*	*miskúi*	*si measkă*	*meshti*	*miskutŭ*

The present indicative goes—

> *mésku, méshti, meáshte, mishtémŭ, mishtêtsĭ, mésku.*

THE THIRD CONJUGATION mainly contains verbs of the Latin third conjugation and makes the infinitive in *eare* and the preterite in *u.*

spuneare to tell (Latin *exponere*).

Ind. Pres.	Imperf.	Pret.	Subj. Pres.	Imper.	Part. Pres.
spúnŭ	*spuneám*	*spúshu*	*si spunŭ*		*spunăndălui*
spún'i	*spuneaí*	*spuséshĭ*	*si spun'i*	*spune*	Part. Past.
spúne	*spuneá*	*spúse*	*si spună*	*si spună*	*spusŭ*
spunémŭ	*spuneámŭ*	*spúsimŭ*	*si spunemŭ*		
spunétsĭ	*spuneátsĭ*	*spúsitŭ*	*si spunetsĭ*	*si spunetsĭ*	
spúnŭ	*spuneá*	*spúsiră*	*si spună*	*si spună*	

Future, *va si, vai* or *va spunŭ*, etc.　Conditional, *vrea spunŭ*.
Compound perfect and pluperfect, *am spusă, aveam spusă*.

Other compound tenses for the subjunctive, etc., can be formed on the model of *aveare*.

As other examples we can take—

Ind. Pres.	Imperf.	Pret.	Subj. Pres. Third Pers.	Imper.	Part. Past.
tindeare to spread or stretch—					
tíndu	*tindeám*	*téshu, tímshu*	*si tindă*	*tinde*	*tesŭ, tímtu*
frăndzeare to break—					
frắñgu	*frăndzeám*	*frédzhu*	*si frăñgă*	*frăndze*	*frímtu*
fătseare to make—					
fákŭ	*fătseám*	*fétshu*	*si fakă*	*fă*	*faptu*
dutseare to lead—					
dúkŭ	*dutseám*	*dúshu*	*si dukă*	*du*	*dusŭ*
trădzeare to draw or drag—					
trágŭ	*trădzeám*	*trápshu*	*si tragă*	*tradze*	*traptu*
arădeare to laugh—					
arắdŭ	*arădeám*	*arắshu*	*si arắdă*	*arắde*	*arắsŭ*
dzătseare to say—					
dzắkŭ	*dzătseám*	*dzắshu*	*si dzắkă*	*dză*	*dzắsŭ*

THE FOURTH CONJUGATION contains verbs of the fourth and third Latin conjugations, the infinitive is in *ire* and the preterite in *ii*. To this conjugation can also be reckoned all the verbs in *esku* which are almost without exception foreign verbs incorporated in Vlach such as—

> *pistipsesku* I believe, from the Greek πιστεύω,
> *g'izirsesku* I wander, from the Turkish *gezmek* to go, *gezdirmek* to cause to go, and
> *mutresku* I look at, from the Slavonic root *motri* to see, as in *s-motrêti* to look at.

In the case of borrowed Greek verbs *esku* is always added to the aorist stem, e.g. ἀλλάζω ἤλλαξα I change, becomes in Vlach *alāksesku* with the infinitive *alāksire*.

durn'ire to sleep (Latin *dormire*).

Ind. Pres.	Imperf.	Pret.	Subj. Pres.	Imper.	Part. Pres.
dórmu	durn'iám	durn'iĭ	si dormu		durn'indălui
dórn'i	durn'iái	durn'ishĭ	si dorn'i	dorn'i	Part. Past.
doárme	durn'iá	durn'i	si doarmă	si doarmă	durn'itŭ
durn'imŭ	durn'iámŭ	durn'imŭ	si durn'imŭ		
durn'itsĭ	durn'iátsĭ	durn'itŭ	si durn'itsĭ	durn'itsĭ	
dórmu	durn'iá	durn'iră	si doarmă	si doarmă	

> Future, *va si, vai* or *va dormu*, etc.   Conditional *vrea dormu*.
> Compound perfect and pluperfect *am durn'ită, aveam durn'ită.*

Other compound tenses can be formed for the subjunctive, etc., as in the case of *aveare*.

Another example is—

avdzāre to hear (Latin *audire*).

Ind. Pres.	Imperf.	Pret.	Subj. Pres. Third Pers.	Imper.	Part. Past.
ávdu	avdzāám	avdzăĭ	si ávdă	avde or avdzā	avdzātŭ

The verbs in *esku* conjugate as follows :

Ind. Pres.	Imperf.	Pret.	Subj. Pres. Third Pers.	Imper.	Part. Past.

pulimsire to fight, from Greek πολεμῶ ἐπολέμησα—

| pulimsésku | pulimsiám | pulimsiĭ | si pulimseáskă | pulimsiá | pulimsĭtŭ |

hrānire to feed, to keep, from Slavonic *chraniti*—

| hrānésku | hrāniám | hrāniĭ | si hrāneaskă | hrānia | hrānitŭ |

bitisire to finish, from the Turkish *bitmek* through the Greek—

| itisésku | bitisiám | bitisiĭ | si bitiseaskă | bitisiá | bitisitŭ |

Irregular Verbs

It will have been seen that not all the verbs given above as typical examples of their respective conjugations can be described as regular, especially in the third conjugation. In this case the different methods of forming the preterite and past participle depend on the Latin originals. Further as regards the imperative it seems that the old fashion was that in the singular at least it should have a special form, e.g. *tinde, avde, spune*, etc. ; but now it is more usual for the second person singular of the present indicative to be used, e.g. *vedzĭ, avdzĭ*. Three verbs—*dutseare, dzātseare* and *fātseare*—have still retained their peculiar Latin imperatives *du, dzā* and *fă*. *Dutseare* owing to the common habit of dropping unaccented *u* has bye-forms which are in ordinary use because in its reflexive form *mi dukŭ*, I go, is perhaps the most used of all Vlach verbs. Thus *nā dutsiámŭ* is *nā tsiámŭ, vā dutsétsĭ* is *vā tsetsĭ* and *dutsétsĭ vā* is *tsez vā*, and these are hard to distinguish from the corresponding forms of *dzātseare tsiamŭ, tsetsĭ*, etc. Of verbs that may be really called irregular the following six are the commonest :

Ind. Pres.	Imperf.	Pret.	Subj. Pres.	Imper.	Part. Past.
dare to give (Latin *dare*)—					
dau	dideám	dedúĭ	si dau		datŭ
dai	dideái	didéshĭ	si dai	dă	
da	dideá	deáde	si da	si da	
dămŭ	dideámŭ	deádimŭ	si dămŭ		
datsĭ	dideátsĭ	deáditŭ	si datsĭ	datsĭ	
dau, da	dideá	deádiră	si da	si da	
l'are to take (Latin *levare*)—					
l'au	luám	loáĭ	si l'au		loatŭ
l'ai	luái	loáshĭ	si l'ai	l'a	
l'a	luá	lo	si l'a	si l'a	
lomŭ	luámŭ	lomŭ	si lomŭ		
loatsĭ	luátsĭ	loátŭ	si loatsĭ	loatsĭ	
l'au, l'a	luá	loáră	si l'a	si l'a	
stare to stand (Latin *stare*)—					
stau	stăteám	stetúĭ	si stau		statŭ
stai	stăteái	stetúshĭ	si stai	stă, stei	
sta	stăteá	stetú	si sta	si sta	
stămŭ	stăteámŭ	stetúmŭ	si stămŭ		
statsĭ	stăteátsĭ	stetútŭ	si statsĭ	statsi	
stau, sta	stăteá	stetúră	si sta	si sta	

Ind. Pres.	Imper.	Pret.	Subj. Pres.	Imper.	Part. Past.
beare to drink (Latin *bibere*)—					
beaŭ	beám	biúi	si beau		biutŭ
bĕai	beái	biŭshĭ	si beai	bea	
beá	beá	biŭ	si bea	si bea	
bĕmŭ	beámŭ	biŭmŭ	si bemŭ		
bĕtsĭ	beátsĭ	biútŭ	si betsĭ	betsĭ	
beaŭ, bea	beá	biúră	si bea	si bea	
vreare to want, to like (Latin *velle*)—					
voiŭ	vreám	vrui	si voiŭ		vrutŭ
vrei	vreai	vrushĭ	si vrei		
va	vreá	vru	si va		
vremŭ	vreámŭ	vrumŭ	si vremŭ		
vretsĭ	vreátsĭ	vrutŭ	si vretsĭ		
vórŭ	vreá	vrură	si va		
yineare, *yinire* to come (Latin *venire*)—					
yinŭ	yin'iám	vin'u	si yinŭ		yinítu, vinítŭ
yin'i	yin'iai	vinishĭ	si yin'i	yină	
yine	yin'ia	vine	si yină	si yină	
vinimŭ	yin'iamŭ	vinimŭ	si vinim		
vinitsĭ	yin'iátsĭ	vinitŭ	si vinitsĭ	yinitsĭ	
yinŭ	yin'iá	viniră	si yină	si yină	

Throughout this verb the *v* and *y* are interchangeable
except in the preterite, and with the dropping of the unaccented
i one gets forms like *vn'am* or *n'am* for *yin'iam* or *vineam*.

Passive and Reflexive

In all verbs that are transitive these may be formed by
putting the pronouns *mi, ti, si, nă, vă* and *si* in front of the
corresponding persons of the verb, e.g.

> *mi spelŭ,* I am washed, or I wash myself.

But in addition there is another kind of reflexive which
is formed by putting the pronouns *n', ts, sh, nă, vă* and *sh*
in front of the persons of the verb. This is used when one
does something which one imagines will be to one's advantage or disadvantage, e.g.

> *niveasta va n' ti adarŭ,* I will make you my bride ;
> *n' spelŭ stran'ile,* I am washing my clothes ; but *spelŭ stran'ile,*
> I am washing the clothes.

SYNTAX

Vlach syntax is very simple and the language is paratactic and not syntactic.   That is subordinate or dependent clauses except of the most ordinary kind are rare.   They even prefer to say—

> *akatsă di ghrăpseashte,* he starts and writes, instead of *akatsă tră si ghrăpseaskă,* he starts to write.

Consequently conditional clauses are not complicated, and only the simplest forms are in use.   Remote possibility is indicated thus (we take the examples from a Samarina folk-tale published by Papahagi in *Basme Aromăne,* pp. 490, 491) :

> *S aveai puïl'lu hrisusit ka tine altu nu vai eara tu lume.*
> If you were to have the golden bird, there would not be another like you in the world.
>
> *Ka tine altu nu vai eara si avuriĭ tine Mushata-Loklui.*
> There would not be another like you, if you were to have the Beautiful One of the World.
>
> *S avearim niñgă vără ndoi poate vrea mi satur.*
> If I were to have another one or two, perhaps I would be satisfied.

THE DIALECTS

Like all languages Vlach divides into many dialects, but it is not easy to draw any hard and fast line between any two and to say that one peculiarity occurs in one region and nowhere else.   The speech of one region shades off into that of another and the pronunciation varies from individual to individual.   Still working on broad lines divisions may be made.   In the East about Seres there seems to be no particular dialect and this is not surprising, for the Vlachs here have come from many different villages.   Only in Rhodope do the Gramosteani seem to have preserved their own dialect.   In the Meglen there is a peculiar dialect, very much under Bulgarian influence, which links on the one hand to Roumanian proper and on the other to Vlach.   But of this region as also of the Seres district and of the Farsherots we have no personal knowledge and our information is drawn mainly from the works of Weigand. In the West we may divide the Vlachs into three groups. The Northern group begins round Monastir and passes through Okhridha to Muskopol'e and the Albanian border. Of this we have some, but no deep personal knowledge. The Central group is represented by Neveska and Klisura, where we have a fair knowledge of the local dialect. The Southern group splits up into several others: (1) the Verria villages, (2) the Olympus Vlachs, (3) the Pindus villages reaching from Samarina to Turia, (4) Metsovo and the Zaghori, (5) the Aspropotamos Vlachs, all those south of Turia and Metsovo and including Malakasi, Kornu, Siraku, Kalarites, Gardista and Halik'i. Of these districts we know the first, the third and the fourth well, especially the third, but we have only a moderate knowledge of the second and very little of the fifth. In the following accounts of the dialects of these regions where our own knowledge is at fault we have based our remarks on the researches of Weigand.

The North

Between the North and the South in general the following differences are constant :

The NORTH says—

> *lipseashte*, it must, for *prinde*,
> *esku* for *h'iu*, *eshti* for *h'ii*,
> *va si* for *vai* in the future of verbs,
> *shă* and *să* for *shi* and *si*,
> *ak'ikăsesku*, I understand, for *duk'esku*,
> *aistu*, this, for *aestu*,
> *mine* for *eu* with verbs, e.g. *mine esku* for *eu h'iu*.

MONASTIR-KRUSHEVO DISTRICT.—Here the marks of the dialect are :

> very little difference between *ā* and *ă*, e.g. *lănă, mănă, făntănă*, etc.
> *shtshiĭ* for *shtiĭ* and *eshtshii* for *eshti*, etc.
> *tsi* in the plural becomes *tsă*, e.g. *multsă, muntsă, alantsă, altsă*, etc.
> Greek sounds such as *th, dh, gh*, are not well pronounced and become *h', d* and *g*.

GOPESH-MOLOVISHTE.—Here the peculiarities are :

> the use of *g'* for *y*, *g'iptu* for *yiptu*, *g'inŭ* for *yinŭ*, *ag'ine* for
> *ayine*, and even in Greek words *g'atru* for *yatru*
> doctor, *g'ilie* glass for *yilie* ;
> of *zh* for *dzh*, e.g. *zhone* for *dzhone*, *zhokŭ* for *dzhokŭ*,
> *azhuñgu* for *adzhuñgu*, etc. ;
> of *z* for *dz*, e.g. *zuă* for *dzuă*, *avzăm* for *avdzăm*, *vizuı*
> for *vidzuı*, etc.

The article in the masculine and neuter is both *ul* and *lu* ;
the former occurs after two consonants, e.g.

> *lukrul, preftul, lemnul,* but *barbatlu, kallu, Greklu,* etc.

OKHRIDHA-LUNKA.—Here the main features are :

> *ă* for *e* after hissing sounds and *r*, e.g. *moashăle* for *moashele,*
> *matsăle* for *matsele,* etc. ;
> an extra vowel is often inserted between two consonants,
> especially when one of them is *r* or *l*, e.g. *kaluguru* for
> *kalugru, lukuru* for *lukru, kăsenŭ* for *ksenŭ, garambo* for
> *gambró,* etc.

The Centre

NEVESKA AND KLISURA.—Here Greek influence on the
pronunciation begins. Thus we have :

> *nd* for *nt, alandă* for *alantă, munde* for *munte* ;
> *ñg* for *nk, iñgrunare* for *inkrunare, iñ gasă* for *in kasă,* and thus
> a confusion arises between *niñgă* near and *ninkă* again ;
> *mb* for *mp, skumbu* for *skumpu, m bade* for *m pade, imblinŭ* for
> *implinŭ.*

In the present indicative in the verbs of the third conjugation the accent in the first and second persons plural
falls not on the final syllable as elsewhere, but on the pen-
ultimate, e.g.

> *fátsim, dútsim, frăndzim, spúnim, depúnim,* etc.

Here too one first hears as one goes from north to south
eu or *io* for *mine.*

But of course since this district is on the border line between
the two big regions both northern and southern forms can be
used, for instance both *ak'ikăsesku* and *duk'esku* are in use.

The South

THE VERRIA VILLAGES.—Here the dialect is mainly that of Avdhela about which more is said below.

THE OLYMPUS VLACHS.—Here we have a kind of lisp and for

> *tsh* we get *ts*, *fitsorŭ* for *fitshorŭ*, *fetsu* for *fetshu*, etc. ;
> *sh* we get *s*, *si* for *shi*, *isire* for *ishire*, etc. ;
> *dzh* we get *dz*, *dzone* for *dzhone*, *dzokŭ* for *dzhokŭ*, etc. ;
> *zh* we get *z*, *Kozani* for *Kozhani*, etc.

On the other hand before *i* and *e ts* and *dz* sometimes almost become *tsh* and *dzh*, e.g.

> *atshia* for *atsia*, *tshem* for *tsem*, *fätshém* for *fätsém*, *dzheană* for *dzeană*, *tradzhĭ* for *tradzĭ*, etc.

It is probable that this lisp of the Olympus Vlachs is due to the very strong Greek influence amongst them. The Modern Greek in most districts cannot pronounce sounds such as *tsh*, *sh*, *dzh*, *zh*, etc., and we have heard this in a native of Samarina who was for twenty-five years continuously in Athens having left his home when a boy of eight. He came back to his village for the summer and though he could talk Vlach perfectly, could not say *sh*, *tsh*, *dzh* and *zh* ; he would say *sedŭ* for *shedŭ*, *dzone* for *dzhone* and so on. Since this peculiarity also occurs amongst the Aspropotamos Vlachs who have all been living for the last thirty years within the kingdom of Greece where education in Greek is nominally compulsory, it seems at least reasonable to attribute it to the conquering influence of Modern Greek.

The PINDUS VILLAGES around Samarina split up into two groups. The first consists of Smiksi, Avdhela, Perivoli, Turia, Ameru and Baieasa and probably too of some of the villages lying between Turia and Malakasi. The second consists of Furka, Samarina, Briaza, Armata, Pădză and Palioseli.

Some features are common to both these groups. These are :

The survival of the perfect subjunctive, e.g.

> *furim*, *avearim*, *băgarim*, *skularim*, *akătsarim*, *videarim*, *vrearim*, *yinearim*, *ptearim*, *agudearim*, *durn'arim*, *vindearim*, *loarim*, etc.

The second person singular of the preterite in the third conjugation is accented on the first syllable, e.g.

spúsishĭ for *spuséshĭ, feátshishĭ* for *fitséshĭ, plĭmsishĭ* for *plimséshĭ, dúsishĭ* for *duséshĭ, vínishĭ* for *vinîshĭ, deádishĭ* for *didéshĭ*, etc.

But the survival of *tseshĭ* and *atseshĭ* for *duséshĭ* and *aduséshĭ* shows that this was not always so.

The dropping of unaccented *i* and *u* is very strong and the change of unaccented *e* and *o* to *i* and *u* also very marked, e.g.

skăndră for *skăndură, l'epri* for *l'epure, iavá* for *eavá*, etc.

Unaccented *ă* and *a* except when initial become *ā*, e.g.

alăgai, alăksesku.

Unaccented *ā* drops, *mkai* and *ñgai* for *măkai* and *măñgai*. *I* after *ts* and *dz* becomes *ā, mundză, altsă*, etc.

The differences between the two groups are that in the AVDHELA group they say—

yiñgits for twenty, as usual.

Before *l', d* and *t* in the combinations *dz* and *ts* drop, e.g. *munzl'i, frasl'i*; and in some cases the *s* becomes *z*, e.g. *frazl'i, sozl'i*; and it even infects words with the article *le, văzle* the cows, for *vătsăle, biserizle* the churches, etc.

a'em, a'ets, a'eam, etc., are commonly used for *avem, avets, aveam*, etc.

At SAMARINA and the villages allied to it—

The passion for *ā* is very strong, *pălăthivi, părăkălsesku*, etc.

Before *l'* the *d* and *t* of *dz* and *ts* are still very slightly heard.

For *yiñgits* they say *yigindz* and this is at times abbreviated to *yindză*.

Măkare to eat, for *măñgare*,

Puñye and *frañye* are used for *punte, frănte*.

For the first person plural of the perfect there is another old form now almost obsolete and only used in a few cases, as *adrasim, fudzisim, vinisim, vidzusim, kădzusim*. This was probably a pluperfect such as occurs in Roumanian where we have *adunasem, tăcusem*, etc.

In the ZAGHORI and at METSOVO the Greek influence in pronouncing

> *nd, ñg* and *mb-*for *nt, nk* and *mp* is not so marked,
> *ts* and *dz* remain unaffected before *l'*,
> *fitséshĭ, didéshĭ*, etc., are the regular forms.

The ASPROPOTAMOS VLACHS have the same lisping pronunciation as their kinsfolk on Olympus, at least those with whom we have spoken had. Otherwise there is little to be said about their dialect, for no one so far has studied it. One noticeable word is *letŭ* or *litesku* I go out, which is used for *esŭ (exeo)* ; this has the infinitives *litire* and *liteare*, the present is *letŭ, letsĭ, leate, litem, litets, letŭ*, the imperfect *liteam*, the preterite *litiĭ*.

But one peculiarity of the Aspropotamos and Metsovo districts is that some words of Latin origin still survive which are unknown elsewhere among the Vlachs, e.g.

> *sănŭ* well, Latin *sanus* ;
> *nămal'u* an animal (used of sheep and cattle), Latin *animal*—
> these two words occur at Samarina as well ;
> *intselegŭ* I understand, Latin *intelligo* ;
> *negru* black (of coffee only), Latin *niger* (cf. the place-name
> K'atra N'agră at Samarina);
> *nkredŭ* I trust, Latin *incredo* ;
> *sintu* I feel, Latin *sentio* ;
> *amo* now, Latin *modo* ;

and a few words of Slavonic origin, e.g.

> *pi gor* downhill.

All these are known in Roumanian, and it is curious that they should still occur in a region where Greek is steadily advancing. Most Pindus Vlachs count and reckon in Greek, because their arithmetic was learnt at the Greek school, and they at times speak a tongue that is really Greek tinged with Vlach, as

> *Easte pramatikos ună apofasi teliusită*,
> It is practically a settled determination ;

and we get words such as

> *efthinitate* cheapness, *alăksimindu* a change of clothing,
> *alăksesku* I change, and so I dress, from the Greek ἀλλάζω
> and its opposite *dislăksesku* I undress ;

apostusesku I am tired, from the Greek ἀποσταίνω, ἀπόστασα, and its opposite *dispostusesku* I cease to be tired, I rest ; *uspitlik'e* friendship, from the Vlach *oaspe, oaspitsĭ* with the Turkish termination *liq*.

Perhaps the reader will be inclined to agree with the old woman who told us—

" *Limba anoastrǎ easte ka ma anapudhǎ di tute,*
Our language is the most upside down of all."

CHAPTER XII

THE HISTORY AND ORIGIN OF THE BALKAN VLACHS

Părămith shteam, părămith aspush,
Nu shtiu kum fetshu, ma nu v arāsh.

I knew a tale, I have told a tale,
How well I do not know, but I have not deceived you.

Conclusion of *Vlach Folktale*

OF the early history of the Vlachs no detailed account
is possible ; all the Byzantine and mediæval histories
are written from the towns, the plains and the coasts,
and what was happening in the hills is generally not recorded,
even if it were known to the writers themselves. So as long
as the Vlachs remained in the hills of the interior they were
outside the sphere of history and wherever or if ever they
descended from the hills and settled in the plains they easily
escaped notice by becoming absorbed into the surrounding
population.

As early as the sixth century A.D. the existence of Vlachs
in the Balkan peninsula may be inferred from the list of forts
and fortified towns recorded by Procopius ; for among a
number of place names including some clearly Italian in
sound like Kastello Novo, we find others such as Skeptekasas,
Burgualtu, Lupofantana and Gemellomuntes which are un-
mistakably Vlach, showing that by that period if not earlier
Vlach was a separate language among the Romance tongues.
Later in the same century the first Vlach words as opposed to
place names are recorded by Theophylactus. In 579 A.D.
Commentiolus with a Byzantine army was pursuing the
Avars in the passes of the Balkans. The pack on one of the
baggage animals began to slip at a time when the muleteer in
charge was walking some distance ahead. A shout of " *Retorna* "

in the native dialect intended for the muleteer alone was misinterpreted at large as a signal for retreat, and the army " turned back " in confusion thinking the Avars were upon them. Theophanes, who tells the same tale, in place of " *Retorna*," gives the words " *Torna, torna fratre* " which add more point to the story and are better Vlach. " *Torna, torna fratre* " almost certainly refers to the baggage and means " It is slipping, brother," and not " Turn back " which is the usual interpretation given. It is also possible that " *se torna* " a reflexive form should be read in place of " *retorna*."

After the sixth century there is a long interval before Vlachs are again referred to ; it is possible perhaps that Latin or Romance names such as Paganus and Sabinus among the Bulgarian chieftains of the eighth century imply a Vlach element, but no certainty is possible. About the year 976 A.D. we read in the pages of Cedrenus that David the brother of Samuel Tsar of Bulgaria was slain between Kastoria and Presba at a spot called the Fair Oaks by certain wandering Vlachs. This is the first mention of Vlachs as such, but soon afterwards references to them and mention of them become frequent, and we find several large districts called after their name. Great Vlachia for several centuries was the name given to Thessaly and Southern Macedonia ; and Little Vlachia comprised parts of Acarnania, Ætolia and Epirus. In both these cases however the Vlach population was probably confined to the hills in the main and occupied the same general position as to-day. Similarly in Dalmatia which falls outside the scope of the present work there were two districts of Morlachs known as Great and Little Vlachia respectively. How much the Vlachs were involved in the Bulgarian empire under Samuel can only be conjectured ; but it is probable that at least they fought in the Bulgarian armies and secured their share of plunder. When the Byzantines surprised the army of the Tsar at Okhridha in 1017, a few years after Samuel's death there is perhaps a hint of Vlach troops among the Bulgarian forces. When the surprise occurred a shout, it is said, arose among the Bulgarians of " Βεζειτε Ω Τζεαρ " which according to Xylander is " Fugite

O Cæsar." It is difficult to explain the existence of any form of Latin or Romance speech among the Bulgarian troops except by the presence of Vlach allies.

In the Strategikon of Kekaumenos there is a description of the Vlachs in Thessaly around Trikkala and Larissa in the eleventh century A.D. Their manner of life then was similar in certain respects to what it is now; for from April to September their flocks and families lived in the mountains of Bulgaria, which then included all Macedonia. Morally they are described as treacherous, faithless towards all mankind and with no fear of God in them; as cowards with the hearts of hares, and brave only through cowardice. This is precisely the character one would expect them to have in the towns which presumably suffered considerably from their depredations. Thessaly was then full of Vlachs, for Kekaumenos mentions that a river near Pharsala flowed through the midst of Vlach villages. We also hear of the appointment of an official to be the ruler of the Vlachs in the province of Hellas.

Barely a hundred years later we have another description in the journal of the Rabbi Benjamin of Tudela, who travelled by land up the eastern coast of Greece about 1160.

" Sinon Potamo or Zeitun is a day's journey further; R. Sh'lomo and R. Ja'acob are the principal of its fifty Jewish inhabitants. Here are the confines of Wallachia, a country of which the inhabitants are called Vlachi. They are as nimble as deer and descend from their mountains into the plains of Greece committing robberies and making booty. Nobody ventures to make war upon them, nor can any king bring them to submission, and they do not profess the christian faith. Their names are of Jewish origin and some say they have been Jews which nation they call brothers. Whenever they meet an Israelite they rob, but never kill him as they do the Greeks. They profess no religious creed."

Zeitun is the modern Lamia, so the confines of Wallachia were the range of Othrys in the south of Thessaly. Jewish names such as Simeon, David, and Samuel are found at the time among the Bulgarians, and may have occurred also among the Vlachs, especially as the races were then closely united.

For the century between these two accounts there are a few references in Anna Comnena : The Emperor Alexius on his march into Thessaly passed close to " a hill called in the common tongue of the nations Kissavos " and then " descended to Exeva, a Vlach town situated near Andronia." Kissavos is a second name for Mt. Ossa which still survives in ordinary use, but Exeva cannot be identified. Elsewhere the same author notes in connection with Ænos that " some of the Bulgarians and those who are nomadic folk are commonly called Vlachs." Pudilius is named as a prominent Vlach leader in Thrace, and the Vlachs are mentioned as acting as guides to the Comans in the Balkan mountains.

Towards the end of the twelfth century the Vlachs suddenly come into prominence. For some time past the state of the Byzantine Empire had been becoming more precarious, and when in 1186 in preparation for his marriage the Emperor Isaac increased the taxes and took toll of the flocks and herds, the Bulgarians and Vlachs in the north promptly rose in open rebellion. The leaders of the rising were two brothers Peter and Asan by name and Vlachs by race according to Nicetas the contemporary historian. From the very first they appear to have aimed at an independent kingdom, for we read that Peter crowned himself with a golden chaplet and assumed scarlet buskins, the sign of Byzantine sovereignty. Their followers were roused to a pitch of religious frenzy ; it was commonly believed that God himself was on the side of the Vlachs and that Demetrius, the martyr and patron saint of Salonica had left his shrine to help their cause. The first attempts of the rebels ended in disaster ; they were defeated by the imperial troops and driven across the Danube like the Gadarene swine in the Gospel to quote Nicetas' own simile. Returning across the river reinforced by Scythian bands they met with another defeat in the following year, but the victorious general being superseded owing to jealousy the fortune of war changed. An army under John Cantacuzenus who had imprudently encamped in the open plain, was attacked at night by Peter and Asan. The surprise was complete, the army was utterly routed and immense booty fell into the hands of the Vlachs. Eventually Isaac took the field in person, and making Adrianople his base advanced with a picked force of cavalry against the Vlachs. Nicetas who seems to have been present gives some account of the battle which was probably typical of the Vlach and Bulgarian tactics. Sending off their booty to the hills, the Vlachs received the Emperor's onset with volleys of spears and arrows. Then retreating a short distance they halted and repeated the process, until they had enticed their opponents on to rough ground when they drew their swords and fell on them with shouts and yells. The result of the day was unfavourable for the Emperor who though escaping actual defeat had to withdraw to Adrianople. In later engagements Isaac seems to have met with more success, but no decisive victory had been gained when the approach of the third crusade made a temporary peace prudent. Although Frederick Barbarossa before starting had secured permission from the Emperor to march through Bulgaria and Thrace, every obstacle was put in his way and relations between the two were strained to the utmost. Peter and Asan in this crisis offered Barbarossa the aid of 40,000 men, and expressed their willingness to hold their kingdom as his lieges, but their offer was refused on the grounds that the crusade was against infidels and not christians. As soon as the crusaders had passed on their way to the east Isaac reopened the war against the Vlachs and Bulgarians. In the interval Peter and Asan had repaired the hill forts and the new campaign went in favour of the Vlachs. In 1192 a Byzantine army retreating through a narrow pass was utterly routed and the Emperor almost captured. This battle was a turning point in the war for the Vlachs now ventured to attack the towns, Anchialos was sacked, Varna captured and Sardica partially destroyed. The loss of a second army in 1194 forced Isaac to look to the king of Hungary for aid, and early in the next year together with his brother Alexius he set out on a final campaign. Treachery now came to the aid of the Vlachs, for Alexius deposed and blinded his brother and the projected expedition was abandoned. The new emperor Alexius offered terms to the Vlachs, which were indignantly rejected and Asan raiding the country around Seres, retired with numbers of captives in safety to Bulgaria. Among these captives, says Nicetas, was a priest well skilled in the Vlach tongue who foretold to Asan that he would soon be murdered. This prophecy was fulfilled by a friend of Asan's called Ivan, who seduced the sister of Asan's wife and on being discovered murdered Asan to save himself. Soon afterwards Peter was also murdered and there was civil war between the Vlachs and Bulgarians, which ended in Ivan flying for safety to Alexius who made him governor on the Balkan frontier and in Johannitius a younger brother of Peter and Asan becoming sole king of the Bulgarians and Vlachs.

The reign of Johannitius, Joannice or Johanizza as he is variously called began in 1196 or 1197 and lasted beyond the Frankish conquest of Constantinople till 1207. Shortly after his accession Chryses, a Vlach in the Byzantine service who had taken no part in the revolt of Peter and Asan and was governor of Strumnitsa suddenly revolted. He seized Prosakon a ruined fort on a lofty cliff overhanging the Vardar, quickly repaired the walls and awaited the attack of Alexius. After a long and stubborn siege and a successful sally of the Vlachs in which the Byzantine camp was plundered, Alexius recognised Chryses as ruler of Prosakon and Strumnitsa together with the surrounding country. Thus in 1199 a semi-independent state under a Vlach chief and with a certain Vlach population, how large it is impossible to say, was established on the Vardar. The striking success of Chryses inspired Ivan to revolt from his new allegiance in the following year. His attempt was however less successful, for deceived by Alexius' terms of peace he rashly came to Constantinople and was immediately thrown into prison. He had however previously routed an imperial army and captured its general Kamytses, and this indirectly led to the second revolt of Chryses. As soon as Ivan began to come to terms with Alexius, the captive general was removed to the camp of Johannitius who was making the best of the occasion by plundering far and wide. Chryses then paid the ransom asked for Kamytses, and meanwhile Alexius came to terms with Johannitius and confiscated

Kamytses' property, and so to recover the money spent
Chryses with the ransomed general embarked on further
conquests. They easily overcame Prilapus and Pelagonia
and Kamytses advancing from the north entered Thessaly
by the pass of Tempe. Details of this expedition which may
have been an attempt to raise the Vlachs of the south are
unfortunately not recorded, but the final result was failure.
Kamytses lost all his new possessions and Chryses was deprived
of Strumnitsa. From these minor revolts we may return to
Johannitius.

Early in his reign Johannitius had conceived the idea of
finding support in the west, and had despatched with this
intent embassies to Rome to appeal for recognition. The
first embassy had miscarried and had been intercepted by
Byzantine officials, but one successfully reached Rome just
after Innocent III had ascended the papal throne. The appeals
of Johannitius were graciously received by the Pope, who
despatched in reply an answer by the Bishop of Brundusium.
This was the beginning of a series of letters between the Pope
and the king, which have been preserved in the *Gesta Inno-
centi*. In these letters Johannitius in making his various appeals
lays stress on the Roman origin of the Vlachs, a claim which
the Pope admits and proceeds to grant as the king requests
formal recognition of his kingdom and the privilege of coining
money. These negotiations had already taken place when the
fourth crusade began and the Latins arrived at Constantinople
ostensibly at first to place the young Alexius on the throne.
It may safely be presumed that Johannitius expected his
claim as King of Wallachia and Bulgaria to be recognised by
the crusaders ; if so he was disappointed for in the pages
of Villehardouin we read how all did fealty to the young Alexius
excepting one John of Wallachia and Bulgaria who had conquered nearly half the land on the west side of the straits of
St George. The accession of Baldwin, Count of Flanders, to
the Byzantine throne a few months later brought no change
in the Frankish attitude towards the Wallachian king ; an
embassy from Johannitius was informed that their master must
sue for pardon, and touch the imperial footstool with his

forehead in token of submission. So with a Latin Emperor in Constantinople the Vlach and Bulgarian war continued only on a larger scale than before, as Johannitius in addition to 40,000 Comans was now helped by the Greeks. From the war that followed we can estimate Johannitius' qualities as a general.

In a battle outside Adrianople the crusaders were utterly defeated, Dandolo the blind Doge of Venice and Villehardouin by a masterly retreat at night saved a portion of the army, but the Emperor Baldwin was captured and the appeals of Innocent III failed to secure the release of the royal captive, who died or was done to death a few months later in Bulgaria. Shortly afterwards Seres fell into the hands of the Vlachs and was destroyed ; and early in 1206 at Rusium the crusaders lost more than a hundred knights. Johannitius' policy of destroying all the cities that surrendered soon alienated his Greek allies. A new ally however arose in the person of Theodore Lascaris who by threatening Constantinople from the east enabled Johannitius to do as he wished in the west until in 1207 the crusaders made peace with Lascaris and so became free to oppose Johannitius in force. Henry had succeeded Baldwin as emperor at Constantinople, and the Marquis Boniface at Salonica was ruler not only of the district round the city, but of South Macedonia and Thessaly as well. These two were to combine forces and undertake a joint expedition against the Vlachs. It was arranged that in late summer they should meet at Adrianople, but the meeting never took place, as the Marquis Boniface was killed by a roving Bulgarian band. His head was cut off and sent in triumph to Johannitius. In the same year Johannitius himself was found stabbed outside Salonica ; he was probably murdered by one of his own men, but the pious inhabitants of the city attributed his death to the lance of St Demetrius.

Johannitius was succeeded by his sister's son Borilas who reigned until 1218 when he was driven out by a son of Asan who was known as Johannitius Asan or Johannitius II. Johannitius II, whose capital was the Bulgarian Tirnova, held the throne for twenty-three years and by employing diplomacy as well as war, and by using the reviving power of the Greeks to counteract the Latins extended his boundaries in all directions. In the south his power reached to the borders of Thessaly or Great Vlachia, in the west to Illyria and in the east to Seres. On his death in 1241 his kingdom soon fell to pieces ; there was no heir of full age to succeed, and twenty years later the kingdom of the Vlachs and Bulgarians lost all its former importance.

It is perhaps impossible to decide the relative position of the Vlach and Bulgarian races in the kingdom of the Asans. It may however be considered certain that the Vlachs were in a minority, and that there was a continual tendency for them to be merged into the Bulgarians. The emphasis laid by the rulers on their Vlach origin was probably due to the exigencies of foreign politics and a desire to obtain help from Rome ; it does not necessarily imply that within the kingdom itself the Vlachs were either numerous or powerful. While the Vlach and Bulgarian kingdom in the north was rapidly declining the Vlachs in the mountains of Epirus and Thessaly suddenly acquired political importance.

At the division of the Byzantine Empire, when Great Vlachia and Salonica had fallen to the share of Boniface, Little Vlachia or Epirus, Ætolia and Acarnania had remained Greek, and its mixed population of Greeks, Albanians and Vlachs united in their hatred of the Franks were ruled by Michael Angelus as despot of Epirus. Shortly after the death of Boniface the kingdom of Salonica declined, the Greek rulers in the west extended their borders eastwards, and a new independent state with a population mainly Vlach not long afterwards arose. John Ducas, a natural son of the second despot married the heiress of Taron a hereditary Vlach chieftain, and so was enabled to make himself prince of a Great Vlachia with a capital at Hypate or Neopatras in the Spercheus valley. He was succeeded by his son and grandson, but in 1308 the line failed and Great Vlachia as an independent state ceased to exist ; the Spercheus valley fell into the hands of the Catalans, and Thessaly was annexed to the emperor at Constantinople. In 1334 Cantacuzenus records that the Thessalian mountaineers who owned no king, Albanians, Malakasians, Buians and Mesarites, up to the number of twelve thousand submitted to the emperor Andronicus III because of winter.   In 1350 Little Vlachia was conquered by the Servians, and its history from then till the coming of the Turks is one of incessant warfare.   Lists of battles and rulers are recorded but of the fate of its mixed population no details have been preserved.

Thus in the fourteenth century generally the history of the Vlachs fails and there is a long gap until after the Turkish conquest.   In the interval it is true there are several notices of Vlach troops employed against Dushan and in other wars ; a few individual Vlachs are also from time to time mentioned such as Urban who cast cannon for Mohammed at the siege of Constantinople, but for the history of the race as a whole there is little or no information.   Their fortunes after the conquest have been told in previous chapters, and it only remains to consider the vexed question of their origin.

It was generally recognised in antiquity that the Vlachs were connected with Roman colonists ; and, as we have just seen, the claim of Johannitius King of Bulgaria and Wallachia to be of Roman blood met with immediate recognition from Pope Innocent III.   This instance, if it stood alone, might perhaps be explained away as a convenient political fiction acceptable at the time to both sides alike, but no such solution is possible in view of other evidence.   Writing in 1150 some fifty years earlier than the papacy of Innocent, the Presbyter of Dioclea had expressly identified the Morlachs or Black Vlachs of Dalmatia with the Roman colonials and had translated their name as " Nigri Latini."   The same view worked out in greater detail is to be found in the *De Regno Dalmatiæ et Croatiæ* of Lucius of Trau who lived in the seventeenth century.   Cinnamus centuries earlier regarded the Vlachs north of the Danube as Italian colonists and the fantastic derivation of the name Vlach from Flaccus the Roman conqueror of the Getæ, which appears in Æneas Sylvius' (Pius II) description of Europe, may also be cited as evidence for the widespread belief in a Roman origin.   Modern authorities have treated the question of origin from a somewhat different standpoint, and accepting a connection with Rome, which is obvious from the language alone, have asked what this connection is, and what is the relationship between the Vlachs of the Balkan peninsula and those north of the Danube. These further questions were to some extent recognised in antiquity, but were never fully answered. Kekaumenos believed that the Vlachs had come south into Thessaly, Macedonia and Epirus after Dacia was abandoned by the Romans, and that they were the descendants of the Getæ and Bessi. Thus presumably he regarded them as Romanised tribes rather than descendants of actual Roman colonists. Lucius on the other hand regards the Vlachs mainly as Roman colonists, and instead of a movement from north to south, believes in a migration in the opposite direction. Generally however those north of the Danube were held to be Roman colonists from the time of Trajan, and the origin of those in the Balkans was rarely separately considered. Modern opinion like ancient has been far from unanimous in its answers.

The Roman colonisation of the Balkan peninsula was not confined to the northern half, and in the south there were the important Roman cities of Corinth and Patrae. Nevertheless though a language of Latin origin still survives to-day in the north, there is no trace of one in the south except for a few Latin words that have been adopted into modern Greek. This may be due to two causes ; either Roman colonisation was on a far larger scale in the north than in the south, or else what may be termed the opposition language was different in the two districts. As it was, both these causes were in operation.

It was a characteristic of the Roman Empire that in the east generally where Latin met Greek, Greek invariably prevailed. It was this that led first to the division of the empire and later to that of Christendom, so that it seems legitimate if we find a Romance language surviving in the east to infer that it arose in an environment which linguistically was not Greek. What is known from history is quite in accordance with such a conjecture. In the south from very early times Greek was the sole language, but in the north it was otherwise. From both Herodotus and Thucydides it appears that in the fifth century B.C. Hellenism was very partial even on the coasts of Macedonia, Thucydides even mentions bilingual tribes on the peninsula of Athos and the existence of a non-hellenized population presumably formed the basis of Demosthenes' denial that Alexander was a Hellene. By the time of the Roman conquest Hellenic influences had doubtless increased greatly and it may perhaps be assumed that Greek was practically the sole language on the coasts, and the chief language in the principal towns. Strabo nevertheless, who wrote in the first century A.D., records the existence of bilingual peoples in Western or Upper Macedonia ; the languages spoken are not stated, but it is almost certain that if Greek was one it was not the mother tongue. A more striking example perhaps is in the description of Greece which used commonly to be attributed to Dicæarchus ; it is there stated that the inhabitants of Chalcis in Eubœa were Greek and spoke Greek, a statement which seems meaningless unless the existence of another language even so far south was just conceivable. The Bessi afford an interesting example of the survival of a separate language ; they were a Thracian tribe who lived in the mountains of Hæmus and Rhodope and possessed in Strabo's time a wide reputation for robbery. Herodotus regards them as a division of the Satræ. Thucydides almost certainly referring to the same people calls them ' the sword-bearers,' and as *Satrer* in Albanian means ' knife ' to-day, they may have some connections with the modern Albanians. At the end of the fourth century A.D. the Bessi were converted to Christianity by Niceta of Remesiana, and in the following century a monk Theodosius built a monastery near the Jordan with four chapels in it, one of which was for the Bessi to worship in in their own language. What this language was is unknown ; it may have been a form of Thracian, but whatever it was its survival is important as indicating that various languages continued in the hills.

The fact that Greek was far from being the universal language in Macedonia and the northern part of the peninsula would undoubtedly help the spread of Latin in the interior and especially in the hills which were opened up first by Roman roads and Roman trade. As against this must be noted that most of the inscriptions found are in Greek, and excepting in the northern districts Latin inscriptions are few in number. It has therefore been urged that by the second century A.D. the peninsula was thoroughly hellenized. Epigraphical evidence however need have very little bearing on the language commonly spoken, for inscriptions are mostly official and always in the educated tongue. The epigraphical evidence for the Balkan peninsula in the eighteenth century for example would suggest that the population was almost exclusively Greek or Turkish. The Slav-speaking peoples might be recorded but the Albanians and Vlachs would escape all notice. For the fifth century A.D. although literature was nearly all in Greek there is evidence for Latin being used in the interior. Niceta, Bishop of Remesiana, used Latin not Greek ; Latin was the native tongue of Justinian who came from Dardania ; but a passage from Priscus is perhaps the best illustration of the position Latin then held. Priscus when in Scythia acting as envoy of Theodosius II to Attila was addressed by a man in native garb in Greek. The circumstance surprised him because Latin was the language used for communication with strangers and only the slaves from the coasts of Thrace and Illyria ever spoke Greek. The man in question happened to be a Greek who was living with the Huns.

It is not possible to give a complete list of the Roman colonies and settlements in the various Balkan provinces, but it is nevertheless certain that their distribution if accurately known would not correspond with the Vlach districts to-day. The Vlachs as we have seen belong essentially to the hills, but the Roman colonies would be placed on the lower slopes or in the plains. The Vlachs, who are found to-day in towns that were once the site of Roman colonies, have only settled there in comparatively recent times. The view has nevertheless been put forward that Aemilus Paulus colonised the hills with Roman troops in order to guard the passes, and that the Vlach districts in the hills including that round Verria correspond with the Æmilian settlements. Unfortunately for any such

theory the Vlachs at Verria only came there after the end of
the eighteenth century and the colonies of Æmilius are mainly
if not entirely mythical. If the Vlachs are the actual descendants of earlier Roman colonists, some changes in position
have to be assumed, though this in itself is no objection if the
warlike history of the country is taken into account. A more
serious objection arises from the general characteristics of
Vlach life. As far back as we can trace them the Vlachs
have been nomadic, many of their present settlements are of
quite recent origin, and in the past there seems no doubt that
nomadism was far more prevalent among them than it is now.
As we have already seen, modern Vlach possesses no words
of Latin origin for any but the bare essentials of a hut or
house. There is strong prejudice among them against agriculture or the mason's trade ; it is also noticeable that the
Vlach words now found in modern Greek are chiefly connected
with flocks and herds, and that the muleteering words in Greek
such as *kapistri* (a halter) are largely of Latin origin. Thus
what evidence there is, suggests that from the first the Vlachs
have led a more or less nomadic life and have been in the main
dependent on flocks and herds. It is therefore more than
mere chance that their first mention in history concerns a
muleteer. It needs but little consideration to realise that this
is not the kind of life which the descendants of Roman colonists
might be expected to follow. To become a shepherd in the
first instance capital is needed ; a nomad life involves self-
reliance, requires a long training probably from birth,
and is perhaps the last form of life a settled population could
adopt with success. The opposite change from a nomadic
to a settled life is easy and is constantly taking place. The
increase of trade, as we saw in the case of the Vlachs themselves,
led to a great increase in settled villages during the eighteenth
century ; a decrease in the number of flocks and herds by
disease, war or robbery produces the same result, for the town
is the last refuge of the nomad who has lost his flocks. It
appears therefore on the whole probable that the Vlachs are
in main the descendants of Romanised hill tribes, rather than
of actual Roman colonists who would long since have been

absorbed by the other town-dwelling races, and in particular by the Greeks. This solution however involves the larger question, which has lately been much discussed, the origin of nomadism in the Balkans generally.

Directly to the north of the peninsula are the open plains of the eastern Danube ; on two sides they are enclosed by mountains, by the Carpathians in the west and by the Balkans in the south ; to the north and north-east between the mountains and the sea they join the Russian steppes which in turn lead to the Asian plateau. Hence from one point of view the plains of the Danube form a *cul-de-sac* for the Asiatic nomad tribes driven westwards into Europe from off the plateau, and each successive inroad would drive the one that preceded it closer against the hills. Thus two Turko-Tartar tribes are now settled in Europe ; the Magyars, who after a brief stay in what is now Roumania, were pushed still further west into their present territory, and the Bulgars who have drifted southwards over the Balkans. The Finns, also of Asiatic origin, have reached their position in a somewhat similar way by moving northwards to avoid the mountains. Are the Vlachs also an Asiatic tribe, and do the traces of nomadic life that survive among them point to a former home on the Asian plateau ? That their language is Romance is in itself of little consequence, for the Bulgars are an example near at hand of a race that has changed its language. In connection with such a theory it is conceivable that anthropological evidence alone could give a definite answer, but apart from the doubt among anthropologists as to how environment and inter-marriage affect physical types, evidence of an anthropological kind for the Vlachs is very meagre. It has frequently been said that the Vlachs have an Italian appearance, but the only statement on the question which, as far as we know, can possibly possess any scientific value is that of Mr. Sokolis the Greek doctor at Metsovo in 1861. In his judgment the Vlachs are neither of a Hellenic nor Albanian type, but more akin to Slavs. This however, if true, may easily be a peculiarity of the Metsovo Vlachs, for the country round is noted for the number of Slavonic place names that still exist. We would describe the Vlachs as a race of medium size and slight build ; with often a white skin and high complexion as compared with the olive tint of the Greeks.   The hair is rarely black, usually dark brown and sometimes quite fair especially in youth ; and many of the children with fair hair, rosy cheeks and blue eyes could pass unnoticed in northern Europe.   At the same time there is a great variety of types and the features vary extremely ; in some faces they are clean cut and refined, in others broad and heavy.   Such personal impressions however have very little scientific value without being supported by measurements and statistics ; for the exceptional types by contrast make a deeper impression on the memory than the normal.   Failing adequate anthropological evidence it is perhaps impossible to refute the theory of a Turko-Tartar or Asiatic origin.   It is certainly true that central Asia is a great centre of nomadic tribes who have two definite homes, one for summer and one for winter ; and that tribes from that quarter have come into Europe in all ages seems to admit of little doubt.   Asia probably was the home of the Scythians, and possibly also of " the proud Hippemolgoi that drink mare's milk," who are mentioned in the opening lines of the thirteenth *Iliad*.   But though such a theory cannot be refuted, it need not for that reason be true ; it assumes that central Asia is the home of all nomadism and neglects the possibility or rather probability that it is indigenous elsewhere ; it tends also to argue from similarity of custom to similarity of race, neglecting to inquire into the important question of environment.   To make any such theory of external origin necessary for the Vlachs, it would have to be shown that though they possessed nomadic customs they were living in a land where nomadism was impossible. Yet the possibility of nomadism in the Balkans is proved by the Vlachs themselves ; and to some extent a nomadic life is essential to all Balkan shepherds, who have to seek different pastures for winter and summer.   Thus the Greek and Albanian shepherds live a life similar in many ways to the Vlachs ; but the peculiarity of the nomadism among the Vlachs is that it is more developed, extends outside the shepherd class and seems once to have included the whole race.

There is therefore no necessity on the grounds of nomadism alone to look for the ancestors of the Vlachs as far afield as Asia or even outside the Balkan peninsula.   They can be found in the shepherd tribes of the hills who compelled to move down each winter to the lower slopes for pasture would come under the influence of the Roman colonists and so become Romanised. Here however the question arises of the connection between the Vlachs of the Balkans and the inhabitants of modern Roumania.   According to one theory, which believes that when the Romans left Dacia all Roman settlers were withdrawn, the modern Roumanians are the results of a later movement from the Balkans northwards.   An opposite theory to this is that the Roumanians are autochthonous Romanised Dacians and the Balkan Vlachs the result of a movement to the south. Both these theories, which as we have seen were suggested in antiquity, have been fully developed by several modern writers.   The truth in all probability lies between these two extreme views.   When the Romans left Dacia it is most improbable that all the Roman settlers and Romanised tribes withdrew also, and on the other hand it is most probable that the factors that Romanised Dacia were also operative in the Balkans.   Thus both the Vlachs in the Balkans, and the Roumanians in Roumania are in the main indigenous, though at different periods the centre of the race has shifted.   To-day it is north of the Danube, in the middle ages it was to the south, and earlier still it may have been nearer its present position.   We may therefore conclude that the Balkan Vlachs are for the most part the Romanised tribes of the Balkan peninsula, reinforced perhaps at times by tribes from over the Danube.   Thus the Vlachs in the west would be for the most part Romano-Illyrians, in the south they might be Atha-manians or other hill tribes mentioned by Strabo, but in the east and along the central mountain range there would be a large Thracian and Bessian element.

Macedonia became a Roman province in 146 B.C. and the Romanisation of the hills probably began early.   In the fifth century A.D., as we have seen, the use of Latin had extended to the native tribes ;   then in quick succession came a series of invasions which resulted in a Slav-speaking district in the centre of the peninsula.   The effect of this was important ; the Vlachs in the hills of the interior became probably more isolated than ever before from the Greek-speaking districts on the coasts, and from the Byzantine towns.   The Slav and Bulgarian conquests have perhaps more than anything else preserved Vlach as a language by delaying the inevitable advance of Hellenism.   Greek influence on Vlach apparently did not begin till after the Slavs themselves had begun to give way to Greeks, and in fact not until the trade revival in the eighteenth century did Hellenism spread rapidly among the Vlach districts in the hills.   This is clear from the Greek and Slav loan words that are used in Vlach to-day ; the Slav words belong to an early stratum and contain such words as *maikă* mother, but the Greek words more recently acquired are largely words for abstract ideas, reading, writing, and other refinements of civilisation.

Though much of the history of the Balkan Vlachs is obscure, one fact stands out clearly, that from the time when they first appear in history they have been allowing themselves to be absorbed gradually by the larger nations that surround them. The natural increase of the hill population, the Turkish conquest and the slow advance of education and trade have all been causes that have retarded their extinction.   Nevertheless their numbers have been steadily, but slowly diminishing, and they themselves have helped this by their lack of national feeling, their dispersion and their power of self-effacement. Sir Arthur Evans has found abundant traces in the north about Uskub and throughout Dardania and Dalmatia that the Slavs have there absorbed a Vlach-speaking people, and the same process is going on in the Meglen to-day.   In the west the Farsherots are gradually becoming Albanians.   Finally in the south it is well known that Greece herself has drawn into Hellenism large numbers of Vlachs and that in Thessaly a large proportion of the town population is of Vlach origin.

APPENDIX I

I. THE GREEK TEXTS OF THE INSCRIPTIONS IN THE CHURCHES AT SAMARINA

IN the texts which follow the conventional epigraphic signs for marking missing letters where such are necessary to the sense, the resolution of abbreviations and the ends of lines are used. All the texts are in an archaic style, which is thought suitable for ecclesiastical purposes and is far removed from the Greek which Vlachs speak. They contain in consequence many errors in syntax, grammar and spelling, which a Greek scholar will notice at once.

1. Inscription in the Church of Great St Mary's, Samarina

† ἱστορήθη οὗτος ὁ θεῖος κὴ πάνσεπτος ναὸς τῆς ὑπερευλογημένης ἐνδόξου Δεσποίνης | ἡμῶν Θεοτόκου Μαρίας ἀρχιερατεύοντος τοῦ πανιερολογιοτάτου μητροπολίτου κ(υρί)ου κ(υρί)ου Ἀνθίμου | ἱερατεύων δὲ ἐν ταύτῃ τῇ ἐκκλησίᾳ Μηχαὴλ ἱερέυς κ(αὶ) προτοπαπὰς κ(αὶ) Χρῆστου Ζήση Στέργιου | Γεωργίου καὶ Χρήστου τῶν ἱερέων ἐπιτροπεύοντος δὲ Γερασίου Τριανταφύλου κ(αὶ) τοῦ αὐτοῦ δαπάνῃ κὴ ἐπιστασίᾳ κὴ διὰ συνδρομῆς τοῦ τιμιοτάτου Ἀδὰμ Τζούτρα[1] κὴ ἑτέρων χριστιανῶν | τῶν ἐν τῇ χώρᾳ ταύτῃ εἰς μνημόσυννον αἰώνιον (vacat) | καὶ διὰ χειρὸς Χρήστου ἱερέος καὶ Ἀντωνίου ἀδελφοῦ αὐτοῦ υἱοὶ παπᾶ Ἰωάννου ἐκ τῆς ἰδίας χώρας | ἐν ἔτει τῷ σωτηρίῳ α̅ω̅κ̅θ̅ ἐν μηνὶ Ἰουλίῳ 30.

2. Inscription in the Church of St Elijah, Samarina

† ἱστορήθη οὗτος ὁ θεῖος κ(αὶ) πάνσεπτος ναὸς τοῦ ἁγίου ἐν|δόξου προφήτου Ἠλίου τοῦ θεσβύτου[2] ἀρχιερατεύων|τος τοῦ πανιεροτάτου μητροπολίτου κυρ(ίου) κυρ(ίου) Ἀνθίμου ἱ|ερατεύοντος δὲ τοῦ αἰδεσιμοτάτου κυρίου Μηχα}ὴλ ἱερέως κ(αὶ) οἰκονόμου καὶ Γερασίου ἱερεώς καὶ Χρήστου ἱερέως ἐπιτροπεύοντος Ἀδὰμ Χοντρὲ[3] τοῦ καὶ | Σαμαρᾶ κ(αὶ) διὰ χειρὸς Χρήστου ἱερέως ὑ(ι)οῦ τοῦ παπᾶ | Ἰωάννου ἐκ τῆς ἰδίας χώρας ἐν ἔτι τῷ σωτηρίῳ α̅ω̅κ̅η̅ Φευρουαρίου κ̅ τέλος.

---

[1] τζ is a common Greek way of writing the sound *tsh*.

[2] Probably an error for θεοφήτου.

[3] His descendants have changed their surname to Hondrozmu, supposed to be a bye form of the Greek Χονδροσῶμα.

3. Inscription in the Church of Little St Mary's, Samarina

Παναγία[1] Θεοτόκε βοίθισε τοὺς δούλους (σ)ου τοὺ|ς κατηκοῦ(ντ)ας νε τί χόρα
ταύτι ἀρχιερατέβουντος Γαβ|ρὴλ τοῦ πανιεροτάτου κὲ θεοπροβλίτου τὶς ἁγιουτάτης
ἱμ|ὸν μιτροπόλεος Γρεβενοῦ ⦿ ἔξαρχε[2] διὰ ἐξόδους | Στερ(γ)ιογ(ι)άνι ἐν ἔτι 1799
Μαίου 28 Ζίσι μάστορας.

4. Inscription in the Church of Little St Mary's, Samarina

Ἡ μὲν καὶ παλαὶ ναὸς τῆς Παναγίας περίβλεπτος οὗτος πόλεως Σαμαρίνας |
ἀλ(λ)ὰ καὶ αὖθις περικαλὴς εἰς κόσμον ἀνεκτίσθη δὴ δόξα Θεοῦ τῶν ὅλων | ἱεραρ-
χοῦντος τῆς ἡμῶν ἐπαρχίας κλεινοῦ Γενναδίου λάτρου τε τῆς | σοφίας, ἐπιμελίᾳ δὲ
πολ(λ)οῦ μετὰ ζήλου Ζήση 'Εξάρχου γενεᾶς Χατ(ζ)ημί|χου. γέροντες ἔλθετε,
ἀνέλθετε νεοὶ, γυναίκες δράμετε, ἐδῶ ὼ | παρθένοι, καὶ προσκυνῆτε Θεῷ τῷ οὐρανίῳ
ἐν φόβῳ ψυχῆς καὶ | καρδίας　　ἐν ἔτι 1865 Αὐγούστου 2 Μάστορας Γιάνης.

5. Inscription in the Church of the Monastery of Ayia Paraskevi, Samarina

Οὗτος ὁ ναὸς τῆς | ἁγήας ἐνδόξ(ου) ὁσηοπ|αρθενομάρτηρος | τ(ο)ῦ Χριστοῦ
Παρασκεβ|ῆς ἐκτήσθη † ἀπὸ τῆ|ς ἐνσαρκίησην ἔτι 1713.

6. Inscription in the Church called Ayios Sotir at the Monastery of Samarina

† ἱστορίθει οὗτος ὁ θεῖος κ(αὶ) πάνσεπτος ναὸς τῆς ἁγίας ἐν|δόξου ὁσιοπαρθενο-
μάρτυρος κ(αὶ) ἀθληφόρου τοῦ Χ(ριστ)οῦ Παρασκευῆς | ἀρχιερατεύοντος τοῦ
πανιεροτάτου κ(αὶ) θεοπροβλήτου μητροπο|λίτου ἁγίου Γρεβαινῶν Κ(υρί)ου
Κ(υρί)ου Βαρθολομαίου δι' ἐπιστασίας | κ(αὶ) συνδρομῆς τῶν εὑρισκομένων ἁγίων
πατέρων ἐν τῇ ἁγίᾳ | μονῇ ταύτῃ διὰ χειρὸς τῶν εὐτελῶν Δημητρίου κ(αὶ) | Μηχαὴλ
ἀναγνώστου κ(αὶ) ἀναγνώστου Παπ(ᾶ) Ἰω(άννου) ἐκ τῆς ἰδίας χώρας | Σαμαρίνας
ἐν ἔτει τῷ σωτηρίῳ a͞ωι͞θ ἐν μηνὶ | 'Οκτομβρίῳ ι͞ε ἐτελειώθη δόξα τῷ ἁγίῳ Θεῷ.

---

[1] Except for the last two words which are in cursive characters the inscription is
throughout in capitals.

[2] We are unable to explain these two words satisfactorily. We have been told
that ⦿ is an abbreviation for Χατζὴ (Hadzhi, pilgrim) which does not seem to help
much. It might stand for χώρας and the phrase might mean "exarch of the land of
Ghrevena."

APPENDIX II

II. BETROTHAL, WEDDING AND OTHER FESTIVAL SONGS

MOST of the songs referred to in Chapters VI and VII have been published elsewhere as will be seen in the notes and consequently there is no need to give the original texts. But in a few cases the songs do not seem to have been published or else the published versions are different from those used at Samarina. So we give the original texts of those songs as we took them down on the spot. Here and in Appendix III our object has been to write the Greek songs so that a Greek scholar can understand them and at the same time to indicate how the Vlachs pronounce Greek. They speak one of the North Greek dialects in all of which the rule is that unaccented *i* and *u* disappear and unaccented *e* and *o* become *i* and *u*. The Greek letters are to be pronounced as in Modern Greek, *i.e.* β is the English *v*, ντ is *nd*, μπ and μβ are both *mb*, γ before *i* sounds is equal to an English *y* and γγ and γκ are like the *ng* in *finger*. Latin letters are used to indicate sounds for which the Greek alphabet has no symbols ; *b* and *d* are the same as in English, *g* is the hard English *g* as in *gape*, σh is the English *sh* and dζh the English *j*. Three common Vlach sounds occur of which two λ′ (=Italian *gl*) and ν′ (=Italian *gn*) occur in Greek as well and so are represented by Greek letters. The third is the peculiar Roumanian vowel ā for which we use the same symbol as in Vlach.

1. BETROTHAL SONG

Πέτρα σὲ πέτρα πιρπατῶ, λιθάρι σε λιθάρι.
Ποὺ νὰ 'βρω σύντρουφου γαλὸ, καλὸ κὶ τιμημένου ;
Σὰν δ' ἄλουγου τοῦ γρήγουρου, σὰν dου γοργὸ ζιϑγάρι,
Σὰν dὴ γυναίκα τὴ γαλὴ, ναπού τιμάει τὸν ἄνδρα τς,
5 Σαν δυὸ ἀδιρφάκια ἀγγάρδιακα ναπούνι ἀγαπημένα,
Κὶ τώρα 'μβῆκι πειρασμὸς γιὰ νὰ τοὺς 'ξιχουρίσῃ,
Κὶ τ' εἶν' ἡ 'φορμὴ νὰ τοὺς ἰβρῇ γιὰ νὰ τοὺς 'ξιχουρίσῃ ;
'Ισεῖς ἀμπέλια ἔχιτι, χουράφια νὰ μοιράστι,
Ὅσα 's τὴ μέση κὶ καλὰ, πάρι τα ἡ ἀφεντιά σου,
10 Κ' ὅσα 's τὴ ἄκρα κὶ κακὰ, δώσ' τα 's τὸν ἀδιρφό σου,
Τέθοια 'φορμὴ νὰ τοὺν ἰβρῇς νὰ πᾶς νὰ τὸν σκουτώσῃς.

2. Song for the Shaving of the Bridegroom

'Σ τὴ πέτρα κάθιτι γαμβρός,
Κ' ἡ πέτρα ἀπόλυκι νιρό
Γιὰ νὰ ξυρίσουν τὸ gαμβρό.
Τὸ χείρι ποὺ τοὺ 'ξύριζι
5 'Εχει κουμμάτι μάλουμα
'Αργυρὸ ξυράφι
Σύρνι ἀγάλεα, ἀγάλεα
Νὰ μὴ ῥαΐσῃ τρίχα.

3. Song for the Dressing of the Bride

Σεὰ ἀνώγεια, σεὰ κατώγεια,
Σεὰ τὰ 'ψηλὰ σεραΐγια,
Ρουχίτσha μου κρυμμένα,
Σύρε μάνα μου, πάρ' τα,
5 Νύφη θέλου νὰ γίνου
Νὰ σταυρουπρουσκυνήσου
Κὶ χείρια νὰ φιλήσου.

4. Song for the Combing of the Bride's Hair

Ναργυρό μου χτένι
Σύρνι ἀγάλεα, ἀγάλεα,
Νὰ μὴ ῥαΐσῃ τρίχα,
Τρίχα ἀπὸ τοὺ κιφάλι,
5 Κὶ τὰ πέρνει ξένους,
Κὶ τὰ κάνει ἀμάγια.

5. Song when the Bride is brought out

Loară n' ti, arāk'iră n' ti,
mor mushată mea !
Kseanile n' tsi deadiră,
mor gugutshă mea !
5 kseanile zh dipartoasile,
mor mushată mea !
Di tse afurn'ie, mor mumă mea,
di mi aghunish di kasă n' ?
Nu ti aghuniï mor feată mea
10 kă ti pitrek a kasă ts
shi la nikuk'irată ts.

6. Song when the Bride's Family departs

Νισεὶς παντὰ θὰ φύγητι, ὥρα σὰς καλή.
Σὰν βᾶτι ἀπὸ τὴ μανοὖλα μου, χιριτήματα.

7. Song when the Bride's Family departs

Κινήσαμι μὶ τὸν ἥλιου, πᾶμι ἀργὰ μὶ τοὖ φιγγάρι.
'Ιγ' ὄρχουμι κὶ σὺ κοιμάσι, 'ξύπνα μωρὴ νὰ ζῆς κὶ νᾶσι.
Μώρ' καυμένη Πλαταμώνα τὶ 'νι τὰ κουράσια π'όχεις;
Ρουμν'ιοπούλες, Τουρκουπούλες, κὶ μικρὲς ἀρχουντουπούλες.
5 Κάθουντι 'ψηλὰ σὶ κιόστι κὶ ἀγναντεύουν τὰ καράβια
Πόρχουντι ἀπὸ τοὖ Μισήρι φουρτουμένα μὶ φκιασίδι.

8. Song when the Bride's Family reaches home

Λείπει κόρη ἀπ' τὴν αὐλή,
Λείπει ιὶ ἀπ' τοὖ μαχαλᾶ,
Λείπει κὶ ἀπ' τὴ μάνα τς,
Λείπει κὶ ἀπ' τὰ ἀδίρφιά τς.

9. When the Bride goes to fetch water

Σὰν ἔρθῃ 'Ανθίτσα γιὰ νιρό,
Νιρὸ νὰ μὴν δῆν δώσῃτι.
Μόν' γὶ νὰ τὴν 'ξιτάξῃτι,
Νανθίτσα ποιὸν ἀγαπᾶς;
5 Τὸν Γιάννη τὸμ βραμάτευτή.

10. When the Bride draws Water

Umble soră, vearsă frate,
Tră inatea ali surate.

11. When the Bride returns from the conduit

Νὰ ἐξιβρῇ ἡ πιθιρά μου
Π'όρχουμι ἀπ' τὴ βρύσι
Κρυουμένη, παγουμένη,
Νὰ 'βρῶ τὴ φωθιὰ νὰ μένῃ,
5 Κὶ τὴμ βήτα φουρνιασμένη.

12. Song when the Arumana procession starts

Ea mundritsā tsi i mushată
Alb, aroshă ka k'irauă !
Ea mundritsā di pri k'eptu
kā si pare birbek aleptu !
5 Ea mundritsā di pri poale
kā si pare ka kash di t foale.

13. Song when the Arumana reaches a conduit

Βρυσοίλα πιτρουκάγγιλα
Δώσ' μὰς νιρὸ νὰ πιοῦμι
Νὰ ἰδῆς πῶς τραγουδοῦμι.

14. Song for Christmas Eve

Kolindä, melindä,
dă n' maie kulaklu,
kā s afiă Hristolu
tu pāhnia a boilor
5 di frikă uvreilor.

15. Song for Christmas Eve

Κόλινδα, μέλινδα,
Δώ μου báβου κλόυρα,
Νὰ πᾶμι κὶ παρεκιά.
Σὰ 'φέτου, παλλικάρια,
5 Σὰ 'φέτου κὶ τοῦ χρόνου.

APPENDIX III

III. THE GREEK KLEPHTIC SONGS USED TO ILLUSTRATE THE HISTORY OF SAMARINA

THE following songs all of which are referred to in the history of Samarina in Chapter V were collected by us in the village itself and are as far as we know unpublished with the exception of the first, of which a version has been printed.

I. YANNI AL PREFTU

Τὶ εἶν' τὰ βαϊριάκια π'όρχουντι ἀπ' τ' Ρουμν'ιὸ τὴ ῥάχη;
Κ' ἡ Γιάννης χαμουγέλασι, τᾱράζει τοῦ κιφάλι,
"Μ' βέρνει ἡ ζώνη τὸ σπαθὶ, πέρνει κὶ τὸ δουφέκι."
Κὶ κάνει τὸν ἀνήφουρου σὰν 'μόρφο πελιστέλι,
5 Κ' ἡ μάνα τ' ἀπού κοντὰ τοῦ σκούζει κὶ βιλάζει,
"Ποῦ πᾶς Γιαννή μου μουναχὸς διχὼς κανὰ κοντά σου;"
"Κὶ τὶ τοὺς θέλου τοὺς πουλλοὺς; πάνου κὶ μουναχός μου."
Σὰν βάνει κὶ χουχούτιζι σὰν ἄλουγου βαρβάτου.
"Ποῦ πᾶτι σκύλ' 'Αρβανιθιά, κὶ σεῖς βρὲ Κουλουν'ιώτες;
10 'Ιγὼ εἶμ' ἡ Γιάννης τ' παπᾶ, Γιάνν' τοῦ Παπᾶ Νικόλα.
Δὲν εἶν' ἰδὼ τὰ Γριβινά, δὲν εἶνι τοῦ Ζαγόρι,
Δὲν εἶν' ἰδὼ ἡ Λαϊστά, κὶ ὅλα τὰ Βλαχουχώρια.
'Ιδὼ τὸ λὲν 'ψηλὰ ἰβουνά, 'ψηλὰ 's τὴ Σᾱμᾱρίνα,
14 Ποῦ πουλιμοῦν μικρὰ πιδιά, γυναίκις κὶ κουρίτσια.

Versions of this song have been published by Aravandinos, Ἄσματα Ἠπείρου, p. 44, No. 51 ; and Khristovasilis, Ἐθνικὰ Ἄσματα, p. 188, No. 39 ; cf. Papahagi, *Litteratura Poporană*, p. 1008, No. xiii.

2. DHUKAS

Τ' εἶν' δοὺ κακὸ ποὺ γένιτι τούτην τὴν ἰβδουμάδα;
Μοῦ 'γέλασαν, μοῦ 'πλάνιψαν οἱ σκύλοι οἱ βρατίμοι,
Κὶ μὄυπαν, "Α'ίδι Δοῦκα μου 'ψηλὰ 's τὴ Σᾱμᾱρίνα
βρατίμοι γιὰ νὰ γένουμι 's τὰ δώδεκα 'βαγγέλια."
5 Σταυρὸ 'κρατοῦσ' 's τὰ χέιρια του, 'βαγγέλια 'χιριτοῦσι,

281

Κ' ἡ παγάνιὰ τοὺς 'πέτρουσι τρουγύρι 's τ' μοναστήρι.
Τὸν Δούκα ἐὰ νιφώναζαν, τὸν Δούκα ἐὰ νιλέγουν,
"Ἐὰ ἔβγα, ἔβγα Δούκα μου, ἔβγα νὰ προσκυνήσῃς."
"Δὲν εἶμι νύφ' νὰ προσκυνῶ, κὶ χείρια νὰ φιλήσου.
10 Ἰγὼ 'μι Δούκας 'ξακουστός, 's τὸ γόσμο 'ξακουσμένος.
Μινὰ μὲ 'ξέρ' ὁ βᾱσιλ'ιάς, μὶ 'ξέρει κὶ ὁ βιζύρης."

3. LEONIDHA AL HADZHIBIRA

Δὲ θέλου μάνα κλιάματα, δὲ θέλου μυριουλόγια.
Μένα μὶ κλέγουν τὰ ἰβουνά, μὲ κλὲν τὰ Βλαχουχώρια,
Μὲ κλαίει ἡ νύχτα κὶ αὐγὴ, τ' ἄστρο κὶ τὸ φιγγάρι,
Μὲ κλὲν κ' οἱ νύφες τοῦ Χαδζῆί, νύφες τοῦ Χαδζῆιβίρου.
5 'Σ τοῦ πᾱλᾱθύρι 'κάθουνταν κὶ 'ψιλουτραγουδοῦσαν,
"Οσοι διαβάτι κὶ ἂν περνοῦν ὅλοὶ τοὺς ἐρουτοῦσαν·
"Μήν εἴδατι τὸν υἱόκα μας αὐτὸν τοὺν Λιουνίδα;"
"Νιμεῖς ἰψὲς τοὺν εἴδαμαν σε κλεφτικὰ λημέρια,
Νεῖχαν ἀρνάκια π'όψιναν, κριάρια σουβλημένα,
10 Τοὺν Λιουνίδα 'βάρισαν τοῦ ὑρῶτου καπιτάνου,
Ποὺ ἦταν ὑαριάκι 's τὰ ἰβουνὰ κὶ φλάμβουρου 's τοὺς κλέφτις."

4. DHIMITRAKI AL PAZAIITI

Τὸ 'μάθιταν τὶ γένιτι νιτούτην τὴν ἰβδουμάδα;
Νιτούτην ἰβδούμαδα τὸν Δημητράκη 'βάρισαν.
'Παΐγησε ὁ μαῦρος 's τοῦ χωριὸ 'ψηλὰ 's τὴ Διμηνίτσα
Νὰ πάρῃ τὰ ἀβγιλ'ιὰ νὰ παΐῃ 's τοῦ Λιουνίδα.
5 Τὴ στράτα ἀποὺ 'παΐγινι, τὴ στράτα ποὺ πηγαίνει
Τρεῖς Τοῦρκοι νισταύρουσι 's τὴ ἰκκλησιὰ ἀπ' τὰ δένδρα.
Τρία μαρτίνια τᾱδουσαν τὰ τρία 's τὴν ἀράδα,
Νένα τοὺν ὑέρνει ἰξώδιρμα κὶ τὸ ἄλλο 's τοῦ πουδάρι,
9 Τοῦ τρίτου τοῦ φαρμάκιρου κατακαρδὶς τοὺν ὑέρνει.

5. YEORGHAKIS KARADZHAS

Ἰσεῖς πουλιὰ ἀπ' τὸ Γριβινὸ, κὶ ἀηδόνια ἀπ' τὸ Κουμάτι,
Σὰν πᾱτι κάτου 's τ' Ἄγραφα, κὶ κάτου 's τοῦ Ῥωμαίικου,
Δώστι χαμβέρι 's τη γλιφτουριὰ κὶ 's ὅλους τοὺς καπιτάνους,
Το Gαραδζῆὰ τὸν βάρισαν 's τοῦ ἔρημου Κουμάτι.
5 Βγῆκε 'μπροστὰ 's τὲς φαμιλ'ιὲς γιὰ νὰ τοὺς χαρατσώσῃ.
Πουλὺ χαράτσι ἰγύριβι 'πὸ 'νὰ μιδζῆιὰ τὸ πράμα.
'Μπροστὰ τοῦ ὑέρνουν μὶ τοῦ καλὸ νὰ πάνι 's τὸ καλό του.
"Κάτσι Γιωργάκη φρόνιμα, κάτσι τὰ πινουμένα,
Νιψὲς μᾱς ἰξιγύμνουσι αὐτὸς ὁ σκύλος Zhούρκας,
10 Μᾱς 'πῆρι λίρις ἱκατὸ κὶ ἰβδουμίντα κάππις."

"Αὐτὸς καλὰ σᾶς ἔκαμι, κὶ 'γὼ τὶ θὰ σᾶς κάνου;"
Πουλὺ χαράτσι ἰγύριβι 'πὸ 'νὰ μιδζhὶd τὸ πράμα.
Σὰν δόκουσι ὁ Dίλι Ζήσ' πουλὺ τοῦ κακουφάνγι,
Κὶ τὸ τσικούρι ἄδραξι κὶ 's τὸ κιφάλι τ' χώνει.
15 Σὰν δένδρο ἀραΐστικι, σὰν κυπαρίσσι πέφτει.
Μαύρα πουλιὰ τοὺν ἔκλιγαν, κὶ ἄσπρα τ' τρογυροῦσαν.

6. YEORYIOS YIOLDHASIS

Τρεῖς πιρδικούλες κάθουνταν 's τὴ Σμόλικαν dὴ ράχη·
Νιμν'ιὰ τηράει τὰ Γιάννινα, κ' ἡ ἄλλη κατ' τὴν Góντσα,
Τοῦ τρίτου τοῦ μικρότιρου τηράει τὴ Σᾶμᾶρίνα.
Σήκου ναπ' αὐτοῦ Γεώργι μου, 'ψηλὰ 's τὸ καραούλι.
5 Νη παγανιὰ μᾶς 'πέτρουσι, μᾶς 'πήραν dὰ κιφάλια,
bροστὰ μᾶς φέρουν dὰ ψουμν'ιὰ, κὶ 'πίσω ἡ παγάνα.

7. GHUSHU AL DHISPULI

Τὸ μάθιταν τὶ γένιτι τούτου τοῦ καλουκαίρι;
Οἱ κλέφτις ἰπρουσκύνησαν κὶ ὅλα τὰ καπιτανάτα.
Τοὺς 'γέλασι, τοὺς 'πλάνιψι ὁ δόλιους κουμαντάρους·
Τοὺς εἶπι, "Γιὰ κουπιάστι ἰδὼ πουσούλες νὰ σᾶς δώσου."
5 Κὶ αὐτοὶ μαυροὶ 'γιλάστηκαν κὶ 'κλείσκαν 's τὴ αὐλή dου.
Ἦταν ἡ ὥρα ἑξ, ἰφτὰ κατὰ τοῦ μισημέρι.
Μουχτὰρ 'Αγὰς σὰν δόκουσι, πουλὺ του κακουφάνγι.

8. GHUSHU AL DHISPULI.

Μοῦ 'γέλασαν, μοῦ 'πλάνιψαν τὰ τρία Βλαχουχώρια,
Ναβέλα, κὶ τοῦ Πιριβόλι κ' ἡ δόλια Σᾶμᾶρίνα.
Μοῦ 'γέλασαν κ' οἱ φίλοι μου νοι σκύλοι πατριώτι,
Κὶ μοῦπαν, "αἴδι ἀρχηγέ, ναιδὶ νὰ προυσκυνήσῃς,"
5 Κὶ μοῦπαν, "αἴδι Γούσhου μου, ναιδὶ νὰ προυσκυνήσῃς,
Νὰ προυσκυνήσῃς 's τοὺν βασhὰ μέσ' τοῦ Πᾶgᾶτσ' τοῦ σπίτι."
Μᾶς 'πήραν κὶ μᾶς ἔδησαν νοι σκύλοι 'Αρβανίτι.
Μᾶς κάνουν δίπλα τὰ ἰβουνὰ, διπλὰ κάτ' τοῦ διν'ιάλι,
Εἰς τὴν Φούρκαν μᾶς 'ξημέρουσαν, 's τὰ Γιάννινα μᾶς πάνουν.
10 Μᾶς 'πήραν κὶ μᾶς 'κρέμασαν νοι σκύλοι 'Αρβανίτι.

Line 8. διν'ιάλι is unintelligible : probably the line should read, Μᾶς
κάνουν δίπλα τὰ ἰβουνὰ κατὰ τοῦ δειλινάρι.

9. THE TROUBLES OF 1886

'Ρύbουλα ἀπὸ τοῦ Σμόλικα, πεύκα ἀπ' τὴ Σᾶμᾶρίνα,
Φέτου νὰ μὴν ἀνοίξιτι, φέτου νὰ μαρανθῆτι.

Νοι Βλάχοι δὲν μᾶς 'φάνγαν 'ποὺ μέσα ἀπ' τοῦ 'Ρωμαίικο.

῎Αλλοι 'πάγησαν κατ' τ' ῎Αγραφα, κὶ ἄλλοι κατὰ τὴ 'Ρένδα

5 Πιρσότεροι 's τὴ Σλίτσhανη, κανὰς δὲν θὰ 'πουμείνῃ,

Κὶ ἄλλοι ἔμιναν κατακαμπὶς, κατακαμπὶς 's τοὺς κάμπους.

Πανάθιμα τὸν αἴτιον τὸν Ζήσι Dζhιμουζhόga.

Αὐτὸς εἶνι ὁ αἴτιος, αὐτὸς γίνγι ἰτία.

'Πῆρι τὸ gόσμο 's τὸ λαιμὸ κὶ ὅλα τὰ Βλαχουχώρια.

10 Μένουν κουρίτσια ἀνύπανδρα, πιδιὰ ἀρραβουνιασμένα.

10. THE WAR OF 1897.

Μᾶς ἦλθι ἄνοιξι πικρή, τοῦ καλουκαίρι μαύρου.

Δὲν κλέτε χώρες κὶ χουριὰ κὶ σεῖς βρὲ βιλαέτια ;

Τ' εἶν' δοὺ κακὸ ποὺ γένιτι τούτου τοῦ καλουκαίρι ;

'Φέτου θὰ γείνῃ πόλιμους, Ἰλλὰς μὶ τὴ Dουρκία.

5 ῎Ηταν παρασκευόβραδου, Σαββάτο τοῦ Λαζάρου,

Κ' οἱ Τούρκοι ἰνίκησαν, 'πῆραν dὴ Θεσσαλία.

'Εδὲμ Πασhὰς ῥουβόλιασι 'ποὺ μέσ' 's τὴν 'Αμιλόνα,

'Σ τοῦ Τούρναβου 'ξιμέρουσι, 's τὴ Λάρσσα γιοματίζει.

Λάχει 'μέρα τὴ bασχαλιὰ μί τὸ Χριστὸς ἀνέστη.

10 'Βρίσκει τὰ κόκκινα τ' αὐγὰ, κριάρια σουβλημένα.

Κὶ πέρνει ἀdζβάρνα τὰ χουριὰ μιχρὶ τοῦ Βιλισhτίνου.

APPENDIX IV

IV. SELECT TEXTS TO ILLUSTRATE THE VLACH LANGUAGE

THE few texts here printed have been chosen to illustrate Chapter XI and the account there given of the Vlach language. With the exception of the first two, the songs and tales have been collected by us ourselves during our travels amongst the Vlachs. As regards the folk songs it is to be noted that the old songs are as a rule in short lines and do not rhyme. A song in which the lines rhyme in pairs is new and probably not more than thirty years old. We have given three such modern songs from Samarina, Nos. 10–12 below. Of these three the first has references to Samarina customs such as their fondness for wine, and their nomadic habits. The third deals with families staying in the plains and not coming up to the village for the summer, and also with the emigration of the able bodied young men to America. The second of the three is one of a large class of personal songs which are very popular at Samarina. There are two men in the village who continually compose new ones which they sing at festivals. They do this not for gain, but for amusement ; and neither of the two song writers can be said to have had much education. This song writing is not due to the Roumanian propaganda, for every now and again some one else will make up a topical and personal song, and we have heard muleteers singing them. That Samarina delights in such songs and thinks no ill of them shows how cheerfully they take life in the summer. The translations appended have been left in as simple a style as possible so that with their aid the original texts may be understood quite easily.

A. FOLK SONGS

1. LUNKA

Tsintsi an' n'i alăgai	Five years long I walked
pri niñg amare,	near the sea,
shă altsă tsintsi mi primnai.	and another five I wandered.
Tru grădină vruta n'i aflai	I found my beloved in a garden
5 iu durn'a sum trandafir.	where she was asleep under a rose tree.

Disfeatse okl'i atsel' lăil'i	She opens her eyes those black eyes
di mi mutreashte ;	and looks at me ;
disfeatse gura di asime	she opens her mouth of silver
shă mi zburashte ;	and addresses me ;
10 " Iu eshti dzhone tută iara	" Where are you boy all winter long
kănd n'i easte rākoare ;	when I am cold ?
ma yin primăveara	But you come in the spring
kănd mi h'ivreashte ? "	when I have fever."

This we have taken from Weigand, *Die Aromunen*, ii. p. 90, No. 60. A Greek version of it is known at Samarina and at Verria. It is probably an old Vlach song that has been translated into Greek.

2. VLAHO-LIVADHI

Bre dzon, fitsorĭ di Kozani	Ho gallant lads of Kozhani
di naparte d arău,	from beyond the river,
kar si vă tshets Kastoria	if you go to Kastoria
tshe easte hoară mare	which is a large town
5 si pitritshets un masturŭ,	see you send a mason,
si h'ibă dzhone multu,	let him be very skilled,
si pilekseaskă marmare,	let him cut marble
s adară groapă mare.	to make a big tomb.
Să stau mbrostu tri si ved	Let me stand upright that I may see,
10 si ved să polimsesku,	that I may see to fight,
să dhipla mihrisesku.	and bend double.
Tshez vă să dzăts a mum mea	Go and tell my mother
kă eu m insurai ;	that I have married ;
soakră mindai ploatsile	as mother-in-law I have taken the slabs,
15 să lailu lok mg'are.	and the black earth as my wife.

We have taken this from Weigand, *Olympo-Walachen*, p. 116, No. xii. The idea of the last six lines occurs in many Greek klephtic songs, *e.g.* Passow, *Carmina Popularia*, Nos. civ, cv, cvi, clii, clvi, clx, clxv. It is possible that these, like the Samarina klephtic songs (see Appendix II), were written by Vlachs, and therefore there seems no reason to suppose that the idea has been borrowed by Greek from Vlach or *vice versa*. In any case this song seems to be an old one.

3. VERRIA

Naparti di lai amare	Beyond the black sea
sh alavdară sh nă mushată.	they praised a beautiful maid.
Kum si n' fak lailu si u vedŭ ?	What am I to do, poor wretch, to see her ?
Ñgallikă ts kallu dzhuneali	Mount your horse boy,
5 zh du ti, dă ts pān di mushata.	and go, away to the beautiful maid.
Bună dzuă lea mushată.	Good day fair maiden.
G'ini vinish lai dzhuneali.	Welcome boy.
Iu n' ts u māta lea mushată ?	Tell me where is your mother, fair maiden.
Mum mea dusi la nā numtă,	My mother is gone to a wedding,
10 la nā numtă văsilkeaskă	to a royal wedding
di si fatsi prota nună.	and is become first godmother.

The Verria Vlachs sing this at betrothals. It is also known at Baieasa, Weigand, *Aromunen*, ii. p. 8, No. 6.

4. AMINTSHU

Dzhokă pionellu	The peacock dances
tu livădzle verdʒă.	in the green meadows.
Roaoă shi lun'ină,	Dew and sunlight,
feata si nverină.	the maiden is downcast.
5 Peanile l' kadŭ,	His feathers drop,
dzonile l' arape,	the youth seizes them,
feata si nverină	the maiden is downcast.
Mor nu ti nverină,	Come maiden do not be downcast
kă pri poartă ts trekŭ,	for before your door I pass,
10 Salona mi dukŭ.	to Salona I go.
Dzā n' tsi vreĭ s ts adukŭ.	Tell me what you wish me to bring you.
Baire din Pole	Necklaces from Stamboul,
shi funde di sta Seara,	and tassels from Seres,
k'aptine di Verria,	a comb from Verria,
15 pudhimate di Larsa.	boots from Larissa.

This song is also known at Turia and Ameru.

5. BAIEASA

Fudzi, fudzi fumŭ !	Go away, go away smoke.
Kātră iu s mi dukŭ ?	Where am I to go to ?
La k'atra k'ipitoară.	To the peaked rock.
Tsi si māku, ţsi z beau ?	What am I to eat, what am I to drink ?

5 Unŭ pulishorŭ.	A little bird.
Ku tsi si lu tal'u ?	With what am I to kill it ?
Ku parlu di la struñgă.	With the post from the sheepfold.
Parlu iu easti	Where is the post ?
L arsiră fokurli.	The fires burnt it.
10 Fokurli iu sundu ?	Where are the fires ?
L asteasiră ploiurli.	The rains put them out.
Ploiurli iu sundu ?	Where are the rains ?
Li biură kăprili.	The goats drank them.
Kăprili iu sundu ?	Where are the goats ?
15 Li mākară luk'l'i.	The wolves eat them.
Luk'l'i iu sundu ?	Where are the wolves ?
Loară kalea di Briaza.	They took the road to Briaza.

6. LAKA

More Armănă sh mor mushată	Vlach maiden, beautiful maid
tsi n' stai mărămnată ?	why do you stand so melancholy ?
Tats lai dado, nu mi kreapă	Hush mother, do not worry me,
kă n'i dzhonile l am tu kseane.	for I have my lad in foreign parts.
5 Dzatse an'i am tsi l ashteptu ;	For twelve years I wait for him ;
nikă treĭ an'i vai l ashteptu,	for three more years will I wait for him,
shi dapoiă vai mi măritŭ,	and then will I marry,
shi n'i l'au un dzhone aleptu,	and I will take a chosen lad,
aleptu shi prămăteftu.	a chosen lad and a merchant.

This song is known at Baieasa, and Weigand, *Aromunen*, ii. p. 86, No. 56, has a version from Monastir.

7. SAMARINA

La patru tsindză marmare,	By marbles four or five,
la shassile făndān'i	by fountains six,
aklo doarme feată siñgură,	there sleeps a maid alone,
siñgură shi isusită.	alone and yet betrothed.
Shi dadăsa ma l'i dzătsia,	And her mother said to her,
shi dadăsa l'i dzătse,	to her her mother says,
" Ea skoală, skoală h'il'e amea	" Arise, arise oh daughter mine,
niveastă va n' t adarŭ,	a bride will I make you,
kă yin kuskril'i tră s ti l'a,	since the kinsfolk come to take you,
10 kuskri di la ghambrolu."	kinsfolk from the bridegroom."

This is one of the three regular songs sung at a betrothal at Samarina, see p. 107. A Greek version, probably a translation, is known at Verria and in Epirus, Ζωγραφεῖος Ἀγὼν, p. 166, No. 310.

8. SAMARINA

Nu ti arāde featā n'ikă,	Make no mistake little girl,
nu yinu la noi.	do not come to us.
La noi are vale mare.	By us there is a great river.
Nu vai pots s u tretsā.	You will not be able to cross it.
5 Peashte mare vai mi fakŭ,	I will make myself a big fish,
zh valea vai n' u trekŭ,	and I will cross the river,
sh eu la voi vai yinŭ.	and I will come to you.
Nu ti arāde featā n'ikă,	Make no mistake little girl,
nu yinu la noi.	do not come to us.
10 La noi are mundz analtsā.	By us there are lofty mountains.
Nu vai pots tră s tretsā.	You will not be able to cross them.
Pitrunikl'e vai mi fakŭ,	I will make myself a partridge,
sh munzl'i vai n' l'i trekŭ,	and I will cross the mountains,
sh eu la voi vai yinŭ.	and I will come to you.
15 Nu ti arāde featā n'ikă,	Make no mistake little girl,
nu yinu la noi.	do not come to us.
La noi are soakră arauă.	By us there is a cruel mother-in-law.
Nu vai pots z bānedzā.	You will not be able to live.
Soakră arauă, noară bună,	Cruel mother-in-law, good daughter-in-law,
20 doaule vai tritsem,	we will get on the two together,
zh doaule vai bānăm.	and two together we will live.

9. SAMARINA

Doi mundzā analts sh grei ;	Two mountains tall and cruel ;
după munde nā livadhe vearde ;	behind the mountain a green meadow ;
tu livadhe nā fāndānă aratse.	in the meadow, a cold spring.
Mi aplikai z beau theam di ap aratse,	I stooped to drink a little cold water,
5 di n' arkai okl'ulu andreptu,	and I cast my eyes ahead,
di n' vidzui un dzhone aleptu,	and I saw a chosen lad,
di sh avea sh un mer arosh tu mānă.	and he had a red apple in his hand.
Dzhone kāt āl dai merlu ?	Boy for what do you give the apple ?
Featā un okl'u di atău.	Maiden one of your eyes.

A version of this song from Monastir is given by Weigand, *Aromunen*, ii. p. 86, No. 57.

19

10. SAMARINA

Dumnidzalekāt h'iĭ mare,	Lord how great thou art,
dai la tuts kāt unǎ hare.	thou givest all a talent each.
N avem sh noi lail'i nā hare.	We too poor wretches have a talent.
Kānd bem yinŭ vrem kāndare.	When we drink wine we want to sing.
5 Sāmārina hoarǎ mare	Samarina is a big town,
kathe dzuǎ ka pāzare.	each day is like a market.
Tsi mshatǎ hoarǎ n avemŭ !	What a fine town we have !
Toamna vdzimŭ, u alāsǎmŭ.	In autumn we go, we leave it.
Prumuveara di pri Martsŭ	In spring about March
10 nā fudzi mindea diñ gapŭ.	our mind goes out of our heads.
Nā bāgǎm mare frundidhǎ	We put great thought upon ourselves
kum s ishim tu pātridhǎ.	how to get up to our home.
S nā bāneadzǎ atsel'i tsi au oi ;	Long life to those who have sheep ;
dupǎ el'i vnim shi noi.	after them we come too.
15 S nā bāneadzǎ tshelnikazl'i ;	Long life to the shepherds ;
dupǎ el'i yin k'iradzhazl'i.	after them the muleteers come.
Nā vnim tuts ku hārauǎ	We all come with joy
kā skāpǎm di iarna greauǎ.	because we have escaped from hard winter.

11. SAMARINA.

Nu vā avdzātsā voi lai Sām-rān'atsā,	Oh Samariniats have you not heard,
Yari la li la, iu duts lca Yanǎ mea ?	Yari la li la where go you Yana mine ?
Tsi s featse la Baktshilarlu ? etc.	What happened at Baktshilar ? etc.
S isusi sh Adhamlu al Tshutra, etc.	Adham al Tshutra became betrothed, etc.
5 di shi lo sh nā kupatsharǎ, etc.	and took a kupatshar, etc.
Avdzārǎ shi niposl'i al Guda, etc.	Guda's nephews heard, etc.
Dusirǎ pān la kāravi, etc.	They went as far as the ferry, etc.
H'il'u al Biti al Mihula, etc.	The son of Biti al Mihula, etc.
shi u arak'i sh u lo nāvcasta, etc.	seized her and took her for his bride, etc.

When this song is sung a *sirto* can be danced to it.

12. SAMARINA.

Estan lipsesk fumel'i di ñg'os,	This year families from below are wanting,
lipsesk feate di h'ima ;	girls from below are wanting ;
nu nā yinŭ Sāmārina.	they do not come to us to Samarina,
Plāñg laile, plāñg maratile	The poor things weep, they weep in misery,
5 pri t anoyi, pri t katoyi.	upstairs and downstairs.
N au laile s plāteaskă aghoyi.	The poor wretches cannot pay their fare.
Panathima l'a etiulu	Curse take the reason
tsini s featsi itie.	which became the cause.
Fug fitshori t Amerik'ie.	Boys go to America.
10 Fug fitshori, fug suratsā,	Boys go, married men go,
fug fitshori tu ilik'ie.	boys of age go.
Featile bagă aghrāpnie.	The girls keep vigil.

B. Folk Tales

I. MUMA SHI FEATA

Eara ună feată shi ună mumă shi muma nu vrea pri feata. U agudia multŭ, shi adră lemnu. Măsa u bāgă tu fokŭ ; arkă tshinusha tu grădina. Di s adră sakurafă. U lo sh u hipse tu dăvani. Shi ună dzuă măsa nu avea apă. Feata s sklă shi adră pită, shi năsă nu iara a kasa shi z duse tă s l'a apă. Shi ndribă pri mbl'erile, " Kari n' adră pita ? " Shi alnă pri dăvani feata. Shi apoia alandă dzuă mbl'earea vrea si z dukă la bisearika shi s askumse după usha shi u akātsă shi u tsānu ñ gasa. TURIA

I. MOTHER AND DAUGHTER

There was a daughter (lit. girl) and a mother and the mother did not like the daughter. She beat her much and made her wood. Her mother put it in the fire ; she threw the ash in the garden. She became a packneedle. She took it and stuck it in the ceiling. And one day her mother had no water. The daughter got up and made a pasty, and she was not at home and had gone to get water. And she asked the women, " Who made me the pasty ? " And the daughter had gone up on to the ceiling. And another day afterwards the woman wanted to go to church and she hid behind the door and she caught her and kept her at home.

2. Kukotlu shi Gălina

Shi eara ună mai ku un pap, avea un kukot ku nă gălină. Imnă, imnă mai ku paplu shi kukotlu s alnă sti alunŭ. Kukotlu kănta shi gălina shdea m pade shi l' tsia, "Kukoate, kukoate arukă n' nă alună." Shi arkă nă alună shi skoase okl'u a gălinil'ei. Metagri gălina, "Kukoate, kukoate arukă ninkă ună." L' arkă ninkă ună shi l' skoase sh aland okl'u. "Kukoate, kukoate arukă ninkă ună." Ăl' skoase un tshor ; metagri gălina pali, "Kukoate, kukoate arukă ninkă ună." Shi arkă ninkă ună shi l' skoase aland tshorŭ. Plamplum gălina la katilu. Gălina ku maia ăl' dzăsiră a katilui, "Afendi m, afendi m, brea n' okl'l'i, brea n' tshoarle, tsi n' adără kukotlu!" Katilu kl'imă kukotlu, "Atsets kukotlu aoa!" Adusiră kukotlu aklotse ; "Tsi ai di gălina?" "N' arupse smeana alunlu." Katilu aduse alunlu, "Tsi aveai di smeana a kukotlui?" "Tsi mănkă frăndzile kapra?" dzase alunlu. "Atsets kapra aoatse," dzăse napoi katilu. "Tsi nu m păshtia gine pikurarlu?" Pikurarlu ăl' dzăse, "Tsi nu n' didea păne doamna mea?" Doamna dzăse, "Tsi mănkă poarka alotlu?" "Atsets poarka aoa!" Poarka nu gri tsiva ; "N' eara foame," dzăse, shi skăpă.   Amintshu (Metsovo)

2. The Cock and the Hen

And there was an old woman with an old man, she had a cock with a hen. The old woman with the old man walked and walked, and the cock climbed on a nut tree. The cock was crowing and the hen was sitting down, and was saying to him, "Cock, cock throw me a nut." And he threw a nut and knocked out the hen's eye. The hen called again, "Cock, cock throw one more." He threw her one more and knocked out her other eye too. "Cock, cock throw one more." He knocked off her leg ; the hen called again, "Cock, cock throw one more." And he threw one more and knocked off her other leg. Plam plum the hen is off to the judge. The hen with the old woman said to the judge, "Master, master, look at my eyes, look at my legs, see what the cock did to me!" The judge called the cock, "Bring the cock here." They brought the cock there ; "What have you with the hen?" "The nut tree tore my drawers." The judge brought the nut tree, "What had you with the cock's drawers?" "Why did the goat eat my leaves?" said the nut tree. "Bring the goat here," said the judge again. "Why did not the shepherd feed me well?" The shepherd said, "Why did not my mistress give me bread?" The mistress said, "Why did the sow eat the yeast?" "Bring the sow here!" The sow did not call out at all ; "I was hungry," she said, and that's all.

3. Aushlu shi Moasha

Eara un aush ku ună maosha sh avea un kukot sh ună plitsă. Vine oara si ñgătshară moasha ku aushlu, sh kăftă di si mbărtsără. Plitsa kădzu ale moasha shi kukotlu kădzu al aush ; shi kăftă kukotlu si z dukă tu kseane. Tatăsu nu l alăsă. " Oh'i, va mi pitrets tu kseane, vai mi dukŭ." E, tatăsu tsia, " Nu ti pitrekŭ," shi apufăsi di l pitriku. Alko iu z duse tu kseane, duse di skălsia la palate al văsil'e, zhdiskălsire multă tsi fătsia află ună flurie. " Kă kă kă ! " dzăse elu, " aflai nă flurie." Avdi h'il'lu al văsil'e sh ease di l' u l'a fluriea, Tsi adară elŭ ? Di părăkălia multă lo napoi tu baktshe di skălsi di s umblu di flurii. Dzăse elŭ vine oara si z dukă la tatăsu. " Tora " dzăse a tatăsui " spindzură mi sh l'a nă drămă sh agudia si vedz tsi vai kadă." Lo shi tatăsu drăma shi l agudish kade k'isavro di flurii. S toarnă tatăsu zh dzăse " Fitshori si lom tagharia shi l' numirăm." Duk la moasha, kaftă tagharia, shi moasha aundze tagharia di katrani ta si s alăkeaskă flurii. Aushlu l akătsă inatea sh akătsară di z bătură doil'i aushan'i tsi eara mbărtsătsă. Tradze un, tradze aland zh vătămară moasha tu lok shi muri. Samarina

3. The Old Man and the Old Woman

There was an old man with an old woman and they had a cock and a hen. The time came and they quarrelled the old woman with the old man, and she asked and they parted. The hen fell to the old woman and the cock fell to the old man ; and the cock asked to go to foreign parts. His father would not let him. " No, you will send me to foreign parts, I will go." His father was saying, " I am not going to send you," and he decided and sent him. There where he went to foreign parts, he went and was scratching by the king's palace, and from all the scratching he did he found a gold piece. " Ka ka ka," said he, " I have found a gold piece." The king's son hears and comes out and takes the gold piece from him. What does he do ? With much entreaty he got back to the garden and scratched and filled himself with gold pieces. He said the hour had come to go to his father. " Now," said he to his father, " hang me up and take a switch and beat me to see what will fall." And his father took the switch and beat him and a treasure of gold pieces falls. His father turns and said, " Boys let us get the bag and count them." They go to the old woman, ask for the bag and the old woman smears the bag with pitch so that the gold pieces should stick. Anger seized the old man and they set to and they beat one another the two old people who had parted. One hits, the other hits, and they killed the old woman on the spot and she died.

4. Uvreulu shi Pikurarlu

Eara nă oară shi un g'iro un tshelnik mare shi mult nikuk'ir sh avea un pikurar mult pisto shi năundru tu nămăl'i avea sh un birbeatse mult mare, shi l' tsia l'aru. Zh vinea pikurarlu a kasa; āl' tsia "Kali mera afendiko." "Kalo s ton bistiko, kum l ai oile shi l'arlu?" Shiună dzuă loară zbor ku un uvreu mult nikuk'ir tră pikurarlu shi tshelniklu āl' tsia kā pikurarlu easte mult pisto shi nu poate si l arădă kan, shi bāgară stihimă ku uvreulu kā vai poată si l' dzākă mindzhune. Bāgară tută periusie sh adrară simvoli ghrapte, ka z dzākă mindzhune pikurarlu si l'a tută periusia al tshelniku shi ka si dzākă alithia si l'a tshelniklu a lui. Si mtă uvreulu, bāgă alte stran'e, alāksi furishaoa shi z duse la oi shi mundria tră si l akumbără l'arlu. Shi pikurarlu āl' dzāse, "Nu ts u dau." Āl' deade dzatse lire shi nu l' u dādea. Dutse, s mtă uvreulu. Ts s adară? Z dutse a kasa shi l'a mbl'earesa shi u aduse aklotse la oi shi pikurarlu s arāse shi l' deade l'arlu tră mbl'earesa. Di kar āl' lo l'arlu uvreulu, lo shi mbl'earesa shi z duse a kasa la tshelniku, shi tshelniklu dapoia pitriku un om si l' greaskă al pikurarŭ. Shi pikurarlu k'insi shi vnea kalea, tsia ku mindea ale kārlibană. Bāgă kātshula pri kārlibana shi zbura ku ea shi l' tsia, "Καλὴ 'μέρα ἀφενδικό!" "Καλὸ 's τὸν βιστικό, τὶ χαβάρια;" "Καλά." "Πῶς τ'άχεις τὰ πρόβατα;" "Καλά." "Τὸ λ'αρο πῶς τὸν ἔχs;" "Ψόφσι." "Nu dutse," āl' tsia ku minde. Vnea ma îgoa shi u bāgă napoi kātshua shi tsia, "Καλὴ 'μέρα ἀφενδικό!" "Καλὸ 's τὸν βιστικὸ, τὶ χαβάρια;" "Καλά." "Πωs τ'άχεις τὰ πρόβατα;" "Καλά." "Τὸ λ'άρο πῶs τὸν ἔχs;" "Τὸν ἔφαγι ὁ λύκος." "Oh'i nu dutse." Yine la poarta al tshelniku shi bāgă napoi kātshua si l' tsia, "Καλὴ 'μέρα ἀφενδικό!" "Καλὸ 's τὸν βιστικὸ, τὶ χαβάρια;" "Καλά." "Πωs τ'άχεις τὰ πρόβατα;" "Καλά." "Πῶs τὸν ἔχs τὸ λ'άρο;" "Πῆγε γιὰ κορηφί-λημα." "Aest easte bun, aest vai dzākŭ." Shi alnă analt la tshelniklu shi află multă lume aklo, atsel'i tsi adrară ghraptele sh ashtiptară pikurarlu tsi vai dzākă, mindzhune i alithia. Shi l' dzāse al tshelniku, "Καλή 'μέρα ἀφενδικό!" "Καλό 's τὸν βιστικό," āl' dzāse tshelniklu, "τὶ χαβάρια;" "Καλά." "Πῶs τ'άχεις τὰ πρόβατα;" "Καλά." "Τὸ λ'αρο πῶs τὸν ἔχs;" Shi pikurarlu āl' dzāse, "Παίει γιὰ κορηφίλημα." Shi epidhis kā spuse alithia āl' lo tută periusia al uvreu shi skāpă. Shi earam shi eu aklo shi n' dādea dzhumitate sh io nu vream kā am multsă.

Samarina

4. The Jew and the Shepherd Boy

Once upon a time there was a great and very wealthy shepherd and he had a shepherd boy who was very trusty and among the sheep he had a very big ram and he used to call it piebald. And the shepherd boy used to come to his house, he used to say to him, "Good day master!" "Welcome to the trusty shepherd boy, how have you the sheep and the piebald ?" And one day they disputed with a very wealthy Jew about the shepherd boy, and the shepherd was telling him that the shepherd boy was very trusty and that no one could deceive him, and they made a wager with the Jew that he would be able to tell him a lie. They wagered all their fortune and made a written contract, if the shepherd boy tells a lie the Jew should take all the shepherd's fortune, and if he tells the truth the shepherd should take his. The Jew bestirred himself, put on other clothes, changed his dress and went to the sheep and was looking to buy the piebald. And the shepherd boy said to him, " I am not giving it to you." He offered him ten pounds and he would not give it to him. The Jew goes away ; he bestirred himself. What should he do ? He goes home and takes his wife and brings her there to the sheep, and the shepherd was deceived and gave him the piebald for his wife. When the Jew took the piebald he took his wife too and went to the shepherd's house and the shepherd sent a man to call to the shepherd boy. And the shepherd boy started and was coming on his way ; he was talking in his mind to his crook. He put his fez on his crook and was talking with it and saying to it, " Good day master !" " Welcome to the trusty shepherd boy, what news ? " " Good." " How have you the sheep ? " ". Well." " The piebald how is it ? " " It's dead." " It does not do," he was saying in his mind. He came nearer and put his fez again (on his crook) and was saying, " Good day master ! " " Welcome to the trusty shepherd boy, what news ? " " Good." " How have you the sheep ? " " Well." " The piebald how is it ? " " The wolf ate him." " No, it does not do." He came to the shepherd's door and put his fez back again and was saying, " Good day master !" " Welcome to the trusty shepherd boy, what news ? " " Good." " How have you the sheep ? " " Well." " How is the piebald ? " " It's gone for a kiss." " This is good, this is what I'll say." And he went upstairs to the shepherd and found many people there, those who had made the contract, and waited for the shepherd boy what he would say, a lie or the truth. And he said to the shepherd, " Good day master ! " " Welcome to the trusty shepherd boy," said the shepherd to him, " what news ? " " Good." " How have you the sheep ? " " Well." " The piebald how is it ? " And the shepherd boy said to him, " It's gone for a kiss." And since he told the truth, he took all the Jew's fortune and that's the end. And I was there too and they offered me half and I would not have it because I have much.

NOTES AND BIBLIOGRAPHY

CHAPTER I

THE principal writers who have dealt with the Balkan Vlachs in general are the following :—

Ἀραβαντινός, Χρονογραφία τῆς Ἠπείρου, and Μονογραφία περὶ Κουτσοβλάχων.

Bărbulescu, I., *Relations des Roumains avec les Serbes*, etc.

Bérard, V., *Pro Macedonia*.

Brailsford, *Macedonia, its Races and its Future*.

Bratter, *Die Kutzowalachische Frage*.

Diamandi, V., *Renseignements Statistiques sur la Population des Balkans*.

Eliot, Sir C., *Turkey in Europe*.

Evans, Sir A., *Antiquarian Researches in Illyricum, Archæologia*, vols. 48, 49.

Fortescue, A., *The Orthodox Eastern Church*.

Λαμπρίδης, Ἠπειρώτικα Μελετήματα.

Lazar, V., *Die Südrumänen* (this contains a useful bibliography).

Leake, *Researches in Greece*, and *Travels in Northern Greece*.

Philippson, *Thessalien und Epirus*.

Pouqueville, *Voyage de la Grèce*, and *Mémoire sur l'Illyrie*, etc., in *Mém. de l'Acad. des Inscrpt.*, vol. xii.

Σχινάς, Ὁδοιπορικὸν τῆς Μακεδονίας.

Tomaschek, *Die alten Thraker*, and *Zur Kunde der Hämus Halbinsel*.

Tozer, *Highlands of Turkey*.

Weigand, *Olympo-Walachen, Vlacho-Meglen, Die Aromunen* and his articles in the *Jahresberichte* of the Roumanian Seminar at Leipzig.

Χοϊδάς, Ἡ Ἱστορία τῆς Μακεδονικῆς Ὑποθέσεως.

Χρυσοχόος, Βλάχοι καὶ Κουτσόβλαχοι.

Other sources of information are the *Encyclopædia Britannica*, the Μακεδονικὸν Ἡμερολόγιον, 1908–1912 (published in Athens), and the linguistic papers of Miklosich in the *Wiener Denkschriften*.

P. 6. The book in question is the Εἰσαγωγικὴ Διδασκαλία of Daniel which was probably printed at the press of the Greek Patriarchate at Constantinople. The signatures are in Greek type, and this feature and the same ornaments are to be found in the Κανονικὸν ἤτοι οἱ Θεῖοι Κανόνες συνειλεγμένοι παρὰ Χριστοφόρου Μοναχοῦ which was printed at the Patriarchate press in 1798. There are copies of both these books in the British Museum.

CHAPTER II

P. 18. Hashia. In Greek the district is called Χάσια (pronounced Khashia), but the name is probably derived from the Turkish *khassa*, private or personal. This would suit a country full of chiftliks. In this connection it is worth noting that till 1840 the villages of Pelion and Magnesia were divided into Khasia and Vakuphia. The former according to Maghnis seem to have been like chiftliks, but Yeoryiadhis' account does not agree with this. See Urquhart, *Spirit of the East*, i. p. 313 ; Philippson, *Thessalien und Epirus*, pp. 152, 170 ; Μαγνής, Περιήγησις τῆς Θεσσαλίας, p. 43 ; Γεωργιάδης, Θεσσαλία², pp. 104, 186 ; Ἀραβαντινός, Χρονογραφία τῆς Ἠπείρου, ii. p. 176.

P. 22. For accounts of the war of 1897 see, Rose, *With the Greeks in Thessaly* ; Bingham, *With the Turkish Army in Thessaly*.

P. 22. For the history of the bishopric of Ghrevena see, Gelzer, *Patriarchat von Achrida*, esp. pp. 8, 16, 20, 35 ff., 117 ff., 136, 142 ; *Byzantinische Zeitschrift*, 1892, pp. 256, 257 : 1893, pp. 43, 59 ; *Athenische Mitteilungen*, 1902, p. 435 ; Le Quien, *Oriens Christianus*, ii. pp. 294, 323 ; Miklosich-Muller, *Acta et Diplomata*, ii. p. 250 ; Νέος Ἑλληνομνήμων, vii. p. 154.

P. 23. For information about the early history of Ghrevena see, Passow, *Carmina Popularia*, Nos. xxi–xxiii, cviii, cx, cxxvi ; Pouqueville, *Hist. de la Régénération de la Grèce*, pp. 61, 338 ; *Parl. Papers 1854*, Correspondence respecting the Relations of Greece and Turkey, p. 227 ; Ἀραβαντινός, Χρονογραφία, i. pp. 64, 174, 195, 379 ; Ἄσματα Ἠπείρου, Nos. 27, 48, 61, 71, 81, 91, 93, 97, 98, 100–103, 113, 116, 117 ; Χρηστοβασίλης, Ἐθνικὰ Ἄσματα, pp. 289, 294 ; Περραιβός, Ἱστορία Σουλίου καὶ Πάργας, i. p. 23 ; Λαμπρίδης, Ἠπειρ. Μελετήματα, iii. pp. 69 ff., v. p. 39, ix. p. 61.

P. 27. For further particulars about Ghrevena see the books already given in the bibliography to Chapter I, especially Leake, Pouqueville, Weigand, Ἀραβαντινός, and Σχινάς, cf. also Nicolaidy, *Les Turcs et la Turquie Contemporaine*, ii. p. 229 ; Μελέτιος, Γεωγραφία (Venice, 1728), p. 396.

P. 28. The word Varoshi which in modern Greek means suburb is according to Gustav Meyer of Magyar origin and is connected with the word *varos* town, and *var* castle. Throughout Thessaly and South Macedonia it occurs as the name of suburbs at Serfije, Okhridha, Elassona, Pharsala and elsewhere. Since under Turkish rule the christians were compelled to live in the suburbs and not in the centre of a town the word Varoshi has come to mean the christian quarter of a town. How the word strayed down into the Southern Balkans is obscure, but it even occurs as far afield as Famagusta in Cyprus.

P. 29. On the Valakhadhes see, Weigand, *Aromunen*, i. p. 128 ; Nicolaidy, *Les Turcs et la Turquie Contemporaine*, ii. p. 216 ; Μακεδονικὸν Ἡμερολόγιον, 1911, p. 113. Their principal villages are Dovratovo, Kublari, Subeno, Krivtsi, Tsurkhli, Triveni, Kastro, Dovrunista, Great Serini,

Dovrani, Kira Kale, Vriashteno, Ventsa, Meseniko, Torista, Angalei, Tshotili, Vaipes, Pilori, Bubushti, Yiankovo, Breshtiani, Nestimi, Zeligoshti, Vrostani and Dhislapo.

P. 30. On the Kupatshari see, Weigand, *Aromunen*, i. p. 130 ; 'Αραβαντινός, Χρονογραφία, ii. pp. 342 ff. Their principal villages are Bura, Divrani, Vravonishta, Tshuriaka, Mesoluri, Dhelvino, Tuzhi, Dusko, Philippei (in Vlach Filkl'i), Vodhendzko, Sharghanei, Lavdha, Lipinitsa, Tishta, Spileo, Zalovo, Riakhovo, Paleokhori, Kosmati, Sitovo, Mavranei (in Vlach Mavranle), Mavronoro, Kipurio which Leake calls Vlach, Zapando, Labanitsa, and Monakhiti. Aravandinos also gives Pulitsari and Kusko, which is perhaps an error for Dusko, as speaking Greek and Vlach. But he omits several of the above, and states that Samarina speaks Greek and Albanian, so his information is probably not absolutely correct.

P. 32. For the summer climate in Macedonia and Epirus see, Leake, *Northern Greece*, i. pp. 115, 268, iv. p. 114 ; Hogarth, *Nearer East*, pp. 99 ff. ; Philippson, *Mittelmeergebiet*, pp. 123 ff. ; Tozer, *Highlands of Turkey*, ii. p. 199.

CHAPTER III

P. 46. For the population of Samarina see, Weigand, *Olympo-Walachen*, p. 6; Nicolaidy, *Les Turcs*, etc., ii. p. 228 ; Cordescu, *Istoricul Şcoalelor Române din Turcia*, pp. 148 ff. ; 'Αραβαντινός, Χρονογραφία, ii. p. 341 ; Σχινάς, 'Οδοιπορικόν, i. pp. 50, 57.

P. 48. Aigl'a is a corruption of the Greek "Αγιος 'Ηλίας.

P. 56. For an account of Vlach boys' games see, Papahagi, *Din Literatura Poporană a Aromânilor*, pp. 71–186.

CHAPTER IV

A general account of Vlach dress is given by Weigand, *Aromunen*, i. pp. 260 ff. ; cf. also his book *Vlacho-Meglen*, p. xxix.

CHAPTER V

Pp. 87 ff. The original texts of the inscriptions in the churches are given in Appendix I.

P. 87. The Church of St Elijah is mentioned in a klephtic song referring to Totskas, Passow, *Carmina Popularia*, No. xxi. l. 24 ; 'Αραβαντινός, "Ασματα 'Ηπείρου, No. 71, l. 24 ; Χρηστοβασίλης, 'Εθνικὰ "Ασματα, No. 104, l. 26.

P. 94. For Vlach houses in other villages see, Weigand, *Aromunen*, i. p. 268 ; Papahagi, *Basme Aromâne*, p. viii.

CHAPTER VI

A description of the betrothal and wedding customs at Samarina has been given by Παπαγεωργίου in Λαογραφία, ii. pp. 432 ff., and those at Blatsă are recorded in the Μακεδονικὸν Ἡμερολόγιον for 1912, pp. 212 ff. The small book by Cosmescu, *Datini Credinţe şi Superstiţii Aromâneşti*, contains a brief account of the customs at birth, marriage and death. Weigand in *Die Aromunen*, ii. pp. 32 ff., 200 ff., briefly describes the marriage and burial customs. Some Vlach customs are mentioned by Marianu in his books on Roumanian folklore, which may be compared for parallel Roumanian observances. For Modern Greek customs the *Volksleben der Neugriechen* of B. Schmidt can be referred to and also the works of Politis. A Greek wedding in the Zaghori is described in Ἑλληνικὸς Φιλολογικὸς Σίλλογος, vol. 19, pp. 223 ff. The best account of Albanian customs is von Hahn's *Albanesische Studien*.

P. 103. The text is in Παχτίκος, Ἑλλήνικα Ἄσματα, p. 269, No. 173 with four extra lines.

P. 107. The original text is given by Παπαγεωργίου, Λαογραφία, ii. p. 434, No. 1.

P. 107. The text is given in Appendix II, No. 1.

P. 107. A version of the text is given by Παπαγεωργίου, *op. cit.*, p. 435, cf. Passow, *Carmina Popularia*, No. DII.

P. 113. The text is given in Appendix II, No. 2.

P. 113. The texts of songs for the dressing of the bride and the combing are given in Appendix II, Nos. 3, 4.

P. 115. Παπαγεωργίου prints the text, Λαογραφία, ii. p. 440.

P. 115. The text is given by Παπαγεωργίου, *op. cit.*, p. 439, No. 1.

P. 116. The Vlach text is given in Appendix II, No. 5.

P. 116. Παπαγεωργίου gives the text of this and the three following songs, *op. cit.*, p. 441.

P. 119. The texts are given by Παπαγεωργίου, *op. cit.*, p. 444, No. 1 ; p. 443.

P. 120. The texts of this and the next two songs are in Appendix II, Nos. 6–8.

P. 121. The text of this song to the *nunŭ* is in Παπαγεωργίου, *op. cit.*, p. 445.

P. 123. The texts of these songs are in Appendix II, Nos. 9–11.

P. 125. The text is in Παπαγεωργίου, *op. cit.*, p. 437.

P. 126. Vlach dirges are given by Weigand, *Aromunen*, ii. pp. 202–210, and Papahagi, *Din Literatura Poporană*, pp. 963 ff. ; cf. Fauriel, *Chants populaires de la Grèce moderne*.

CHAPTER VII

For Vlach folklore the most comprehensive work is Papahagi, *Din Literatura Poporană a Aromânilor* ; much will be found in the works of Cosmescu referred to for Chapter VI and in Weigand, *Aromunen*, ii. pp. 116 ff. Papahagi, *Basme Aromâne* is a good collection of folk tales. Parallel Roumanian, Albanian and Greek customs are treated by Marianu, von Hahn, B. Schmidt and Politis whose books have already been quoted in Chapter

VI. Other books on Greek folklore are Lawson, *Modern Greek Folklore*, and Hamilton, *Greek Saints and their Festivals*.

P. 129. For the fair of Mavronoro see Pouqueville, *Voyage de la Grèce*, ii. p. 495 ; Ἐπετηρὶς Παρνασσοῦ, 1902, p. 142.

P. 130. The texts of the first two songs are in Appendix II, Nos. 12, 13. A version of the third is given by Weigand, *Aromunen*, ii. p. 88, No. 59.

P. 132. For Pirprună songs see Weigand, *Aromunen*, ii. p. 136, No. 80, and Papahagi, *Literatura Poporană*, pp. 723–729.

P. 137. These Christmas songs are in Appendix II, Nos. 14, 15.

P. 138. On Karkandzal'i see Lawson, *op. cit.*, pp. 190 ff.

P. 138. For the mumming at Epiphany see *Annual of the British School at Athens*, xvi. pp. 232–253. The Thracian festivals are described by Dawkins, *Journal of Hellenic Studies*, 1906, pp. 191 ff., and Katsarow, *Archiv. f. Religionswissenschaft*, 1908, pp. 407 ; for its relation to the Greek drama see Ridgeway, *Origin of Tragedy*, and Nilsson in *Neue Jahrbücher f. d. klassische Altertum*, xxvii. pp. 677 ff. For the Albanian custom see von Hahn, *Albanesische Studien*, i. p. 156.

CHAPTER VIII

P. 114. Baldacci's journey is described in Ἐπετηρὶς Παρνασσοῦ, iii. pp. 152 ff.

P. 146. For the *tshelnikŭ* system see Weigand, *Aromunen*, i. p. 186.

P. 148. References to Yanni al Preftu will be found in Ἀραβαντινός, Χρονογραφία, Λαμπρίδης and Χρηστοβασίλης, Ἐθνικὰ Ἄσματα.

P. 149. The text is given in Appendix III, No. 1.

P. 149. The text is in Ἀραβαντινός, Ἄσματα Ἠπείρου, No. 50 ; cf. Papahagi, *Literatura Poporană*, p. 912, No. xxiv.

P. 150. The text is in Ἀραβαντινός, *op. cit.*, No. 52, and Χρηστοβασίλης, *op. cit.*, No. 46.

P. 152. The tale of Demetrius is in Pouqueville, *Hist. de la Régénération de la Grèce*, i. pp. 339 ff.

P. 154. The song is in Ἀραβαντινός, *op. cit.*, No. 92.

P. 155. For the rising of 1854 see Finlay, *Hist. of Greece*, vii. pp. 221 ff. (ed. Tozer), *Parliamentary Papers 1854, Correspondence respecting Relations of Greece and Turkey*, Ἀραβαντινός, Ἄσματα Ἠπείρου, Nos. 27, 32.

P. 157. The song is in Appendix III, No. 2.

P. 159. For the rising of 1878 see Σεϊζάνης, Ἐπανάστασις τοῦ 1878.

P. 161. The song is in Weigand, *Olympo-Walachen*, p. 131, No. xx.

P. 162. This song and the next are in Appendix III, Nos. 3, 4 ; cf. Papahagi, *Literatura Poporană*, p. 1014, Nos. xxi, xxii.

P. 163. For the tale of Karadzhas, see Zuca, *Istorioare din Epir*, pp. 39 ff. ; the song is in Appendix III, No. 5. A pamphlet describing Zhurkas as a hero was published in Athens in 1880, Ἀνδραγαθήματα τοῦ Βασιλείου Ζούρκα, by Koritsias, Papadhopulos and Bosos.

P. 165. This and the next two songs are in Appendix III, Nos. 6, 7, 8.

P. 166. For the exploits of Katărah'ia, see Chirol, *'Twixt Greek and Turk*, pp. 82 ff. : he refers to Leonidha on p. 173 and Davelis on p. 170.

P. 168. This song and the next are in Appendix III, Nos. 9, 10.

CHAPTER IX

For other books on this district see Weigand, *Aromunen*, i., Ἀραβαντινός, Χρονογραφία, Λαμπρίδης, Ἠπειρώτικα Μελετήματα, and Ζαγοριακά, and Cordescu, *Istoricul Şcoalelor Române din Turcia.*

P. 183. Mr. Sokolis' paper is in the Ἐπετηρὶς Παρνασσοῦ, 1883, p. 298, and is called Περὶ Ἠπείρου καὶ Ἀλβανίας.

P. 192. For the epic of Ali Pasha see Σάθας, Ἱστορικαὶ Διατριβαί, pp. 123 ff. ; cf. Ἀραβαντινός, Ἱστορια τοῦ Ἀλὴ Πασιᾶ, pp. 523 ff. ; Leake, *Northern Greece*, i. pp. 463 ff.

P. 193. For Ayios Kosmas see Σάθας, Νεοελληνικὴ Φιλολογία, pp. 487 ff.

P. 197. The song is given by Papahagi, *Literatura Poporană*, p. 1026, No. xlii.

P. 203. For the tale of the mountain demons see Zuca, *Istorioare din Epir*, pp. 46 ff. ; Papahagi, *Başme Aromâne*, No. 3 ; Παρνασσὸς, 1890, pp. 347 ff.

CHAPTER X

For this chapter apart from our own researches the principal authorities are the works of Leake, Weigand and Diamandi mentioned in the bibliography to Chapter I. There is also some information to be found in the periodical *Lumina* which used to be published at Monastir.

P. 215. For Muskopol'e see the songs in Weigand, *Aromunen*, ii. p. 150, No. 91 ; Papahagi, *Literatura Poporană*, pp. 994, 1010, Nos. i, xvi, xvii.

P. 220. For the Gramos Vlachs in the Meglen see *Lilicea Pindului*, i. p. 65.

CHAPTER XI

For books on the Vlach language see the works of Weigand quoted in the bibliography to Chapter I, the various articles in the *Jahresberichte* of the Roumanian Seminar at Leipzig ; Densusianu's *Histoire de la langue roumaine* and Miklosich's publication of the books of Kavalliotis and Daniel in the *Wiener Denkschriften* for 1882. In Greek the best book is the Λεξικὸν τῆς Κουτσοβλαχικῆς Γλώσσης of Νικολαΐδης, to which Capidan has published a *Réponse Critique*. G. Meyer's *Neugriechische Studien* and Murnu's *Rumänische Lehnwörter in Neugriechischen* illustrate its relations with Greek. For neighbouring languages the Albanian, Bulgarian and Roumanian grammars of Weigand, G. Meyer and Puşcariu may be consulted. The best works on modern Greek are Thumb's *Handbuch* which has been translated into English and Hatzidakis' *Einleitung*. A

good collection of Vlach texts is given by Papahagi in his *Basme Aromâne*.
The earliest students of Vlach were Lucius who collected a few words in his
De Regno Dalmatiæ et Croatiæ and Thunmann in his *Geschichte der
östlichen europaischen Völker*. The oldest monuments of Vlach are the
lexicons of Kavalliotis and Daniel and the *Codex Demonie* published in the
Jahresberichte of the Roumanian Seminar at Leipzig. There is no Vlach-
English dictionary, but the works of Weigand and Papahagi contain useful
glossaries ; Nikolaidhis' lexicon is also useful, but the employment of the
Greek alphabet is a very serious inconvenience. There are two Vlach-
Roumanian dictionaries by Dalametra and Mihaileanu. Modern Vlach
literature is represented by two or three local newspapers such as *Dreptatea*
published in Salonica and periodicals like *Lumina, Graiu Bun, Lilicea
Pindului*, all printed in Bucharest, and *Flambura* printed in Salonica. The
four volumes of the *Biblioteca Lumina* of which Zuca's *Istorioare din Epir*
is the second were issued from Bucharest, but Zicu Araia's version of "Enoch
Arden" was published at Monastir. Both Zuca and Araia write in the
Samarina dialect.

CHAPTER XII

The chief ancient authorities have been mentioned in the text and most
if not all of them are to be found in the Bonn Corpus of Byzantine Historians.
The later period of the Asan kingdom is dealt with by Georgius Acropolita ;
most of the Byzantine Histories and many of the Chronicles of the Crusaders
contain references to Vlachs. Besides the main modern authorities mentioned in the bibliography to Chapter I are the following :

Arginteanu, *Istoria Românilor Macedoneni.*
Boga, *Românii din Macedonia.*
Finlay, *History of Greece.*
Iorga, *Geschichte des rumänischen Völkes.*
Jireček, *Geschichte der Bulgaren.*
Miller, *History of the Ottoman Empire.*
Murnu, *Vlahia Mare.*
Pič, *Ueber die Abstammung der Rumänen.*
Roesler, *Romänische Studien.*
Rubin, *Les Roumains de Macédoine.*
Thunmann, *Geschichte der östlichen europäischen Völker.*
Xenopol, *Les Roumains au Moyen Age* ; *Histoire des Roumains* ;

and Peisker's chapter on the "Asiatic Background" in the first volume of
the *Cambridge Medieval History.*

VOCABULARY

In this vocabulary will be found all the Vlach words in the text and appendices. It is hoped that it will prove useful to any readers who wish to translate for themselves the texts given with the aid of the grammar in Chapter XI. The abbreviations used are those common in dictionaries, v. for verb, n. for noun, and so on. As regards verbs the form given is the first person singular of the present indicative, and the infinitive and preterite, where known, are added. The numbers I, II, III, IV indicate the conjugations of the verbs in question, which are explained on pages 242–248. The letters *g'*, *h'*, *k'*, *l'*, *n'* and *ñ* are grouped under *G, H, K, L* and *N*, and *ă* and *ā* under *A*.

A

a, prep.; with acc. *at, to* ; with gen. and dat. of nouns, pronouns and adjectives as a sign of the case, see pp. 234, 235, 238.

adarŭ, v. I, *make, do* ; adrare, adrai.

adete, n. fem., *custom.*

adhimtă, n. fem., *fine home-spun.*

adukŭ, v. III, *bring, fetch* ; adutseare, adushu.

adunare, n. fem., *meeting.*

adzhuñgu, v. III, *arrive, reach, be enough* ; adzhundzeare, adzhumshu.

aestu, pron., *this.*

afendi, n. masc., *master.*

aflu, v. I, *find* ; aflare, aflai ; reflexive, mi aflu, *I am born.*

afstriaku, n. masc., *Austrian gold piece.*

aghoyie, n. fem., *hire of mules and horses, fare, cost of journey.*

aghrāpnie, n. fem., *vigil, watch-night service.*

aghunesku, v. IV, *drive away, expel* ; aghunire, aghuniĭ.

agudesku, v. IV, *hit, strike, attack* ; agudire, agudiĭ.

ahāntu, rel. pron., *as many as.*

aieri, adv., *yesterday.*

aistu, dialectic form for aestu.

akatsu, v. I, *seize, start* ; akātsare, akātsai.

ak'ikăsesku, v. IV, *understand* ; ak'ikăsire, ak'ikăsiĭ.

aklo, aklotse, adv., *there.*

akresku, v. II, *grow, increase* ; akrishteare, akriskui.

20

akumbărŭ, v. I, *buy* ; akumbărare, akumbărai.
ăl', dialectic form for l'i.
al, abbreviation for alŭ.
alagŭ, v. I, *wander* ; alăgare, alăgai.
alăk'esku, v. IV, *stick* ; alăk'ire, alăk'iĭ.
alăksesku, v. IV, *change one's clothes, dress* ; alăksire, alăksiĭ.
alăksimindu, n. neut. ; *change of clothing.*
alantu, pron., *the other.*
alasŭ, v. I, *leave, let alone, abandon* ; alăsare, alăsai.
alavdu, v. I, *praise* ; alavdare, alavdai.
albu, adj., *white.*
ale, the gen. and dat. sing. of the fem. article.
alegŭ, v. III, *choose, pick out* ; aledzeare, alepshu.
a l'ei, pronom. adj. indecl., *her* ; see a lui ; also gen. and dat. fem.
    sing. of elu.
alinŭ, v. I, *climb, ascend* ; alnare, alnai.
alithia, n. fem., *truth.*
aliura, adv., *somewhere else.*
alkă, n. fem., *cream.*
a lor, pronom. adj. indecl., *their* ; also gen. and dat. plur. of elu.
alotŭ, n. neut., *yeast.*
altu, indef. pronoun, *other.*
alŭ, gen. and dat. sing of the masc. article.
alună, n. fem., *nut.*
alunŭ, n. masc., *nut tree.*
a lui, pronom. adj. indecl., *his* ; fem. a l'ei ; really gen. sing. masc.
    and fem. of elu.
am, v. II, *have* ; aveare, avui.
amare, n. fem., *sea.*
amerŭ, see merŭ.
ameu, pronom. adj., *my, mine.*
amintu, v. I, *obtain, acquire, take* ; amintare, amintai.
amo, adv., *now.*
analtu, adj., *high, tall.*
analtu, adv., *up, upstairs, aloft.*
anapudhu, adj., *upside down, mixed, disturbed.*
andihristu, n. masc., *Antichrist* ; fem. andihristă.
andreptu, adv., *straight ahead.*
andri, n. masc., *robe* ; see p. 64.
anemi, n. fem., *skein-holder.*
Añglie, n. fem., *England.*
anostru, pronom. adj., *our.*
anoyie, n. fem., *upper room.*
anŭ, n. masc., *year.*
aoa, aoatse, adv., *here.*
aoaltari, adv., *the day before yesterday.*
aoatse, see aoa.

apă, n. fem., *water.*
apală, n. fem., *loose lump of carded wool.*
aplekŭ, v. I, *bend, stoop* ; aplikare, aplikai.
aplikatoară, n. fem., *milch-ewe.*
apofasi, n. fem., *determination, decision.*
apoia, adv., *afterwards.*
apostusesku, v. IV, *be tired* ; apostusire, apostusiĭ.
aproape, adv., *near.*
apufăsesku, v. IV, *decide, determine* ; apufăsire, apufăsiĭ.
arădŭ, v. III, *laugh, deceive* ; arădeare, arăshu.
arapŭ, n. masc., *Arab.*
arapŭ, v. IV, *seize, snatch* ; arak'ire, arak'iĭ.
aratse, adj., *cold.*
arău, n. neut., *river.*
arău, adj., *wrong, harmful.*
ardu, v. III, *burn* ; ardeare, arshu.
arkoare, n. fem., *cold*, dialectic form of răkoare.
aroshu, adj., *red.*
arsarŭ, v. IV, *jump, leap* ; arsărire, arsăriĭ.
arugă, n. fem., *exit from sheep fold.*
arukŭ, v. I, *throw* ; arkare, arkai.
arumănŭ, n. masc., *Vlach* ; fem. arumănă.
arupŭ, v. III, *tear, break* ; arupeare, arupshu.
asăns, adv., *to-day.*
ashteptu, v. I, *wait, wait for, expect* ; ashtiptare, ashtiptai.
asime, n. fem., *silver.*
ashi, ashitsi, adv., *so, yes.*
askundu, v. III, *hide* ; askundeare, askumshu.
aspargu, v. III, *spoil, break, change a large coin for small change* ;
    aspardzeare, asparshu.
aspunŭ, see spunŭ.
astiñgu, v. III, *quench, extinguish* ; astindzeare, asteshu.
atău, pronoun, adj., *thy, thine.*
atsets, contracted form of adutsetsĭ from adukŭ.
atseu, pron., *that.*
atsia, adv., *there, here.*
atumtsea, adv., *then.*
auñgu, v. III, *anoint, smear* ; aundzeare, aumshu.
aushu, n. masc., *old man.*
avdu, v. IV, *hear, listen* ; avdzăre, avdzăĭ.
Avgustu, n. masc., *August.*
avostru, pron. adj., *your.*
ayine, n. fem., *vineyard.*
azborŭ, only in phrase si dutseare azborŭ, see p. 52.
azhuñgu, dialectic form of adzhuñgu.

B

bade, dialectic form of pade.
bāghānikă, n. fem., *batter cake.*
bagu, v. I, *put, place* ; bāgare, bāgai.
bairŭ, n. neut., *necklace.*
baktshe, n. masc., *garden.*
bană, n. fem., *life.*
bānedzu, v. I, *live* ; bānare, bānai.
bārbatŭ, n. masc., *man, husband.*
bātal'e, n. fem., *beetling mill.*
batŭ, v. II, *beat, hit* ; bāteare, bātui.
beau, v. II, *drink* ; beare, biui.
birbeatse, dialectic form for birbekŭ.
birbekŭ, n. masc., *ram.*
bisearikă, n. fem., *church.*
bitisesku, v. IV, *finish* ; bitisire, bitisiĭ.
bou, n. masc., *ox.*
brānŭ, n. neut., *sash.*
bre, exclam., *ho ! hi !*
bresku, dialectic form for mundresku, mutresku.
bufŭ, n. masc., *owl.*
bubghală, n. fem., *a sweet*; see p. 122.
buhare, n. masc., *chimney.*
bunŭ, adj., *good.*

D

d, abbreviation of di.
da, affirm., *yes.*
dadă, n. fem., *mother.*
dală, n. fem., *buttermilk.*
dapoia, adv., *afterwards.*
dau, v. irreg., *give* ; dare, deduĭ.
davani, n. fem., *wooden ceiling.*
depunŭ, v. III, *descend, make to descend* ; dipuneare, dipushu.
dhipla, adv., *double, by side of.*
di, prep., *of* ; di tu, *from* ; di pri, *out of.*
di, conj., *and.*
dineavra, adv., *just now.*
dipartosŭ, adj., *distant.*
dipŭ, adv., *altogether, completely.*
dipunŭ, see depunŭ.
disfakŭ, v. III, *unfasten, open* ; disfătseare, disfetshu.
dislāksesku, v. IV, *undress* ; dislāksire, dislāksiĭ.
dispostusesku, v. IV, *stop from being tired, rest* ; dispostusire, dispostusiĭ.
doamnă, n. fem., *mistress.*

doi, num., *two* ; fem. doauă.
domnu, n. masc., *master.*
dormu, v. IV, *sleep* ; durn'ire, durn'iĭ.
dosprădzatse, num., *twelve.*
dramă, n. fem., *switch.*
drāshteală, n. fem., *washing and bleaching tub.*
duk'esku, v. IV, *understand* ; duk'ire, duk'iĭ.
dukŭ, v. III, *lead* ; dutseare, dushu : most common in reflexive
form mi dukŭ, *I go.*
dulape, n. fem., *cupboard.*
dultse, adj., *sweet.*
dulumă, n. masc., *woman's long coat.*
Dumnidzeu, n. masc., *God.*
după, prep., *after.*
dzākŭ, v. III, *tell, say* ; dzātseare, dzāshu.
dzatse, num., *ten.*
dzeană, n. fem., *cheek, mountain ridge.*
dzhibadane, n. fem., *waistcoat.*
dzhokŭ, v. I, *dance* ; dzhukare, dzhukai.
dzhone, n. masc., *young man, youth, gallant.*
dzhumitate, v. fem., *half.*
dzhuncale, n. masc., *young man, youth.*
dzuă, n. fem., *day.*

E

ea, exclam., *see !*
eapă, n. fem., *mare.*
efthinitate, n. fem., *cheapness.*
elu, pron., *he* ; fem. ea, *she* ; see p. 238.
epidhis, conj., *since.*
esku, v. aux., *be* ; h'ire, earam, fui ; see h'iu.
estan, adv., *this year.*
esŭ, v. IV, *go out* ; ishire, ishiĭ.
etiu, n. masc., *cause of, reason for* ; always personal.
eu, pron., *I.*

F

fagŭ, n. masc., *beech tree.*
fakŭ, v. III, *make* ; fātseare, fetshu.
fāndānă, n. fem., *spring, source* ; dialectic form of fäntänă.
făntănă, n. fem., *spring, source.*
fără, prep., *without.*
fatsă, n. fem., *face.*
feată, n. fem., *girl, daughter.*
fitikă, dim. of feată.

fitshorŭ, n. masc., *boy, son.*
flokŭ, n. neut., *flock of wool.*
flurie, n. fem., *gold florin.*
foale, n. fem., *skin bag* (for carrying cheese, wine, water, or the like).
foame, n. fem., *hunger.*
fokŭ, n. neut., *fire.*
frăndză, n. fem., *leaf.*
frăñgu, v. III, *break* ; frăndzeare, fredzhu.
frapsinŭ, n. masc., *ash tree.*
frate, n. masc., *brother.*
frikă, n. fem., *fear, fright.*
frundidhă, n. fem., *thought, care.*
fugŭ, v. IV, *flee, go away* ; fudzire, fudzăĭ.
fukară, adj., *poor.*
fumeal'e, n. fem., *family.*
fumŭ, n. masc., *smoke.*
fundă, n. fem., *tassel.*
furkă, n. fem., *distaff.*
furishaoă, n. fem., *costume, dress.*
furtatŭ, n. masc., *groomsman.*
furtutiră, n. fem., *loading pole.*
furŭ, n. masc., *thief, robber, brigand.*

G, G'

găleată, n. fem., *milk pail.*
gălină, n. fem., *hen.*
gambro, n. masc., *bridegroom* ; dialectic form of ghambro.
gamilă, n. fem., *camel.*
gapŭ, dialectic form of kapŭ.
garambo, dialectic form of gambro.
garvanitshu, n. masc., *homespun* (medium).
garvano, n. masc., *homespun* (coarse).
gasă, dialectic form of kasă, but only in phrase iñ gasă.
g'atru, dialectic form of yatru.
gavŭ, adj., *blind.*
ghălikă, n. fem., *basket.*
ghambro, n. masc., *bridegroom.*
ghrăpsesku, v. IV, *write* ; ghrăpsire, ghrăpsiĭ.
ghrapto, adj., *written.*
g'ilie, dialectic form of yilie.
g'ine, adv., *well* ; adverb of bunŭ.
g'inŭ, dialectic form of yinŭ.
g'iptu, dialectic form of yiptu.
g'iro, n. masc., *time, season* ; dialectic form of k'iro.
g'iză, n. fem., *boiled butter milk.*

g'izirsesku, v. IV, *wander* ; g'izirsire, g'izirsiĭ.
glarŭ, adj., *mad.*
gor, only in adv. phrase pi gor, *downhill.*
grădină, n. fem., *garden.*
grekŭ, n. masc., *Greek.*
grendă, n. fem., *tree-trunk, log.*
gresku, v. IV, *call, shoʌt* ; grire, griĭ.
greu, adj., *heavy, serious.*
groapă, n. fem., *hollow, grave, pit.*
grossu, adj., *thick.*
gugutshă, n. fem., *darling.*
gură, n. fem., *mouth.*
gustu, n. neut., *taste, pleasure.*

H, H'

hăiate, n. fem., *cloister.*
hăirlitka, exclam., *Here's to the wedding !*
hambla, adv., *downstairs* ; sometimes almost as a noun, *ground floor.*
hani, n. fem., *inn, resting-place.*
harauă, n. fem., *joy, pleasure, wedding.*
hare, n. fem., *talent, inclination, disposition.*
hasku, v. I, *gape, yawn* ; hăskare, hăskai.
hazo, adj., *mad, silly.*
h'erbu, v. III, *boil, cook* ; h'irbeare, h'ershu.
h'igŭ, v. III, *fix, insert* ; h'idzeare, hipshu.
h'il'e, n. fem., *daughter.*
h'il'u, n. masc., *son.*
h'ima, adv., *below* ; used mainly of the lower country, *the plains.*
h'iu, v. aux., *be* ; h'ire, earam, fui ; see esku.
h'ivresku, v. IV, *have fever* ; h'ivrire, h'ivriĭ.
hoară, n. fem., *village.*
hrănesku, v. IV, *feed, cherish* ; hrănire, hrăniĭ.
Hristo, n. masc., *Christ.*
hrisusesku, v. IV, *gild, make of gold* ; hrisusire, hrisusiĭ.

I

i, dialectic form for easte, 3rd pers. present indic. of esku and h'iu.
i . . . i, conj., *either . . . or.*
iară, n. fem., *winter* ; dialectic form of iarnă.
iara, adv., *again.*
iara, dialectic form of eara.
iarbă, n. fem., *grass.*
iarnă, n. fem., *winter.*
ilik'ie, n. fem., *full age, right age, age.*

imblinu, adj., *full* ; dialectic form of implinŭ.
imnu, v. I, *walk* ; imnare, imnai.
impartu, v. IV, *divide, separate* ; impărtsire, impărtsiĭ.
implinŭ, adj., *full*.
in, prep., *in*.
inate, n. fem., *anger*.
indregŭ, adj., *whole, complete*.
ing'os, adv., *below*.
iñgrunare, n. fem., *crowning, marriage*.
iñgrunŭ, v. I, *crown, marry* ; iñgrunare, iñgrunai.
inkallikŭ, v. I, *mount a horse, ride* ; inkallikare, inkallikai.
insorŭ, v. I, *marry* (of a man) ; insurare, insurai.
intselegu, v. III, *understand* ; intseledzeare.
invesku, v. II, *clothe, dress* ; invishteare, inviskui.
io, dialectic form of eu.
ishire, see esŭ.
isusesku, v. IV, *betroth* ; isusire, isusiĭ.
itie, n. fem., *cause, reason*.
iu, adv. rel. and interrog., *where*.
iuva, adv., *nowhere*.

K, K'

ka, conj., *like, as*.
ka, intensive part., *more*.
kā, conj., *that, because, since*.
ka si, conj., *if*.
kadŭ, v. II, *fall* ; kădeare, kădzui.
kaftu, v. I, *ask for, look for* ; kăftare, kăftai.
kairŭ, n. neut., *handful of carded wool*.
kaldu, adj., *warm, hot*.
kale, n. fem., *road*.
k'ale, n. fem., *skin, hide*.
kali mera afendiko, *good day, master* ; a Greek phrase.
kalo s ton bistiko, *welcome to the trusty shepherd boy* ; a Greek phrase.
kăltsuvetă, n. fem., *garter*.
kalŭ, n. masc., *horse*.
kalugru, n. masc., *monk*.
kămeashă, n. fem., *shirt*.
kănale, n. fem., *mill-stream*.
kanda, conj., *like, as if*.
kăndu, v. I, *sing* ; kăndare, kăndai ; dialectic form of kăntu.
kăndu, conj., *when* ; also interrogative.
kăne, n. masc., *dog*.
kanŭ, indef. pron., *one, some*.
kapitin'u, n. masc., *pillar, cushion*.
kapră, n. fem., *goat*.

k'aptine, n. masc., *comb.*
kapŭ, n. neut., *head.*
kar si, dialectic form of ka si.
kara, conj., *when.*
kāravi, n. fem., *boat, ferry boat.*
kare, rel. and interrog. pron., *who ?*
kārlibană, n. fem., *shepherd's crook.*
karkalanzā, n. masc., *a demon.*
karkandzā, n. masc., *a demon.*
kārklikŭ, n. masc., *forty para piece.*
kārnu, adj., *snubnose, a person with a bridgeless nose.*
karte, n. fem., *letter, book.*
kārută, n. fem., *water shoot for mill.*
kasă, n. fem., *house, hut.*
kashari, n. fem., *shepherd's camp and cheese factory.*
kashŭ, n. masc., *cheese* ; kash kaval, *special kind of cheese* ; in Italian, *caccia cavallo.*
katasarku, n. masc., *flannel.*
kāte, distrib., *apiece, each.*
katfe, n. masc., *a kind of stuff.*
kathe, adj. indecl., *each, every.*
kati, n. masc., *judge.*
kātoyie, n. fem., *storeroom on ground floor.*
kātră, prep., *towards, about.*
k'atră, n. fem., *rock, stone.*
katrani, n. fem., *pitch.*
kātse, interrog. adv., *why ?*
kātshuă, dialectic form of katshulă.
kātshulă, n. fem., *fez.*
kātŭ, rel. and interrog., *how much ?* or, *as much as.*
kāzane, n. fem., *cauldron.*
k'eliposhe, n. fem., *embroidered fez* ; see p. 65.
k'eptu, n. neut., *breast, chest.*
k'ibape, n. fem., *roast meat* ; see p. 42.
k'in'isesku, v. IV, *start, move* ; k'in'isire, k'in'isiï.
k'inŭ, n. masc., *pine tree.*
k'ipeñg'i, n. fem., *wooden balcony* ; see p. 98.
k'ipitorŭ, adj., *peaked, sharp, pointed.*
k'iradzhi, n. masc., *muleteer.*
k'irauă, n. fem., *Turkish woman.*
k'isavro, n. masc., *treasure.*
kleaie, n. fem., *key.*
kl'emu, v. I, *call* ; kl'imare, kl'imai.
klidhonă, n. fem., *trinket for fortune telling.*
klinŭ, n. neut., *pleat, fold.*
koadă, n. fem., *tail.*
koastă, n. fem., *rib, side.*

kofă, n. fem., *wooden flask.*
korbu, n. masc., *crow* ; or metaphorical, *poor wretch.*
kornu, n. neut., *cornel, cornel tree.*
kornu, n. neut., *horn.*
krepŭ, v. I, *crack, worry* ; kripare, kripai.
krishtinŭ, n. masc., *Christian,* fem. krishtină.
ksenŭ, adj., *strange, foreign* ; also used as a noun, fem. kseană.
ku, prep., *with.*
kukotŭ, n. masc., *cock.*
kukuveauă, n. fem., *owl.*
kulakŭ, n. masc., *cake, bun, loaf of bread* (of a special kind, see p. 101).
kulauz, n. masc., *guide, informer.*
kumŭ, rel. adv., *how ?*
kunak'e, n. fem., *camp, governor's office.*
kundushu, n. masc., *jacket for a man.*
kunosku, v. II, *know* ; kunushteare, kunuskui.
kupatsharŭ, n. masc., *Kupatshar* (see p. 30) ; fem. kupatshară.
kupatshu, n. masc., *oak tree.*
kurkubetă, n. fem., *vegetable marrow.*
kuskru, n. masc., *relation by marriage, wedding guest.*
kusurinŭ, n. masc., *cousin* ; fem. kusurină.
kutarŭ, n. neut., *sheep fold.*
kutsutŭ, n. neut., *knife.*

L, L'

l, abbreviation for la, lă, or lā.
l', abbreviation for l'i.
la, prep., *to* ; pri la, *on to.*
lă, lā, pronom. adj. enclitic, *their.*
lai, a polite form for addressing men to call their attention when one does not know or does not wish to use the personal name.
laiŭ, adj., *black.*
lakŭ, n. neut., *lake, pool.*
lākrimă, n. fem., *tear.*
lală, n. masc., *uncle.*
lānă, n. fem., *wool.*
lapudă, n. fem., *sock.*
lapte, n. masc., *milk.*
largu, adj., *wide.*
l'arŭ, adj., *piebald.*
l'au, v. I, *take* ; l'are, loai.
lea, fem. of lai.
lemnu, n. neut., *wood, timber.*
l'epure, n. masc., *hare.*
letŭ, v. IV, *go out* ; litire (liteare), litiĭ.

l'i, pron., gen. and dat. fem. and masc. of elu.
l'i, pronom. adj. enclitic ; *his, her, its*.
ligutsharŭ, n. masc., *mummer*.
lilitshe, n. fem., *flower*.
limbă, n. fem., *tongue, language*.
lipon, interj., *well*.
lipsesku, v. IV, *be wanting* ; lipsire, lipsiĭ; impersonal use, lipseashte, *it must, it is necessary*.
liră, n. fem., *pound*.
lishk'itorŭ, n. neut., *skein-winder*.
litesku, see letŭ.
livadhe, n. fem., *meadow*.
lokŭ, n. neut., *place*.
lukredzu, v. I, *work* ; lukrare, lukrai.
lukru, n. neut., *work, business*.
lukume, n. fem., *Turkish delight*.
lume, n. fem., *world, people*.
luñgu, adj., *long*.
lun'ină, n. fem., *light*.
lupŭ, n. masc., *wolf*.

M

m, abbreviation for mi or mu.
m, before b, abbreviation for in.
ma, conj., *but*.
ma, adv., *more*.
maie, n. fem., *mother, old woman, grandmother*.
maikă, n. fem., *mother*.
Maiu, n. masc., *May*.
maka, conj., *if*.
mākare, n. fem., *food* ; see mākŭ.
mākŭ, v. I, *eat* ; mkare, mkai ; cf. māñgu.
malliotŭ, n. masc., *woollen overcoat*.
mānă, n. fem., *hand*.
mānc, adv., *to-morrow*.
māñgu, v. I, *eat* ; mañgare, mañgai ; see maku.
maramnatŭ, adj., *melancholy, unhappy*.
marañgo, n. masc., *carpenter*.
maratŭ, adj., *unhappy*.
mardzine, n. masc., *edge*.
mare, adj., *big, great*.
māritŭ, v. I, *marry* (of a woman) ; māritare, māritai.
mārkatŭ, n. masc., *yiaurti, a kind of junket*.
marmarŭ, n. neut., *marble, marble block*.
mārtare, n. fem., *marriage*, see maritŭ.
Martsu, n. masc., *March*.
măsa, contraction for mumă sa.

maseauă, n. fem., *jaw.*
masturu, n. masc., *mason, skilled craftsman.*
māta, condensed form of muma ta.
mathimă, n. fem., *lesson.*
mātritsă, n. fem., *milch-ewe.*
matsu, n. neut., *entrails*, usually in plural only.
mbartu, dialectic form for impartu.
mbl'eare, dialectic form of ml'eare.
mbrostu, adj., *upright*, dialectic form of improstu.
measă, n. fem., *table.*
merŭ, n. neut., *apple, apple tree.*
mesku, v. II, *treat* ; mishteare, miskui
metagresku, v. IV, *call again* ; metagrire, metagriĭ.
mg'are, dialectic form of ml'eare.
mi, acc. of eu.
mihrisesku, v. IV, *bend, make smaller* ; mihriseir, mihrisiĭ.
mindārlik'i, n. fem., *dais, platform* ; see p. 96.
mindŭ, dialectic form of amintu.
mindzhune, n. fem., *lie, untruth.*
mine, acc. of eu ; sometimes used as a nom., *I.*
minte, n. fem., *mind, sense.*
misandră, n. fem., *cupboard, sideboard* ; see p. 96.
mishkāturǎ, n. fem., *scrap, fragment.*
misohori, n. fem., *central square or market-place of a village.*
ml'eare, n. fem., *woman, wife.*
moarte, n. fem., *death.*
moashă, n. fem., *old woman.*
molonoti, conj., *for all that.*
mor, exclam. ; addressed to woman only, generally used with terms of endearment.
morminde, n. masc., *grave, monument.*
morŭ, v. IV, *die* ; murire, muriĭ.
mshatŭ, see mushatŭ.
mu, pronom. adj. enclitic, *my.*
multu, adj., *much, many.*
mumă, n. fem., *mother.*
munde, dialectic form of munte.
mundresku, v. IV, *look at* ; mundrire, mundriĭ ; cf. mutresku.
munte, n. masc., *mountain, hill.*
mushatŭ, adj., *beautiful.*
mutresku, v. IV, *look at* ; mutrire, mutriĭ ; . mundresku.
mutŭ, v. I, *move, disturb, bestir* ; ıntare, mtaı.

N, N', N

n', abbreviation for n'i ; also reflexive pronou· first pers. sing.
ñ, before g, abbreviation for in.

n, abbreviation for nă, nā or nu.

nă, nā, abbreviation for ună.

nă, nā, pronom. adj., enclitic, *our*.

nă, nā, gen. and dat. of noi ; also reflexive pronoun with verbs for first pers. plur.

năfoară, adv., *outside*.

n'agră, adj., obs., fem. of negru.

nakă, adv., *perhaps*.

nāmal'u, n. neut., *animal, a head of sheep or cattle*.

naparte, adv., *on the other side*.

napoi, adv., *after, next, then*.

năskāntsi, indef. pron., *some*.

năsŭ, pron., *he* ; fem. năsă.

nātheamă, adv., a *little*.

năundru, adv., *within*.

ndoi, see doi.

ndrebŭ, v. I, *ask, question* ; ndribare, ndribai.

ne, affirm., *yes*.

negru, adj. obs., *black* ; fem. n'agră.

neka . . . neka, conj., *neither* . . . *nor*.

ñgatshu, v. I, *be angry, quarrel* ; ñgātshare, ñgātshai.

ñgallikŭ, dialectic form of inkallikŭ.

ñgoa, adv., *on this side, near*.

ñgrunare, see iñgrunŭ, iñgrunare.

n'i, gen. and dat. of eu.

n'i, pronom. adj. enclitic, *my*.

ni . . . ni, conj., *neither* . . . *nor*.

n'ikŭ, adj., *small*.

nikuk'iratǎ, n. fem., *household, household property*.

nikuk'irŭ, adj., *rich*.

n'ile, num., *a thousand*.

niñgă, prep., *near*.

ninkă, adv., *still, again*.

nipotŭ, n. masc., *nephew, grandson*.

niruh'ite, n. fem., *sink*.

niveastă, n. fem., *bride*.

nkredŭ, v. II, *trust, believe* ; nkredere, nkridzui.

noară, n. fem., *daughter-in-law*.

noauă, num., *nine*.

noi, pron., *we*, plur. of eu.

nomŭ, n. neut., *law*.

nou, adj., *new*.

nu, neg., *not, no*.

n'u, pronom. adj. enclitic, *my*.

nudă, n. masc., *room, sitting-room* ; cf. udă.

numirŭ, v. I, *count, number* ; numirare, numirai.

numtă, n. fem., *wedding*.

nună, n. fem., *godmother.*
nunŭ, n. masc., *godfather.*
nverinŭ, v. I, *be melancholy* ; nverinare, nverinai.

O

o, pron., acc. fem. of elŭ.
oaie, n. fem., *sheep.*
oară, n. fem., *hour, time.*
oaspe, n. masc., *guest, friend.*
obdzātse, num., *eighty.*
oh'i, neg., *no.*
oi, plur. of oaie.
okl'u, n. masc., *eye.*
omos, conj., *however.*
omŭ, n. masc., *man.*
optu, num., *eight.*
ou, n. neut., *egg.*

P

pade, n. fem., *meadow, green, level space.*
pāhnic, n. fem., *stable.*
paimāne, adv., *the day after to-morrow.*
palate, n. fem., *palace.*
pālāthiri, n. fem., *window.*
pali, adv., *again.*
palto, n. neut., *greatcoat.*
pampordzhi, n. masc., *captain of a steamer.*
pānă, prep., *as far as.*
panathima, exclam., *curse upon.*
panayirŭ, n. neut., *feast, festival.*
pāne, n. fem., *bread.*
papŭ, n. masc., *grandfather.*
para, n. masc., *money* ; *a para.*
pārākālie, n. fem., *entreaty, prayer.*
pārākālsesku, v. IV, *request, entreat* ; pārākālsire, pārākālsiĭ.
părămithŭ, n. neut., *tale, story.*
pārinte, n. masc., *parent, priest.*
parte, n. fem., *part.*
parŭ, v. II, *appear, seem* ; pāreare, pārui ; usually impersonal, pare, *it seems*, etc.
parŭ, n. masc., *post.*
pasku, v. II, *pasture, feed* ; pāshtcare, pāskui.
patridhă, n. fem., *fatherland.*
patru, num., *four.*
patrudzatse, num., *forty.*

patŭ, n. neut., *bottom, base.*
pāzare, n. fem., *market, market-place, market-day.*
peashte, n. masc., *fish* ; dialectic form of pesku.
penitadhă, n. fem., *farewell gift* ; see p. 42.
periusie, n. fem., *property.*
pi, dialectic form of pri.
pikurarŭ, n. masc., *shepherd.*
pileksesku, v. IV, *cut, hew, carve* ; pileksire, pileksiĭ.
pionellu, n. masc., *peacock.*
pishli, n. masc., *jacket for a man.*
pistipsesku, v. IV, *believe, think* ; pistipsire, pistipsiĭ.
pisto, adj., *trusty, faithful.*
pită, n. fem., *pasty.*
pitreku, v. II, *send* ; pitritseare, pitrikui.
pitrikă, n. fem., *lump of loose wool.*
pitrunikl'e, n. fem., *partridge.*
pitrupŭ, n. masc., *warden, overseer, church warden.*
plāñgu, v. III, *cry, weep* ; plāndzeare, plimshu.
plātesku, v. IV, *pay* ; plātire, plātiĭ.
plimshu, preterite of plāñgu.
plitoñ, n. fem., *horn.*
ploaie, n. fem., *rain.*
ploatshă, n. fem., *plate, slab.*
poală, n. fem., *apron.*
poarkă, n. fem., *sow.*
poartă, n. fem., *door.*
podhimă, n. fem., *boot.*
politie, n. fem., *city, large town.*
pomŭ, n. neut., *fruit, fruit tree.*
potŭ, v. II, *be able* ; p(u)teare, ptui.
prămāteftu, n. masc., *merchant.*
pramatikos, adv., *practically.*
pravdă, n. fem., *beast of burden.*
preftu, n. masc., *priest.*
pri, prep., *upon, on* ; di pri, *out of* ; pri la, *on to.*
primăveară, n. fem., *spring.*
primnu, v. I, *walk, wander* ; primnare, primnai.
prinde, v. impers., *it must, it is fitting* ; the only other tense in use
    is the imperfect prindea.
protŭ, num. adj., *first.*
pruksinitŭ, n. masc., *envoy.*
prukuk'ie, n. fem., *progress, advance.*
prumuveară, n. fem., *spring* ; dialectic form for primăveară.
psofŭ, adj., *dead* (of animals).
pudhimate, plur. of podhimă.
puillu, see pul'u.
pulimsesku, v. IV, *fight* ; pulimsire, pulimsiĭ.

pulishorŭ, dim. of pul'u.
pul'u, n. masc., *bird* ; articulated puillu.
punte, n. fem., *bridge*, see puñye.
puñye, n. fem., *bridge*, see punte.
pute, adv., *never*.

R

roaoă, n. fem., *dew*.
rugatshune, n. fem., *prayer*.

S

s, abbreviated form for si or să.
să, dialectic form for si.
sakurafă, n. fem., *pack needle*.
samarŭ, n. masc., *pack saddle*.
sănŭ, adj., *well, healthy*.
sărbătoare, n. fem., *holiday, festival*.
sare, n. fem., *salt*.
sarkă, n. fem., *long coat with loose sleeves*.
saturŭ, v. I, *satisfy* ; săturare, săturai.
seară, n. fem., *evening*.
sh, abbreviated form for shi or sha.
sh, third personal reflexive pronoun, singular and plural, and all genders.
shă, dialectic form for shi.
shapte, num., *seven*.
shasse, num., *six*.
shedŭ, v. II, *sit* ; shideare, shidzui.
sheidzătse, num., *sixty*.
shi, conj., *and, also, even*.
shilivări, n. masc., *breeches*.
shoarikŭ, n. masc., *mouse*.
shoputŭ, n. neut., *conduit head*.
shtiu, v. IV, *know* ; shtire, shtiĭ, or shtiui.
si, conj., *that, to* ; cf. tră si, ka si.
si, pron. reflexive, third person, sing. and plur.
siharik'e, n. fem., *gift given in return for congratulations*.
sintu, v. IV, *feel* ; sintsire, sintsiĭ.
simvoli, n. fem., *agreement, contract*.
siñgurŭ, adj., *alone*.
skălsesku, v. IV, *scratch*; skălsire, skălsiĭ.
skăndură, n. fem., *plank, board*.
skapŭ, v. I, *escape, get rid of* ; skăpare, skăpai ; also impers. skapă, *it is done*.
sklavŭ, adj., *slave, prisoner*.

skolŭ, v. I, *get up, raise* ; skulare, skulai.
skotŭ, v. III, *take out* ; skuteare, skoashu.
skumbu, adj., *dear* ; dialectic form for skumpu.
skumpu, adj., *dear.*
slabŭ, adj., *bad.*
smeană, n. fem., *drawers.*
soakră, n. fem., *mother-in-law.*
soră, n. fem., *sister.*
sotsŭ, n. masc., *friend, companion.*
spelŭ, v. I, *wash* ; spilare, spilai.
spindzurŭ, v. I, *hang* ; spindzurare, spindzurai.
spunŭ, v. III, *tell, explain* ; spuneare, spushu.
stau, v. irreg., *stand* ; stare, stetui.
steauă, n. fem., *star.*
stefanŭ, n. neut., *bridal crown.*
sterpu, adj., *barren, sterile.*
sti, prep., *on, upon.*
stih'imă, n. fem., *bet, wager.*
stran'u, n. neut., *garment.*
struñgă, n. fem., *sheep fold.*
su, pronom. adj. enclitic, *his* ; fem. sa, *her.*
sum, prep., *under.*
sumă, n. fem., *lump of carded wool.*
supra, adv., *above.*
surată, n. fem., *bridesmaid.*
suratŭ, for insuratŭ past part. of insoru.
susŭ, adv., *above.*
sută, num., *a hundred.*

T

t, abbreviated form for ta, ti, or tu.
ta, dialectic form for tră.
taghari, n. fem., *bag, small sack.*
taha, conj., *as if.*
tălăganŭ, n. masc., *overcoat.*
tal'u, v. I, *cut, kill* ; tăl'are, tăl'ai.
tămbare, n. fem., *cape of goats' hair.*
tată, n. masc., *father.*
teliusesku, v. IV, *finish, settle* ; teliusire, teliusiĭ.
tendă, n. fem., *rug, blanket.*
tetă, n. fem., *aunt.*
theam, abbreviation for năthcamă.
ti, dialectic form for tră.
tindu, v. III, *spread, stretch* ; tindeare, teshu or timshu.
tine, pron., *thou.*
tin'ie, n. fem., *price, honour.*
21

tin'isesku, v. IV, *honour* ; tin'isire, tin'isiï.

toamnă, n. fem., *autumn.*

tora, adv., *now.*

tră, prep., *for.*

tră, si, conj., *in order that.*

tragŭ, v. III, *draw, drag* ; trădzeare, trapshu.

tramă, n. fem., *yarn, thread.*

tramvaidzhi, n. masc., *tram conductor* or *driver.*

trană, n. fem., *skein.*

trandafirŭ, n. neut., *rose, rose tree.*

tredzătse, num., *thirty.*

trei, num., *three* ; treil'a, *third, the third time.*

trekŭ, v. II, *pass by, run, get on* ; tritseare, trikui.

tri, dialectic form of tră.

tropŭ, n. neut., *custom, manner.*

tru, dialectic form of tu.

ts, pronom. adj. enclitic, *thy.*

ts, abbreviation for tsi, tsă, tsă, gen. and dat, sing. of tine.

ts, reflexive pronoun, second pers. singular.

tsănŭ, v. II, *hold, keep* ; tsăneare, tsănui.

tsară, n. fem., *earth, soil.*

tsaruhă, n. masc., *cobbler.*

tsaruh'e, n. fem., *out-door shoe.*

tsayă, n. fem. *spool.*

tse, see tsi.

tsea, see atseu.

tseapă, n. fem., *onion.*

tseară, n. fem., *candle, taper.*

tsets, for dzătetsï from dzăkŭ, but vă tsetsï is for vă dutsetsï from mi duku.

tshelnikŭ, n. masc., *shepherd, head shepherd.*

tshikrik'e, n. fem., *spinning-wheel.*

tshinuse, n. fem., *ash.*

tshoariku, n. masc., *legging, gaiter.*

tshokotŭ, n. neut., *hammer.*

tshorgă, n. fem., *rug, mat.*

tshorŭ, n. neut., *foot, leg.*

tsi, rel. indecl., *who, which, what.*

tsi, interrog., *who ? which ? what ?*

tsi, pron. gen. and dat. fem. and masc. of tine.

tsia, contracted form of dzătsia from dzăkŭ, but si tsia is for si dutsia from mi dukŭ.

tsikettă, n. fem., *jacket for a girl.*

tsini, for tsi.

tsintsï, num., *five.*

tsipune, n. fem., *coat* (for a man).

tsisprădzatse, num., *fifteen.*

tsiva, adv., *nothing, something.*
tu, prep., *in, at* ; di tu, *from.*
tu, pronom. adj. enclitic, *thy.*
turka, only in phrase a la turka, *according to Turkish reckoning or custom.*
tutŭ, adj, *all.*

U

u, dialectic form of i (for easte) in certain phrases, usually after ts.
u, acc. sing. fem. of elŭ.
udă, see nuɑ̆.
umblu, dialectic form of umplu.
umplu, v. II, *fill* ; umpleare, umplui.
umtŭ, n. neut., *butter.*
unŭ, num., *one.*
urdu, n. neut., *a kind of cheese.*
ureakl'ă, n. fem., *ear.*
ushe, n. fem., *door.*
uspitlik'e, n. fem., *friendship.*
usprădzatse, num., *eleven.*
usprăyiñg'itsĭ, num., *twenty-one.*
usturㆍă, n. fem., *yarn for weaving.*
uvreu, n. masc., *Jew.*

V

va, abbreviated form of va, vă or vā.
vā, pron. reflexive, second pers. plur.
vā, gen. and dat. plur. of voi.
vă, vā, pronom. adj. enclitic, *your.*
va, vai, particles by which the future of a verb is found.
vakă, n. fem., *cow.*
vale, n. fem., *stream, valley.*
valitshe, n. fem., *small stream, small valley*, dim. of vale.
vărŭ, indef. pron., *one, some.*
văsil'e, n. masc., *king.*
văsilik'esku, adj., *royal.*
văsiloan'e, n. fem., *queen.*
vatămu, v. I, *kill, murder* ; vătămare, vătămai.
vatră, n. fem., *hearth.*
vdziră, dialectic form for fudziră from fugŭ.
vearde, adj., *green.*
vedŭ, v. II, *see* ; videare, vidzui.
versu, v. I, *pour, pour out* ; versare, versai.
vilendză, n. fem., *rug, blanket.*
vindu, v. II, *sell* ; vindeare, vindui.

vinitŭ, adj., *blue.*
vitsinŭ, n. masc., *neighbour* ; fem. vitsină.
voi, pron., *you,* plur. of tine.
voiŭ, v. II, *wish, want, love* ; vreare, vrui.
vreare, n. fem., *good-will* ; see voiŭ.
vrutŭ, past part. of voiŭ.

Y

yatru, n. masc., *doctor.*
yermu, n. masc., *worm.*
yiftesku, adj., *gipsy.*
yig′indz, dialectic form of yiñg′itsĭ.
yilie, n. fem., *glass, tumbler.*
yiñg′itsĭ, num., *twenty.*
yinŭ, v. III, *come* ; yineare, vin′u.
yinŭ, n. neut., *wine.*
yiptu, n. neut., *corn, wheat.*

Z

z, dialectic form of s for si or să.
z, dialectic form of ts for tsi, tsă or tsā.
zanate, n. fem., *trade.*
zborŭ, n. neut., *word.*
zburăsku, v. I, *speak, talk* ; zburare, zburai.
zh, dialectic form of sh for shi or shă.
zhokŭ, dialectic form dzhokŭ.
zhone, dialectic form of dzhone.
zuă, dialectic form of dzuă.
zvaltsă, n. fem., *shuttle.*

INDEX